The Canadian Rockies

Pioneers, Legends, and True Tales

By Roger Patillo (B.A., M.S.W., M.B.A.)

Trafford
PUBLISHING

Order this book online at www.trafford.com/05-0525
or email orders@trafford.com

Most Trafford titles are also available at major online book retailers.

Note for Librarians: A cataloguing record for this book is available from Library
and Archives Canada at www.collectionscanada.ca/amicus/index-e.html

Printed in Victoria, BC, Canada.

ISBN: 978-1-4120-5627-4

Typed and edited by Amberlea Press

Published by:
Amberlea Press
P.O. Box 1682
Aldergrove B.C. V4W 2V1
and
Trafford Publishing

*We at Trafford believe that it is the responsibility of us all, as both individuals
and corporations, to make choices that are environmentally and socially sound.
You, in turn, are supporting this responsible conduct each time you purchase a
Trafford book, or make use of our publishing services. To find out how you are
helping, please visit www.trafford.com/responsiblepublishing.html*

*Our mission is to efficiently provide the world's finest, most comprehensive
book publishing service, enabling every author to experience success.
To find out how to publish your book, your way, and have it available
worldwide, visit us online at www.trafford.com/10510*

www.trafford.com

North America & international
toll-free: 1 888 232 4444 (USA & Canada)
phone: 250 383 6864 ♦ fax: 250 383 6804
email: info@trafford.com

The United Kingdom & Europe
phone: +44 (0)1865 722 113 ♦ local rate: 0845 230 9601
facsimile: +44 (0)1865 722 868 ♦ email: info.uk@trafford.com

14 13 12 10 9

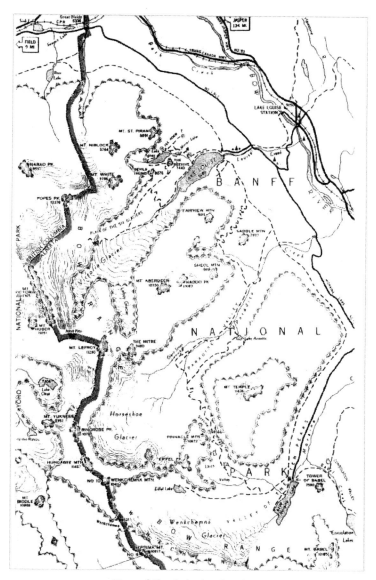

Map of the Lake Louise Area

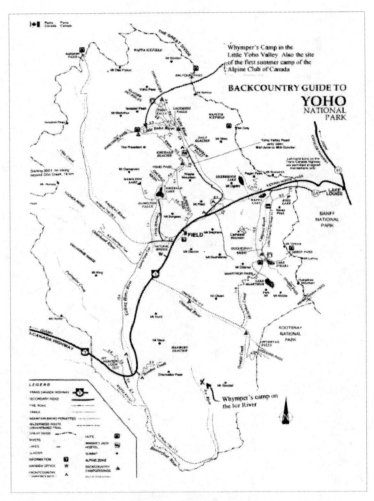

Map of the Yoho Area showing Whymper's camps

Dedication

This book is dedicated to my wife Donnie, who has been most patient and supportive as I have spent countless hours researching and preparing this manuscript.

It is also dedicated to the memories of those who shared so much of their knowledge and their experience with me so many years ago. They are in no particular order: **Ernest, Walter, and Edward Feuz, Lawrence Grassi, Phyllis Munday, H.A.V. "Harry" Green, Nick Morant, Walter Perren, Jimmy Simpson, John Linn, and Phyllis Hart**.

Finally, it is dedicated to all those that I have shared the mountain trails with over the years, and to those who love the Rockies and continue to cherish the memories of days gone by.

Lake O'Hara
"Catching the evening rise"

Thanks and Acknowledgements

There are many people to thank when one attempts to put together a book such as this.

I would first like to extend my thanks to **Dr. Charles (Chuck) Roland** who kindly gave me his notes, personal reflections, and thoughts regarding the tragedy on Mt. Victoria that took place on July 30, 1954 when four Mexican climbers plunged to their deaths into Abbot Pass.

Thanks are also due to **Jon Whelan** of Banff who sent me a copy of Sir Edward Whymper's long lost journals.

I have quoted liberally from a number of books and journals and these are found in the bibliography. In particular, **Esther Fraser's** excellent book *Wheeler* on the life of A.O. Wheeler was most helpful as was **J.M. Thorington's** book *Where the Clouds Can Go* on the life of Conrad Cain. The books of **E.J. Hart** of Banff were invaluable as were those of **Grant MacEwan.** Ian Anderson's book *Sitting Bull's Boss*, **Sam Steele's** book *Forty Years in Canada*, and **David Cruise and Alison Griffith's** The *Great Adventure–How the Mounties Conquered the West*, were helpful in writing the early life of Tom Wilson and setting the stage for what was to follow.

My personal copies of the **Canadian Alpine Journals** dating back to the first one printed in 1907 were invaluable sources of information and photos.

I would also like to thank the staff of the **Vancouver Public Library** and the staff of the **Canadian Archives** in Ottawa, who assisted me in finding out-of-print books, and photos. The **Glenbow Museum and Archives** in Calgary and the **Whyte Museum and Archives** in Banff were also most helpful.

Finally, special thanks are due to **Phil Sherwood,** who edited the manuscript and made many valuable suggestions to improve the content and presentation.

Table of Contents

Map of the Lake Louise Area — iii

Map of the Yoho Park Area — iv

Dedication — v

Thanks and Acknowledgements — vi

Photo Credits — xi

Introduction — 1

Chapter 1 – Tom Wilson – A Man for all Seasons — **7**

Growing up in Ontario — 12
Tom Wilson and the North West Mounted Police — 13
The March West — 14
What happened to them all — 35
    Chief Sitting Bull — 35
    Major James Walsh — 41
    Colonel James Macleod — 42
    Sam Steele — 42
    Louis Riel — 44
    Jerry Potts — 47
    Frank Dickens — 49
    Chief Crowfoot — 50
    Paddy Crozier — 52
    Lt. Colonel A.G. Irvine — 52
Rogers and Wilson – A Dynamic Duo — 55
Tom Wilson – Master Guide and Outfitter — 61
How Banff Became Banff and a National Park was created — 68
Tom Wilson Makes a Discover – Finding Lake Louise — 69
How Banff Indian Days Began — 76
Santa Claus Comes to the Rockies — 82
Home for Christmas – Tom has a Close Call — 96
Memories of Golden Days — 98

Chapter 2 – Tom Boys — **105**

James and Fred Tabuteau — 105
Wild Bill Peyto — 106
Ralph Edwards — 117
Fred Stevens — 120
Tom Lusk — 120
Bob Campbell — 121
Jimmy Simpson — 121

Chapter 3 – Early Visitors to the Rockies   **133**

James Joseph McArthur – Surveyor and Mountaineering Pioneer   133
Reverend William Spotswood Green and Reverend Henry Swanzy   135
Harold Topham, Carl Sulzer and Emil Huber   141
Dr. Charles E. Fay   142
Walter Wilcox and the Boys from Yale University   142
Naming the Ten Peaks   146
1894: A New Chalet at Lake Louise   149
The First Recorded Mountaineering Accident, July 12, 1894   151
Discovering Paradise Valley   153
Early Mountaineering Technique   158
The Climb of Mt. Temple (11,636 feet)   159
Early Visitors to Lake O'Hara   160
Winter comes to the Rockies in 1894   163
The Summer of 1895   164
The Appalachian Mountain Club Arrives   165
Wilcox Explores beyond Bow Pass   166
An Early Tragedy: The First Recorded Mountaineering Death
in the Rockies   167
1897 – A Professional Guide Comes To The Rockies and
Mt. Lefroy Is Conquered   174
The First Ascent of Mount Victoria   176
Collie, Dixon, and Baker – The Climbers From England   176
A Daring Rescue   181
Collie and Barker Explore the Mount Forbes Area.   182
Did Professor Jean Habel Discover the Yoho Valley?   183
In Search of Mounts Hooker and Brown – 1898   185
Fay and Curtis Climb Mt. Niles in August of 1898   187
The First Trip from Lake Louise to Lake O'Hara via Abbot Pass   188
The Climbing of Mt. Balfour – 1898   189
Other Early Climbers   190

Chapter 4 – Early Swiss Guides in the Rockies   **193**

Introduction   193
Professional Guides Introduced to the Rockies   193
Peter Sarbach – the First Professional Guide in the Rockies   194
Fuez and Haesler Begin a Dynasty   195
Building Abbot Pass Hut   200
The Plain of Six Glaciers Teahouse   201
Glacier House Burns to the Ground   201
Learning the Mountain Pace   209
Other Notable Swiss Guides   215
Christian Haesler Jr   215

Rudolf Aemmer   216
The Rescue of Mrs. Stone – 1921 As told by Rudolf Aemmer   216
How the Guides Were *Really* Treated!   222

Chapter 5 – The Saga of Sir Edward Whymper   **227**

Introduction   227
Who was Sir Edward Whymper?   227
The Conquest of the Matterhorn   228
The Disastrous Descent   238
Why Did This Tragedy Happen?   241
Life After the Matterhorn   244
The Lion of the Matterhorn comes to Canada   245
Whymper's Journeys in 1901   245
The Climbing of Mt. Assiniboine   269
1903 – Whymper Returns to the Rockies   272
A Walk Through The Rockies   273
Sir Edward Passes Away   278

Chapter 6 – A.O. Wheeler – Lion of the Rockies and the Alpine **283**
Club of Canada

The Early Years   283
The Founding of the Alpine Club of Canada (ACC)   291
An Early Mountaineering Tragedy   295
A Permanent Clubhouse in Banff   299
The Saga of Mount Robson – Who climbed it first?   300
The Later Years   317

Chapter 7 – More Exceptional Personalities of the Rockies   **319**

Conrad Kain (1883–1934) Mountain Guide Extraordinaire   319
Byron Harmon – Pioneer Photographer of the Rockies   336
Lawrence Grassi – Trail Builder of the Rockies   341
Erling Strom   346
The Mount Temple – Skoki Ski Area   348
Georgia Engelhard – That Girl Could Climb!   353
Katie Gardiner – An International Climber   355
Walter Perren   357
Phyllis Munday   358
H. A. V. Harry Green   362
Lillian Gest   365
Marshall Diverty and Bud Brewster   365
Arnold Brigden   366
An Interesting Ride from Banff   367
Nick Morant's Grizzly Bear Encounter   370
Norm Luxton – A Pillar of Banff   374

Bruno Engler – A man for the mountains.   377
Ken Jones   378
Hans Gmoser   379

Chapter 8 – Two Mountaineering Tragedies

Introduction   383
Death on Mt. Victoria   385
Reflections   411
Tragedy on Mt. Temple: The worst climbing accident   414
          ever recorded in the Rockies
The Aftermath   419
The Inquest   424

Chapter 9 – Final Thoughts, Reflections and Concerns   429

Bears and Humans Don't Mix Well   433
Is the Bear Population in Canada at Risk?   441
How to Save the Banff Grizzlies   443
Other Blunders   446
Park Users Must Accept Responsibility for Their Own Stupidity   447

A Glossary of Terms   451

Bibliography   455

Photo Credits

SUBJECT	SOURCE	PAGE
Symbols: CAJ – Canadian Alpine Club Journal	**RWP – Roger W. Patillo**	
Front Cover	RWP	
Map of Lake Louise Area		iii
Map of Yoho Park	RWP	iv
Lake O'Hara	Dedication Page	

Introduction

Crossing the S. Saskatchewan	Carl Rungius	3
Joy Kimball at Plain of Six Glaciers	RWP	4
Plain of Six Glaciers Teahouse	RWP	5

Chapter 1

Tom Wilson	CAJ	10
Tom Wilson at Cabin	Canadian Archives	11
Tom Wilson	Canadian Archives	12
Major General Sir George French	Canadian Archives	15
Colonel James F. Macleod	Canadian Archives	15
Jerry Potts	Fort Macleod Historical Society	16
Fort Whoop-up Trail	Fort Macleod Historical Society	17
Indian Women at Fort Whoop-up		18
Lieutenant Colonel George Custer	Fort Macleod Historical Society	20
Sitting Bull	Fort Macleod Historical Society	21
Fort Walsh	RWP	25
Major James Walsh	Fort Macleod Historical Society	26
Major James Walsh	Fort Macleod Historical Society	31
North West Mounted Police at Ft. Walsh	Fort Macleod Historical Society	32
Fort Walsh 1878	Fort Macleod Historical Society	32
Sitting Bull at Fort Walsh in 1878		37
Colonel James MacLeod	Unknown	38
Chief Crowfoot	Unknown	38
Sitting Bull's Monument at Wood Mountain	RWP	39
Sitting Bull's Monument at Wood Mountain	RWP	40
Sam Steele	Unknown	46
Louis Riel	Unknown	47
Francis Dickens	Unknown	53
Jean Louis Legare	Unknown	54
Lieutenant Colonel A. G. Irvine	Unknown	54
Major A.B. Rogers	Unknown	59
The Driving of the Last Spike on the CPR	Unknown	60

SUBJECT	SOURCE	PAGE
Silver City	Unknown	64
Banff 1884 and 1887	Canadian Archives	65
Tom Wilson and Family	Whyte Museum & Archives	66
Tom Wilson and George Fear	Whyte Museum & Archives	66
Walter Wilcox in 1896		67
Lake Louise 1882		78
Lake Louise after storm		79
Tom Wilcox	RWP	79
Lake Louise—In late April & May	RWP	80
Banff Indian Days	Unknown	84
Wilson and Brewster	Whyte Museum & Archives	85
Walter Wicox, Chief Hunter, Tom Wilson		86
Chief Walking Buffalo—George MacLean	Byron Harmon	87
Chief Buffalo Calf—Hector Crawler	Byron Harmon	88
Chief George Crawler	Byron Harmon	88
Tom Wilson on snowshoes		97
Tom Wilson's Plaque	Canadian Archives	99
Lake Agnes in Summer	RWP	100
Tom Wilson and His Wife Minnie	Whyte Museum and Archives	101
Tom Wilson	Whyte Museum & Archives	102
Tom Wilson's Grave	RWP	103

Chapter 2

Fred Tabuteau	Whyte Museum & Archives	107
Bob Campbell	Whyte Museum & Archives	107
Wild Bill Peyto	Whyte Museum & Archives	108
Wild Bill Peyto & Ulysse LaCasse	Whyte Museum & Archives	109
Fred Stevens	Whyte Museum & Archives	110
Bill Peyto	Whyte Museum & Archives	113
Peyto Lake	Whyte Museum & Archives	113
Bill Peyto	Whyte Museum & Archives	114
Ralph Edwards	Whyte Museum & Archives	118
Tom Lusk	Whyte Museum & Archives	118
Jimmy Simpson	Canadian Archives	119
A Young Jimmy Simpson	Unknown	122
Fording the Stream	A painting by Carl Rungius	123
Jimmy Simpson	Crag and Canyon Newspaper	124
Water Color by Jimmy Simpson	Mr. P. Williams	125
Num-Ti-Jah Lodge	from Paining by Catharine Whyte	125
Watercolor by Jimmy Simpson	Whyte Museum & Archives	127
"Old Billy"	A painting by Carl Rungius	127

SUBJECT	SOURCE	PAGE
"Lord of the High Country"	A painting by Carl Rungius	128
Carl Rungius	Unknown	128
Num-Ti-Jah Lodge	RWP	129
Jimmy Simpson	Whyte Museum & Archives	129
The Simpson Sisters	Whyte Museum & Archives	130
Bow Lake	RWP	130

Chapter 3

James J. McArthur	CAJ	134
Reverend William Spotswood Green	A. O Wheeler	136
Green & Swanzy on Mt. Bonney	W. S Green	136
Green and Swanzy on Mt. Bonnie	W.S. Green	138
Lake Louise in 1888	W.S. Green	139
Sulzer and Huber	A.O. Wheeler	140
Map of Mt. Sir Donald	A.O. Wheeler	140
First Chalet at Lake Louise	Unknown	143
Second Chalet at Lake Louise	Walter Wilcox	144
First Guests at the Second chalet	Walter Wilcox	144
Moraine Lake	RWP	148
Moraine Lake	RWP	149
Paradise Valley	RWP	154
101 Wilcox Camp in Paradise Valley 1894	Walter Wilcox	155
The Giant Steps	RWP	155
Mount Temple	Walter Wilcox	156
Sam Allen at Opabin Plateau	Walter Wilcox	157
The Mitre and Mt. Lefroy	RWP	157
Lake Agnes	RWP	158
Lake O'Hara	Unknown	161
Lake O'Hara	Unknown	162
Abbot Pass	RWP	162
Abbot Pass	RWP	169
Phil Abbot	CAJ	170
Tom Wilson Recovering Abbot's Body	Whyte Museum and Archives	172
Members of Appalachian Mnt. Club	CAJ	177
Peter Sarbach	CAJ	178
Professor Charles Fay	CAJ	179
Mt. Victoria	RWP	180
Mt. Victoria—Summit Ridge	RWP	180
Mt. Des Poilus	Robert Simms	186
Mt. Athabaska	RWP	187
Jim Brewster		189

SUBJECT	SOURCE	PAGE
Norman Collie and H.E. Stutfield	CAJ	19
Val Fynn	CAJ	192
Mrs. Berens	A.O. Wheeler	192
Mrs. Berens	A.O. wheeler	192

Chapter 4

Feuz Family	Unknown	197
Ed Feuz Sr.& C. Heasler Sr.	A.O. wheeler,	198
Early Swiss Guides	A.O. Wheeler	199
Early Swiss Guides	A.O. Wheeler	199
Edward Feuz Sr.	A.O. Wheeler	200
Pack train to Abbot Pass		203
Plans for Abbot Hut	CAJ	204
Abbot Hut	RWP	205
Basil Gardom	RWP	206
The Swiss Guides	Nick Morant	207
Swiss Chalet at Lake Louise	Ernest Feuz	208
Ernest Feuz and Georgia Englehard	unknown	210
Ernest Feuz and Georgia Englehard	CAJ	210
Swiss Chalets at Eidelwiss (Golden)	RWP	211
Stephen House	Canadian Archives	212
Glacier House	Canadian Archives	212
Swiss Brides Arrive in Golden	Whyte Museum & Archives	218
Ernest Feuz & Rudolf Aemmer	Nick Morant	219
Rudolf Aemmer & John Barrymore	unknown	219
Camilla Horn	unknown	220
Rudolf Aemmer	. Nick Morant	220
Ernest Feuz	Nick Morant	221
Bronze Statue	RWP	222
Edward Feuz Jr.	Byron Harmon	223
Walter Feuz	Nick Morant	224
Grave Markers	RWP	225
Ernest Feuz	Nick Morant	226

Chapter 5

The Matterhorn	The Alps	229
The Matterhorn	The Alps	230
The Matterhorn	The Alps	230
Edward Whymper	British Alpine Club	233
Michel Croz	British Alpine Club	234
Douglas Hadow	British Alpine Club	234

SUBJECT	SOURCE	PAGE
Rev. Charles Hudson	British Alpine Club	235
Lord Francis Douglas	British Alpine Club	235
Old Peter Taugwalder	British Alpine Club	236
Young Peter Taugwalder	British Alpine Club	236
The Matterhorn	RWP	239
Apparition on the Matterhorn	British Alpine Club	240
Sir Edward Whymper	CAJ	247
Whymper's Guides	CAJ	248
Twin Falls	RWP	264
Takakkaw Falls	RWP	264
The Reverend James Outram	CAJ	270
Christian Bohren	CAJ	271
Whymper and Hector	ACC	280
Edward Whymper	ACC	281
Quarter Way House At Lake Louise	Byron Harmon	282

Chapter 6

Mrs. Young	A.O. Wheeler	287
Rogers and the Swiss Peaks	A.O. Wheeler	288
Glacier House	A.O. Wheeler	289
Glacier House	A.O. Wheeler	289
Pacific Express	A.O. Wheeler	290
Remains of Glacier House	RW P	290
Founding Members ACC	CAJ	292
Elizabeth Parker	CAJ	293
Founding Members from Banff	CAJ	293
First Camp–in Yoho Valley	CAJ	295
First Graduates ACC Camp	CAJ	296
ACC Camp at Laughing Falls	CAJ	297
Lady Climbers on Mt. Burgess	CAJ	298
Lady Climbers on Mt. President	CAJ	298
ACC Club House in Banff	CAJ	303
ACC Club House (Interior)	CAJ	303
A.O. Wheeler	CAJ	304
ACC Camp –Lake O'Hara	CAJ	304
A.O. Wheeler	CAJ	306
Donald "Curly" Phillips	CAJ	307
Reverend George Kinney	CAJ	307
Mt. Robson	Phyllis Munday	309
Kain, MacCarthy, Foster	CAJ	309
Wheeler, Phillips	CAJ	310

SUBJECT	SOURCE	PAGE
Reverend George Kinney.	CAJ	310
Kinney's Flag	Unknown	312
Clara Wheeler	CAJ	313
Emmeline Savatard	CAJ	313
Elizabeth Parker Hut	CAJ	314
Elizabeth Parker	CAJ	314
Wheeler	CAJ	315
A.O. Wheeler Hut at Rogers Pass	RWP	316
Wheeler's grave in Banff	RWP	316
The ACC Crest	CAJ	318

Chapter 7

SUBJECT	SOURCE	PAGE
Conrad Kain	Byron Harmon	320
Kinney, Kain and Phillips	A. O. Wheeler	321
Conrad Kain	CAJ	324
Conrad Kain on Mt. Robson	CAJ	325
Mt. Robson	Phyllis Munday	325
Conrad Kain on Mt. Cook	J. M. Thorington	334
Conrad Kain on Mt. Resplendent	Byron Harmon	335
Byron Harmon	CAJ	337
Byron Harmon	CAJ	338
Bow Lake–Bob Bapti	Byron Harmon	339
Ulysse La Casse	Byron Harmon	340
Lawrence Grassi	CAJ	343
Lawrence Grassi in O'Hara	CAJ	343
Lawrence Grassi–on the trail	CAJ	344
Lawrence Grassi Hut	ACC	346
Ike Mills in Skoki	unknown	349
Skiing in Skoki	unknown	349
Post Hotel	unknown	350
Skoki Ski Lodge	unknown	350
Mt. Temple	RWP	351
The Herring Bone	Byron Harmon	351
Skoki Area		352
Georgia Englehard	ACC	355
Katie Gardiner	ACC	356
Walter Perren	unknown	359
H.A.V. "Harry" Green	Calgary Herald	359
Don and Phyllis Munday	Phyllis Munday	360
Phyllis Munday	Phyllis Munday	360
Lillian Gest	Uknown	363

SUBJECT	SOURCE	PAGE
Bud Brewster and Chief	Nick Morant	364
Nick Morant	Nick Morant	373
Mt. Rundle	Nick Morant	374
Spiral Tunnel	Nick Morant	374
Norm Luxton	Byron Harmon	375
Bruno Engler	Nick Morant	376
Ken Jones	Unknown	376
Hans Gmoser	Unknown	381
Hans Gmoser	Unknown	382

Chapter 8

SUBJECT	SOURCE	PAGE
Mexican Climbers	Calgary Herald	388
Mexican Climbers	Chuck Roland	389
Mexican Climbers & Abbot Pass	Chuck Roland	390
Offilea Fernandez	Chuck Roland	392
Mexican s on Mt. Victoria	The Albertan	394
Mt. Victoria – Line of fall	RWP	394
Surviving Mexican Climbers	Calgary Herald	395
Ofelia Fernandez	Calgary Herald	395
Surviving Mexicans	Calgary Herald	396
Abbot Pass and Mt. Victoria		397
Three Rescuers	Calgary Herald	399
Ernest Feuz	Calgary Herald	399
Roland and Wehner	Chuck Roland	401
Wehner, Stanfield, Roland	Chuck Roland	402
Two Rescuers	Calgary Herald	403
Pack Train	Calgary Herald	404
Two Rescuers	Chuck Roland	404
Mt. Lefroy	RWP	411
The Rescuers	Chuck Roland	413
Mt. Temple – accident site	The Albertan	416
Surviving boys	Calgary Herald	417
Surviving boys	Calgary Herald	417
Mt. Temple – Line of the avalanche	Warden's Service	422
Mt. Temple – Location of the bodies	Warden's Service	423
The Summit – Mt. Temple	RWP	427
Elizabeth Parker Hut in O'Hara	Unknown	428

Chapter 9

SUBJECT	SOURCE	PAGE
Grizzly Bear	B.C. Wildlife Br.	435
Black Bears	B.C. Wildlife Br.	436

SUBJECT	SOURCE	PAGE
Grizzlies	Unknown	444
Bronze Statue – Lake Louise	RWP	449
The author with his daughter at O'Hara	RWP	449
Mt. Fay	RWP	457

Introduction

This book describes many of the colourful characters and events that shaped the history and the legends of the Canadian Rockies. Different writers have recounted some of these stories but others have never been told. Most of the events and the descriptions are factual, but in seeking to capture the spirit and the excitement of the times, I have taken some literary licence. I have also tried to provide as much background history as possible in order to help the reader appreciate the uniqueness of the characters and the times in which they lived.

The exceptional span of 115 years, from 1870 until 1985 when the last of the Feuz brothers died, saw many changes, both in western Canada and the world at large. These included the formation of the North West Mounted Police (NWMP), the Battle of the Little Big Horn, the Riel Rebellion, the building of the Canadian Pacific Railway (CPR), the Boer War, the invention of the telegraph and the telephone, the sinking of the Titanic, the introduction of the automobile and the airplane, the First and Second World Wars, the Great Depression, the invention of the television and the microchip, and a man walking on the moon. Many of the remarkable characters described herein played important roles in some of these earlier events. During this time, world-class luxury hotels were built and maintained at Banff, Lake Louise, Rogers Pass, and Field to receive well-to-do and adventuresome tourists from around the world. These hotels were situated in the rugged wilderness with wild animals literally on their doorsteps. Even today grizzly bears, black bears, elk, deer, moose, coyotes, and the occasional cougar wander through Banff, Lake Louise, Field, and Jasper.

From as early as the 1880s, adventurers, mountaineers, and naturalists from all over the world, came to the Rockies to explore, to study the flora and fauna, to hike the trails, and to ascend the virgin, snow-capped mountains. Their exploits and adventures, as well as those of the men who guided them, were the stuff from which many tall tales and legends grew. Those living and working in the rough-and-ready western frontier around Banff and the Bow River Valley, were aware of a much more sophisticated world beyond their wilderness, as their annual clients came from the elite of Europe, England, and the United States.

The early visitors to the area, and the pioneer outfitters and guides that served them were a remarkable collection of larger-than-life characters. **Sir James Hector** and **Major A.B. Rogers** both explored routes through the Rockies in the 1860s and 1880s. **Tom Wilson**−the notorious and unequalled pathfinder, packer, and raconteur of Banff−became a legend in his own time when, on the golden morning of August 21st, 1882, he became the first white man to lay eyes on the beauty of Lake Louise. Wilson is also credited with being the first white man see Emerald Lake, Takakkaw Falls, Twin Falls, and the beautiful Yoho Valley. He also was the first to blaze a trail into Mt. Assiniboine−the "Matterhorn" of the Canadian Rockies. He also cut a trail over Simpson Pass to the Vermillion River and then out to Castle Junction−a route that later became the Banff-Windermere Highway. With the exception of a few wasted years, Tom Wilson made Banff and the Bow River Valley his home from 1881 until his death on the crisp, autumn afternoon of September 20th, 1933, in Banff,

Walter Wilcox and his resolute colleagues from Yale University were the first to explore, map, and name most of the peaks, valleys, creeks, and glaciers in the Lake Louise-Moraine Lake area in the 1890s. **Rudolf Aemmer, Christian Haesler Jr.,** and the Feuz brothers—**Edward, Earnest and Walter**—were early Swiss guides from Interlaken, Switzerland and together with the great Austrian guide **Conrad Kain** they began a rich tradition of mountaineering in the Canadian Rockies. The legendary **Sir Edward Whymper** was both arrogant and aloof, but he was also the conqueror of the Matterhorn in Switzerland and he played a major role in making the sport of mountaineering popular in the Rockies. He visited the area in 1903, 1904, and 1905 but endeared himself to no one. **Sir James Outram**, a gifted "man of the cloth" and superb climber from England, was a frequent attendee at the camps of the Alpine Club of Canada around the turn of the century. He made the first ascent of Mt. Assiniboine and is credited with making several impressive first ascents on the spectacular peaks between Bow Lake and the Columbia Icefield.

William and Mary Vaux and their family were frequent visitors to both Lake Louise and Glacier House at Rogers Pass where, among other things, they studied the movements of the great glaciers of the Rockies. **A. O. Wheeler**, the remarkable pioneer land surveyor and visionary, surveyed the Rockies and the Selkirk Mountains for the CPR and later for the Boundary Commission of the government of British Columbia. He was the principal founder of the Alpine Club of Canada in 1906 and promoted it tirelessly for the rest of his life. He played an immense role in encouraging people of all classes to take up hiking and climbing in the Rockies.

Elizabeth Parker was also an early lover of the Rockies and, with Wheeler, one of the principal founding members of the Alpine Club of Canada. In 1913, **Conrad Kain** became the first to climb Mt. Robson. Twenty years later in 1933, he was **Phyllis Munday's** guide when she became the first women to conquer Mt. Robson. He is also credited with introducing skiing and ski jumping to the Rockies. **Professor Charles E. Fay** and **J. N. Collie** from Yale University, and **Dr. Stone** and his wife from Purdue University were also early climbers in the area, as was **Professor Jean Habel** from Germany, who was among the first to explore the Yoho Valley and the Waputic Icefields.

Wild Bill Peyto, the eccentric packer, trapper, and bon vivant also made the Banff and the Bow Valley his home. He was one of the early park wardens in Banff National Park and his exploits literally filled a book—T.J. (Ted) Hart's biography, *Ain't It Hell*. **Tom Lusk, Bob Campbell, Soapy Smith, Curly Phillips,** and **Ulysse La Casse** were also colourful wranglers and guides in the area and all worked for Tom Wilson at one time. **Ray Legace,** who helped built the original Post Hotel in the village of Lake Louise, rented out horses there until the mid-1960s after a working as a packer and camp cook for Tom Wilson.

Jimmy Simpson, the builder of Num-Ti-Jah Lodge at Bow Lake, was also a pioneer wrangler and guide. A superb storyteller, he also worked for Wilson for a number of years before starting his own backcountry guiding business. In his later years he became an accomplished watercolour artist.

Byron Harmon, the pioneer photographer and mountain adventurer, preserved much of the early history of the area with his remarkable photos. Many of these photos are featured in the book *Great Days in the Rockies*. **Nick Morant** was known as the "Gentleman Photographer of the CPR" and he carried on where Byron Harmon left off. He lived in Banff until his death in March of 1999.

Erling Strom introduced modern downhill skiing to the Rockies and built the famous Mt.

Assiniboine Ski Lodge at Sunshine. **Ike Mills,** "The Mad Musher of Skoki" was known for his dog teams and helped build the remote Skoki Ski Lodge.

Jimmy Brewster and his brothers purchased Tom Wilson's packing and guiding enterprise in Banff in 1902 and built a transportation and sightseeing empire there. Over the intervening years the Brewster name has became synonymous with the Canadian Rockies.

The exploits and accomplishments of these remarkable characters all contributed to the legends and lore of the Banff-Lake Louise area of the Rockies. Other personalities that figure prominently include: **Sam Steele, the Rev. George Kinney, Don and Phyllis Munday, Val Fynn, Georgia Engelhard, Lillian Gest, Katie Gardiner, Harry Green, Walter Perren, Bruno Engler, Lawrence Grassi, John Monod, Phyllis Hart, John Linn, Percy "Beef" Woodworth, Hans Gmoser, Bud Brewster, Chuck Roland and Ray Wehner.**

I worked at Chateau Lake Louise during the summers from 1957 until 1964, and over the years I have seldom missed returning at least once each summer to climb, hike and visit old friends again. The late 1950s and the early 1960s was a great time to be in the Rockies as a few of the original pioneers were still living around the Banff and Lake Louise area and others visited the Chateau regularly. Many spent countless hours showing me photographs and telling their stories as well as those of the original pioneers that they knew so well.

The Feuz brothers, Ray Legace and Jimmy Simpson had shared the trails with some of the original pioneers of the Rockies and they were eager share their memories with me so that they would not be lost. Most of these legendary personalities are gone now, but I like to think that they still roam those great shining mountains that lie just beyond the Great Beyond.

So sit back and let me tell you what I know about some of these remarkable characters and the adventures that they had when the Canadian mountain wilderness was still unspoiled. Then I'll have kept some promises that I made to old friends many years ago.

Carl Rungius' painting of Jimmy Simpson crossing
the river at Saskatchewan River Crossing.

Joy Kimball – manageress of the Plain of Six Glaciers Teahouse
This photo was taken on May 30, 2001 – the opening day of the 2001 season.

The Plain of Six Glaciers Teahouse

Chapter 1

Tom Wilson: A Mountain Man for All Seasons

It is appropriate to begin this book with the story of Tom Wilson, who was arguably the greatest of the Canadian mountain men. Tom was a legend in his own time and his influence over the early development of the Banff-Jasper corridor was immense. Tom had a knack of turning up when there was a major event taking place in western Canadian history. Many viewed him as a man to be counted upon to save the day in any situation and he played this role to the hilt. Larger-than-life he was much respected by all those he encountered.

Tom was completely at home with the Sioux and Blackfoot Indians of the Great Plains, as well as the Blood and the Stoney Indians of the foothills. They in turn trusted him. Tom's native friends taught him both the ways of the forest trails and how to survive alone in the mountains. Having once traveled through an area, he could remember every detail about it for years afterwards. These qualities made Tom a man that others consulted before venturing into the mountain wilderness of the Banff-Bow River corridor and beyond. From the late 1880s until his death in 1933, Tom's corral in Banff was usually the first place that climbers and adventurers were sent to get advice about the backcountry.

Tom was equally at home with all manner of men One night he could sit by the campfire with his Stoney Indian friends telling stories as the sparks leapt high into the blackness of the star-studded sky, and the following night he could share a different campfire and more tales with a Marquis from Europe or a financier from New York. White or native, rich or poor, educated at the great colleges and universities of England and the United States, or educated in the ways of the trail and the forests in Mother Nature's classroom, Tom could relate to them all.

Although Tom was adept at spinning some exciting yarns from his past experiences, he had a sterling reputation. He was known for being honest, resourceful, fair, reliable, and a perfect gentleman. He never had to face accusations of being drunk or disorderly, unpleasant, or foul-mouthed. Like his mentors, Walsh, Macleod, and Steele of the North West Mounted Police (NWMP), he was seen as a man of integrity who could be called upon to settle disputes fairly and impartially. It was for this reason that he was appointed as the magistrate for the Banff area and over the years he was elected to various civic positions. He was also the founder of Banff Indian Days and served as its chairman for many years.

Tom played an important role in the history of western Canada. His memories of his encounters with the great Sioux warrior Chief Sitting Bull and the remnants of his once proud nation, as they camped in the rolling, sweet-grass hills of southern Saskatchewan, never left him. He never forgave Sir John A. Macdonald and his political cronies in Ottawa for allowing the Sioux to starve during the brutal winters of 1880 and 1881. Nor could he forgive the manner in which MacDonald's minions failed to support Colonel James Macleod, Colonel Sam Steele, and Major James Walsh, of the NWMP. These men were his heroes and his friends.

Tom's list of accomplishments, and the events he played a role in verges on the unbelievable. As a twenty-one year old recruit with the NWMP at Fort Walsh, Tom rode with Sam Steele, James Walsh, James Macleod, and the venerable Jerry Potts in keeping an eye on Sitting Bull and his band when they camped above the "Medicine Line" after the Battle of the Little Big Horn in June, 1876. (The Indians of the plains referred to the forty-ninth parallel, the border between Canada and the United States, as "the Medicine Line" for its seemingly magical ability to prevent the American soldiers from crossing it.) Wilson greatly admired these men and they him, but he was just a young man at the time and they were seasoned veterans. They taught him a great deal about the ways of men, horses, and nature.

A few years later, Tom led Major Rogers through the Kicking Horse Canyon and on to Rogers Pass as they looked for a route through the mountains that could accommodate the new transcontinental railroad. He was present for the historic driving of the Last Spike at Craigellachie, British Columbia on November 27th, 1885 (he was twenty-six years of age) and he can be seen in the famed photo of that historic occasion. Tom and Major Rogers were not bashful in helping themselves to Adam Smith's private stock of Scotch whiskey later that evening as they entertained William Cornellius Van Horne, and his entourage from eastern Canada, with exciting stories of their experiences in the wilds of the Canadian Rockies.

Tom's solo journey from Lake Louise to Saskatchewan River Crossing and then up and over Howse Pass River along the Blaeberry River to the Columbia River in 1883, to confirm the chosen route through the Kicking Horse Canyon was a remarkable feat of stamina, survival, and outdoorsmanship. He was also the first white person to lay eyes on Lake Louise, Takakkaw Falls, Twin Falls, and Emerald Lake.

After his contract with Major Rogers and the CPR was finished, Tom opened the first guiding service in the Rockies and escorted important visitors from Europe and the United States on hunting, climbing, and exploration trips throughout the untamed wilderness between Banff and Jasper. Tom was the first guide to lead adventurers into the Mt. Assiniboine area, the Skoki and Baker Lake area, the Yoho and the Little Yoho valleys, Lake O'Hara, and Emerald Lake.

When the Riel Rebellion broke in 1885, Tom was one of the first to join Sam Steele's Rangers to help run down Big Bear and Gabriel Dumont. He is also credited with hiring and training most of the great mountain men of the Rockies at one point or another. Wild Bill Peyto, Curly Phillips, Bob Baptie, Ray Legace, Jim Simpson, Bob Campbell, Fred Stevens, and Ray Legasse all worked for Tom during their careers, and some went on to start guiding businesses of their own.

If there was ever any trouble afoot, or an emergency in the area, people knew they could call on Tom. When the unfortunate Phil Abbot fell to his death from the top of Mt. Lefroy in 1894 (becoming the first mountaineering fatality in the Rockies) Tom was there to help pack out Abbot's body from the Plain of Six Glaciers at Lake Louise. He was also on hand to assist A.O. Wheeler when he founded the Alpine Club of Canada and naturally Tom was called upon to help set up the first Alpine Club camp in the Little Yoho Valley in 1907.

The managers of the CPR hotels at Banff, Lake Louise, and Field consulted with Tom regularly, especially concerning problems with guests, locals, or the railway. His innovative solutions usually worked. Tom also took charge when the Banff Springs Hotel, Chateau Lake Louise, Mt. Stephen House, and Glacier House, all burnt down within months of each other in 1923 and 1924 – but that's another story. Was there an arsonist on the loose? That's a mystery that even Tom didn't solve.

Tom, and his wife Minnie, lived in Banff for most of their lives. They were away from the Bow Valley for a few years while he started a horse ranch and trading post at Kootenay Plain near at Nordegg, Alberta. Following this venture he moved to Enderby, British Columbia. As might be expected, the couple soon began to miss the Rockies and it wasn't long before Tom moved the family back to Banff, where he lived as a semi-celebrity and guide for the remainder of his life. He was in constant demand for advice, information, and a story or two and he could always be counted upon to liven up any gathering.

Tom died in Banff, on September 20th, 1933 at seventy-four years of age. Surrounded by the mountains he loved, he now rests in a quiet and shady spot in the Banff cemetery. A short walk leads to a lookout with a fine view of the Bow River Valley and the glacier-hung peaks to the west. He preceded many of his friends in crossing over the Great Divide. His good friend Conrad Kain, died six months later on February 2nd, 1934, in Cranbrook, British Columbia. Mary Schaffer died in 1939, Byron Harmon in 1942, Bill Peyto in 1943, A.O. Wheeler in 1945, Jimmy Brewster in 1947, and Norm Luxton in 1962. All except for Conrad Kain are buried near Tom in the Banff cemetery.

On hearing of Tom's death, his old friend A.O. Wheeler (the founder of the Alpine Club of Canada) wrote the following tribute:

> *His personal charm, fine sense of humour and his unequalled fund of information about Sitting Bull, the North West Mounted Police, the building of the railroad, uncharted mountain areas, wildlife and horses together with an outstanding gift as a raconteur – (story teller) made him beloved by all that knew him. His sympathetic assistance to the Alpine Club of Canada, in its early vicissitudes, will not be forgotten and we trust that his Happy Hunting Ground may contain all that he loved so well and that has made his life so memorable.*

–The Canadian Alpine Club Journal, 1933 pp.203-205).

Tom wore a pointed Royal Canadian Mounted Police (RCMP) style Stetson hat all his adult life and he usually dressed formally. While others scruffed around town dressed in jeans and buckskin jackets, Tom was usually seen in a dark, tweed three-piece suit with a shirt and tie. He always carried a gold pocket watch and chain in his vest pocket. In all the pictures taken of Tom from 1890 until his death in 1933, this was his standard attire. Someone said that Tom was buried with his old Stetson hat on his head. I hope that this was true, because he would have needed it while riding the plains and scaling the high mountain passes with his many friends in that land that lies just beyond the Great Divide.

The following stories tell of Tom Wilson and the many roles he played during the early golden days of western Canada and the Canadian Rockies.

Tom Wilson
Adventurer, Outfitter, Explorer, Mountain Man, Raconteur.

* Assisted Major James Walsh, watching over Sitting Bull and his Sioux Nation 1880–1881 while with the North West Mounted Police at Fort Walsh
* Discovered Lake Louise on August 21, 1882
* Discovered Emerald Lake and Takakkaw Falls
* Led Major Rogers to the summit of Rogers Pass
* Initiated and coordinated Banff Indian Days
* Present for the driving of the last spike of the CPR at Craigallachie
* Packer, outfitter, guide and story-teller for many years in Banff
* A true Canadian hero

Tom Wilson outside his cabin

Tom Wilson seated in the lobby of the Banff Springs Hotel – 1895

Tom Wilson, taken during his later years in Banff

Tom Wilson–Growing up in Ontario

Thomas Edmonds Wilson was born to Irish Canadian parents on August 21st, 1859 in the little town of Bondhead, just north of Toronto, Ontario. Shortly after his birth, his parents moved to Barrie, which at that time was considered to be wilderness. During his youth, Tom learned the secrets of trapping and path-finding and how to survive alone in the wilderness from local Indians. They also taught him how to make and mend snowshoes. This early practical education, together with his understanding of Indian ways, served him well throughout his life.

Tom's father tried to eke out a living by farming, but anyone who knows that part of the country – the lakes, rocks, pine, and sugar-maple forests – can appreciate that farming in that land can be a cruel business. To survive, one must log and trap in the winter, collect maple syrup in the spring, and fish in the summer.

Tom learned to paddle a canoe before he went to grade school, and cavorting with his Indian friends on moccasin clad feet, he would run swiftly through secret forest trails to hidden glades and magical waterfalls known to only a few in the Muskoka region.

Each fall, while still in grade school, Tom and his native friends hunted deer with their bows and arrows, and later with rifles. Seldom did he return without some game – a welcome addition to the family larder. He also learned how to snowshoe and survive in the woods during winter blizzards that sometimes lasted for days. There was little that he was not interested in learning. He learned how to handle horses at an early age and made extra money after school training and gentling everything from Clydesdale draft horses to high-strung thoroughbred stallions. He also became an accomplished blacksmith, which supplemented the family income.

After attending a one-room school near his home, he completed his formal education at the Barrie Grammar School, graduating in 1875 at the age of sixteen. He then worked on local farms as a hired hand, but he was always in great demand for breaking and training colts. Shortly after turning seventeen he decided to see the "Wild West" that he had read so much about in the stories of James Fenimore Cooper and the like. (Cooper wrote *The Leather Stocking Tales – The Pioneers* in 1823, *The Last of the Mohicans* in 1826, *The Prairie* in 1827, *The Pathfinder* in 1840 and *The Deerslayer* in 1841). These stories of the early frontiersmen and their adventures with Indians, buffalo, horses, the wide prairie, and the shining mountains stirred the blood of most strong young men of the day and Tom was no exception. Little did he know that years later a movie would be made of his own life and it would be appropriately called *The Pathfinder*. Tom also followed the exploits of General George Custer in the United States and the newly established NWMP that had been dispatched to the Cypress Hills in southern Saskatchewan to deal with the American whisky traders from Fort Benton, Montana who had massacred of a small group of Assiniboine Indians in the Cypress Hills of southwestern Saskatchewan. It also served to protect Canadian sovereignty north of the Medicine Line (the 49th parallel).

Tom Wilson and the North West Mounted Police

As a teenager, Tom heard much about the 1869-70 Red River uprising in Manitoba and the exploits of Louis Riel. He followed the details of the trial of Thomas Scott, who was found guilty of defying Riel's Provisional Government and was subsequently executed by a Metis firing squad – headed by Ambrose Lepine, one of Riel's lieutenants. He also followed the events of the Wolsely Expedition that was sent to Fort Gary Manitoba in 1870 to deal with hostilities there. Two of his heroes, Major James Macleod and Colonel Sam Steele, were on that expedition and he wished that he'd been old enough to go along with them. Three years later, in May of 1873, the North West Mounted Police was created.

The North West Mounted Police—The March West

Under the inept leadership of the Colonel George French, the NWMP battalion got off to a bad start on its march west from Fort Dufferin, (which was near the U.S. border and south of Fort Gary). The battalion of young recruits was in a high state of excitement when they left Fort Dufferin on the rainy morning of July 8th, 1874. "*I doubt if any expedition ever undertook a journey with such complete faith and such utter ignorance*," reminisced **Sir Cecil Denny**—one of the original recruits and the author of the book, *The Riders of the Plains*. Shortly after getting underway the expedition's horses stampeded and were lost for days. Then a hail and lightning storm blew away their tents and ruined the supplies. With no provisions left the battalion almost starved, and had it not been for the emergence of three phenomenal leaders from within their ranks (James Macleod, James Walsh, and Sam Steele) and the resourcefulness of Jerry Potts (a notorious half-breed scout and tracker) all would have been lost. Potts, who grew up on the plains with the Blackfoot and the Sioux, was hired at Fort Benton, Montana, to be a guide and be a general nursemaid for the young recruits. His knowledge of the plains and its inhabitants saved the young brigade on many occasions. Potts was instrumental in leading the young troops to Fort Whoop-Up in order to close down the illicit whiskey trading activities there.

Fort Whoop-up was built in 1869 at the junction of the Oldman and St. Mary rivers, near the present city of Lethbridge, Alberta, by two unsavory hombres from Montana. Intended to be a "whiskey outpost", Fort Whoop-up was supplied from Fort Benton on the American side of the Medicine-Line. The trail that led from Fort Benton to Fort Whoop-Up became known as the "Whoop-Up Trail".

Colonel French proved to be a totally unsuitable leader and by the time the troop had reached the Cypress Hills, he was close to a nervous breakdown. Some suggested that he was in this condition before the battalion ever left Ontario. To prevent a mutiny from within the ranks, Colonel James Macleod took charge of the force on September 18th, 1874, and Colonel French returned to Ottawa as fast as the riverboat from Fort Benton could take him.

> The humourless commander was as much disliked by his men
> as his second-in-command (Macleod) was cherished. The men
> concluded that French was out of his element, but it was obvious
> that Colonel James Macleod, Major James Walsh, Major Sam
> Steele and a handful of others had found theirs. (Ian Anderson,
> 2000–p.39)

Led by Macleod, Walsh, Steele, and Potts, the revitalized force made short work of the few whiskey traders that were left in the area and closed down Fort Whoop-up. On October 13th, 1874, under Pott's guidance, the building of Fort Macleod commenced on an island in the Oldman River. Colonel Macleod then dispatched Walsh to build a fort in the Cypress Hills, just south of the present-day town of Maple Creek, Saskatchewan. Work begun on June 8th, 1875 and six weeks later the new fort was completed.

From these two posts the NWMP kept a sharp lookout for trouble from whiskey traders and Indians alike and began to bring law and order to western Canada. These early police officers were men of courage, backbone, and integrity with hearts of lions, a sense of justice, and a commitment to fight for the right. It was too bad that their bosses and the politicians in Ottawa didn't share in this integrity as the young force was frequently let down by political decisions and patronage appointments into their ranks. This inevitably sapped their morale.

Major General Sir George French – first Commissioner of the NWMP – Commissioner 1873–1876.

Colonel James F. MacLeod – Assistant Commission of the NWMP 1873-1876 Commissioner 1876–1880.

Jerry Potts
Famous scout, guide, interpreter and general nursemaid to the NWMP during its formative days in the West. Had it not been for Potts the young Force might not have lasted more that three months in the West. He was much feared by both white men and the Indians. There was no greater fighter on the Plains.

The infamous Whoop-up Trail from Fort Benton to Fort Whoop-up.
This was the trail of the whiskey-traders who supplied bad whiskey to the Indians in return for hides.

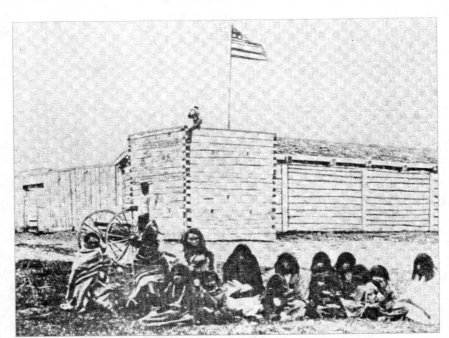

Indian women and children outside Fort Whoop-up
Built in 1868 it was a regional headquarters for the whiskey traders.

In the latter part of 1875, Colonel Macleod was so thoroughly disgusted and frustrated with Ottawa that he resigned as Assistant Commissioner of the NWMP. Major Walsh was the next in line to succeed Macleod and was strongly recommended for the position by Macleod himself. However, thanks to some good old-fashioned political interference, the position was given to the colorless Acheson Gosford Irvine, who hailed from Quebec.

The appointment of Irvine over James Walsh, who was popular among the rank and file, further dampened morale. Irvine was the Quebec born commander of Manitoba's Provisional Battalion of Rifles and like Colonel French before him he was humorless and dull. He had studied civil engineering and then attended military school in Kingston Ontario before joining the Rifles. His main claim to fame was that he had connections in high places in Ottawa and his grandfather was a long-time member of the executive and legislative councils of Lower Canada (Quebec). His men nicknamed him "Irvine the good".

Meanwhile, early in the spring of 1876, the Sioux from the western plains of the United States began drifting north into what is now southern Saskatchewan and Alberta. This greatly disturbed the Canadian Blackfoot Indians and the Cree tribes of the western Canadian plains as the Sioux and the Nez Perce' tribes were their traditional enemies. It was none other than Major James Walsh, usually alone, save for an interpreter and perhaps a scout or two, who rode into the Sioux camps and told them of the rule of law in Canada. Often Walsh would spend days in their camps, sleeping in the chief's teepee at night and wandering freely among the Sioux by day.

Dressed in his scarlet red tunic, with extra gold braid sewn on for more dramatic impact, Walsh's courage in the face of overwhelming odds was remarkable. Occasionally he would even apprehend native offenders, right in their camps, and escort them single-handedly back to Fort Walsh for trial. Walsh soon became a legend among the Indians of the plains on both side of the Medicine Line. He represented "big medicine" to the chiefs of the Sioux, the Blackfoot, and other tribes respected him more than any other white man of the day. Sitting Bull's Lakota Sioux tribe was in awe of him and gave him the name "White Forehead".

Usually alone, and sometimes with only a scout or two, Walsh would fearlessly ride into the Indian camps, sit down with some of the fiercest riders of the plains and calmly outline what the "Great White Mother" (Queen Victoria) expected of them. He also explained the consequences of not complying. Then he'd give them supplies, and even guns and bullets, to hunt the rapidly dwindling buffalo for food.

> *Totally fearless Walsh would confront Spotted Eagle, the war chief of the Sans Arcs, Long Dog the fighting chief of the Hunkpapas Sioux, White Eagle the chief of the Sisseton Sioux and Black Moon the chief of the Lakota Sioux. These war chiefs, who commanded the respect of their fellow warriors, could have wiped Walsh and his fellow red coats off the face of the earth in the twinkling of an eye. They came peacefully however and asked him to plead with the Great White Mother to have pity on them and let them stay in her land. Walsh did not fear them – he believed, as did Colonel Macleod, that honesty, justice, and fair play would win the peace. (Anderson 2000)*

Meanwhile in southern Montana, on the bright Sunday morning of June 25th, 1876, Sitting Bull, the great leader of the Lakota Sioux, was out-witting, out-maneuvering, and out-fighting "Yellow Hair" (General George Custer) and 264 soldiers of the 7th Calvary at the Little Big Horn River. After the massacre the Sioux headed north to the safety of the Medicine Line as fast as they could get there. Sitting Bull believed that the Great White Mother would protect him. He also believed that Major Walsh, her red-coated servant, was a man he could trust.

> *By the winter of 1876, Dark Moon and 2,900 Sioux men, women and children were camped in the Sweet Grass Hills where they were safe north of the Medicine Line. They were a collection of Hunkapapas, Ogalalas, Minniconjous, Sans Arcs, Blackfeet (not to be confused with the Canadian Blackfoot Tribe) and Two Kettles. They were the first of the Sioux refugees from the Little Big Horn to cross the Medicine Line. (Anderson 2000)*

They wouldn't be the last to come. Chief Joseph and his Nez Perce' tribe were also on their way as was Chief Medicine Bear of the Yankton Sioux with his war chief Black Horn and their people. They also took up residence in the Sweet Grass Hills just north of the Milk River ridge.

Lieutenant-Colonel George Armstrong Custer
He pushed the Sioux too far and paid the price at the Little Big Horn River on
June 25, 1876 when he and the 7th Calvary he led were annihilated by Sitting
Bull and a confederacy of the Sioux Nations.

The great Sioux Chief, Sitting Bull

At a meeting of the chiefs, White Eagle introduced Walsh.

This is White Forehead, soldier chief of the Shagalasha—the British Mother's red-coat pony soldiers. He is the law on this side of the Medicine Line. He speaks straight, not like the Americans. You can trust him. (Anderson 2000 p.83)

The newspapers of eastern Canada and the United States were full of stories covering the Custer massacre, the "Indian menace" and their movement into Canada. They frequently mentioned James Walsh quoting him and expressing amazement at how one red-coated "Mountie" could control the fiercest warriors of the plains with such ease. The Fort Benton Record reported regularly from the "front" as it were, and frequently quoted Walsh, who was not bashful about expressing his feelings about how the Indians should be treated. The Fort Benton Record was usually anti-Indian in sentiment but occasionally it condemned its own government's treatment of the Sioux and the Nez Perce'. Walsh was often held up as a model of how to handle the noble savages. The Manitoba Daily Free Press of Winnipeg, the Toronto Globe, the Montreal Witness, the New York Herald, and the Chicago Times all carried exciting stories of the Custer massacre and Sitting Bull and frequently James Walsh was applauded for doing single-handedly what the whole US Calvary had not been able to do.

Surprisingly these accounts were anything but pleasing to Prime Minister Sir John A. Macdonald, Edward Dewdney, the Minister of the Interior, and A.G. Irvine, Walsh's commanding officer. While passing through Chicago, Walsh had the audacity to pay a visit to General Sheridan, the commander of the U.S. Army, to give him some advice on handling the Indians south of the Medicine Line. He suggested that Sheridan take immediate steps to deal with the fraudulent and dishonest Indian agents who were stationed at the U.S. forts along the frontier. His reputation was so well established that President, Rutherford Hayes, invited Walsh to Washington to discuss the Indian problem, "should he ever pass that way". When Walsh suggested to Sir John A. Macdonald that he was thinking of doing just that, Macdonald flew into a rage. Lowly mounted police officers had no right to call on U.S. presidents!

Walsh became the target of much back-stabbing as Sir John A. suggested that he was encouraging the Sioux to stay in Canada in order to enhance his own growing reputation. Irvine seemed to be jealous of the larger-than-life reputation that Walsh was gaining and he undoubtedly saw him as a threat to his own career aspirations.

On September 19, 1877, a great pow-wow (organized by Major James Macleod, Sam Steele, James Walsh, the Reverend John McDougall, (a pioneer Methodist missionary) and Jerry Potts) was held on the Bow River at Blackfoot Crossing or "The Ridge under the Water" near the present southern Alberta village of Gleichen. It resulted in the signing of the last of the major Indian treaties (the Blackfoot Treaty Number 7) in the North West Territories (Saskatchewan and Alberta did not exist then and were a part of the N.W. Territories).

Crowfoot, the revered grand chief of the Blackfoot tribe, played a leading role in bringing the native delegation on side. Other chiefs there for the occasion were: Eagle Tail, chief of the Peigans, Bulls Head, chief of the Sarcee, Weasle Calf and

Old Sun chiefs of the Blackfoot, Buffalo Calf chief of the Stoneys, and Rainy Chief and Red Crow chiefs of the Blood tribes.

The Honorable David Laird, Lieutenant Governor of the North West Territory and Lieutenant Colonel James Macleod each spoke eloquently in favor of the treaty and then the chiefs spoke in turn. Food rations were provided and a peace pipe was passed around many times. Finally on September 22, 1877 the last of the major Indian Treaties was signed. It was a glorious Alberta autumn afternoon – the mountains sparkled in the distance under a fresh sprinkling of snow, and the clear, swift-flowing Bow River rushed by the camp where all were assembled.

When Crowfoot was asked to be the first to sign the Treaty he refused and said:

> *"I'll be the last to sign and I will be the last to break the treaty."*
> *Crowfoot and his people relinquished, surrendered and transferred*
> *their rights, title and interests to Her Majesty the Queen, her heirs*
> *and successors, for all the country between the boundary line*
> *and the Red Deer River, for as long as the sun shines and rivers*
> *run. (Grant MacEwan, Fifty Mighty Men, 1958.)*

Meanwhile back in Barrie, Ontario, Tom Wilson was now in his late teens. He read the stunning account of the battle of the Little Big Horn and how following the massacre, Sitting Bull had led his people to safety across the Medicine Line and into the Sweet Grass and the Thunder Breeding Hills of southern Saskatchewan. He also read accounts of Major Walsh, who was single-handedly gaining the trust and confidence of Sitting Bull and the Indians of the plains. Tom noted that there was much controversy as to whether the Sioux should be allowed to stay in Canada, as many wanted Sitting Bull and his followers sent back to the United States. The names of James Walsh, James Macleod, and Sam Steele become legendary, as each week, stories of their exploits, as well as those of other NWMP officers, filled local newspapers. Tom just couldn't wait to get involved.

In late May of 1878, Sitting Bull and his Lakota Sioux nation were just two jumps ahead of the pursuing U.S. cavalry. They hastened north from the Milk River, crossing the Medicine Line into present-day southern Saskatchewan. They camped at Pinto Horse Butte on the banks of the White Mud Creek–now called Frenchman's River, not far from of Val Marie.

On June 2nd, Major Walsh, dressed in a scarlet tunic and accompanied by his two scouts (Gabriel Soloman and Louis Lavallie) rode with brazen boldness into Sitting Bull's camp. Approaching Sitting Bull's teepee they were met by Spotted Eagle, the war chief of the Sans Arc, who warned them that they were riding into the camp of the highest ranking chief on the plains and to proceed at their own peril.

> *Walsh rode straight to his goal with neither halt nor change of*
> *pace. Nothing like this had ever happened before – a white man,*
> *riding unannounced, and apparently unafraid, into the presence*
> *of the most feared native leader on the continent. The war-weary*
> *Spotted Eagle gazed in astonishment as this mounted man in*
> *immaculate police uniform led his little group to Sitting Bull's*

tipi at a bold gait. ... Sitting Bull had a reputation as a ruthless killer and the police officer was making a reputation as one of the most fearless figures of his time. It was a tense moment, a crucial confrontation in Canadian history. ...The Indian held all the physical advantages. Behind him, within mere minutes traveling time, were 5,000 unhappy Sioux including 1,000 warriors. Immediately behind Walsh were six nervous supporters. The officer halted a few paces from the Chief's tent, bringing the Indian to his feet. For an instant, both men remained motionless gazing at each other, like bulls measuring each other for a fight. Major Walsh broke the spell by dismounting and passed his reins to one of his constables. Striding confidently toward the Chief, he offered his hand in greeting. With surprise bordering on shock, the Chief responded and the two shook hands. (Grant MacEwan, Sitting Bull, 1973)

Major Walsh didn't just exchange pleasantries and leave, he stayed overnight, talking to Sitting Bull and his war chiefs, eating and sleeping in their teepees, and carefully outlining what the Great White Mother's expectations were of them. The respect Walsh commanded was unbelievable. The Sioux thought that he must have "Heap Big Medicine" on his side, as he showed with no sign of fear as he slept peacefully in the camp of the great war-chiefs who had wiped out Custer and the 7th Cavalry just a few months earlier.

The next day, just as Walsh and his men were about to leave, White Dog, a well-known war chief, rode into camp with three of his braves leading a string of five handsome ponies. Walsh's scout, Gabriel Solomon, recognized the ponies as belonging to Father DeCorby, a Catholic priest serving in the Cypress Hills. Stealing each other's horses was considered great sport and the source of much entertainment among the Indians of the plains and it was also the cause of the odd tribal battle. Walsh, however, was not amused. He immediately stepped forward and told White Dog that he was confiscating the horses and placing him under arrest. After some heated discussion, Walsh agreed to let White Dog go with a severe warning, but he led the ponies behind him as he bid Sitting Bull adieu and rode boldly out of the camp.

Sitting Bull must have shaken his head in amazement. What power did this red-coat possess that made him utterly fearless? Those present on that historic occasion never forgot Walsh's bravery and his uncommon courage and they spoke widely about the visit. Each time the tale was told it became more exciting. "White Sioux" as Walsh became known as, had won Sitting Bull's highest respect. (Allen, *White Sioux*,1969). It was not long before all the newspapers of the day carried the story.

After confronting Sitting Bull and the fiercest war chiefs of the plains, it is understandable that Walsh wasn't easily intimidated by the likes of the often-inebriated Sir John A. Macdonald, the ineffective Ed Dewdney or the politicians, bureaucrats in Ottawa. To most Canadians–including Tom Wilson–he was a true hero. Wilson idolized Walsh and hoped that someday soon he'd be able to ride with him.

It was not long before Macdonald and Dewdney decided that the Sioux, the Nez Perce' and other tribes from south of the Medicine Line should return to the United States and the reserves that had been established by Congress. However, the Indians refused, declaring that they loved the "Great White Mother" and "White Sioux" her red-coated chief. Sitting Bull also claimed that his ancestors had always sided with the British. He told of how his people had fought with their British brothers during the Revolutionary War of Independence and again during the War of 1812-1814. He even produced his grandfather's medals from George III to bolster his claim. Macdonald, however, was not impressed when Major Walsh pleaded Sitting Bull's case. He wanted the Sioux gone and he began to blame Walsh for Sitting Bull's refusal to leave.

Fort Walsh nestled in the Cypress Hills

By 1880 the great herds of buffalo that once roamed the Canadian and American plains had been all but wiped out. Both the Canadian and the American governments knew the importance of the buffalo herds to the Indian's nomadic lifestyle. As long as the buffalo roamed free, the Indians would follow them respecting no boundaries, resisting a controlled and contained lifestyle on reservations, and generally posing a threat to settlement and the building of the transcontinental railroads. With this in mind, neither government tried to control the wholesale slaughter of the buffalo and the spread of deadly diseases, such as small pox, among the Indians of the plains. Within a few years all but a few of the great herds, that had once stretched across the plains for as far as the eye could see were gone and so was the Indian's traditional economy and their way of life.

Major James Morrow Walsh in buckskin garb and a hat that was fashionable at the time. General George Custer wore a similar outfit. This photo was probably taken in 1877.

In a particularly poignant letter to his wife Mary, dated June 3, 1880, Colonel Macleod summed up his frustration with the politicians and the bureaucrats who seemingly displayed an utter lack of understanding for what was happening in western Canada: "*The Indians are starving and living on fish. I'm not satisfied with the government's arrangements for supplies. The government appears to think that Indians can hunt for a living, but there is nothing to hunt ... the buffalo are all gone!*

It was so bad on the Canadian plains during the winters of 1879, 1880 and 1881 that the Indians had nothing but roots and their own horses to eat. Walsh and his men at Wood Mountain and the detachments from Fort Walsh, Fort Que'Apelle and Fort Macleod began to share their own meager supplies with the starving Indians. When Sir John A. Macdonald heard of this, he was furious. He reasoned that if the Sioux were allowed to starve for a while, they'd soon pull up stakes and head for the reservations that were waiting for them south of the border. In an infamous letter to the Governor General of the North West Territories, Macdonald wrote: "*When all this is over, I think we must dispense with Walsh's services in the Mounted Police.*"

By the fall of 1879, the plight of the Sioux and their native brothers across the Canadian plains had become desperate. The "long-knives" (the U.S. Cavalry) had set fire to the grasslands between the Milk River and the Missouri River to stop the buffalo from migrating north to the Medicine Line. By the time the icy winds of winter blew across the plains, the Sioux were starving and had to resort to eating their horses. Many were weak and sick and suffering from epidemics. The federal government continued to maintain a deliberate unspoken policy of starving the natives into submission.

Major Walsh, on the other hand, sympathized with Sitting Bull and arranged for his men and his friend Louis Legare to bring wagonloads of food to feed the Sioux. Someone leaked this news to Macdonald (probably Major A.G. Irvine who was hoping to become the next commissioner) and all hell broke loose. Macdonald was furious, and began to believe that Walsh was purposely encouraging the Sioux to stay north of the Medicine Line to maintain the publicity he was enjoying. Walsh was publicly regarded throughout Canada and the United States as the one white man that Sitting Bull respected.

During this time Walsh, James Macleod, and Sam Steele, and other NWMP regulars, were bringing law and order to western Canada. They were also foiling Louis Riel's plans to enlist Indian allies to bolster the Metis Rebellion in Saskatchewan. It is difficult to overestimate the influence Walsh and his colleagues had on western Canada. Without their leadership, things would undoubtedly have turned out much differently.

There was considerable unrest among the Indian tribes of the plains on both sides of the border at this time, owing to the growing disappearance of the buffalo. The Blackfoot, Peigan, Blood and Stoney tribes were particularly anxious, as the great herds were no longer plentiful in the foothills and high plains of the Fort Macleod–Fort Calgary area. They were forced to roam further east toward the Cypress Hills and Wood Mountain where the herds were more plentiful, but where their traditional enemies also hunted. However, Indians of all tribes, now shared a common concern, how to survive against the onslaught of the white man. Soon rumors of an Indian alliance, created to drive the white man from the plains, began to spread across the land.

It was also at this time that the Metis, who harboured many grievances after being driven from their beloved Red River country to central Saskatchewan, decided to make a stand. Led by Gabriel Dumont and Ambroise Lepine and allied with Big Bear, the great chief of the Cree, they once again called on their old friend Louis Riel, who was in exile in Montana, to help them. (Riel had married there and was teaching school in the Judith Basin area.)

Riel, who had led the Red River Rebellion of 1869-70, was a true man of the people. Born in 1844 in St. Boniface, across the river from Fort Garry (Winnipeg), he initially studied for the priesthood. His oratorical abilities, charismatic personality, and strong feeling for natural justice for his people quickly made him their champion. He played this role with vigor and passionate dedication and quickly ran headlong into the insensitive and manipulative policies of Macdonald's government. This led to the Red River Rebellion and eventually to the formation of the Province of Manitoba.

During the rebellion, Riel was accused of orchestrating the murder of the obnoxious Thomas Scott. Subsequently, he was twice elected as a member of Parliament and twice he was expelled from the House of Commons in Ottawa. In 1875 he was banished from Canada for five years. From the Dakota Territory in the United States, he frequently wrote long, passionate articles that outlined his grievances against Ottawa, and those responsible for his exile. John A. Macdonald was definitely not among those included in his Christmas card list.

Ottawa's response to the unrest among of the Metis was to fabricate and promote the myth that Riel was a religious fanatic suffering from delusions of grandeur. He was portrayed as a "troublemaker of the first water" who threatened the development of the nation. In particular he and the free-roaming Metis jeopardized Macdonald's dream of a national railroad. With the buffalo gone, the Indians starved into submission, and Louis Riel and the Metis out of the way, there would be no opposition to eastern Canada's dreams of a nation stretching from sea to sea.

In the fall of 1878, Major Walsh learned that Louis Riel had been secretly visiting the Cree, the Blackfoot, the Sioux, and the Peigan tribes in the Cypress Hills and the Wood Mountain area and had ventured as far a field as Fort Macleod. At the same time news arrived that Ambroise Lepine, Riel's old lieutenant from the Red River Rebellion days, and the one who had captured Thomas Scott and sentenced him to death, was holding meetings in the Metis settlements and the Indian villages throughout the Canadian prairies. Following this, Lepine met with Riel in Fort Benton, Montana.

Major Walsh figured something was afoot and he guessed that they weren't planning the meal menu for the annual Metis summer picnic. He then learned that Riel had convinced the South Assiniboines to enter into an Indian blood alliance to liberate the western plains and return them to the Indians and the Metis. Riel also tried to convince Medicine Bear and Black Horn of the Yankton Sioux to join them in the blood alliance but they refused.

With his characteristic boldness Major Walsh and his scout Louis Daniels rode across the Medicine Line and then some seventy-five miles into Montana Territory to meet with Red Stone, the chief of the South Assiniboine tribe. Walsh stayed in Red Stone's camp for two days and convinced the great chief that he should withdraw from his alliance with Riel. When Riel learned of the withdrawal of Red Stone's support he was furious and vowed that he'd see Walsh dead.

It was about this time that Walsh heard that a big pow-wow was planned for the Big Bend area of the Milk River in Montana. It was here that Riel hoped to win the allegiance of Chief Crowfoot of the Blackfoot[1] nations and Big Bear of the Cree tribes. Riel promised Crowfoot that he would be his right-hand man when he ruled the plains, but to get Crowfoot's agreement, Riel needed more Sioux and Cree to join in the alliance.

Walsh moved quickly. He paid a hurried visit to his old friend Sitting Bull the esteemed chief of the Sioux nation. He convinced them to remain loyal to the Great White Mother. He then ordered his men to seize all the firearms and ammunition held by the traders of the area and store them at Fort Walsh until things quieted down. This prevented Riel and his followers from gaining access to the guns they needed for the uprising. With this accomplished, Walsh rode to the rendezvous at the Big Bend of the Milk River and convinced Chief Crowfoot to take his Blackfoot tribe back home. He also advised the chiefs of the other assembled tribes to complain to their Indian Agents that a large group of Canadian Metis was on their reserve, trying to start trouble.

This they did and by the late fall, a combined force of U.S. marshals, soldiers, and customs officers raided the Big Bend camp, seizing all the weapons and ammunition and ordering the Canadian Metis and their Indian allies back to their own country. Those Metis who claimed to be American were removed to southern Montana. Walsh then sent out the word that Louis Riel was not welcome in Canada and if caught, he would be arrested.

Had Walsh not acted so decisively, to upset the plans of Dumont, Lapine, and Riel, the history of western Canada would have been much different. An Indian blood alliance of the tribes of the plains and foothills, joined by the Metis and the Cree, would have expelled the white man from the area in short order. However, as it turned out, before the snow fell late 1879, Walsh had succeeded in foiling Riel's plans to take back the western plains with himself as the ruler. He got little credit for his crucial action, but it undoubtedly stalled the North West Rebellion and frustrated Riel's plans to attract greater numbers to his cause.

It was a defining moment in Canadian history, ranking equally with Wolfe's daring capture of Quebec on the Plains of Abraham in 1759, Adam Dollard des Ormeaux's heroism in saving the little settlement of Montreal from the blood-thirsty Iroquois in 1660, and the driving of the Last Spike of the CPR in 1885. James Walsh was the right man for the situation all right and its unfortunate that his nervous superiors didn't appreciate his accomplishments. Canada owes him a great debt.

Back home in Barrie, Ontario young Tom Wilson continued to be thrilled by the newspaper accounts documenting the events happening in western Canada. He wanted to meet Walsh, Steele, and Macleod for himself. Like most young men

---

[1] **Note**: John Turner in his book "The Northwest Mounted Police" points out that in Canada; It's *Black-foot*—not *Blackfeet*. "The plural of foot is feet. But it's one Blackfoot, two Blackfoot, ten Blackfoot or a whole band of Blackfoot Indians. ... They are Blackfoot quite irrespective of the number involved in referring to them"

of that day, the romantic notion of wearing a scarlet red tunic and bringing law and order to the wild west was mighty appealing. So at seventeen years of age, he traveled to Detroit, Chicago, and as far as Sioux City, Iowa, picking up odd jobs handling horses and working on farms along the way. Getting homesick, he returned to Barrie in the fall of 1878 and joined the Volunteer Militia of Canada, where he learned the basics of soldiering and military discipline.

In early 1880, the NWMP began to recruit strong, self-reliant, and educated young men from the farms of Ontario. Tom, now twenty-one years of age, was old enough to enlist and on the sunny afternoon of July 19th, he signed up in Barrie, Ontario. In a few days he was headed west – bound for Fort Walsh in the Cypress Hills. Soon he'd be riding patrol in the rolling hills and the flat lands of southern Saskatchewan and dealing with the Sioux refugees and the Canadian tribes. He had no idea how quickly he'd become disillusioned with the NWMP.

Tom's journey west involved a steamboat voyage through the Great Lakes and across Lake Superior to Duluth, Minnesota. A train then took him to Bismarck, North Dakota and from there he traveled by riverboat up the Missouri River to Fort Benton, Montana. Tom was particularly interested in the North Dakota and Montana Territory as he had read a great deal about this traditional hunting ground of the Sioux and the Nez Perce' Indians. The eastern newspapers had been full of stories dealing with Custer's ignominious defeat and the "Indian situation". Some articles sympathized with the Indians but most endorsed their annihilation.

Tom knew every detail of General Custer's humiliating defeat at the battle of the Little Big Horn, which took place on a the sunny Sunday morning of June 25th, 1876. He'd also followed the stories of how Sitting Bull and his Sioux people had taken refuge in the hills just southeast of Fort Walsh. It would not be long he was sure, before he would meet Sitting Bull as well as Chief Joseph, the leader of the Nez Perce nation. Given his background growing up with Indians in Barrie, Ontario he naturally sympathized with the natives.

Tom understood that it was the ignorance and corruption of the U.S. Congress that had caused most of the problems with the Indians of the plains. From the time Lewis and Clarke trekked across the continent in 1805 and 1806 and promised the "protection, love and prosperity" of their "Great White Fathers" in Washington, one promise after another had been broken.

(The final betrayal came in a surprise attack on the remnants of the once-proud Sioux nation at Wounded Knee in southern Montana, on a bitterly cold morning in the first week of January, 1891. The 7th Cavalry, led by the vengeful Major Nelson Miles, slaughtered a group of half-starved old men, sick women, and small children as they tried to defend themselves with sticks and a few bows and arrows. The overwhelmed Sioux were cut down by the Cavalry's swords and trampled into the frozen ground by the Army's steel-shod horses. Wounded Knee was a hollow victory and didn't win the Americans any respect on either side of the forty-nineth parallel.)

James Morrow Walsh of the NWMP

One of Canada's truest heroes, Walsh single-handedly managed Sitting Bull and his great Sioux nation of some 3,000 fearless riders and legendary war chiefs when they high-tailed it across the Medicine Line into Southern Saskatchewan in late May of 1878. Alone, save for a scout and attired in his red serge tunic with extra gold braid sewn on it, Walsh rode into Sitting Bull's camp at Pinto Horse Butte on White Mud Creek (now Frenchman's River), near the present town of Val Marie, and took control. He told him of the Great White Mother he represented and that he would tolerate no nonsense. Amazingly he won Sitting Bull's respect and obedience. It was a defining moment in Canadian History, every bit as significant as General Wolfe's decisive victory over Montcalm on the Plains of Abraham near Quebec City. Equally significant is the fact that later in 1878, James Walsh single-handedly foiled Louis Riel's plans for a "Blood Alliance" to wipe the white-man from the plains. He also saved countless gold seeker's lives when he was appointed as the first Commissioner of the Yukon during the gold rush.

A man of amazing courage, integrity, honor and compassion, it is not surprising that he would run head-long into Sir John A. MacDonald and his minions in Ottawa. Canada owes him a great debt. Had it not been for him, this country would have turned out much differently.

The NWMP officers at Fort Walsh in 1879
F.J. Dickens, the son of the writer Charles Dickens, is in the back row–second in from the left. Seated in the middle row from L. to R. are A. G. Irvine, James MacLeod and Dr. J. Kittson.

Fort Walsh in 1878

In those days Fort Benton, Montana was an important terminal for the distribution of all goods and passengers coming into the west. Paddle wheelers and steam barges could make their way up the Missouri River to Fort Benton all the way from St. Louis. With no competition from the railroads (which were not yet built) all goods, including whiskey came into the territory by the riverboats that landed at Fort Benton. Beyond this point the river was not passable, and so the town grew into a rough and ready center that attracted freewheeling, wild-natured frontiersmen who held life pretty cheap. From Fort Benton it was a two-day ride to Fort Walsh, which was nestled in the Cypress Hills of present day Saskatchewan.

[The present day topography of the Fort Benton area is the same as it was in the 1860's. The river makes a long and lazy "S" turn just before it reaches the town site. From a lookout, high above the Missouri River, east of town, one can imagine the large riverboats and barges nearing their destination. Much of the town has been restored and the large hotel there is well worth a visit. Walking along the tree-lined streets, one can easily imagine what it must have been like to arrive at this wild frontier town after a long journey on the river. It was the biggest commercial centre in the west and it offered all a weary traveller could wish for – and perhaps a few other things as well.]

By the spring of 1880, the pressure and the political interference that Sir John A. Macdonald and his minions were applying to the NWMP came to a head. In June, Colonel Macleod had had enough. He reorganized his command and transferred Major Walsh to Fort Qu'Appelle, effectively removing Walsh from the Wood Mountain area where Sitting Bull was camped. Superintendent Paddy Crozier was assigned to replace Walsh at Wood Mountain. At this point Macleod resigned in disgust. He was a man of great integrity and could no longer tolerate interference from those who had no real understanding, or concern, for what was happening in the western Canada.

Macleod's resignation was a great blow to the morale of the troops, as he was much revered by the young men of the force. They saw him as a father figure who had brought them through when Colonel French had failed them. When it was learned that A. G. Irvine "the Good", not James Walsh, had been appointed to take Macleod's place, the men were devastated.

The members of the NWMP at Fort Macleod, Fort Walsh, Wood Mountain and Fort Qu'Appelle' weren't the only ones disappointed at the news of Irvine's appointment. The Sioux knew that with Irvine in command of the NWMP, their days in Canada were numbered. Both Irvine and Crozier danced on strings pulled by the puppet masters in Ottawa and they were anything but sympathetic to the Indians' cause. It was said of Paddy Crozier that he never let compassion get in his way when it came to managing the Sioux.

In the late June, 1880 Walsh took sick leave and returned to his home in Brockville. From there he sought an interview with the Prime Minister to plead the case of his friend Sitting Bull but Macdonald refused. He reasoned that when Sitting Bull and his people got hungry enough they would return to the reservations that were waiting for them in the Yellowstone area of Montana and Wyoming.

This was the political climate that Tom Wilson rode into when he arrived at Fort Walsh on September 22nd, 1880. It didn't take him long to size up the situation and to learn that one of his heroes, James Macleod had resigned from the force in frustration and disgust. He also learned that diseases such as smallpox introduced to the natives through tainted blankets, were systematically decimating the Indians. Both the American and the Canadian governments turned a blind eye to this despicable practice. Both governments also tacitly approved the over-hunting of the buffalo by the "hiders" as it was reasoned that when the buffalo ceased to roam the plains so would the Indians, and they would be easier to contain on the reserves that had been set up for them.

At Fort Walsh, Tom gained the friendship of Jerry Potts, forming a close bond that would last for many years. Potts, usually a man of few words, filled Tom in on the internal politics of the "honourable force" as they rode out on patrol missions together. Later that fall, as they rode from Fort Walsh to Wood Mountain they visited Sitting Bull in his camp. Potts introduced Tom to the great Chief and he was able to see first hand the desperate state of privation that the once proud leader found himself in.

Wilson and Potts also visited Major Sam Steele who, in Walsh's absence, was in charge of Fort Qu'Appelle. Sam confirmed that things were not well within the NWMP and suggested that Tom keep his eyes open for other opportunities further west. He also mentioned that the newly-established Canadian Pacific Railroad (CPR) would soon be hiring people to build the railroad and survey a route through the Rocky Mountains. During the fall and winter of 1880, Tom rode patrol from out of Fort Walsh and helped keep peace among the tribes, as they often amused themselves by stealing each other's horses and taking the odd scalp.

In the late spring of 1881, Tom visited Sitting Bull's camp for the last time. He stayed two days with the chief and saw how hopeless and helpless his people had become. Sitting Bull was still hoping that Major Walsh would return from the east with news that the Great White Mother had agreed to give his people permanent sanctuary in the hills of southern Saskatchewan. Major Walsh didn't return, but he did sent a letter to Sitting Bull by way of Louis Daniels, his trusted scout at Wood Mountain. Tom read it aloud to the great chief. It told of how Walsh, defying Sir John A. Macdonald's wishes, had travelled to Chicago to talk to General Hammond on behalf of the Sioux. Hammond agreed to give Sitting Bull and his people safe passage to the reserve that had been set up for the Sioux near Fort Bufford. Walsh also had arranged for his friend Jean Louis Legare, who had given Sitting Bull and his people supplies and food, free of charge during the harsh winters of 1880 and 1881, and his former scout Louis Daniels, to go along with the Sioux for moral support. Legare supplied the wagons to carry those who didn't have horses, and those who were too weak to ride. Tom Wilson and Jerry Potts helped Sitting Bull understand that this was his best option under the circumstances.

Finally, with both Walsh's assurance and encouragement from Potts, Legare, Daniels and Wilson, Sitting Bull agreed to leave Canada. Irvine and Crozier took credit for the negotiations and never once mentioned the role played by others, particularly Walsh, Legare, Daniels, Jerry Potts, and young Tom Wilson.

On July 15th, 1881, Sitting Bull and the Lakota Sioux packed up their camp and headed south across the Medicine Line for the last time to confront their destiny in Montana. The reservation where they were escorted was not far from the junction of the Yellowstone and the Little Big Horn rivers where they had handed the U.S. Calvary its only defeat. Accompanying them were Jerry Potts and Jean Legare. Later Legare told Tom that it made him weep when he saw how pathetic the once proud Sioux were on that trip. Most were sick, old, and helpless. The glory days for the great warriors of the plains were finished, as were the buffalo that had been the staple of their economy. It didn't happen often, but it made Tom Wilson tear-up as well. I was told that he did so for years afterward whenever he'd tell stories of Sitting Bull around his corral in Banff.

Frank Dickens, the son of the famous author Charles Dickens, was also a member of the NWMP at the time and his journal and letters were sent back to England. He reported the final surrender of the great chief:

> *When he and his sorry train of Sioux arrived at Fort Bufford, Dakota Territory, and the moment came to surrender to Major Brotherton of the U.S. Army, the old warrior deliberated in the council tent for some time before rising and putting his arm around one of his sons, an eight-year-old, who stood wide-eyed beside him as he spoke:*

> '*I surrender this rifle to you through my son. I wish him to learn the habits of the whites. I wish it to be remembered that I was the last man of my tribe to surrender my rifle, and this day it is given to you.*' (E. Nicols – Dickens of the Mounted 1989)

What Happened to Them All?

What became of the characters that so influenced the history of western Canada, as well as the thoughts and actions of young Tom Wilson?

Sitting Bull, the great chief of the Lakota Sioux, took his people to a reserve in central Montana. He was confined at Fort Randall until 1883 and then he moved to a reserve near Standing Rock. In 1885, he joined **Buffalo Bill Cody's Wild West Show** and toured the United States and eastern Canada. He had been approached on five different occasions to join Louis Riel, but each time he refused. He wanted to remain loyal to Major Walsh and the Great White Mother he represented. On December 14th, 1890, at the age of fifty-four, he was shot and killed with his seventeen-year-old son Crowfoot and six braves in a fight with tribal police at Grant River, South Dakota. Two weeks after he was buried, the 7th Cavalry slaughtered the remnants of the Sioux – over two-hundred sick men, women and children – at Wounded Knee in South Dakota.

Grant MacEwan, in his superb book entitled *Sitting Bull*, 1973, describes the type of man Sitting Bull was.

Only in death did Sitting Bull's struggles end. He won most of the battles he fought but lost the important one – the long war against the oncoming hordes from lands across the sea. Strange people, these newcomers, and crafty. He could not understand them, try as he might. Their way of thinking was so foreign to his ideals. What they wanted was to him morally wrong. He found that he could not trust them. He said so in the speech by which he might be remembered; a speech marked by bewilderment and beauty; a speech revealing the depth of his imagination and the anguish in his heart.

Sitting Bull's last recorded speech was as follows:

Behold my friends, the spring is come: the earth has gladly received the embrace of the sun, and we shall soon see the results of their love. Every seed is awakened and all animal life. It is through this mysterious power that we too have our being and we therefore yield to our neighbors, even to our animal neighbors, the same rights as ourselves to inhabit this vast land.

Yet hear me friends! We have now to deal with another people, small and feeble when our forefathers first met with them, but now great and overbearing. Strangely enough, they have a mind to till the soil, and the love of possession is a disease in them…. They claim this mother of ours, the Earth, for their own use, and fence their neighbors away from her, and deface her with buildings and their refuse. They compel her to produce out of season, and when sterile she is made to take medicine in order to produce again. All this is sacrilege.

This nation is like a spring freshet: it overruns its banks and destroys all who are in its path. We cannot dwell side by side. Only seven years ago we made a treaty by which we were assured that the buffalo country should be left to us forever. Now they threaten to take that from us also. My brothers, shall we submit? Or shall we say to them: First kill me, before you take possession of my fatherland. (Eastman 1924 – Indian Heroes and Chieftains p.119)

The great Lakota Sioux Chief—Sitting Bull at Fort Walsh in 1878
This photo, the only one taken of him in Canada, was taken by T. G. Anderton of the NWMP stationed at Fort Walsh. Many American photographers claimed this photo as their own.

Colonel James MacLeod 1870

Chief "Crowfoot" of the Blackfoot Confederacy

Sitting Bull's Monument at Wood Mountain Saskatchewan

On July 15, 2002, it was a memorable experience for me to sleep under the stars at the foot of Sitting Bull's monument and listen to the same prairie night sounds that he would have listened to–coyote yips, wolf howls and the screeches of night hawks and owls as they hunted and called to one another. Occasionally a horse would whinny in the night from somewhere out in the surrounding hills. At sunrise I looked out on the same rolling hills and grasslands that the great Chief would have gazed upon and I tried to imagine his feelings that last morning at Wood Mountain (July 15, 1881) as Jean Louis Legare's wagons, and a few red-coated Mounties, waited to take him and the remnants of Sioux tribe across the Medicine Line to Fort Bufford, Montana where he surrendered to the U.S. Cavalry and submitted to a life of containment. His way of life, and that of the great riders of the plains, died that day. The wolves and the coyotes still mourn for them across the prairies and you can hear them do so every evening at Wood Mountain.

The Sitting Bull Monument at Wood Mountain Saskatchewan
The plaque reads as follows:

SITTING BULL
BORN ABOUT 1834 IN SOUTH DAKOTA, SITTING BULL WITH OTHER NOTED SIOUX INDIAN CHIEFS AND SEVERAL THOUSAND FOLLOWERS FLED INTO CANADA AFTER THE CUSTER MASSACRE IN 1877. FOR FOUR YEARS HE CAMPED IN THE WOOD MOUNTAIN DISTRICT. FIRMLY BUT FAIRLY TREATED BY THE N.W.M.P AND SUSTAINED BY PROVISIONS FROM THE TRADER LOUIS LEGARE. IN JULY 1881, THE LATTER ESCORTED SITTING BULL AND THE REMNANTS OF HIS BAND BACK TO THE UNITED STATES WHERE THE FAMOUS CHIEF WAS KILLED IN DECEMBER 1890.

Following Sitting Bull's surrender, **Major James Morrow Walsh** returned to Fort Qu'Appelle and remained there for two years. He resigned from the NWMP on September 1st, 1883. His old friend and commanding officer, James Macleod stated in his book, 'The North West Mounted Police and Law Enforcement 1873-1905':

> Macdonald had found a scapegoat and Walsh, although not summarily dismissed, was forced to resign in 1883, after Sitting Bull was safely back in the United States. He served his country well and was rewarded poorly for it. He deserved better.

During his time at Fort Qu'Appelle, Walsh drew the admiration of none other than William Cornelius Van Horne – then the general manager of the CPR. After his resignation from the force, Walsh formed the Dominion Coal, Coke and Transportation Company in Brandon, Manitoba and helped develop coal mining in Manitoba's Souris River Valley district. As providence would have it his biggest customer was the CPR and from this enterprise he was able to amass a fortune. He built an elaborate home in Brockville, Ontario and called it "Indian Cliff".

In 1897, at the height of the Klondike Gold Rush, Walsh was appointed both the Commissioner of the Yukon and the superintendent of the Yukon NWMP reporting directly to the Minister of the Interior rather than the Commissioner of the NWMP. He held this post for over a year and then resigned. His old friend, Major Sam Steele, took his place and became a legend in the Klondike. In his book Forty Years in Canada (2000) Steele later wrote:

> Each man had to bring into the Yukon district at least 1,150 pounds of solid food besides tents, cooking utensils as well as prospectors and carpenters' tools, or he would not be permitted to enter the country. This order, given by Walsh the commissioner of the territory, was one of the wisest ever given in the Yukon and the means of preventing much trouble and privation: needless to say it was strictly enforced.

Walsh's notes, written the day after Sitting Bull's death, sum up the type of man he was and the deep feelings he held for his old friend:

> I am glad to hear that Bull is relieved of his miseries, even if it took a bullet to do it. A man that wielded such power as Bull once did, that of a King, and over a wild spirited people, cannot endure abject poverty.... Without suffering great mental pain and death is a relief.... The Indians were not receiving sufficient food.... Women and children crying for assistance ... his suffering from day to day became worse ... stronger appeals to the Great Spirit ... appearing to the white people as a crazy ... I regret now that I had not gone to Standing Rock and seen him ... Bull was misrepresented. He was not the bloodthirsty man reports made him out to be. He asked for nothing but justice ... He did not want to be a beggar... He was not a cruel man. He was kind of heart. He was not dishonest. He was truthful. He loved his people

and was glad to give his hand in friendship to any man who was honest with him.... Bull experienced so much treachery that he did not know whom to trust.

Walsh made "Indian Cliff" in Brockville, Ontario his final home and he died there at sixty-five years of age. His funeral on July 25th, 1905, was one of the largest ever-witnessed in Brockville.

Shortly after arriving at the Cypress Hills in 1876, **Colonel James Farquharson Macleod** took over command of the North West Mounted Police from Colonel French. With the help of Jerry Potts he organized the Blackfoot Treaty Number 7 at Blackfoot Crossing in September of 1877. Never happy being caught between the realities of life on the western frontier and the demands of politicians and bureaucrats in Ottawa, he resigned from the NWMP in 1880. He later became a judge of the Supreme Court of the North West Territories.

Major Sam Steele wrote glowingly of Macleod.

> *As a soldier, a judge and a gentleman he had few equals. From the time he arrived, in everything for the well being of the people of the North West Territory (west of Ontario) his hand was to be seen. No one was jealous of him: he was the admired of all, and kind to a fault. He had been transferred to Calgary some time before his death, and was much missed in Macleod.*
>
> *When Fenian raids were threatened, he was again in the front, and in 1870, he was the brigadier-major on the Wolseley–Red River expedition. In 1873, he was appointed to the newly formed North West Mounted Police (NWMP), eventually becoming the commissioner of the force, which he maintained at a high state of efficiency until he resigned in 1880. Following this he took an appointment as stipendiary magistrate of the territory, stationed at Macleod–the fort he founded south of Calgary.*

In later years Tom Wilson met frequently with the old commissioner. Together they visited Crowfoot, Father Lacombe, the Reverend John McDougall, and Sam Steele. Occasionally Major Walsh would drop in, and then talk would turn to the early days of the NWMP, the Great March of 1873, their life in the Cypress Hills, and their adventures at Fort Macleod. Colonel James Macleod died in Calgary on September 5th, 1894.

Sir Sam Benfield Steele, born on January 5th, 1849, in Purbrook, Simcoe County, Ontario described early life in his book *Forty Years in Canada* as follows:

> *My riding and shooting I learned under the auspices of my cousins in the township of Oro. I roamed the woods during the holidays and built boats and rafts, assisted them in making gunpowder*

and ball, using a heavy rifle or fowling piece as soon as we could carry them. There was nothing in the life of the backwoods pioneer that we did not know and desire to learn.

Big Sam joined the militia at sixteen years of age and soon qualified for the highest rank in the second battalion of the Leicestershire Regiment. He earned a first place certificate and made 100 per cent on drills and discipline. Events would soon take him to the Canadian prairies.

On November 24th, 1869, Louis Riel took forcible possession of Fort Garry on the Red River, seizing the fort's supplies, guns, and money. He quickly established a provisional government and after a trial conducted by his lieutenant Ambrose Lepine, the hapless Tomas Scott was executed by a firing squad on March 4th, 1870. This galvanized Sir John A. Macdonald into dispatching a militia to the Red River under the leadership of Colonel Viscount Wolseley. Sam Steele joined the expedition on May 1st, 1870, and left immediately for the Red River Valley. It was on this expedition that he met James Macleod who later became his commanding officer in the NWMP.

On May 3rd, 1873, Macdonald introduced a bill into parliament that established the North West Mounted Police, a police force in the North West Territories which included present day Manitoba, Saskatchewan and Alberta. Recruiting began in September under Inspector James Walsh and Sam was one of the first to sign up. He was given the rank of Sergeant Major (his rank upon leaving the Wolseley expedition) and he was placed in charge of breaking the horses and instructing the Non Commissioned Officers how to ride. Walsh took over the duties as adjutant, veterinary surgeon, and riding-master.

Big Sam was with the NWMP on the 1874 march west and he also helped to close down Fort Whoop-up. He then helped establish Fort Macleod and Fort Walsh and served at Fort Qu'Appelle as the adjutant in charge of the district. Later he was placed in command of the detachment that kept law and order in the construction camps as the CPR built the railway across western Canada. He was also present at the driving of the Last Spike of the CPR at Craigallachie B.C. on November 7, 1885.

With the outbreak of the North West Rebellion in May of 1885, Steele was appointed a major of the Canadian militia. Placed in command of the Alberta Field Force, he was charged with raising a mounted corps known as "Steele's Scouts." For reliable recruits, he turned to his old friends from his NWMP days. Tom Wilson from Banff and the reverend John McDougall from Morley were among the first to sign up. The hard-riding Steele's Scouts assisted in apprehending Louis Riel, and then they "put the run" on Big Bear.

In 1885 Sam became the Superintendent of the NWMP and on December 8th, 1888, he was placed in command of the Macleod District. After ten years of exemplary service in southern Alberta, he was appointed to keep law and order in the Yukon during the gold rush of 1898. After this he commanded the Canadian troops in both the Boer War and the First World War. In 1918 he was knighted by King George V. A year later he died in London, England – a victim of the great flu epidemic.

Fort Steele in British Columbia and Mount Steele in the Yukon were named in honour of "The Lion of the West". His funeral was one of the largest in western Canada and caused a break in the violence and turmoil of the General Strike in Winnipeg. Someone said: "Sam wouldn't have had it any other way." Not bad for a kid from Ontario who never completed high school.

Louis Riel. In 1884, a delegation of Metis, who had abandoned the Red River country in Manitoba in favour of a freer life in Saskatchewan, rode down to Sun River, Montana to convince Louis Riel to champion their cause once again. On March 15th, 1885 the North West Rebellion broke out when a Metis–Cree Indian alliance attacked a NWMP brigade from Fort Carlton, near Duck Lake between Prince Albert and Battleford. The leader of the NWMP troop was none other than the ubiquitous Paddy Crozier and he unwittingly led his men into an ambush.

This event sparked great panic throughout the West, as everyone feared that Crowfoot, the chief of the Blackfoot tribe, would join with the Sioux, the Cree, the Peigans, the Bloods and the Stoneys to form a blood alliance. In Calgary there was pandemonium in the streets as frantic dispatches for help were sent to Ottawa. An immediate mobilization took place and every available man in the West was pressed into action. Among those rushing to Saskatchewan on the newly completed CPR railroad was Tom Wilson, who joined his old friend Sam Steele for the emergency.

When Riel was captured, he was quickly charged with treason, tried, and convicted. On November 16, 1885, he was hanged at the NWMP barracks in Regina. Some contended that his trial was rigged, saying that it should have been held in Winnipeg before a more sympathetic jury. Crafty old Sir John A. Macdonald gave the order to hasten the trial and to hold it in Regina, where a jury friendly to the crown would guarantee the desired result. Macdonald wanted Riel dealt with quickly before support for him grew too great, especially in the Province of Quebec where there was great sympathy for him.

In a letter sent home to England on November 20, 1885, Frank Dickens, who was on the scene at the time, described Riel's death:

What does God say, one wonders, about people who paraphrased His commandment by killing Louis Riel? No, my dear, I did not witness the hanging. Nor did I attempt to visit him in his cell, to repay the courtesy of his Montana hospitality. Besides, Riel did not want for attention. The eyes of the entire Canadian nation – of both nations, French and English – were upon the man about to walk to the gallows.

The morning of the execution was so gentle, a thing of mist and hoar frost, that it was as if the Almighty were denying anyone an excuse to absent himself from the scene. Morbid curiosity is not paramount among my failings, yet I too was drawn forth by the sparkling pageant, into the compound where a rather self-conscious crowd had gathered. Outside on the road shuffled those latecomers who were disgruntled because limited space had denied them their wish to observe the hanging in the barracks yard. I stayed well beyond the flagged cordon, desirous to be only in the vicinity, should an angel of the Lord appear with silver sword to slash the black flag atop the staff, and pluck the prisoner from the noose, to bear him off to higher ground and prove, yes, indeed, God is Catholic.

Unlike the doomed Sidney Carton,[the protagonist of Charles Dickens' novel, A Tale of Two Cities] Louis Riel in his last moments was not subjected to a cicada chorus of knitting needles. I'm told that the only sound was the occasional nervous laugh from the troopers on guard, at the kind of joke that we use to buffer a situation that is larger than life. At last, even I heard the thud, the thrum of a rope suddenly taking the full weight of a sturdy, pinioned man. Someone said: "The son of a bitch is gone for sure now."

It was an accolade of a sort, quite in keeping with the respect shown by the compatriots of Madame Defarge. The French execute an Englishman, the English execute a (mostly) Frenchman, and the story is sad in both tongues. I'm told that Riel, too, died bravely, stoutly refusing the legal defence of insanity, to the end. On the scaffold, he prayed for so long that the sheriff had to set a time limit, and when Riel reached the part of the Lord's Prayer "deliver us from..." the sheriff signaled for the trap to be sprung. The noose knot slipped from beneath Riel's ear during the drop, so that the fiery champion of the oppressed was strangled to death – a process that took two minutes. Carton's guillotine was more charitable. ...

(E. Nicol– *Dickens of the Mounted* 1989)

Sam Benfield Steele– "The Lion of the North"

Louis Riel, the Metis leader who tried to help his people and preserve their way of life. An eloquent orator, he was twice chosen to represent his people in Ottawa but found it a hopeless cause. He tried to fight off the domination of the West by Eastern interests but that too was a hopeless cause. Spin-doctors in the East called him a madman, a fanatic, a religious zealot, and a traitor. He was captured at the Battle of Batoche, taken to the NWMP barracks in Regina where he was quickly tried, convicted and hung on November 16, 1885.

Jerry Potts the great scout, Indian fighter, and interpreter was the unofficial nursemaid to the NWMP during their march west in 1874 and during their early days at Fort Walsh and Fort Macleod. He served the NWMP for twenty-two years, leading a remarkable life on the plains. His father was a Scot, in charge of the American Fur Trading Company post at Fort Benton, and his mother was a Peigan princess. Jerry could be either an Indian or a white man as the mood struck him.

It was Jerry Potts who suggested to Colonel George French and Colonel James Macleod that they build Fort Macleod was on an island in the Old Man River. It was also Potts that led the fresh-faced NWMP when they closed down the infamous Fort Whoop-up and "put the run" on the ruthless whiskey traders from Fort Benton. He was constantly making daring rescues of one kind or another and was utterly fearless in the face of great danger—even when hopelessly out-numbered. It was said that pound for pound, Jerry Potts was the most feared fighter, Indian or white, ever to ride the plains. He gave no quarter and expected none.

In February of 1885, Sergeant W. D. Antrobus and ten members of the NWMP left Fort Macleod in hot pursuit of a group of American whiskey traders who were operating illegally in the High River area. Potts was the police officer's guide and interpreter. It was bitterly cold on the open plains and the patrol encountered numerous blizzards. During one violent storm, the patrol's tents were blown away and the posse had to take shelter in the snow with only a few willow bunches to protect them. To keep from freezing, the men slept in pairs under their buffalo-hide blankets. Later Sergeants Antrobus reported on his misfortune of having to sleep next to Captain Paddy Crozier during the storm. It was too cold for either to get much sleep, but he observed that Jerry Potts simply rolled up in his buffalo hide, snuggled down in the blowing snow, and slept soundly.

At Pine Coulee they came across an abandoned trading post and here they waited out a blizzard that lasted for several days. When the storm abated, the culprits were apprehended near High River. On the return to Fort Macleod, the patrol got separated between Old Fort Campbell and High River. Antrobus, Scott, Dunbar, and Bliss were following behind the main party when another blizzard suddenly sprang up. Dunbar later related their ordeal:

When we got our packs properly arranged, we mounted, but imagine our feelings when the track was no longer to be seen. So thickly was the snow falling that we could not see 50 yards on any side. We could not be guided by the wind because it did not blow five minutes at a time from the same direction. Some of the boys became greatly alarmed at the thought of becoming lost, and one of them wanted to get back at once to Fort Campbell, about eight miles away. I refused, saying that Jerry would return for us when Captain Crozier found we did not come up with him in reasonable time. Poor Scott was in an awful plight, feeling sure that we would all perish. Just as I was beginning to give up all hope of any of our boys coming back for us, and thinking seriously of returning, Jerry and Crozier came upon us without being visible until within 30 yards. We then all started off for High River, arriving at 10 p.m.

This Jerry Potts is justly called the best guide in the country, for I do not believe there is another man who could have guided us through that storm as he did. We struck High River about a mile from the old camping ground. Fort Macleod was reached in three days' travel, the last day being a particularly hard one, 56 miles; we left Pine Coulee at 4 am and arrived at Macleod at 11:30 p.m. Two horses played out on the way and we left one at The Leaving, and the other at Cut Bank. When we arrived at the fort we put the prisoners in the guardhouse and sent the horses to the herd. After a good meal and a smoke, I went to bed and had a comfortable night's rest. (Hugh Dempsey The Early West)

Frank Dickens, mentioned earlier, was the celebrated fifth son of novelist Charles Dickens and a member of the NWMP during its formative years, from May of 1873 until the spring of 1886. He provides an interesting description of Potts in a letter written from Fort Macleod on October 19th, 1881.

> *The recent months have afforded me the opportunity to become better acquainted with a Great Man of this region. I speak of Jerry Potts, the intrepid trailer-cum-scout-cum-interpreter who founded this fort by leading Colonel Macleod and his Troops to what must be the most pleasant desert isle this far from the South Pacific – such is the admiration and respect in which Jerry Potts is held, by the Blackfoot and the Metis and the Force alike, that the man can do no wrong. The result of the mating of a Scots trader with a Peigan woman to produce the worst features of each race. Potts' underpinning is so bowed that he walks as lurching parentheses. Not until a pony is inserted between his legs do the man and beast become a marvelous entity, a totally effective synthesis in motion. Above the waist, Jerry in repose was not prepossessing. He is slouch-shouldered, his arms longer than his legs, and his squat torso announces nothing of its strength, which is Samsonian. His round face, equally taciturn, is trifurcated by his nose and his Mongolian moustaches into three equal segments. He tops off this ill-assembled visage with a brimmed hat worn jauntily to the right to counterbalance the revolver slung on his hip, butt forward.*
>
> *Who can wonder at my curiosity about Jerry Potts and that I crave to know more about a man who kills, ruthlessly, and kills again, yet enjoys the regard and trust of everyone in the Territories. My inquisitiveness overcame the normal bounds of conversation between an NWMP officer and a half-breed guide. Encountering Jerry on the road, I feigned a problem with my pony's hoof and while he examined it I asked him: "Jerry, how does it feel to kill a man?"*
>
> *He glanced at me with his accustomed impassiveness and said: "Feels good." It was not the reply I had hoped for. I had to press him further, "It is told that in a famous victory over the Crees you took nineteen scalps. What, to you was the meaning of that primitive act?"*
>
> *Jerry's eyebrows rose slightly. He shrugged and said: "Same like when you English cut off de head." His hand made a violent chopping motion at his neck, and then he grinned and grunted, "Don't see nudding wrong with your pony," he remarked and went on his way." (E. Nicol – Dickens of the Mounted, 1989).*

Grant MacEwan (1958) describes how Jerry Potts took part in one of the last major Indian battles on the plains. The Blackfoot, Peigans and Bloods were on one side and the Crees were on the other.

> *Jerry Potts was hunting with the Bloods and Peigans in good buffalo country, now called southern Alberta. Chief Piapot's Crees – 600 to 800 of them, made a sortie into that part, looking for enemy scalps. They attacked a small cluster of Blood and Blackfoot teepees on the Belly River and massacred many of the occupants – mostly old people and children. The few defending warriors were far outnumbered but word was carried to the Peigans who were camped by the St. Mary River, above Fort Whoop-up. The Peigans smeared themselves with war paint and commanded Jerry Potts to lead them in a counter-attack. It was bound to be a bitter fight because Crees and the tribesmen of the Blackfoot group hated each other at any time. The Crees were from what would today be the province of Saskatchewan and the Blackfoot alliance were from Alberta soil The Peigan scouts located the Crees resting beside the river, just across from the present City of Lethbridge. Jerry and his Peigans came up quickly. They had the advantage of the more modern guns and when they attacked, the surprised Crees were forced to fall back. The retreating Indians drew toward the river and made their stand in a coulee within view of the Galt Hospital built there about twenty years later.*
>
> *For a time there was a stalemate with the Crees in one coulee and the Peigans in another. Then Jerry led the Peigans in a frontal attack and made it a bad day for the Crees. The latter were forced back, obliged to plunge into the river and as many were shot in the water as were killed on the land. According to Jerry's telling, the river was so full of fleeing Crees that all a pursuer had to do to kill one was to point his gun at the water and fire. The Crees were almost wiped out. Jerry Potts was the victor's hero. (MacEwan, Fifty Mighty Men, 1958)*

Jerry Potts passed on to the Happy Hunting Ground on July 17th, 1896, and was buried with full military honours in the police plot at Fort Macleod. Tom Wilson, who knew and admired Jerry greatly, was at the ceremony along with Sam Steele. Also in attendance were many of the original troops of NWMP that he had rescued and guided during their formative years on the plains. A bronze statute of Jerry, commemorating his contribution to the settling of the Canadian West stands in the museum at Fort MacLeod.

Chief Crowfoot, "Chief of Chiefs," played a significant role in maintaining peace between the Blackfoot nations and the representatives of the Great White Mother. Crowfoot was fiercely loyal to James Macleod and James Walsh, and he steadfastly resisted overtures from Louis Riel, Gabriel Dumont, and Big Bear to join a blood alliance to drive the white man from the plains. Grant MacEwan suggests that Crowfoot was born somewhere south of the Red Deer River in 1821. His real name was "Crow Big Foot" but Jerry Potts, who knew the chief well, shortened his name to "Crowfoot."

> An old Indian at Gleichen recalled that he was 12 years old when he first saw Crowfoot. It was at Fort Whoop-up and the impression lingered. Even at that time, the chief was recognized as a great warrior whose score was over a hundred victories. He was a distinguished horseman and always rode a spotted horse. The man was tall and erect; his hair was long and unbraided, and he ruled with a firm hand. Bravery and horsemanship—that's the way he won the leadership. He always rode the best horse and, in a run after buffalo, he rode the fastest.

Crowfoot played a major role in the signing of the Blackfoot Treaty on September 27th, 1877, at Blackfoot Crossing on the Bow River. He remained loyal to the Treaty, especially in 1885 when he refused to join the Crees to support Riel. For his loyalty, the Council of the Northwest Territories gave him a gift of fifty dollars. William Van Horne of the CPR upstaged the bureaucrats by presenting the old chief with a lifetime pass for the CPR railroad. After the North West Rebellion, Crowfoot and some other chiefs were given a luxurious trip to eastern Canada and Ottawa where they could see the might of the new nation. Their trusted friends, Reverend John McDougall and Father Lacombe, accompanied them on the trip and it had a great impact upon them. On his return to his people, Crowfoot put the idea of a "blood revolt" out of their minds. "The white people." he said, "are as thick as flies in the summertime." His advice was to go into cattle ranching.

When Crowfoot died on April 25th, 1890, at age sixty-nine, his best horse was shot and his saddle and rifle were buried with him because he would need a good horse and saddle in the Happy Hunting Ground. He was buried at Blackfoot Crossing where Treaty Number 7 had been negotiated and signed. Four years later, his friend James Macleod joined him in the Great Beyond where the high plains run wild and free.

Tom Wilson often talked of Crowfoot, whom he had come to know well while he was with the NWMP. They maintained their friendship until the Chief's death and some say that it was the old chief who gave Tom the idea for Banff Indian Days. Tom attended Crowfoot's burial, as did a number of the former members of the NWMP, who had known him during their time in the West. Later Wilson named the large multi-fingered glacier that over looks Bow Lake and Num-ti-Jah Lodge, in honor of the heroic chief. Sadly there is neither a marker nor a plaque to commemorate the signing of Treaty Number 7 at Gleichen, or any evidence of Crowfoot's grave.

Paddy Crozier's career went downhill quickly after he led his troops into an ambush at Duck Lake in 1885. He was also blamed for exercising poor judgment during the North West Rebellion campaign. When Sir John A. Macdonald overlooked him in the appointment of a new Commissioner of the NWMP in 1886, he resigned in disgust and remained a rather bitter man for the rest of his life.

Lt. Colonel A.G. Irvine's career also deteriorated following the North West Rebellion, as he was accused of ineptitude. He resigned from his position of Commissioner of the NWMP in 1886. Sam Steele always felt that Irvine was treated badly and that both he and the NWMP deserved more credit than they received for controlling the hostilities during the rebellion.

> *The presence of the NWMP at Prince Albert saved that settlement from falling into the hands of the Metis and their fierce allies. The place was the key position in that part of the northwest, and had it been taken, there is no doubt the rebellion would have assumed greater proportions. During the whole of the campaign, Colonel Irvine's scouts performed valuable services under their daring and capable leader, Mr. Thomas Mackay. They were constantly in touch with General Middleton's force and repeatedly drove back Riel's scouts. Their presence was so dreaded by Riel that he threw up strong entrenchments on the left bank of the South Saskatchewan opposite Batoche.*

> *Yet during the whole of the operations the eastern press teemed with aspersions against Colonel Irvine and his men; the newspapers containing these were read in the militia camp daily by all ranks. The war correspondents who were there published such stuff as "What is Colonel Irvine doing? What are the Mounted Police doing? Why do they not come out and attack Riel?" Attack him! With two hundred men and leave Prince Albert open to rapine and murder! Such was the tenor of many articles; but in spite of the fact that they were known to headquarters, no effort was made on the part of the officers responsible for Colonel Irvine's movements to disabuse the mind of the public, poisoned as it was by the slanders sent abroad.*

> *The resignation of Lt.-Col. Irvine, our commissioner, came as a great shock to all that knew him. He was a great favorite throughout the west, a hard-working conscientious officer who had served his country faithfully for many years. He was still in the prime of life, and for my part I could see no reason why he should retire, particularly after the good work that he had done during the rebellion. (S. Steele, Fifty Years in Canada)*

Inspector Francis Jeffrey Dickens of the NWMP
The third son of Charles Dickens, Inspector Dickens was on the "Great March" West. He had run-ins with the likes of Sitting Bull, Jerry Potts, Big Bear, Gabriel Dumont, Sam Steele, Louis Riel and his superiors. Plagued with a number of chronic ailments he also stuttered and was hard of hearing. His superiors thought that he was down right lazy and some claimed that he was an alcoholic. His commanding officer A.G. Irvine considered him to be a "complete incompetent" Even if this was all true he was, above all, a survivor. When put in charge of Fort Pitt during the Riel Rebellion he nettled his superiors by abandoning the fort without firing a shot. He apparently holds the record as the only man in the force never to get a promotion for a period of over twelve years. He served in the NWMP from 1874 to 1886. For a great read and more insight into this remarkably inept character, Eric Nichol's book "Dickens of the Mounted" provides further details.

Jean Louis Legare a French Canadian trader in Southern Saskatchewan. Jean-Louis befriended Sitting Bull and his people and gave them food and supplies. He also supplied wagons and escorted Sitting Bull and the remnants of his once proud tribe to a reservation near Ford Buford, Montana.

Lieutenant-Colonel A.G. Irvine, Third Commissioner of the NWMP – 1880–1886
He was reported to have been a humorless individual and the men sarcastically called him "Irvine the good". He had friends in high places in Lower Canada (Quebec) and was appointed Commissioner over James Walsh.

Sir John A. Macdonald saw the completion of the great transcontinental railway that he and the young country had dreamed of, but he was unable to avoid the many charges of graft and corruption that followed him like a bad odor. In 1891 he was defeated in the general election and Sir John Abbot became the Prime Minister. James Walsh became active in Liberal politics, campaigning against the Conservative Party and the manner in which the NWMP was being managed. In 1896, Sir Wilfred Laurier led the Liberal Party to victory and became Prime Minister of Canada. This resulted in reforms in the NWMP and an appointment for Walsh as Commissioner of the Yukon in 1897.

By the end of 1885, Sir John A. McDonald and his government of the day had over one thousand Mounties and over two dozen NWMP detachments scattered throughout the west. The Blackfoot Treaty was signed and Sitting Bull was routed from the safety of the Sweet Grass Hills, and escorted back across the border. The U.S. soldiers who were waiting for him and his people then arrested him. The Indians from the Great Lakes to the Rockies were rounded up and herded onto reservations. The buffalo were just a memory, Louis Riel was dead, and the last spike of the Canadian Pacific Railway had been driven home." (D. Cruise and A. Griffiths, The *Great Adventure*, 1996)

Rogers and Wilson – A Dynamic Duo

In May of 1881 Tom heard that good men with experience working and living in the wilderness were needed to scout, pack, and blaze trails for the new transcontinental railroad that Sir John A. Macdonald planned to build across the country. The main hiring centre was at Fort Benton Montana, so on May 16th, 1881, Tom bid farewell to the NWMP, Fort Walsh, and the friends he'd made there. Before leaving however, he paid a final visit to Sitting Bull's camp and Fort Qu'Appelle where he met with Sam Steele.

Tom had been a member of the NWMP for just eight months but by then he knew that it wasn't for him. He just couldn't be a part of an outfit whose senior officers were manipulated by Ottawa politicians and forced into treating both the Indians and its own members shabbily. Sam Steele recognized this and wished Tom well as he headed for Fort Benton. They didn't know that their paths would cross many times in the years to come.

Many thoughts crossed Tom's mind as he pointed his buckskin pony toward the southwest and rode through the Sweet Grass Hills toward Montana. He crossed the Medicine Line near the present border crossing of Wild Horse and headed across the flat lands to the Missouri River and Fort Benton. A new chapter of his life was about to unfold.

Tom didn't have to wait long at Fort Benton before hiring on with P.K. Hyndman, Major Rogers' chief engineer in charge of the mountain section of the CPR line. Starting work as a teamster and scout, he helped move supplies and materials from Fort Benton to Old Bow Fort near the junction of the Bow and the Kananaskis rivers in present day Alberta, where a temporary headquarters for the survey team had been established. From this post the supplies were transported by pack-horse into the mountains.

When Tom and his pack train arrived at the Stoney Indian Mission at Morley, John McDougall, the pioneer Methodist missionary, welcomed him. Tom knew McDougall well, as he was legendary among the natives of the plains – on a par with Father Lacombe in their hierarchy of respect. The Indians of the Canadian plains respected these two men greatly as both lived with their parishioners and fought against the evils of the "firewater" sold by the whiskey traders. Lacombe and McDougall were paternalistic about the native tribes they shepherded and fiercely protected them from exploitation. Thanks largely to these men of God, Indian warfare on the plains became almost non-existent. Both Father Lacombe and Reverend McDougall were present at the signing of the famous Blackfoot Treaty of 1877 at Blackfoot Crossing, and they offered their counsel to Chief Crowfoot of the Blackfoot nation and to Chief Buffalo Calf of the Stoney tribe.

From Old Bow Fort the supplies for the survey were moved further into the mountains and Reverend McDougall's brother David helped Tom move the pack train to Bow River Gap. Here Tom waited for Major Rogers who had been trying to find a suitable route for the railroad through the Selkirk Mountains. On July 15th, 1881, a discouraged and exhausted Major Rogers staggered into Tom Wilson's camp near Banff. He had failed to locate an acceptable route, but after resting for a day or two, the indomitable little Major had Tom Wilson accompany him further up the Bow River Valley to the Continental Divide. This was Tom's first introduction to the towering, glacier-hung mountains of the Canadian Rockies. This territory would soon become his personal domain, and for years to come few would venture into the area without engaging his services as a guide or seeking his advice.

At the Continental Divide, Tom and Major Rogers camped under the shadow of Cathedral Mountain at Wapta Lake and waited for the Major's nephew, Allan Rogers, to bring a pack train up the precipitous Kicking Horse Canyon from Golden. When it appeared that young Al was lost, Tom headed out to find him. A day later he heard three rifle shots in quick succession and answered them with three shots from his own Winchester. Within minutes, Al's pack train came into sight and soon he and his impetuous uncle were re-united.

In the fall of 1881 Tom headed back to Fort Macleod. He then visited old friends at Fort Walsh, Wood Mountain, and Fort Qu'Appelle and caught up on the latest news of the NWMP. After visiting with Crowfoot, he headed for Montana where he spent the winter trapping for furs. In the spring of 1882, he made his way back to Morley and then on to his camp on the Bow River near Banff where he signed on with Major Rogers for another season.

During the late summer, Tom camped on the Bow River, near the junction of the Pipestone River, One day he thought that he heard thunder which struck him odd as the sky was cloudless. When he questioned his Stoney Indian packer, Eddy "Gold Seeker" Hunter, about it, Eddy told him that it was the "Great Spirit" speaking up at the Lake of Little Fishes in a valley high above them. The next morning – August 21st, 1882 – was Tom's birthday and he and Eddy set out to find the lake, which turned out to be one of the great discoveries of the Rockies. He initially named the magnificent tarn "Emerald Lake" but in 1884, the name was changed to honour Princess Louise – a daughter of Queen Victoria and the wife of the Marquis of Lorne. For years, however, the locals of the area referred to it simply as "Tom's Lake".

A few days later, while tracking some packhorses that had slipped their hobbles just east of the present town of Field, Tom discovered the "Natural Bridge," where Emerald Creek rushes into the Kicking Horse River. Continuing to search for his horses, he followed Emerald Creek along a lightly travelled trail through the lodge pole pines. After about two hours of bushwacking, he broke into a clearing and discovered Emerald Lake – the second of the four jewels of the Rockies (the others being Lake Louise, Moraine Lake, and Lake O'Hara).

A year later, while exploring the upper reaches of the Yoho River, Tom also discovered Takakkaw Falls – the second highest falls in Canada. Later he said that his first sight of the stupendous waterfall took his breath away. He stood in awe as he gazed up at the thundering plume of water cascading more than twelve hundred feet down the face of the cliff and sending out spray and mist for hundreds of feet in all directions. Jimmy Three-Toes told him that "Takakkaw" was the Cree word for "wonderful" and Tom decided to camp near the foot of the falls for the night. The following morning he hiked further up the valley and discovered Laughing Falls. Proceeding still further and standing near the site of the present Twin Falls teahouse, he also became the first white man to see the impressive Twin Falls cascading down the cliffs from high above.

In 1882, Major Rogers asked Tom Wilson to explore the feasibility of using Howse Pass as an alternative route to the Kicking Horse Canyon for the railroad. Howse Pass had been the old fur traders' route from the Columbia River to Saskatchewan River Crossing. The route then proceeded over David Thompson Pass to Rocky Mountain House and the prairies beyond. Alone and without a guide, Tom left his camp on the Pipestone River and headed up the Bow River Valley to the right of Bath Creek. He continued past Hector, Peyto, and Bow lakes on old Indian game trails. This made him the first white man to see these lakes and the expansive ice fields of the surrounding peaks. At Bow Lake, Tom named an impressive glacier that overhangs the lake after his old friend, Chief Crowfoot.

Proceeding on to Saskatchewan River Crossing, he then turned left and made his way past towering peaks, wild rivers, and a tangle of forest blow-downs and deadfall. Following the fading blazes left by the old fur traders as best he could he descended along the wild Blaeberry River canyon and eventually reached the Columbia River Valley where an anxious Major Rogers was waiting. Rogers had given Wilson ten days to make the journey and had grown more and more apprehensive as the days slipped by. *"If that boy don't show up, what'll I do?"* exclaimed Rogers. *"No one but a fool would send a lad on such a trip alone and no one but a fool would try to make it alone."* (The Last Spike, P. Berton)

But Tom was no fool and he made the journey in just thirteen days. When he staggered, half-starved, out of the forest, Rogers hugged him like a long-lost son and gave him a fifty dollar bonus for his efforts. It was a remarkable journey through uncharted mountain wilderness and it required great stamina, mountain savvy, and resourcefulness to do it alone. His trek confirmed that the Kicking Horse – Rogers Pass route was the best choice for the transcontinental railway. The trip had an added benefit for Wilson. He had an exceptional memory and once he explored a territory, the features remained fixed in his mind. This would serve him well in the future.

After the 1882 season with the CPR came to an end, Tom was hired to help control some Indians who were causing trouble and annoying the CPR survey crew near Medicine Hat. Tom's relationship with Crowfoot enabled him to visit the venerable old chief and soon the problems were resolved. He also visited James Macleod and Paddy Crozier at Fort Macleod, and Colonel Irvine and Frank Dickens at Fort Walsh.

During that winter, Tom hired on with Colonel James Walker, another NWMP acquaintance, to work on his timber lease at the famous Cochrane Ranch. In the spring of 1883, he moved to Morley where he stayed with Dave McDougall and took serious notice of Dave's lovely daughter Minnie for the first time. In early June, Tom resumed his survey work with Major Rogers and the CPR on the Kicking Horse Canyon route through the mountains. Later that summer, Tom was put in charge of escorting Sir Sandford Fleming and the Reverend George Grant (the Principal of Queens University) from Banff to Rogers Pass. This was Tom Wilson's first experience guiding dignitaries from the East, but it wouldn't be his last. All went well and Sir Sandford wrote a glowingly report about his experiences on the trail with Tom Wilson as his guide.

In early 1884, Tom left the employ of the CPR and took up residence at the base of Castle Mountain, where the boomtown Silver City was expanding rapidly. He prospected for a while and then moved to Holt City (later called Laggan and then the Village of Lake Louise, where he and his partner Jimmy Wright built a cabin. Shortly after this, Tom renewed his acquaintance with the beautiful Minnie McDougall who was working at a boarding house at Silver City, and this time she swept him off his feet. On seeing her again Tom thought: "This is the gal for me!" He proposed marriage and Minnie accepted.

The happy couple planned to marry in the spring of 1885 but they had to postpone the wedding following a telegram from Sam Steele. Louise Riel and the Metis, along with Chief Big Bear and his Cree, were creating unrest in Saskatchewan and Steele needed help to get things under control. Tom had spent some time with Steele at Holt City (Laggan) the previous winter, as Sam was stationed there to maintain law and order in the CPR construction camp. Given their friendship, it was only natural for Steele to seek Tom's assistance and offer him a place in his troop of Steele's Scouts

Tom packed his bag in less than two hours, kissed his bride-to-be goodbye, and jumped aboard the train headed for Calgary where Steele was waiting with his other handpicked men. They headed immediately for Fort Pitt in Central Saskatchewan, The Fort was supposed to be under the command of their friend Frank Dickens but it was under siege by Chief Big Bear and his Cree warriors. When Steel's Scouts arrived they discovered that Dickens had abandoned the fort, taking the Scottish settlers to safety. The hard-riding Scouts soon "put the run" on Big Bear and his men and chased them north but somehow the wily chief eluded them and escaped.

When Major-General Dobson Middelton and his troops arrived by rail from the East, there was a brief skirmish at Batoche and Louis Riel was captured. A hurried trial was convened in Regina and Riel was hung in the NWMP barracks there on November 16th, 1885. Tom didn't wait around for the hanging. instead he caught the first train back to Laggan, packed his best three-piece suit, and then headed for the McDougall household in Edmonton where he wed Minnie on October 19th, 1885.

Major A.B. Rogers
Major Rogers, master surveyor for the C.P.R, and Tom Wilson blazed the route for the railroad from Calgary to the Shushwap. Their route took the railroad line through Kicking Horse Canyon from Field to Golden and then along the Columbia River over Rogers Pass to Revelstoke. From there the tracks proceeded through Eagle Pass and Three Valley Gap to the North Okanagan Valley

After the marriage, the happy couple honeymooned on their way back to Morley where they planned to live with Minnie's uncles – David and the Reverend John McDougall. However, no sooner did they arrive than Tom got word that a special train filled with CPR officials was headed from Calgary to Craigellachie British Columbia for the ceremonial driving of the "Last Spike". Tom was invited to attend and on November 5th, along with Chief Crowfoot, Father Lacombe, and the Reverend

John McDougall, he caught the train at the Morley station. On board were Cornelius Van Horne, Donald Smith, Sam Steele, James Walsh, Major Rogers, and a host of dignitaries from eastern Canada.

As Tom boarded the train, Major Rogers jumped from his seat and gave Tom a welcoming bear hug. Soon the flasks came out and many tall tales were told as the train proceeded through Banff, Laggan, Field, and Golden on its way to the summit of Rogers Pass. Surrounded by his old friends once again Tom was in his element. They all knew that it would probably be the last time they would be together, and they intended to make the most of it.

On a cold and rainy November 7th, 1885, a group of some of the most important and influential men in Canada gathered at Craigellachie, a nondescript whistle stop just west of Revelstoke. They had come together to witness one of the most important events in the county's short history: the driving of the "Last Spike" on the Canadian Pacific Railway. With that steel spike – not gold or silver – the national dream of a ribbon of two steel rails linking the country together from the Maritimes to the Pacific was realized.

Donald Smith driving the historic Last Spike of the Canadian Pacific Railway on November 7, 1885, just west of Revelstoke at Craigallachie, B. C. Tom Wilson is wearing the light gray Stetson to the left of Smith in the foreground.

Among the dignitaries present on that historic day was the official party that had come out by train from Montreal, Ottawa, and Winnipeg. William Cornelius Van Horne, the flamboyant and hard-driving general manager of the CPR led the group. Donald A Smith, a director of the railway, Sir Sanford Fleming, the engineer-in-chief of the project, John McTavish, the land commissioner, and George Harris, a financier from Boston were also in attendance. Andrew Onderdonk, who had pushed the rails from Savona to Three Valley Gap, and then through Eagle Pass to Revelstoke, met the train as it was coming down from Rogers Pass. His private railway car from Port Moody British Columbia. brought Michael Haney and Harry Cambie to the ceremony.

Major A.B. Rogers, the feisty, hard-cussing, little man with the huge mutton-chop whiskers, and Tom Wilson had grown to be fast friends while working on the railroad. Rogers knew that had it not been for Tom he might not have found a route through the Rockies and the Selkirks. He was also indebted to Sam Steele and Major James Walsh, both of whom maintained law and order along the line during the construction of the railroad in western Canada.

Finally the rails were joined and the ceremonial iron spike was put in place. The dignitaries gathered close in for the photographer as Donald Smith raised the sledgehammer and aimed a mighty blow at the spike. The camera flash ignited and a small burst of smoke momentarily surrounded the photographer. It was done! No one cared that the blow was a bit off centre and bent the spike. The old spike was pulled out and another was put in its place. The onlookers gathered round once again and had a few laughs. The ceremonial bottle of Scotch whiskey was passed around and as the photographer had a good swig everyone prepared for another historic photo.

This time Smith's blow was straight and true and the spike sank deep into the oil-soaked timber of the tie as the flash ignited once again. A second crushing blow sent the spike home. A cheer went up as hats were tossed in the air and the locomotives let out long shrill whistles. Hand shakes, bear hugs, and claps to the back followed as a second bottle of Scotch whiskey was consumed. No two men hugged each other with more enthusiasm and greater joy than Major A.B. Rogers and Tom Wilson. They knew that they had played a major role in an important chapter of Canadian history.

Tom Wilson—Master Guide and Outfitter

The driving of the Last Spike marked the end of another chapter in Tom's Wilson's life. Now that he was a married man he had to settle down and establish himself. During the winter of 1885-1886, he and Minnie ran a boarding house at Silver City. When very little silver or gold was found in the area and rumours started that gold had been discovered near Golden, the town pulled up stakes and moved almost overnight. The gold seekers took everything with them, including the windows and the doors. With the population of Silver City reduced to twenty or so stragglers, Tom and Minnie abandoned the boarding house and moved back to Morley, where they homesteaded north of town. There they built a home, a barn, and a few corrals and went into the horse and cattle business. It was during this time that Tom registered his famous Powder Horn brand.

To supplement their meager income Tom did odd jobs for the CPR. One of his first assignments was to improve his original trail from Laggan up to Lake Louise. Upon completion, he escorted Mrs. Ross and Mrs. Brothers, the wives of two CPR engineering officials up the trail to the lake. These women thus hold the distinction of being the first recorded tourists to actually visit the magnificent lake that, in less than twenty years, would become a destination for travellers from around the world.

In 1887 Wilson cut a wider trail up from the station at Laggan up to Lake Louise. A boat was then hauled up the trail. Shortly after this a crude log chalet was constructed just back from the lakeshore and not far from the site of the present Swiss guides' cabin. That fall Tom guided his first hunting party into the Rockies, beginning a career that would last for the rest of his life.

In 1886 the CPR began building the Banff Spring Hotel in Banff and just two years later it opened. Adventures began flocking to the Banff and the new hotel looking for excitement in the wild Canadian Rockies. Tom Wilson was just the man to give it to them, with pack trips and hunting excursions into the mountains. Tom convinced W.L. Matthews, the manager of the new hotel, and his friends in the hierarchy of the CPR, to allow him to advertise his business as "Tom Wilson the guide to the CPR".

He instantly had a large pool of clients, mainly drawn from the hotel's guest list. Shortly after this, he leased and eventually purchased a property at the corner of Banff Avenue and Buffalo Street where he built a large corral and a cabin. This became the headquarters of his outfitting business for many years. Later, in partnership with his friend George Fear, he opened a store that specialized in outdoor gear and camping supplies.

In his book *The Rocky Mountains of Canada*, (1916), one of the first books that described those 'rough and ready' early days in the Canadian Rockies, Walter Wilcox gives a vivid description of the excitement found at Tom Wilson's corral:

> *During the summer season "Wilson's" is frequently the scene of no little excitement when some party is getting ready to leave. There you may see ten or fifteen wicked-eyed ponies; some in a corral and the rest tied to trees, ready for packing. If the horses are making their first trip of the season there is considerable bucking and kicking before all is ready. Several men are seen bustling about, sorting and weighing the packs, and making order out of the pile of blankets, tents, and bags of flour and bacon. The cayuses are saddled and cinched up one by one with many a protesting bite or kick. The celebrated "diamond hitch" is used in fastening the packs, and the struggling men look picturesque in their old clothes and sombreros as they tighten the ropes, bravely on the gentle horses but rather gingerly when it comes to a bucking bronco.*
>
> *A crowd of the businessmen of Banff, who usually take about 365 holidays each year, stands around to offer advice and watch the sport. Then the picturesque train of horses with their wild looking drivers files out through the village streets under a fusillade of snapshot cameras and the wondering gaze of new arrivals from the east. (Walter Wilcox, 1916)*

Wilson's outfitting business grew quickly, due largely to the steady flow of guests from the Banff Springs Hotel. His clients represented the rich and famous from Europe, eastern Canada and the United States. In his first year of guiding, he led his customers over Vermillion Pass and became the first white person to see Marble Canyon. He also guided clients to first ascents of Mt. Wind (Lougheed) and Storm Mountain.

In 1893, Tom was the first white person to make his way to the base of Mt. Assiniboine. He blazed a trail up Healy Creek and then proceeded up and over Simpson Pass into the valley of the Simpson River, which he followed to the junction of the south branch. From there he cleared a path up to the next ridge and then on to the top of Ferro Pass. Finally, he blazed a trail down into the Mitchell River Valley and from there it was an easy task to ascend to the turquoise lakes at the foot of Mt. Assiniboine to set up camp. Tom's client on that historic trip was Robert L. Barrett, a Chicago businessman and paper manufacturer. Later, in a letter to Tom, dated November 1st, 1924, he described his impressions on seeing Mt. Assiniboine up close for the first time:

> *"I don't think that even old K2, the 28,000 ft. peak of the Himalayas, looked as high and imposing, and as terrible as old Assiniboine when you and I finally won through to where we could have a good look at him."*

On the return trip to Banff, Tom followed the Simpson River to Vermilion Pass and visited Marble Canyon once again. The original trail that Tom Wilson blazed into Mt. Assiniboine became the standard route into the area for future climbers, skiers and adventurers. Later, when **Erling Strom** built the Sunshine Village Lodge at the foot of Mt. Assiniboine, the first road that was built into the area followed Tom Wilson's original trail.

In the summer of 1893, Tom Wilson met two students from Yale University, Walter Wilcox and Samuel Allen. They were eager to climb and explore the area. They would visit the Rockies on many more occasions over the years and leave their mark upon them forever. Allen had first visited the Rockies and the Selkirks in 1891 when he climbed the Devil's Thumb above Lake Agnes near Lake Louise. Wilcox had also visited the Selkirks in 1891 and his description of the aspiring climbers staying at Glacier House at the time has often been quoted:

> *"We found a group of enthusiasts who were accustomed to gather every evening around a blazing fire and read section's from William Spotswood Green's "Among the Selkirk Glaciers" just as our forefathers were wont to read a daily chapter from the Bible."*

Silver City in about 1895
Situated at the foot of Castle Mountain just 18 miles from Banff, Silver City was a booming place where Tom Wilson met his wife Minnie in 1884.

'Home Sweet Home' at Silver City – 1885

Banff in 1884
The store to the left of the picture is called "The People's Store". Later it would become Wilson and Fear. One thing that hasn't changed in all these years is Cascade Mountain. It still dominates the town.

Banff in 1887
Some say that the goat in the picture belonged to the Brewsters who owned Banff's first dairy.

Tom Wilson with wife Minnie and their family of five children.
This picture was taken in the spring of 1896. The children from right to left are:
Bessie, John, Rene, Ada and Tom Jr. (Eddie).

Wilson & Fear—Outfitters for Adventurers
Tom Wilson is standing in the doorway to the right and partner George Fear
is standing in the left. Taken in 1885.

Walter Wilcox in an early fall snowstorm in 1896. He is on his way back from Mt. Assiniboine. Walter and his colleagues made many trips to the Rockies and they were the first to attempt to climb Mt. Assiniboine and Mt. Lefroy. They were the first to climb Mt. Temple and the first to explore Paradise Valley and the Valley of the Ten Peaks.

In 1892, Allen toured Europe and the Alps and climbed the Matterhorn, which had been first conquered by Sir Edward Whymper in 1865. In 1893, while waiting in Banff for Wilcox to join him, Allen ascended Mt. Rundle and got the first recorded view of Mt. Assiniboine. When Wilcox joined Allen in Banff a few days later, they learned that the chalet at Lake Louise had recently burnt to the ground. As they were planning to climb in the Lake Louise area, they bought some emergency camping equipment and supplies from none other than "T. E. Wilson's Outfitters of Banff". While making their purchases, they met Tom Wilson and were soon quizzing the "Pathfinder of the Rockies" about the area with growing awe and admiration.

1893 was a good year for Tom. Not only did he firmly establish his guiding business, but his unrivalled knowledge of the area was in great demand. He had few competitors and was highly respected in the community. The fact that Walter Wilcox wrote a book that extolled his services, and those of his chief packer Wild Bill Peyto, didn't hurt his business either.

How Banff was named "Banff" and a National Park was created

In 1881 Tom Wilson, who had just signed on as a packer for the proposed new railway through the Rockies, was busy escorting Major Rogers along the Bow River corridor and over the Great Divide to the Kicking Horse River near the present town of Field, British Columbia. He routinely organized and led pack trains loaded with supplies from Morley, and the main railway supply depot at Padmore, to Castle Junction. From there they pushed through to Laggan, and then to a camp at the Great Divide. One of Tom's favourite spots to camp along the way was at the base of Cascade Mountain, on the banks of a little stream that later became know as Whiskey Creek. He usually stayed in a meadow, where the creek enters the Bow River, as it provided good grazing there for his horses.

In 1882, Tom's Stoney Indian friend, **Chief Hector Crawler,** told him of some hot springs and caves at the base of neighbouring Sulphur Mountain. Tom checked them out and occasionally visited them for a refreshing dip after a hard day in the saddle.

In 1883, the **McCardell** brothers, William and Thomas, together with their pal **Frank McCabe**, quit their jobs with the railway and decided to do a little prospecting for gold. They built themselves a raft and manoeuvred it across the Bow River, not far from where the present bridge in the town of Banff. Following an old and well-travelled trail, they came to a hole in the ground above a large cave. Lowering themselves down to the floor of the cave, they discovered a small lake of hot sulphur-smelling water.

The boys figured they'd found a real "tourist trap" and immediately set out to build a fence around the opening. Later they constructed a crude log cabin at the site and filed a claim on the property. They then applied to get it registered. Later that fall when the lads were out hunting, they thought they saw steam rising from the lower part of Sulphur Mountain, just above their cave. It didn't take the budding entrepreneurs long to find the Upper Hot Springs and to stake the area as well. They had some mighty big plans for the sites and they couldn't wait to hang out their shingle.

By 1884, the leases for the land containing the hot springs were still ungranted, so McCabe, being a bit tight for money, sold his interests in the hot springs to **D.B. Woodworth,** a budding entrepreneur from Kings, Nova Scotia, who was camping with some friends near Cascade Mountain at Siding 29. Apparently crafty Frank McCabe sold Woodworth the rights to the leases for $1,500 with $500 to be paid up front as a down payment. The only thing wrong with the deal was that he neglected to tell his partners – the McCardell brothers.

When Bill and Tom McCardell learned of the scheme, they became downright angry and engaged the services of a young lawyer who just happened to be hanging around Siding 29, hoping for some business – as many lawyers are wont to do. The young lawyer was none-other than **Jim Lougheed** who later he became Sir James Lougheed. After being briefed on the details of the disputed transaction, Lougheed, wired the Honorable **Thomas White**, Minister of the Interior in Ottawa explaining that the deal between Woodworth and McCabe had not yet been consummated. He suggested that White buy the hot spring sites on behalf of the federal government, and told him to stand by for more details. Lougheed then went to court on behalf of the McCardell brothers and succeeded in having the McCabe-Woodworth deal quashed. At that point, White, with Lougheed's assistance, acquired the squatter's rights to the springs from the three original adventurers. (Lougheed obviously acted in conflict of interest, but in those days it was "anything goes!")

By 1885 Tom Wilson's favorite camping spot had became a small community and another settlement was developing further to the south around the base of Tunnel Mountain. Later that year **William Pearce**, Superintendent of Mines for the Dominion of Canada, visited the area and decided that the hot springs should be preserved for the public. (I suspect that it was Tom Wilson that proposed the idea to Pearce as he guided him about the area.) Tom had also heard of Jim Lougheed's efforts to save the hot springs from Woodworth, McCabe, and the McCardells boys, and he undoubtedly encouraged Pearce to work with Tom White in Ottawa to create the reserve. Wilson also guided **P. R. Belanger** of the Dominion Topographic Survey when the hot springs were being officially surveyed, and he would have used this opportunity to pass on his vision to protect the region for future generations.

On November 25th, 1885, an Order-in-Council in Ottawa set aside a ten square-mile reserve around the Sulphur Mountain hot springs. The following year, surveyor **George Stewart** laid out the town site and the roads on the north side of the Bow River. Shortly after this, **Donald Smith** and **George Stephen** of the CPR arrived at Siding 29 by railcar. They were immediately impressed with the beauty of the area and Smith (later known as Lord Strathcona) named the new village "Banff," after his own birthplace in Scotland. Soon after this, Parliament passed an Act extending the original Order-in-Council from ten square miles to 260 square miles, thus creating the Canada's first national park. Tom's friend **George Stewart**, was appointed as the park's first superintendent, and the rest is history.

Tom Wilson Makes A Discovery–Finding Lake Louise*

It was just about noon on August 20th, 1882, and Tom Wilson, packer, pathfinder, and surveyor for the CPR and his two Stoney Indian companions were making good time on their trip to the Continenal Divide from Castle Junction. Tom was a good-looking young man, just twenty-three years of age at the time and in his prime. He was about six feet tall and had a sinewy body, a powerfully-built chest, narrow hips, and long legs. He had a generous shock of coal-black hair under his

---

* This story is also told in my book *Lake Louise at its Best: An Affectionate Look at Life at Lake Louise By One Who Knew It Well.*

stained Stetson hat and his wide-set, dark brown eyes had a special twinkle to them that foretold of his fun-loving and easy-going nature. There wasn't much on the trail or in the sky that escaped his darting glance. Except for a poorly-trimmed, black moustache, he was clean-shaven. His nose was well-proportioned, but it had been broken in his late-teens while training a hot-blooded, young colt. In later years, Tom recalled the incident.

> *I got on this rank, young stud colt and it threw its damn' head right back into my face after its first jump. Sure taught me to put a 'tie-down' on young colts when try'n to break 'em, and ta keep my feet out and my head back, when get'n aboard a pony that likes to buck some.*

Tom wore a thick grey wool shirt, a heavy tweed over-jacket, and long, grease-stained, deerskin leggings that he'd acquired from a Sioux brave while he was stationed at Fort Walsh. He had traded a good knife for two pairs of leggings and a buckskin shirt as well. He wore the leggings over his tough, twill pants to protect them from the wear and tear of the trail. He also wore high-topped, leather, packer-style boots that laced up to just below the knee. He packed a big Colt revolver on his right hip and he carried a new lever- action Winchester rifle in one of his saddle scabbards. A long-barrelled, big-bore, Hawkin muzzle-loading, cap-lock rifle was in a second scabbard. Here was a man for the mountains – strong, fit, tough, and intelligent, with a natural curiosity for the ways of both man and nature.

Tom and his two Indian packers had left Castle Mountain junction at first light and the traveling had been easy along the narrow trail that wove its way westward through the thick lodge-pole pine and aspen forests along the banks of the fast-flowing Bow River. Tom noticed that the pine forests swept up the slopes on either side of the river until they reached the timberline and the high alpine and sub-alpine regions where the saw-toothed, snow-capped mountain peaks racked the deep blue sky.

The trail was in good shape. It had been a warm summer in the Rockies – not a lot of rain, but just enough to prevent things from becoming too dry. Now the iron shod horse's hoofs kicked up small clouds of light, brown dust with each step. It was a hot afternoon and Tom, who had long since shed his coat, looked up at the sun and reckoned that it was just about four thirty. There wasn't a cloud to be seen. It was one of those special days that come along every so often in the mountains during the last few weeks of August.

As Tom rode along he could see a saddle-shaped mountain to his left. A few years later Walter Wilcox and his colleagues from Yale University would name it Saddle Peak. Towering high above it was a huge, glacier-hung mass that seemed to be the highest peak around. It would later be come known as Mt. Temple and at 11,621 feet it would prove to be the highest mountain in Banff National Park. Some sixty years later it would be the scene of a significant mountaineering tragedy, but that's another story.

Majestic peaks now surrounded Tom and a bit further to the west, and almost directly south of where he rode, was a grouping of snow-capped mountains, two of which had massive glaciers on them. One would later be called Mt. Lefroy, after

Sir John Henry Lefroy, a prominent scientist of the day. It measures 11,227 feet and would prove to be one of the most treacherous mountains in the area. In 1896 it would be the scene of the first recorded mountaineering fatality in the Rockies. The neighbouring peak of 11,362 feet held huge upper and lower glaciers. Originally called "Green's Peak", it would later become known as Mt. Victoria after the Queen of England. Its long knife-like ridge would become one of the classic mountaineering challenges in the area and be the scene of several mountaineering tragedies.

Straight ahead, Tom could see a large glacier and a solitary black peak rising from it at the crest of the Continental Divide. The intrepid adventurers Walter Wilcox and Samuel Allen would soon name them Bath Glacier and Waputik Peak (9,036 ft.).

At the Great Divide, a little creek emerges from Ross Lake, high above the valley. This creek is the first to actually flow to the west. Further on, and a bit to Tom's right, was a massive solitary peak that looked like a rabbit. It would later be named Mt. Hector (11,135 ft.) in honor of Dr. James Hector of the famous Palliser Expedition.

Also to Tom's right, just east of Pipestone Creek, were a group of peaks that would later be named Mt. Richardson (10,122 ft.), Mt. Ptarmigan (10, 033 ft.), Mt. Whitehorn (8,754 ft.) and Mt. Redoubt (9,518 ft.). Along the valley between Whitehorn Mountain and Redoubt Mountain lies Ptarmigan Lake and Boulder Pass. The valley eventually leads to the Skoki Lakes and the beautiful Skoki Valley. Mt. Whitehorn would much later become the site of the world-famous Lake Louise ski resort.

Tom pulled his pony to a halt at the edge of the Bow River and looked across at a sparkling little creek that ran down the steep slopes of the pine and spruce forest from some unseen hanging-valley high above them. It emerged from the steep slopes at the edge of the forest and meandered to the right of a lightly-treed meadow that spread out from the banks of the Bow River. Tom wondered where the creek came from, but he quickly put it out of his mind. He couldn't follow every little stream into the valleys above the Bow River Valley corridor. He had a deadline to meet and he was already a few days behind schedule. He'd whooped it up too long in Banff and then his Indian guides had arrived two horses short, delaying his departure yet another day while he found replacements at Canmore.

The air in the shade of the large aspen where Tom's pony stood was cool and fresh, scented with the smell of the spruce and pines. On the opposite side of the river, the ground was dry and sandy and nicely carpeted with sparse high-country mountain grass, pine needles, leaves and an array of wild flowers. There were Western Daises, Indian Paint Brushes, Western Columbine, Oregon Lilly and a few others whose names Tom didn't know. The aspens and the lodge-pole pines were nicely scattered with lots of open space between them, and Tom figured that this would make a good place to graze the horses, build a small corral, and set up a camp. There was no evidence that any man had ever ventured into this little grove, as there were no old campfires pits or tree blazes to be seen – just a well-worn game trail beside the little stream that wandered from above to the right of the meadow.

Through the trees, Tom could see four or five cow elk lying down with their eyes closed and their legs tucked under them, resting in the heat of the afternoon.

A big bull elk with a massive rack of horns was hunkered down beside his harem unperturbed by Tom's presence. It was siesta time in the Rockies and the elk had picked a good place for a light afternoon nap. The light breeze that accompanies the Bow River, and the wispy, pine-scented zephyrs that play along the little creek, kept all but the most persistent of mosquitoes and horseflies away from the animals. From time to time the big bull would flick an ear to divert a horsefly or a mosquito from its bloody pursuit. Nothing seemed to be stirring except for the rushing sound of the Bow River as is hurried by on its way toward the prairies. Even the whiskey jacks and the large black mountain ravens were having a snooze.

Tom's hawk-like eyes caught sight of a Richardson ground squirrel as it scurried busily from tree to tree on some unknown quest, but that was all. Because the waters were flowing in an easterly direction, Tom knew that he was still on the eastern slope of the Continental Divide and he reckoned that this was a good place to camp for awhile.

From where Tom sat resting his pony, the water of the river appeared to be as clear as crystal. The Bow River had lost a lot of its early-season volume, as it had been an early spring and a hot summer in the Rockies. Most of the spring run-off had taken place by early July, and now that it was late-August, the river flowed clear and fresh. There were several good spots nearby where the horses would have no trouble fording the river, so he nudged his sure-footed, buckskin pony in the ribs with the heels of his high-top boots.

The horse was of uncertain breeding but it was tough and sure-footed and it moved easily down the little bank of sand and gravel into the river. As they splashed across, Tom lifted his feet from the stirrups, leaned back against the high cantle of his stock saddle, and pulled his knees up to keep his boots dry. The pony humped its way up the gentle gravel embankment on the far side with little effort and began to graze on the lush mountain grass at its feet. Tom relaxed the reins and swung out of the saddle. He then loosened the saddle's cinch and straightened the saddle blanket. His legs and back were stiff from his ride, so he stretched and swung his arms around in windmill fashion, rotating his shoulders as he did so.

Throwing his sweat-stained Stetson at the base of a nearby aspen tree, Tom sat down and leaned his back against its rough trunk. Soon his Indian packers were also across the river and they too dismounted and stretched their stiff muscles.

"It's a good place ta camp for a few days boys," Tom drawled. "This is as pretty a place as I've seen all day. Good graz'n here for the horses too. We can put up a little corral and we'll be protected from the wind, if one should come up. This nice little breeze will keep the 'squita's away and we probably won't have to start a smudge fire tonight cause it's gonna be clear and cold. I'd planned to camp at Pipestone Creek and it's not that far away. We can easily use this as our base camp. Start set'n up camp, boys," he instructed. "This will be home for a few days."

As the packers started to untie the diamond-hitches to unload the five pack-ponies, Tom closed his eyes allowing his mind to slowly drift back to his days at Fort Walsh and his friends James Walsh, Sam Steele, and Frank Dickens of the NWMP.

The NWMP had not been for Tom and he knew it—too much politics, too much bickering, and too much interference from Ottawa. He had longed to see the shining mountains that the old trappers from Fort Whoop-Up and Rocky Mountain House spoke of when they stopped at the fort on their way back across the prairies with their big loads of furs.

Tom, who was then twenty-two years of age, resigned from the NWMP on May 16, 1881. He bid good-bye to his friends in the force and headed for Fort Benton, Montana to get a job with the CPR. As he shook hands with Major Walsh, Frank Dickens, he was caught in Walsh's steely gaze. "Good luck Tom," Major Walsh said.

"Take this with you and remember what you've seen here. The great herds of buffalo, once so numerous that they stretched across the landscape for as far as the eye could see are all but gone now. And the mighty Indian nations that camped among the hills here will soon be all gone as well. The way of life for the people of the plains will never be the same again."

With that Walsh, who knew that his days with the NWMP were also numbered, cleared his throat and handed Tom something in a small, well-oiled, leather bag with a drawstring. Tom took it, loosened the drawstring and shook a medium-sized pocketknife into his rough palm. On one side of the bone handle were engraved his initials "T.E.W.". On the other side was the inscription "NWMP-1881".

Next the venerable Jerry Potts shook Tom's hand. *"Keep safe Tom," he said. "Watch the trail ahead and keep an eye for what's comin' up from behind. Always camp where it's high and dry and above all, trust your instincts."*

Jerry then rode to Fort Benton with him.

Tom heard that things hadn't gone well for Major Walsh after that. He always thought that Walsh was a true Canadian hero, but the politicians and bureaucrats in Ottawa were angry that he had tried to help Sitting Bull. They removed him from his post and forced him to resign from the NWMP in 1883.

Suddenly Tom woke from his dreams of the past, startled by the sound of distant thunder. Looking for clouds he saw none; it was as calm as when he had first settled down. Closing his eyes and settling back against the tree again he once more heard thunder. Puzzled, he stood up for a better look at the sky.

"What's that thunder I've been hear'n?" he asked his Indian packer Eddy Hunter. Eddy replied that it was the "Great Spirit" speaking at the "Lake of Little Fishes". He said that the little creek that ran by their camp came from the lake.

Tom was deep in thought as the two packers got things unloaded and began to set up camp. The horses were unpacked, unsaddled, hobbled, and then put out to roll and graze in the meadow. Tom looked over to where the elk had been, but they had moved on. He took the leather pouch from his jeans and took out the knife that Major Walsh had given him the year before. Opening it, he carved "T.E.W. 20/08/82" in large letters on the side of the big aspen that he had slept under. Then he carefully cleaned the knife's blade, folded it, and put it back in the pouch. Just as he was about to put it safely back in his pocket, he noticed that one of the horses had slipped its hobbles and was ambling off toward the river. As he ran to catch the escapee, the leather pouch along with the knife fell to the ground and was half-covered by a large yellow aspen leaf. The next moment, one of the packers, who was building a fire-pit with a ring of large stones, placed one of the rocks over the leaf and the unseen knife below it. After completing the fire pit, he went in search of dry firewood.

After camp was set up and their meal of roast ptarmigan had been consumed, Tom was aware that the thunder of the Great Spirit continued intermittently throughout the evening. He decided to get up at first light and see the Lake of Little Fishes for himself.

It was one of those special nights in the Rockies. A large full moon lit up the meadow and the snow-capped mountains high above them. The fast-flowing Bow River beside their camp sparkled and flashed in the soft, honey-coloured moonlight. Finding it hard to get to sleep, Tom sat for a long time smoking his pipe and soaking in the spellbinding scene. He could hardly wait for morning to come, as he was anxious to see the lake that Eddie had told him about.

The first rays of sun were streaming up the Bow River Valley from the east and Tom and Eddy Hunter were up and having coffee, some biscuits and the leftovers of the ptarmigan they had enjoyed the night before. It had been a clear, cool night—not cold enough to lay the first frost on the ground, but just enough to keep the mosquitoes away. They packed some bannock and pemmican in a light pack and made ready to start up the trail beside the little brook that flowed from the Lake of Little Fishes. They left camp at about nine o'clock, Tom carrying a medium-sized, double-bitted axe in case he had to clear a trail. Jimmy Three-Toes was left to build a small corral and watch over the camp and the horses.

As they started up the well-used game trail, Tom instinctively felt the right thigh of his deerskin leggings for the customary bulge of his pocketknife. When he realized that it wasn't there, he checked his other pockets. Pausing for a moment, he decided to search for it when he returned to camp. He hoped that he hadn't lost it, as it meant a lot to him.

The trail was fairly easy-going at first but then it grew steeper for half a mile before levelling out and hugging the brook closely. Tom knew that if he kept within hearing distance of the stream, it would lead him to the lake. Every so often he stopped to clear away branches and deadfall from the trail. Once or twice he saw moccasin footprints on the trail but they weren't fresh. The deer tracks were however, and he spotted four deer grazing just off the trail above them to the left. There were cold bear droppings on the trail, but no bears were seen. It was a pleasant trip through the lodge-pole pine forest and Tom noticed that as they gained elevation, the trees became smaller in girth.

Looking back across the expanse of the Bow River Valley toward Whitehorn Mountain and down the Pipestone Valley, a dark peak seemed to stand out from the rest in the distance. One day it would be named the "Black Douglas" and it would be to this mountain that Ernest and Edward Feuz (two of the Swiss guides working at Lake Louise) would carry a long pole so they could shinny up it to surmount a 40-foot cliff face that had turned them back on a previous attempt to climb the mountain.

Tom and Eddie continued along the trail. It was rather level now and they walked easily. Then the terrain grew steeper and the creek tumbled over a series of boulders for about a quarter-mile. The sun was warm on their backs and as they made their way up the final steep incline, Tom reckoned that they had been on the trail for about three hours. Then, through the trees they could see massive peaks and glaciers ahead of them and glimpses of the Lake of Little Fishes.

In a few moments, Tom was at the lake's edge. He fell to his knees in awe of the most breathtaking scene he had ever beheld. The jade-green lake was wild, untouched, and bathed in the golden August sunlight. He had no idea that in the not-too-distant future, a series of chalets, hotels, and chateaus would be built near the spot where he knelt, and that countless thousands of tourists from around the world would visit it each summer.

There wasn't a ripple on the tarn's glassy surface and the towering mountains and the glaciers above Tom and Eddy were perfectly reflected, as if in a gigantic mirror, causing them almost question which was real. So silent and breathtakingly perfect was the scene that they were left utterly speechless. Later Tom would recall that special moment.

> As God is my judge I never in all my explorations saw such a matchless scene. On the right and left, forests that had never known an axe came down to the shores, apparently growing out of the blue-green water. The background, a mile and a half away was divided into three tones of white, opal and brown, where the glacier merged with the shining water. The sun, high in the noon hour, poured into the pool, which reflected the whole landscape that formed a horseshoe.

As Tom gazed at the incredible scene, kneeling and resting on the heels of his high-topped boots a huge avalanche rumbled down the snowy, upper glacier of Mt. Victoria at the far end of the lake. Slowly it gathered momentum and slipped over the edge of the cliff falling free for some fifteen hundred feet before crashing to the lower glacier at the entrance to "The Death Trap" at the Plain of Six Glaciers. The tremendous booming thunder of the avalanche reached Tom's ears a few seconds later.

A minute or two later, another avalanche started high up on the glacier of the peak to the left of Mt. Victoria, which later became known as Mt. Lefroy, named after the Astronomer General, Sir John Henry Lefroy. The snow, rock, and ice seemed to be in free-fall for a long time as it cascaded down the sheer, three thousand foot north face of the mountain and crashed to the glacier below, sending up a puffy cloud of snow and ice. A few seconds later, Tom heard the thunderous boom. He felt that the Great Spirit was speaking directly to him, just as his Indian guides had said it would. The date was August 21st, 1882, Tom's twenty-third birthday.

Tom remained transfixed for a long time, watching the miraculous scene and the numerous avalanches that continued to fall from the peaks. Finally, he and his native companion ate some bannock and pemmican and started down the trail to their camp on the Bow River. Their two-hour trip was easy going and Tom took the opportunity to blaze and improve the trail. When they returned it was almost four o'clock and Jimmy Three-Toes was waiting for them with the horses packed and ready to go.

"Hey Jimmy! What's up? Why are you packed and ready to move out?" Tom called out. Jimmy replied that while Tom was gone, Major Rogers had been by and given orders to meet him at his camp on the Pipestone River, a little further up the Bow River. Rogers planned to explore Kicking Horse Pass the following morning and he wanted Tom–pronto!

"Have you boys seen my pocket knife?" Tom asked, as he checked his coat pockets and looked over the ground where he had sat and slept the day before. Both of the Indians shook their heads. Tom reluctantly swung into his saddle, neck-reined his pony sharply to the left and gently dug his heels into the horse's flanks. They then splashed smartly across the Bow River and headed west toward the Pipestone River for their reunion with Major Rogers.

That night Tom told the Major about the lake that he'd found and how he'd decided to call it "Emerald Lake". Two years later, in 1884, Dr. G. M. Dawson, the head of the Geological Survey, officially re-named Tom's mountain jewel, "Lake Louise" in honour of the Royal Princess and the wife of the Governor General of Canada.

Fifty years to the day, after Tom first beheld the "Lake of Little Fishes", his friend Byron Harmon took a special photo of him. The 50th Anniversary Dining Room menu at Chateau Lake Louise described the photo as follows:

> *Pipe in mouth and seated on a rock at the lake's shore he's gazing wistfully over his lake's broad, blue-green expanse. In his eyes an expression of wonder and admiration glows as ardently as when a younger pair of eyes beheld the same scene for the first time on a late August day, half a century before. [See photo on page 79]*

Tom Wilson went on to become arguably one of the greatest mountain men this country has ever known. Conrad Kain, Wild Bill Peyto and Jimmy Simpson may have equalled him in terms of toughness, resilience, and stamina. However, they never surpassed the resourcefulness and ingenuity of the strapping lad who left Ontario at an early age to play a major role in the opening up of the Canadian West and the mountains that he loved so well.

What happened to Tom's pocketknife? Well, in 1959, while looking for worms to tantalize some feisty trout in the Bow River, near where Tom had camped in August of 1882, I found it in its tattered leather case under a blackened rock that had been used to ring a fire pit. I cleaned it up and oiled it and carried it proudly for a week or so. Then I lost it again in the Bow River when the raft I built with Jimmy Miller capsized as we attempted to ride it from Lake Louise to Banff. For the full story read my book *Lake Louise At Its Best: An Affectionate Look at Life at Lake Louise By One Who Knew It Well.*

How Banff Indian Days Began

In the fall of 1886, construction began on the Banff Springs Hotel. Supplies and materials were packed up Lynx Street to the Bow River and hauled across a pontoon bridge built by George Stewart. From there they were transported to the construction site.

Designed by architect **Bruce Price**, the father of **Emily Post** ("Miss Manners") the French chateau-style hotel boasted three main stories, a domed roof, and a rotunda with elaborate overhanging balconies. It had oriel windows, dormers, and turrets, and featured ninety-two masters' rooms and eighteen servants' rooms. The estimated construction cost was in the order of $95,600 – an incredible amount in those days.

> *Opening in June of 1888, the hotel's first season accommodated some 1,500 guests and the rooms fetched $3.50 per night. The guest list was made up of 53% Canadian, 26% American, 19% from Great Britain and 2% from other countries. In 1891, 3,389 guests registered for the summer season with 56% from America and 26% from Canada. The Hotel became so popular, that annually the CPR, had to renovate the three-storey building with its 259 beds and ten bathrooms. (Parker, 1990)*

During the inaugural season the hotel was open from June 1st, until September 30th, and it was an overwhelming success. Based on this, manager W.L. Matthews and his congenial staff expected an even bigger season the following year. As the news of this luxurious hotel in the heart of the Canadian Rockies and its overall ambiance spread across Canada, Europe, and the USA, reservations soared.

The 1889 season was going well until early July, when torrential rains and rockslides wiped out the railroad tracks to the west at Field, British Columbia and at Canmore to the east within a few hours of each other. This left the guests at the Banff Springs Hotel cut off, with nothing to do. It was estimated that it would be at least a week, perhaps two, before the tracks were repaired. Desperate, for ways to entertain his guests, Manager Matthews sent out an urgent plea for help to Tom Wilson. A fast rider was dispatched to fetch him from Red Earth Creek, where he was guiding some dudes from Europe on a hunting and fishing trip.

Tom had lots of time to think about the problem as he rode his big black stallion 'Midnight' back to Banff and to the Banff Springs Hotel. The seeds of a solution were already sown in his mind as he shook the trail dust from his clothes and headed though the massive doors of the hotel and down the lobby to manager Matthews' office.

Matthews described the problem and after a few moments, Tom put forward the idea of asking his old friend, Chief Buffalo Calf (also known as Hector Crawler) of the Stoney Indian Band at Morley, to come to Banff with tribe members and horses to hold a four-day Indian festival. He suggested that the Indians could dress up in their ceremonial costumes, the kind they wore for the old-time rendezvous with the fur traders, and have a parade down the main street of Banff each day. He also suggested that there could be some contests of skill and daring, native dances, and traditional Indian food. Finally he proposed that the event be held near the base of Cascade Mountain on the outskirts of Banff and that it be called "Banff Indian Days."

Thrilled with the idea, Mathews offered Tom a case of the CPR's finest Scotch whiskey if he could pull it off. Pleased at the prospects of planning the big event,

Tom took four bottles with him and the following morning he rode Midnight to the Stoney's camp near Morley.

Chief Buffalo Calf greeted Tom warmly when he arrived and later, seated around the campfire with most of the tribe, the two exchanged the latest news and reminisced about the days gone by. As Chief Buffalo Calf got his ceremonial pipe ready, Tom proposed the idea of "Banff Indian Days." They all agreed that it was a good idea, and to seal their agreement, the ceremonial pipe was lit and passed around.

Lake Louise in all its summer glory as Tom Wilson would have first seen it on August 21, 1882.

Lake Louise in mid August after a sudden summer storm

Tom Wilson sitting beside Lake Louise
Byron Harmon took this picture on August 21, 1932–fifty years to the day
after Tom discovered the lake on August 21, 1882. It was also his birthday.

Lake Louise in Late May

Lake Louise in late April

The following morning Tom rode back to the Banff Springs Hotel to speard the word that the first annual Banff Indian Days Celebration would be held four days later. Tom himself would be the Master of Ceremonies for the event, and the CPR would be the official sponsor – offering prizes and refreshments for the participants of each event as well as food for all the Indians who attended. The "official" Indian Days photographer would be George Fear as his photographer friend Byron Harmon did not yet live in Banff.

Two days later one-hundred and fifty Stoney Indians left Morley for Banff, travelling on horseback and by wagon, Some horses even pulled travios. The first night they camped out near Canmore in a place known as "Indian Flats." The next day they reached the Indian Days Encampment, which had been set up just east of Banff on a broad plain where the "Buffalo Paddock" and the Banff airport were later located.

With great excitement and some kicking and biting, the animals were marshalled into position and the first Banff Indian Days Parade got underway. Leaving the campground a little behind schedule, the proud entourage was enthusiastically applauded by the appreciative onlookers as it proceeded down Banff Avenue. Tom Wilson led the way, dressed in the buckskin garb of a mountain man and cradling his long-barrelled, Hawkin rifle in the crook of his left arm while guiding his prancing black stallion with his right. Beside him Chief Buffalo Calf rode bareback on a spirited paint gelding with a traditional rope bridle and dressed in his ceremonial deerskins and a flowing headdress of eagle feathers. The two were an impressive sight as they led the historic parade under a cloudless mid-July sky.

The two leaders were followed by a large number of Indian braves who also rode bareback on painted ponies. Younger warriors followed behind dressed in fierce-looking costumes and war paint and carrying bows, spears, and tomahawks. Next came the women with the younger children. Many led dogs and horses that pulled travois behind them. George Fear had his camera strategically set up on a rooftop at the intersection of Bear Street and Banff Avenue and he took many photos of the historic event. It was quite a sight!

Tom Wilson, Chief Buffalo Calf, and those that followed them were greeted with more hurrahs and appreciative applause at the bridge as they crossed over the Bow River, but the loudest applause came when they entered the grounds of the Banff Springs Hotel. The guests were crowded on balconies and patios and they were delighted at seeing the natives in their ceremonial garb. Most had read the popular stories about General George Custer, Buffalo Bill Cody, Major Walsh, Sitting Bull, and the Wild West Shows. Tom Wilson grinned from ear to ear as he gave a thumbs-up salute to manager Matthews, who was standing on the top step of the hotel and surveying the scene with pride and amusement. It was indeed an historic occasion.

Following the parade, the hotel guests were transported in horse-drawn wagons and coaches to the Indian encampment where foot races, wrestling matches, horse races, target shooting, tomahawk and knife-throwing contests, and trick riding exhibitions took place. Tom and Chief Buffalo Calf kept order and congratulated both the winners and the also-rans of each hotly-contested event. The guests of the CPR could scarcely believe their eyes as they were allowed to walk around, enter teepees, buy native handicrafts, eat bannock and jerky, and take many photographs.

Never before had such an event been held in North America. It took a man like Tom Wilson to come up with the idea, organize it, and see it through. Manager Matthews was delighted with the way Tom had solved his problem of how to entertain the stranded guests. A few days later, regular train service was re-established. Manager Matthews was true to his word and paid his debt with a case of the CPR's best Scotch whiskey. Tom loaded a side of beef into a wagon and headed for Morley with some of his friends. There they and the Chief held a feast and celebrated their success.

Word soon spread about the remarkable event, and manager Matthews and the CPR urged Tom and Chief Buffalo Calf to make it an annual affair. From then on, Banff Indian Days took place each year in mid July. Tom organized the event until 1915 and then he passed it on to others. For many years Norman Luxton, editor of the much-read *Crag and Canyon* newspaper Jimmy Brewster and Dave White did an outstanding job of organizing the spectacle. Luxton and Claude Brewster often subsidized it out of their own pockets. Many other civic-minded individuals also worked to keep the event alive over the years. It is all well-described in Patricia Parker's excellent book, *Feather and Drum*.

The author witnessed the event on several occasions in the late 1950s and the early 1960s and it was indeed an event not to be missed. Sadly, owing to lack of help organizing and managing the event, Banff Indian Days came to an end in 1979. The buffalo were rounded up and removed from the Buffalo Pound and the Indians who camped there for so many summers camped there no more.

Recently there have been renewed efforts to revive the spectacle but it will never have the free-wheeling excitement of the original event. Now permission must be obtained from Parks Canada bureaucrats to do anything in Banff National Park, and of course, there are always insurance issues, in case a horse sneezes on someone, or a spectator gets sick on a hot-dog and decides to sue for damages.

Santa Claus comes to the Rockies

[In 1962, a white-haired lady by the name of Mrs. West told me many of the details of the following story at the old Post Hotel one rainy afternoon in late August. She was in her late sixties then, and her father had worked for a lumber camp at the Great Divide in the early 1900s. Jimmy Simpson filled in the rest of the essential details for me as we chatted and looked out over Bow Lake at his Num-Ti-Jah lodge one warm August evening in 1962. I have embellished the account considerably to flesh out the story and help it to come alive.]

The summer of 1911 had been a short one in the Rockies and winter seemed to set in early. It started snowing in late October and continued day after day—this kept the rail crew busy clearing the tracks between Field and Banff. One afternoon during the first week of December, **Tom Wilson, Byron Harmon, Norman Sanson, George Fear,** and **Jimmy Brewster** were having a bracer or two of the CPR's Scotch whiskey in Tom's cabin on the outskirts of Banff. **Minnie Wilson** had a big pot of elk stew on the stove and the stories were flying thick and fast. **Dr. Brett** dropped in for a "snort" and then **Jimmy Simpson** and **Wild Bill Peyto,** ambled in and shook the snow from their big buffalo-skin coats. Finally **Norm Luxton,** of the *Crag and Canyon* newspaper arrived, lit his pipe, and joined in the conversation. They talked about all that had transpired that season and the fact that Tom had just received the news that Sir **Edward Whymper,** a man they all knew well, had passed away in Chamonix, France on September 16th. This provoked a lively session of "Sir Edward" stories. [Chapter 5 recounts the true story of Sir Edward Whymper in Canada.]

After a few more drinks, the talk turned to Christmas. Tom, who had five children of his own at the time, suggested that they plan a spectacular event for Banff to take place on December 23rd. Having conceived of Banff Indian Days in July of 1889, and having managed it for many years, Wilson was no stranger to organizing elaborate community events. Everyone knew that if there was something to be done, whether it was a trip into the wilderness, a schoolteacher to be hired, or a community event to plan, Tom Wilson was the one to call upon.

Tom told the others that he had read about a Santa Claus Parade in Toronto and suggested that it would be a great surprise for the kids of Banff if Santa were to come to town. He proposed that Santa arrive in a sleigh at about four o'clock in the afternoon on the day before Christmas Eve and gallop up Banff Avenue to a stage that would be set up at the Bow River bridge. Elves could toss candy from the sleigh to the children and families lining the street. A large Christmas tree could be erected near the bridge, where Santa could give out gifts and candy. Everyone thought that it was a great idea!

Byron Harmon suggested that his wife Maud and Jim Brewster's wife "Lade" (her real name was Tressa), could check the Eaton's catalogue and order gifts for the girls, while he and Jim did the same for the boys. They'd consult with the churches and the school to make sure that no one was forgotten. Jimmy Simpson reminded the group that there were a few children in Field, Lake Louise, Wapta, and Silver City that shouldn't be forgotten. Norman Sanson then suggested that Santa should also make a quick trip to the Stoney Indian Reservation at Morley with a sleigh full of food and some toys. It was turning into a big event until Tom's wife Minnie asked how all this was going to be paid for. This brought an uneasy silence to the gathering

At this point, Jimmy Simpson broke open his bottle of rye whiskey and Byron Harmon suggested that they should come up with a budget and convince the CPR to foot half of the bill if they could raise the rest. *"Great,"* said Tom. He continued: "I just might know where I can raise the rest of the money. A few years back … in 1896, I helped drag young Phil Abbot down from the Plain of Six Glaciers at Lake Louise after he was killed in a fall on Mt. Lefroy. He was with a group of young duds from the Appalachian Mountain Club. Walter Wilcox, Sam Allen, Lou Frissell, and Charlie Fay were all friends of his. Wild Bill Peyto and I've packed most of 'em into the backcountry a time or two since then. Those boys are loaded and I'm going to telegraph Wilcox and Fay tomorrow morning and ask them to raise the other half of what we need and send it to us. Should be no problem," he drawled.

"Good idea," agreed Wild Bill: "Those boys are pretty well fixed alright, and they sure do love this country. Wilcox and Allen are real interested in the Stoney language. It was them that gave the Ten Peaks at Moraine Lake all those Indian names. They did likewise for most of the glaciers, creeks and passes in that area."

"That's right," said Norm Sanson, "If anyone can help foot the bill, them boys can."

Indian Days in Banff
In the center of the picture is Chief Hector Crawler in his head-dress and Tom Wilson with his pipe, dressed as usual in a three-pieced suit.

High excitement during Banff Indian Days

Tom Wilson (right) with Walter Wilcox and Jim Brewster at Banff Indian Days. Jim Brewster has the woolly chaps on.

Tom Wilson in his later years with his old friend Jimmy Brewster

Walter Wilcox, Chief John Hunter, (Stoney Indian Chief) and Tom Wilson at Lake Louise. Byron Harmon took this photo in July of 1925.

Chief Walking Buffalo – George Maclean

Chief Buffalo Calf–Hector Crawler

Chief George Crawler

"We'll need to get a good-sized sleigh as well as a Santa Claus suit and a few elf costumes," said Tom. "We want this to be a memorable event for everyone."

Jim Brewster said that he had a sleigh that he could paint for the occasion and Dr. Brett volunteered to ask a few of the church ladies to sew some costumes. Byron Harmon was chosen to be Santa Claus and Billy Randell, Janet Whipple and Mabel Fear were elected to be the elves. Tom agreed to drive the reindeer.

"Reindeer!" Byron exclaimed, "Where the hell are we going to get reindeer?"

"We could use elk," volunteered George Fear. "They have big horns and there's lots of 'em around here."

"We could never train 'em in time," said Tom. Bill Peyto quickly agreed.

"We could use horses and strap some deer horns to their heads," suggested Billy Randell. "We could get Tommy Lusk and Fred Stevens to make up some head harnesses for the horses and strap the horns on with 'em."

All agreed that this would be a fine compromise, as Tom had a four-horse team of fawn-colored horses that would fit the bill. Two were real gentle but the other two were a bit of a handful. Tom promised to have them ready to go for the big day. The plan was taking shape and so Norm Luxton proposed another toast.

One final detail still had to be worked out: how to get Santa to Field and Lake Louise. Doctor Brett came up with the idea of loading the sleigh onto a flat-car and having a steam engine pull it down the track to Field. Santa and the elves could ride in a coach and they could cover the sleigh with a tarp so that no one could see it. Lawrence Grassi could have a team of horses ready at Field and they could strap the horns on the horses before they hitched up.

When Santa was finished in Field, they could load the sleigh on the train and head for Lake Louise where Reg West could meet them with another team to pull Santa and the elves around the village. When the festivities were over there, they'd load up the sleigh for the last time and head back to Banff. Dr. Brett suggested brief stops at Hector and Silver City to give out candy and presents. When they got back to Banff, they'd unload the sleigh and get set up for the big parade through town. It was an elaborate plan, but after one more round of drinks, it all seemed quite possible.

The plans all hinged on Tom being able to convince the CPR to come up with half of the needed funds and on Wilcox and his colleagues in New York and Boston coming up with the other half. Within two days, Walter Wilcox telegraphed Tom to tell him that he had wired $750.00 to the Manager of the Banff Springs Hotel. He sent with fond regards to the people of the Bow Valley and best wishes for a very merry Christmas. He also sent his best wishes to Wild Bill Peyto whom he admired greatly.

On receiving the news, Tom didn't waste any time riding over to the Banff Springs Hotel to see Manager G.H. Rawlins. After sending a wire to CPR headquarters in Montreal and receiving approval to match the amount, Rawling wrote Tom a cheque for $1,500. The parade was now a go and they had just two weeks to get everything ready.

As the news of the event spread, the whole community got involved. A Christmas dinner was planned in the Catholic Church basement, to be followed by a pageant at the Anglican Church. As a grand finale, a tree decorating ceremony at the head of Banff Avenue was organized where there would be mulled apple-cider and Christmas carols. The *Crag and Canyon* stirred local interest with an article telling the readers that something special was going to happen on the day before Christmas Eve. Readers of the paper in Field, Hector, Lake Louise, and Silver City were told to expect big things on that day as well.

Preparations moved at a fever pitch for the next two weeks. The Banff Presbyterian women's group was busy sewing the pageant costumes and the Anglican pastor's wife held rehearsals each day after school. Minnie Wilson and the ladies from the United Church were busy with costumes for Santa and the elves and Jimmy Brewster gave his sleigh a new coat of red paint. He trimmed the rails and runners in fresh black enamel and when it was finished he hid it under a tarp beside the train station. The CPR agreed to provide an engine, a coach, and a flatcar and Tommy Lusk and Fred Stevens, assisted by Bill Peyto, secretly made the head harnesses to hold the deer antlers on the horse's heads. Maud Harmon and Lade Brewster finalized the list of the children that would receive gifts at Field, Hector, Lake Louise, Silver City, and Banff and then sent an order to Eaton's in Calgary.

Jimmy Simpson got things organized in Field and Lake Louise and both **Lawrence Grassi** and **Reg West** got their horses, harness, and sleigh bells ready for the big day. The Swiss guides agreed to dress in their traditional costumes and help give out the gifts and sing carols. **Mrs. Legace** and the schoolteacher, **Miss Hume,** volunteered to serve mulled wine and Christmas cookies at the Lake Louise train station and Mrs. Walters and the manageress of Mount Stephen House. **Miss Mollison,** agreed to do likewise at Field. Tom Wilson also sent a message to **Chief Buffalo Calf** at Morley, telling him to expect a visit from Santa on the morning train three days before Christmas.

Tom supervised all the preparations, getting daily progress reports from everyone involved. It appeared that everything was coming together with the precision of a well-crafted Swiss watch. With just two days to go, the costumes were completed and the toys arrived from Eaton's. The final rehearsals for the Christmas pageant were in full swing and the Christmas tree was up and anchored in place at the top of Banff Avenue. Jim Pong, the cook for the Alpine Club camp at Sherbrooke Lake, volunteered to prepare the hot cider and the *Crag and Canyon* ran another notice telling the readers that exciting things were going to take place on December 23rd. Byron Harmon went beyond the call of duty, gaining two or three pounds in preparation for his role as a jolly, well-fed Santa.

On the morning of December 22nd, Tom Wilson and Bill Peyto, and Tommy Lusk drove a team and a sleigh to White's general store and loaded it with the food, blankets and toys for the Stoney Indians. They then drove to the station and loaded the goods on the early train heading east. There were no clouds to be seen in the deep blue sky that morning and it was a crisp ten degrees below zero. The early-morning sun made them glad to be alive and in the Rockies, as they chatted light-heartedly and shared a laugh or two about some of the dudes they'd guided over the years. Soon the train pulled slowly out of the station and headed for the Stoney Indian Reservation at Morley.

Chief Buffalo Calf welcomed his old friends at the station with his usual ceremonial fanfare. Many hands helped load the wagon and then they all headed for the camp. The chief had a good fire going and after the food, blankets, and gifts were handed out, it was time to sit around the fire, have a coffee, and tell a few stories about the success they had been having trapping marten, lynx, fox, and wolves in the foothills. Johnny Three Toes mentioned that he'd seen lots of lynx that season and some large packs of timber wolves. Tommy Lusk reckoned that the early snow and the large herds of elk and deer in the area were probably attracting them. Bill Peyto claimed to have shot three lynx and six wolves just west of the Vermilion Lakes the previous week. Tom Wilson then livened up the coffee with a bit of rum as they chatted together. As the rum began to take effect, the stories became even more exciting.

In the late afternoon, Lusk, Peyto, and Wilson said good-bye to their Stoney Indian friends and caught the four-thirty train back to Banff. When they arrived, they still had time to get Tom's four-horse team hitched to a stone-boat. In the crisp twilight, they worked the team until Tom was sure that they'd be well behaved when hitched to Santa's sleigh the following afternoon.

Tom was up early the next morning, making a final check of all the details. There had been a fresh snowfall during the night and it promised to be another beautiful day in the Rockies. He fed and watered the horses at his corral, had a quick breakfast, and then hurried down to the station to help load the sleigh and meet Santa and the elves. While loading the sleigh, Tom slipped a fresh bottle of Hudson's Bay rum under the seat–this would keep Santa and the elves in a jolly mood throughout the day.

By eight o'clock, a sizable crowd had gathered to wish Santa and the elves a bon voyage. Byron "Santa" Harmon was already in his costume and he was feeling very festive. Billy Randell, Janet Whipple, and Mabel Fear also had their elf costumes on. Lade Brewster and Maud Harmon arrived with the toys sorted for the children at Field, Hector, Lake Louise and Silver City. When these were carefully loaded on the coach and all was ready, Nellie Martin took a series of photographs for the *Crag and Canyon*. Norman Sanson gave the engineer the high sign and with a long blow of the steam whistle, the engine pulled slowly out of the station and puffed its way down the track.

The train came to a stop at the siding just east of Field where **Lawrence Grassi** was dutifully waiting with a team of high-stepping bay horses. Everyone in the little town was in a festive mood and as Santa and his elves came into view, there was spontaneous applause and hoarse cries of "Here comes Santa!"

The sleigh bells jingled crazily as the two horses, each with a set of antlers strapped to their heads, galloped at top speed toward the town. Santa had found the bottle of rum that Tom had slipped into the sleigh and they had all sampled it liberally before climbing aboard the sleigh. The elves tried to hold onto the presents as they all hung on while Tom strained to keep the steeds under control as he guided them through the snow. Fortunately he succeeded in reining them in just in time to bring them to a halt in front of the hotel. Once stopped, Santa and the elves jumped out of the sleigh with a "Ho, Ho, Ho!"

Everyone was in a jolly mood as they headed for the hotel lobby where Miss Mollison was overseeing two large pots of hot mulled wine and hot cider, as well as cookies and venison sandwiches. When all were assembled and the children seated quietly on the floor in front of the small stage, Tom began to call out each child's name. As a child came forward, an elf handed Santa a present, which he in turn gave to the child. Then an elf gave each child a small bag of hard candy while another handed out a fresh orange—a real treat.

"The children were so thrilled. I wish you could have seen their eyes," said Mrs. West, as she related the story to me with tears welling up in her own. "The hotel was decorated with garlands, boughs, candles, and red ribbons. I've never forgotten the scent of the pine boughs mingled with the smell of the mulled wine, the hot cider, and the cinnamon." Her voice broke momentarily.

"Everyone was in such a wonderful mood. When the presents and the candy had been given out, Janet Whipple, Mabel Fear and some of the Swiss guides lead everyone in some Christmas carols. I remember that Tom Wilson and "Santa" Harmon sang with great enthusiasm and when they sang, "Oh Little town of Bethlehem" Jimmy Simpson had to blow his nose and wipe his eyes with his polka-dot bandanna. That hymn meant a lot to him, I guess."

After more carols and more mulled cider, it was time to move on to the station at Hector. Santa and the elves scrambled into the sleigh and Tom cracked his whip. The prancing team sprang into action again and galloped back to where the train was waiting. The antlers had been removed from the horses' heads and tossed into the sleigh during the festivities, but in the excitement Tom forgot to strap them on again for the dramatic dash out of town. No one seemed to notice though, and the horses didn't complain either.

The sleigh was quickly loaded onto the flatcar and preparations were made for the stop at Hector. The engine chugged up the grade through the long spiral tunnels, which had been completed just two years earlier in 1909. At Wapta Lake they stopped briefly at the Hector station and Santa and the elves gave out presents and candy to the children who waited there with their parents. The little train then proceeded down the tracks, passed frozen Sink Lake and over the Great Divide to the village of Lake Louise.

Reg West and a team of pinto ponies were waiting out of sight just around the corner from the station where everyone was waiting. Everything was going according to schedule and as the men got the sleigh hitched to the team, the elves adjusted their costumes and got the presents ready for the Lake Louise children. Reg wrestled with the nervous horses, attaching the antlers to their heads and Tom passed the bottle of rum around again. When all was ready, Tom urged the horses into a trot with a light snap of his whip and the sleigh moved smartly over the powdery snow. As they rounded the corner, the Lake Louise station came into view.

A crowd of locals and about a dozen children waited expectantly outside the station. When they heard the sleigh bells and saw Santa and his helpers approaching in the sleigh, they let out a cheer. Tom handled the team masterfully and brought the "reindeer" to a halt in front of the station where they were met by Ernest Feuz, Christian Haesler, and Rudolf Aemmer—all dressed in their traditional leather knickers, jackets, and Tyrolean hats. Ray Hill, the stationmaster, welcomed Santa and then escorted everyone into the station where he had a large pot of cider steaming on the station's massive woodstove.

Several wooden boxes were pushed together to make a stage and then Tom Wilson introduced Santa and the elves. The presents, candy, and oranges were handed out and then elves Janet Whipple and Mabel Fear, assisted by the Swiss guides, led the singing of a number of carols. After Mrs. Legace and Miss Hume served cookies and a special rum-soaked cake it was time for Santa and the elves to continue on their journey.

When the sleigh was loaded, the engineer blew the steam whistle three times and the little train chugged down the track once again. The next stop was at Silver City, where more presents and candy were given out. Finally, Santa's train began the final leg of the journey back to Banff where the townspeople were waiting with enthusiastic expectations. It was a fine afternoon and all had gone so well that Santa and his helpers decided to celebrate their success with another nip or two from the bottle of rum. The first bottle was finished and another was quickly opened. By the time the train pulled into the Banff train station, Santa and his elves were feeling mighty jovial.

Jimmy Brewster, Bill Peyto, Tommy Lusk, Norm Luxton, and Norm Sanson all turned out to greet Santa's train and help get things ready for the parade down Banff Avenue. Bill and Tommy had already harnessed Santa's team and as the train pulled into the station in a cloud of steam and smoke, the horses reared and pawed the air—one of them doing a "Texas two-step."

By this time the steady intake of rum, cider, and mulled wine was having its effect on Santa and his entourage. Tom Wilson, the first off the train. did not appear to feel the cold. Santa, whose nose was decidedly redder than when he'd left Banff earlier that morning, followed him. Billy Randell was also a bit unsteady on his feet so Jimmy Simpson, who had ridden in the coach with them from Field, had to help him off the train. Janet Whipple and Mabel Fear were giggling and seemed a bit tipsy, but they managed to get off the coach without requiring assistance.

Jim Brewster and Norm Luxton could see that disaster was lurking pretty close at hand so they called for strong coffee while they unloaded the sleigh from the flatcar and filled it with the toys. Tommy Lusk wrestled with the horses to attach the antlers, and it was easy to see that they didn't appreciate having the horns on their heads. The two wilder colts were tossing their heads and trying to rear but Tom Wilson, who was now in the sleigh, jerked the reins and cussed them out a bit to get their attention. Lusk finally lost his temper and hammered one of the horses in the nose with his gloved fist. That seemed to do the trick and the recalcitrant steed settled down and stood quietly. But anyone could see that it was a mighty high-strung animal.

When the horses were properly hitched and adorned with the antlers, Santa and the elves were heaved into the sleigh. Both Bill Peyto and Jimmy Simpson felt that they should lead the front pair of colts but Tom Wilson would have none of it and told them to turn them loose. He was sure they'd settle down before the sleigh reached Banff Avenue.

Peyto and Simpson reluctantly let go of the bridles as Tom urged the team forward and slapped the reins over their rumps. The two lead colts both jumped nervously and jerked the sleigh into motion. The first jerk nearly toppled poor Billy Randell out of the sleigh, but Mabel Fear pulled him back in. After a few more jerks and some frantic sidestepping, the team settled down and began to pull the sleigh along nicely.

"Hang on, Billy!" yelled Jimmy Simpson.

"Hold tight to that team, Tom!" hollered Norm Sanson.

Tom circled the team around the yard of the station a couple of times while everyone got into their sleighs and headed into town. It was now four-thirty and almost dark.

A good-sized crowd had gathered in front of the stores that lined Banff Avenue and they applauded enthusiastically as the skittish horses pulled the heavily-laden sleigh along the parade route. Tom made a wide turn from Wolf Street and guided the prancing steeds down the wide boulevard of Banff Avenue. All was going well.

The sleigh bells jingled merrily with each step and the antlers on the horses' heads looked very impressive. Tom and Santa waved enthusiastically to the cheering crowd and the elves tossed hard candy to the bystanders. "This is a piece of cake," Tom thought to himself as he waved to his wife, who was standing in front of Harmon's Photo Shop with his five children.

Suddenly, from out of no-where, the village dog—a hound of unknown breeding—jumped out of the crowd and began to bark ferociously at the nervous horses. Then the annoying critter swung around and nipped at the lead colt's heels.

"Get that son-of-a-bitch off the street!" Tom yelled to Curly Phillips, as he spotted him in the crowd. "He's scar'n the hell out of these horses."

Just then the left lead colt aimed a vicious kick at the obnoxious mutt with both hind feet—catching it square in the chest and sending it flying across the snow-covered street to the opposite boardwalk. The dog yipped in pain as it dragged itself away through the crowd.

But the damage was done. The right lead horse reared and tossed its head violently, dislodging the antlers so that they slid down its neck with one set of points digging into its chest and the other smacking the left lead horse on the right shoulder. Both horses reared and pawed the air and then they sprang forward, giving the sleigh a terrific jerk forward. This tossed the unsteady Billy Randell and the surprised Mabel Fear out of the sleigh into the snow-covered street. This amused the crowd immensely.

Tom fought to control the team but to no avail. The second pair bounded forward ejecting Santa from the sleigh as well. The antlers on the second pair of horses were now flapping around and digging into the horse, spooking them even more. The parade was quickly becoming a disaster but the crowd seemed to enjoy the Christmas-themed wild west show that was unfolding before their eyes. Someone yelled: "Ride'm Santa" as Santa Harmon and Billy Randell picked themselves up from the snow.

Both Tom Wilson and Santa were cussing the nervous steeds with wild abandon, and the air was blue for a moment or two. Then Jimmy Simpson and Bill Peyto rushed in among the flying hooves with their hunting knives drawn.

"Cut those damn horns off those horses, boys!" yelled Tom as he fought to hold the frightened steeds in check with the reins. In a moment, the deed was done and the tangled antlers were tossed to the side of the street. The horses now stood quietly as Simpson and Wild Bill each held a lead horse. This gave Santa, Billy Randell, and Mabel Fear a chance to scramble back into the sleigh.

"Better lead them until we get to the end of the street where the Christmas tree is boys," Tom instructed.

There was a lot of good-natured jesting as Santa and the elves brushed snow and dirt from their costumes. A member of the crowd wanted to know where Santa had learned to drive, while another pointed out that the reindeer had lost their horns. This brought on a round of laughter and more jeering and catcalls. An embarrassed Santa retorted that it was tough to find good reindeer in Banff.

When the procession finally reached the Christmas tree at the top of Banff Avenue, Tom, Santa, and the elves mounted a large stage to give out the presents. When they were finished, Mabel and Janet led the crowd in a round of Christmas carols. When they sang *God Rest Ye Merry Gentlemen* no one sang with more feeling than Tom Wilson, Jimmy Brewster, Byron Harmon, Jimmy Simpson and Norman Luxton.

After the carol singing the crowd adjourned to the basement of the Catholic Church, where for seventy-five cents a plate, a dinner of roast venison and elk with all the trimmings was set out. Father McInnis said grace and then gave a heart-felt Christmas blessing to all in attendance. After dinner, everyone proceeded to the Anglican Church for the Christmas pageant. The pageant was a success and everyone applauded appreciatively as the Wise Men gave gifts of gold, frankincense, and myrrh to the baby Jesus. A chorus of *Oh Come All Ye Faithful,* brought the evening to an end and then everyone walked home under a starry sky.

Norman Sanson remarked to Tom Wilson and Jimmy Simpson, that there seemed to be something special about the quality of the starlight that lit their way back to Tom's cabin that night. They all felt the spirit and the magical quality of peace that hung over the little town nestled among the snow-covered mountains in the heart of the Canadian Rockies.

That first Santa Claus parade in the Rockies was an unquestioned success, creating memories that lasted a lifetime for the children who had waited with great anticipation for Santa and the elves to arrive. A child of just eight years then, Mrs. West seemed to remember every sight, every sound, and every smell as she talked about the events of that memorable day.

Jimmy Simpson also recalled the events in great detail as we talked at his lodge at Bow Lake. His sparkling, dark eyes filled with tears as he recalled his old friends Tom Wilson, Tommy Lusk, Bill Peyto, Jimmy Brewster and Byron Harmon and the joy they all shared in bringing Christmas to the Rockies. They didn't give gold, frankincense, or myrrh—they gave much more. They gave a gift that lasted a lifetime in the hearts of everyone who was present on that very special day when Santa paid his first visit to the Bow River Valley.

We repeated the event in 1912 and again in 1913, but after that we all had other things to do," Jimmy said wistfully. "It really was someth'n special for the kids of the valley—and for all of us as well."

Home for Christmas—Tom Wilson has a Close Call

A.O. Wheeler told this story after receiving a letter from Tom Wilson. It concerns a seventy-mile trip on snowshoes that Tom made just before Christmas from his horse ranch at Kootenay Plains on the North Saskatchewan River to his home in Banff where his wife and children were expecting him for Christmas The route, which Tom describes as being "lonely, tree-clad, valleys, rock-bound gorges, and wind-swept passes where all nature lay still in the icy grip of winter" began at Kootenay Plains by ascending the trail along the Siffleur River, then up and over Pipestone Pass and down the trail along the Pipestone River to Laggan (the village of Lake Louise). From Laggan, Tom planned to use his lifetime pass on the CPR and catch the train to Banff.

A quick check of a topographical map of the area, confirms the magnitude of such a journey on snowshoes in the dead of winter, but Tom tackled this trip as a matter of course in days when there were no thermal clothing, no gortex or triple-insulated outer wear, and no high-tech winter boots. These were the days when men really were men. In his letter to Wheeler, Tom tells of the trek in a matter-of-fact manner.

There is not much to tell of my trip over the Pipestone Pass. It was simply the case of a man starting on a seventy-mile snowshoe trip across the mountains to eat his Christmas dinner with his wife and family, and getting there and eating dinner, the pleasure being well worth the trip. I rode to within eight miles of the summit and started early the next morning on snowshoes to cross the pass (8,300 feet). It was snowing a little and very cold when I started, and when I got opposite the Clearwater Gap, a blizzard came up. I could not see more than six or eight feet ahead in that grey snow light that makes everything look level. I was on the trail along a mountainside, and was afraid of falling down into one of those steep side collars (which you remember on that side), and of breaking my snowshoes, so I turned and went down the mountain to the creek bottom. The snow was seven or eight feet deep and I fell through a snow bridge, getting both feet wet. It was below zero and a long way up to timber whichever way I turned, but I'd never liked hitting the back trail. It was eight o'clock at night before I crossed the summit of the pass and reached the first timber. I got a fire started, but it was drifting and snowing so hard that the snow covered my socks and moccasins as fast as I could wring them dry, and, owing to the fierce wind, the flames leap in every direction, making it impossible to get near the fire, so at half past nine I gave it up, put on my wet foot gear and snowshoes and started down the valley. I could not see and felt my way with a stick.

By daylight I had made three and a half miles; not much, but it kept the circulation going. In the heavy timber I made a fire and dried out. My feet were beginning to pain as they had been thawed out twice already. I made three miles more that day and finished the last of my grub. The big snowshoes sank fifteen inches in the soft new snow and were a big drag on my frozen toes. I saw it meant three or four more days tramping without grub to make Laggan. I made it in three, but the last day I could only make about fifty yards without resting, and my tracks did not leave a very straight line. The chief trouble I had was to keep from going to sleep; it would have been so much easier to quit than to go on.

Wheeler offered these comments on Tom's strength and resolve:

Think for a moment what it really meant; that every time he put on his snowshoes, his toes got frozen owing to the tight shoe straps; that every time he took them off, his feet had to be thawed out; that every step had to raise a load of ten to fifteen pounds of soft snow; that wood had to be collected and cut to keep alive during the night; that the fierce pain would drive away sleep; that he had no food, and always before him those interminable, slow, dragging miles of snowy wilderness. It must have required iron determination to make it to the end of the never-ending track, to eat his Christmas dinner with his wife and family.

Tom's dry wit did not abandon him during this ordeal and when Doctor Brett examined his badly frozen feet, he is reported to have said: "I hope I won't have to loose them Doc. I've had 'em a long time and I'm sort of used to 'em." He lost several toes on each foot but he always remarked that he couldn't complain as Doctor Brett had left him well balanced by taking the same number of toes from each foot.

❧

Tom Wilson on snowshoes

Memories of Golden Days

While researching this book, I came upon one of Tom Wilson's own tall tales written for the 1924 edition of the Canadian Alpine Club Journal. It sums up his feelings for the days in the Rockies when he was young and so were the trails he blazed.

In looking over some papers some time ago, I ran across a "Certificate of Leave of Absence," dated August 21, 1884 [Tom's birthday] from my mineral claim on Quartz Creek, signed A.W. Vowell, Gold commissioner, and initialed by Sheriff Redgrave. I have sent the Certificate to the David Thompson Memorial Post of the Museum there at Lake Windermere. It had been raining all spring and summer, the worst we ever had in the mountains. I had come down from the head of Quartz Creek and recorded my claims (Judge Vowell and Redgrave had opened the office in Golden while I was out in the hills) and then went to the end of the track for more supplies. I came back to Golden – still raining – and thought I would get a leave of absence from my claims on Quartz Creek, until the end of the track reached Beavermouth. The Sheriff said I did not need it for the Quartz Creek claim, but I insisted and asked him down to my tent on the banks of the Kicking Horse River- still raining. We put a log on the fire and talked some more and went back to the office, and he wrote it out for me.

A lot of the boys had come in from the hills to record claims and get supplies and it was getting late and still raining, and 21st August was my birthday – so went back down to the tent and put another log on the fire. Shan and Jock McKay joined us, and we put on another log; then the Sheriff told us about his favorite saddle horse that had learned to retrieve for him. When he shot ducks or geese on the river or slough the horse would go in and bring them out to him – same with fool hens or grouse on the trail.

Shan looked sorry for a while, and then said he believed him. We put on another log and Shan told the Sheriff about a marten that he had trained to lead other marten to his traps–up on the Middle Forks- said he got the idea from their having trained a steer at the Chicago stock yards to lead the wild ones into the slaughter house. The Sheriff said he believed him – about the trained steer. Just then Archie McMurdo and Dutch Charlie joined the fire, and we put on another log. Archie said he was having a lot of hard work picking the rock out of the gold on his claim up in Caribou Basin. Dutch Charlie said he was going to buy the CPR and finish building it himself – said Jim Ross was breaking all the contractors that wasn't in the ring, and robbing those that was.

Then one-eyed Jim Kane and Tom Wright joined the fire, and we put on another log – still raining. Jim Kane said he was only going to bring a small sack of gold at a time from his claim on Canyon Creek, didn't want to hurt the Market. Tom Wright said he was going to buy some good timber as soon as the end of the track got to Golden and build him a big houseboat – said it was just this kind of weather that gave old Noah the tip to build his. We put another log on as Ben Pugh and Tom Haggerty joined in. Ben said he had not struck anything *but indications of a damn hard winter. Fred Aylmer and Baptiste Morgan came over from the store and we put on a branch or two. Then Frank Armstrong and Arthur Dick and several others came to see if it had stopped raining. At daylight most of the crowd had retired, still raining. Archie had curled up under the little spruce tree and wanted to bet anybody that the only good dry place in the Valley to strike a match was on his tongue. I packed up and hit the trail for the end of the track.*

Good old days on the trail and evenings around the campfire, and when the coffee pot upset just as it was beginning to boil and the sugar and salt got wet, and sometimes the beans went sour and the bacon musty and the wind blew smoke in your eyes, and ashes and sparks on your blankets, and the butt of the biggest bough hit the small of your back, and the mosquitoes almost crowded you out of the tent, and you heard the horse bell getting fainter and fainter, and you knew dam well they would be five miles away in the morning – but just the same, O Lord, how I wish I could live them all over again. (Tom Wilson, Canadian Alpine Journal, 1924, p,123)

Tom Wilson beside a plaque dedicated in his honour by the Trail Riders of the Rockies in 1924. It was moved to the graveyard in Banff on his death. The plaque reads:

Tom Wilson
Trail Blazer of
The Canadian Rockies
Lake Louise 1882
Emerald Lake 1882

"The Lake in the Clouds" – Lake Agnes, the Devil's Thumb, the Needles, and Mt. Whyte.

Tom and his good wife Minnie

One of the last pictures take of Tom Wilson

Tom Wilson's grave in the Banff Cemetery

Chapter 2

Tom's Boys

As Tom Wilson's guiding business grew, he hired and trained men to help accommodate his many clients. Most of the original guides and mountain men of the Rockies were trained by Tom. Under his tutelage they learned the ways nature, path-finding, camping, packing, and handling clientele from among the "rich and famous". After a year or two of working for Tom most learned to tie the "diamond-hitch" (a complicated arrangement of a single rope to hold a large load on a pack saddle) and many went on to become successful guides and outfitters themselves. Wild Bill Peyto, Jimmy Simpson, Fred Stevens, Ray Legasse, Soapy Smith, Tom Lusk, Bob Campbell, Fred Ballard, and even Jimmy Brewster were among this group. From time to time Tom even pressed George Fear, his partner in the dry goods and outfitting business in Banff, into action as an emergency cook.

James Tabuteau

One of the first guides that Tom Wilson hired in the early summer of 1895 was a young Irish immigrant named James Tabuteau. Know for his ability to cuss out unruly packhorses, Tabuteau also won a reputation for being pretty handy with a gun. His first major guiding trip was to take Colonel Robert O'Hara, one of the first tourists to come to the Rockies, up to the enchanted lake that now bears his name.

After a summer working for Wilson, Tabuteau decided to join the NWMP. He did so with Tom's blessing and a recommendation to his old friend and mentor Sam Steele, who was then the Superintendent at Fort Macleod. Tabuteau was stationed in Canmore for a number of years and then he headed to the West Coast, where he became the Chief of Police in the thriving city of New Westminster.

Fred Tabuteau

Fred, or "Tabby" as he was known, was Jim's younger brother and another early member of Tom Wilson's crew. He was also good with clients and became a well-respected backcountry guide, trailblazer, and packer who was described as being: "wild as a hawk but the kind of man who would stick with you through any kind of trouble." Tabby didn't mind a drink or two as he sat around the campfire after a long day on the trail. Occasionally after one or two too many, he'd break into song and regale those who'd listen with a fine repertoire of songs from Ireland. (Hart, E.J. 1979).

Wild Bill Peyto[3]

Ebenezer William Peyto was born in Welling, Kent, England, in 1868. He grew up roaming the hills and dales of southwest England, but he was a free spirit and left for Canada in 1886 at the age of eighteen. Bill travelled Canada from coast to coast and also visited parts of the United States. When he ran out of money he would frequently support himself by engaging in the manly art of prizefighting. He ended up in Moberly, British Columbia, in 1887 and after a short stint working for the railway, he moved to Cochrane where he started a homestead in 1890. Bill developed considerable skills as a woodsman and hunter and taught himself elementary geology. He also earned a modest reputation as a prospector before joining Tom Wilson's guiding and outfitting business in 1895. At first he was hired on as an apprentice guide, but soon he began taking some of Tom's best clients deep into the Rockies on his own.

On one of Peyto's early guiding trips, he took Walter Wilcox into Mt. Assiniboine. Tom Wilson had guided Robert Barrett to Mt. Assiniboine in 1893, the first time that a white man had visited the base of the Matterhorn- shaped mountain. In July of 1895, using the route that Wilson had previously blazed Wild Bill successfully guided Walter Wilcox, Robert Barrett, and J. K. Foster to the mountain.

It was a gruelling trip that involved making a route through thick deadfall and over steep slopes. Awed by the big mountain, Wilcox decided not to climb it on that occasion. He was, however, much impressed with Wild Bill Peyto who sported a big sombrero, a neckerchief, a six-shooter and cartridge belt, and a large hunting knife. His high-cantelled, stock saddle sported Mexican stirrups and two rifles in scabbards. Wilcox later wrote of Wild Bill:

> *I soon grew to admire Peyto… He was efficient, daring, highly imaginative, an excellent man with horses and a good friend. He spoke in the low, quiet voice of the true westerner, but even so he spoke rarely. His forte was doing things, not talking about them…. Peyto always slept with a loaded rifle, his six-shooter and his hunting knife close at hand. When asked about this he commented that "the country was full of grizzlies and there could be an Indian uprising at any time". He liked to be prepared and ready. (Wilcox, 1909)*

It was on this trip that Wilcox took the famous photograph of Wild Bill that he later published it in his book. The photo has been retouched numerous times and reprinted in countless books and promotions.

A few weeks after the trip to Mt. Assinibione, Wild Bill also guided Walter Wilcox and his party along the Bow River Valley to Bow Lake and the Bow Glacier. They then crossed a pass near Dolomite Peak and skirted the slopes of Mt. Hector.

---

3 The material about Wild Bill Peyto has been adapted from an article by Gordon Burles: "Bill Peyto and the Canadian Rockies."–*Canadian Alpine Journal* 1973, and from E.J. Hart's book *Aint it Hell-Bill Peyto's Mountain Journal*, 1995.

Fred Tabuteau

Bob Campbell

Wild Bill at one of his cabins in the Simpson Pass area. He staked a mining claim in this area.

Ulysse LaCasse Served as a packer for Tom Wilson and Jimmy Simpson and later he signed on with the Warden's Service.

Wild Bill Peyto

Walter Wilcox took this picture and published it in his book *The Rockies of Canada in 1900*. The picture has been used countless times in books, pamphlets, and now on web pages. Few know where it came from. Wild Bill was one of a kind, as later stories will attest.

Fred Stevens

Fred was a mountain of a man and one of the best with an axe ever to come to the mountains. He could make short work of cutting a trail through miles of deadfall and blow-downs. He went to work for Tom Wilson in 1896 and was well regarded by all who knew him.

In the off-season, Wild Bill took up trapping along the Pipestone River Valley. He almost died in a blizzard but was saved when his faithful horse, Chiniquay, led him through five-foot high snowdrifts to the safety of his cabin.

In August of 1897, Wild Bill led the noted British climber Norman Collie and Americans Charles Fay, A. M. Baker, C. S. Thompson and their guide Peter Sarbach to the Mt. Balfour region. All the members of this expedition had significant mountains along the Great Divide named after them. Later that month Bill guided Collie, Baker, Richardson, and Sarbach to the Howes Pass area. This was a dramatic trip across big rivers and through deadfall and uncharted forest. The flies were particularly bad on this trip and they had to build smudge fires to keep the pests away. On some occasions when the flies were particularly ferocious, Collie observed Wild Bill covering his horses with bacon grease and driving them into a creek.

It was on this trip that Peyto, while looking for some horses that had ambled off into the forest, came upon a magnificent jade-blue lake. Collie showed his esteem and admiration for Bill by naming the beautiful tarn "Peyto Lake". He also named the large glacier that feeds the lake and a nearby peak after Wild Bill. A viewpoint, high above the lake is now a major tourist stop on the Banff-Jasper highway.

The group made the first ascent of Mt. Sarbach on this trip. While returning to Laggan, the deadfall was so dense in the Howse Canyon area that Bill decided to cross via Baker Pass and head directly for the village of Field. The route was especially difficult and hard on the horses, but they eventually made it back safely. This was the first known crossing of Amiskwi Pass.

In 1898, Wild Bill guided Collie and his party up the Pipestone River, over Pipestone Pass, and eventually to the Saskatchewan River. The deadfall was so intense where the Escarpment River meets the Siffleur River that a horse became crippled and had to be shot. The party finally arrived at the junction of the Mistaya and the Saskatchewan Rivers and then they headed up the North Fork of the Saskatchewan River to the Wilcox Meadows overlooking the Columbia Icefields and Mt. Athabaska. Woolley and Collie made the first ascent of Mt. Athabaska (11,452 ft.) on this trip. Later Wild Bill accompanied them on the first ascent of Diadem Peak (11,060 ft.).

During these guiding trips Wild Bill earned his undisputed reputation for colourful language and his quick action with unruly broncos. He would not hesitate to tune-up a reluctant horse at the slightest provocation, using extremely colourful language in the process. Bill could apparently turn the air blue while trying to urge his pack animals through the miles of deadfall and the pathless forest that he encountered in the Rockies. On one occasion he stored some food and gear for use on the return portion of a trip A few weeks later he returned to the area but couldn't locate the cache. This was the occasion for much cussing and carrying on. The party nearly starved before he eventually found the cache.

With Tom Wilson's blessing Wild Bill joined the Lord Strathcona Horse during the summer of 1900 to fight in the Boer War in South Africa. Serving under the leadership of none-other-than Sam Steele of the NWMP. Bill distinguished himself in battle and displayed great courage and riding ability. For six months he specialized in "drawing fire" which involved riding at break-neck speed infront of the enemy lines to draw their fire and reveal their positions. Three horses were shot out from under him, but he always escaped uninjured. After the war he visited his parents in England where he slept on the floor, as he preferred the hard boards to the luxury of a soft, feather bed.

Wild Bill was a local hero when he returned to Banff in 1901 after the Boer War. He immediately purchased a string of packhorses, as well as some camping equipment and supplies, and opened his own guiding service. He began by guiding clients for his old boss Tom Wilson, and shortly after hanging up his own shingle, he was hired to guide Sir Edward Whymper into the Yoho Valley.

Whymper had an impressive climbing record, with many first ascents in Europe and South America. These included the famous Matterhorn in Switzerland – though this achievement was shrouded in controversy that dogged Whymper throughout his life. Sir Edward was arrogant and condescending in the extreme and expecting everyone to pay him deference. This attitude did not go over well in the Rockies and he endeared himself to no one – even though he was a guest of the CPR. Most, on seeing him in action, felt that his guides must have dragged him up the Matterhorn – as was often the case with the early Victorian mountaineers. In fairness to Whymper though, he was in his sixties by the time he reached the Rockies and no longer as spry or as fit as when he established his reputation as being one of the finest mountaineers in Europe.

Wild Bill, and Bob Bapti, a wrangler, went ahead on the trail into the Yoho Valley with the supplies, after arranging that Whymper would follow along later. However, Whymper was delayed at Field and after a day or so Wild Bill and Bapti became hungry. They decided to open one of Whymper's tightly-sealed pack boxes and eat some of the grub. When Whymper finally arrived in camp, he was outraged and accused the pair of stealing from him. Wild Bill was not a man to be trifled with and took exception to these serious charges. He turned the air blue as he cussed Whymper, in his colourful language, leaving nothing to the imagination. He packed Whymper out of the Yoho Valley at the agreed time, but that was the last that he or any other Banff outfitter, with the exception of Tom Wilson, had to do with him.

During the trip into the Yoho Valley with Edward Whymper, Peyto met the Reverend James Outram. They took an immediate liking to each other. Sitting around the campfire one night, Wild Bill told Outram about Mt. Assiniboine, informing him that the "Matterhorn of the Rockies" was still unclimbed. He offered to pack Outram into the mountain in just two days and assist him with the climb. Outram immediately took Bill up on the offer and they began to plan their adventure. They kept their plans secret from Whymper, leaving him in Field to fend for himself.

Leaving Banff on August 31st, with a wrangler, a cook, and the Swiss mountain guides Christian Haesler Sr. and Christian Bohren, Outram and Peyto followed Tom Wilson's old trail that led along Healy Creek. They then followed Tom's blazes up and over Simpson Pass to Surprise Creek and then over Ferro Pass to the base of Mt Assiniboine. True to his word, Peyto got the group to the base of the mountain in two long days.

Bill Peyto on his great horse Chiniquay
Photo taken by Walter Wilcox in 1895

Peyto Lake with Mt. Patterson in the background

This photo of Bill Peyto was taken by George Noble
It won a prize at the Toronto Fair

On Wild Bill's advice the party ascended the mountain from the southwest side. They made their camp at the 7,200-foot level and on September 3rd, 1901, Peyto accompanied the climbing party a good distance up the mountain. He then decided to return to the base and prospect for minerals. Clouds rolled in that day and the climbing attempt had to be abandoned. The following day the weather cleared and Outram and his guides succeeded in climbing Mt. Assiniboine by the southwest face and descending by the north ridge. The weather remained favourable all day and the climb was completed in just thirteen and one half hours. At that time they felt that it was the greatest climbing achievement in North America.

The journey back to Banff was hampered by poor weather but they made it back in just two days as Peyto had promised. Later in his book, *In the Heart of the Canadian Rockies,* Outram described Wild Bill Peyto as being: "picturesque and workmanlike", and one of the two best packers in the Rockies—the other being Tom Wilson.

On January 6th, 1902, Wild Bill married Emily Wood. In time they had a son that they christened Robin. Tragically, Emily died of a brain haemorrhage on September 6th, 1906, and young Robin was sent to Armstong, B.C. to live with Miss McCleary a friend in the Okanagan Valley. The death of his wife and the dislocation of his son caused him great heartache and remorse.

In 1902, Outram returned to the Rockies and hired Wild Bill to lead him into the mountains once again. This time they headed for Saskatchewan River Crossing. During this trip, Bill was thrown from his horse—one of and few times in his life. We are not told what became of the horse, but I imagine Bill tuned him up some. The air around Saskatchewan River Crossing was probably pretty colourful for some time—even with the Reverend Outram on the scene. Peyto is also reported to have jumped into the river to save one of his horses on this trip.

In 1915, Wild Bill joined the army with the Seventh Brigade of the Canadian Machine Gun Company and was soon shipped overseas. At Hooge, France he was wounded in the thigh, but he refused to be shipped home, giving up his place to another soldier. While at the front, Bill is reported to have saved a fellow soldier's life by amputating his leg. Wild Bill had hunted, killed, and skinned countless grizzlies, black bear, elk and moose, so to amputate a human leg was just another unpleasant chore to attend to.

After the War, Bill returned to Canada as a hero for the second time. A special welcome home celebration was planned in Banff, but the modest Peyto got off the train in Canmore and avoided the crowd.

In 1918, Peyto became one of the first wardens in Banff National Park. His district included Healy Creek, Brewster Creek, Red Earth Creek, the Bow River, and the Mt. Assiniboine region. This was familiar territory to Bill as he had previously built a number of rough trapping shelters in the area and staked several mining claims. He refused to stay in the government's modern log cabin as he preferred his own rough-hewn abodes.

On July 17th, 1921, Dr. Stone, the President of Purdue University and his wife attempted a first ascent of Mt. Eon (the 10,860 feet), a peak just south of Mt. Assiniboine. When they reached the final chimney just below the summit Dr. Stone took off his rope and began to ascend the final 60 feet of the mountain. As he approached the final pitch, he slipped and fell past his wife to his death. In her attempt to find her husband, Mrs. Stone tried to rappel down a steep rock face, but ran out of rope and became stranded on a narrow ledge.

After several days, with no word from Doctor Stone and his wife, Wild Bill was asked to form a search-and-rescue party. He quickly rounded up Rudolf Aemmer, a Swiss guide from Lake Louise, an NWMP constable, and seven trail crew workers, and on July 23rd he packed the rescuers into Assiniboine in just one day, a 45 mile trip. All marvelled at the skill, determination, and stamina of the man.

The next morning the party climbed a 7,800 foot spur on Mt. Eon and discovered Mrs. Stone on a narrow ledge. She had been there for eight days surviving on a mere trickle of water. Rudolph carried Mrs. Stone off the mountain and Wild Bill took her to Banff, where she received medical care from Dr. Brett. On August 5th, Bill guided the mountaineering guides Edward Feuz, Rudolf Aemmer and Conrad Kain, together with A.H. MacCarthy, back into Mt. Assiniboine to recover Dr. Stone's body. Conrad Kain and Edward Feuz found the body well preserved on a glacier on the opposite side of the Mt. Eon and brought it back to Banff. Several months later, the Alpine Club of Canada presented Wild Bill with a special citation for his super-human efforts in rescuing of Mrs. Stone.

Wild Bill continued as a Park Warden until 1933, when he retired. It was during this time that his reputation as an eccentric character grew to larger-than-life proportions. He is reported to have carried a bound, but very much alive, lynx into the bar of the historic Cascade Hotel in Banff. The patrons in the bar cleared out in a hurry, while Bill quenched his thirst with a cool glass of ale. He was said to have set bear-traps around his cabins to discourage intruders, both animal and human. On one occasion the police chased him through the town of Banff on horseback after he locked Jimmy Simpson in a cage with a live lynx. And then there were the stories of how he accused his second wife of trying to poison him, and of how he occasionally he walked down the main street of Banff chewing on a large piece of raw meat. He also had the habit of suddenly disappearing. "He would leave in the middle of the night, in the middle of a conversation, or on Christmas day and stay out in the wilderness, or in one of his cabins, for two to three weeks at a time."

Wild Bill's good friend Conrad Kain, provided a colourful description of the man.

> *Bill is an old Prospector, a trapper, a guide – a western original! I have known him for three years. He is from Banff, the true man of the forest, and has always some new experience to relate. Fortune has not always favoured him but most of the time he has been lucky. Eight years ago he lost his wife. He said: "If she were still alive, I would be 10 or 15 years further from the grave." I know from other people that he was never the same old Bill afterwards. His appearance is rough and coarse. He looks like a wildcat. On seeing him, without talking, one easily understands why people are afraid of him. But that is only outwardly. I think I know better: he is of the old West, quite independent, removes his*

hat to no one, and says whatever he thinks. But if someone comes to him in distress, he finds a soft-hearted man. (J. M. Thorington, 1935, pp 313-314)

Bill Peyto died in 1943 and was buried in the Banff cemetery next to his beloved wife Emile. His burial plot is not far from those of his friends Tom Wilson, Byron Harmon, Norman Sanson, and A.O. Wheeler. Wild Bill will always be remembered by the magnificent lake, peak, and glacier that bear his name. He was one-of-a-kind and his legend lives on in the Rockies. For an intimate portrait of Wild Bill Peyto's life, read to E. J. Hart's superb book entitled: *Ain't it Hell: Bill Peyto's Mountain Journal.*

Ralph Edwards

Born in 1869 at Ramsgate, England, Ralph Edwards was well educated at the City of London School. He came to Canada in 1888 and eventually made his way to Canmore, where he worked in the mine for a year or two before going to work for Tom Wilson. Edwards was also a guide on the Barrett-Wilcox trip into Mount Assiniboine in 1895 with Wild Bill Peyto. In 1950 he wrote a delightful book, *The Trail to the Charmed Land* in which he recalled his experiences in the Rockies.

> *I rise to remark that any one who imagines that following a pack train, in all kinds of weather, over all kinds of country, with the attendant thousand and one jobs that seem to appear from nowhere in particular, does not provide some of the steadiest and most continuous work conceivable, is making just about the biggest mistake of his life. But we who followed the lure of the mountain trail loved the life and would not willingly exchange it for any other. (Edwards R. 1950)*

Edwards had a remarkable career guiding for Tom Wilson at in the 1890,s and the early 1900's. There is little doubt that he and Fred Stevens, guiding Professor Habel, were the first to cross Emerald Pass and descend down to Takakkaw Falls and then to trod up the Yoho Valley to the Yoho and Wapta glaciers. On the way they passed Laughing Falls, and Twin Falls, and the little known Diableret Falls, (about a mile past Twin Falls at the head of the Valley). This intrepid group was also the first to blaze a trail from Takakkaw Falls down the Yoho River to Kicking Horse Flats – just east of Field.

Edwards also was the first to find Dolomite Pass and descend it from the Pipestone Valley to Bow Lake in July of 1899. A full account of his adventures is found in his book *The Trail to the Charmed Land*, 1950.

Ralph Edwards
Employed initially by Tom Wilson in the 1890's, Ralph was born in Kent England. In 1949 he wrote about his experiences in the Rockies in an excellent book called *The Trail to the Charmed Land*.

Tom Lusk
Tom worked for Tom Wilson in the late 1890s. He had the reputation of being as handy with the bottle as he was with horses.

Jimmy Simpson
Mountain man extraordinaire. Note Jimmy's long-barreled Winchester rifle in his saddle scabbard.

Jimmy Simpson with a big horn sheep that he shot

Fred Stevens

Fred Stevens was born in Michigan in 1868. As a teenager, he left home for a life of adventure and headed for Montana, where he worked in lumber camps, and occasionally supported himself by trapping, hunting, and logging. By 1896 he was in Banff, working for Tom Wilson.

Fred was a big man, standing over six feet tall in his stocking feet. His years of physical labor in logging camps had endowed him with an amazing physique. His massive arms and shoulders enabled him to handle most tasks on the trail with ease. He could cut trail through miles of deadfall and blowdowns without seeming to work up a sweat, and he quickly gained the reputation of being one of the best axe-men in the mountains. The noted First World War correspondent, Stanley Washburn, described Fred in his book *Trails, Trappers and Tenderfeet in the New Empire of Western Canada.*

> *Big hands, big feet, and a big soul. He was then, and is today, a big man, as big a one as I have met in travels to many far corners of the world; big not only in bulk, but big in the qualities of the heart and soul that go to make the best type. ... To be Fred Steven's friend is all the introduction that a man needs to get the best that the trail offers. (Washburn, S. 1912)*

Tom Lusk

Tommy Lusk had the reputation of being as handy with a bottle as he was with a horse. His past was a little shady, and the rumours were that the little ranch he started in the 1890's, south-east of Morley, was stocked with cattle he'd rustled somewhere along the Chisholm Trail in Texas. Tom was in his early sixties when he started to work for Tom Wilson in 1896, and he soon developed the reputation of being one of the hardest drinkers around.

Martin Nordeeg, who discovered of the Nordeeg coal deposits, described Tommy as having "glassy eyes".

> *As long as we were in Morley, his eyes appeared glassy to me and I began to believe that this was their normal appearance. But when I noticed the copious drinks, which he took frequently, I had my doubts. At the return to civilization after the season's work; Tom invested his earnings in liquor, retiring with several cases to his cabin in Morley. Tom was methodical in his habits: he divided his cases and bottles carefully into the weeks and months of the long winter allowing himself double quantities for Christmas and New Years Day, thus constituting a whiskey budget. (Nordeeg, M., Pioneering in Canada, 1906-1924)*

Bob Campbell

Robert E. "Bob" Campbell came to Banff in 1896 because Tom Wilson, who was the chairman of the Banff School Board at the time, hired him to teach school in Banff. Tom's keen eye noticed that Bob had a pleasant way with people and that he was also good with horses, so he hired him to guide clients into during the summer months.

Born in Lanark County, Ontario, in 1871, Bob was raised on a farm not far from where Wilson himself grew up. He graduated from the Barrie Collegiate Institute with a teacher's certificate and then studied business at the Northern Business College in Owen Sound. In 1893 he headed west for adventure and taught school in the Moose Jaw area for a while. Someone told Bob that he'd love Moose Jaw because there was a pretty girl behind every tree. However, when Bob got to that southern Saskatchewan prairie community, he was greatly dismayed. There were no trees!

Later in Banff, Campbell became Wilson's partner and in time he bought Tom out. He continued guiding and outfitting for many years and in 1959, wrote a book about his experiences called: "*I Would Do It Again*".

Jimmy Simpson

Justin James MacCartney Simpson was born on August 8th, 1877, in Stamford, Lincolnshire, England. His father was an expert on Roman coins and the family had its own coat of arms. Being a fun-loving lad, some would say, the proverbial black sheep, Jimmy later confessed that on more than one occasion, he poached deer on the estate of the Marquis of Exeter. Poaching was a pastime that Jimmy would later indulge in while living in the Rockies.

In March, 1896, Jim was sent to Canada to make his fortune farming on the prairies. Upon his arrival in the Winnipeg area, he surveyed the situation and quickly came to the conclusion that he didn't think much of farming and even less of the prairies. After one night on a farm, he left early the next morning for the bright lights of Winnipeg. He stopped at the first watering hole and proceeded to try to wash away his fears of having to spend the rest of his life as a "prairie stubble jumper". Within a week, all his money was gone.

Taking this as a sign that it was time to move on, Simpson stowed away on a westbound train. At the thriving boomtown of Silver City, (now called Castle Junction just west of Banff) a vigilant conductor discovered him and unceremoniously booted him off the train. As he dejectedly walked down the lonely stretch of tracks toward Laggan, fortune shone on him once again, for he happened upon an old trapper named Smith who was to greatly influence his life

It's funny how, from seemingly out of nowhere, the Lord sometimes puts the right person in your path just when you need it most and this was the case with Jimmy Simpson. Smith took Simpson in and during the following winter, taught him the ways of the mountains and the secrets of trapping mink, marten, fox, wolf, and beaver. As they made their rounds on Smith's trap-line the old trapper also taught him to snowshoe. Jimmy was a good student, and the backwoods knowledge that he learned from Smith served him well in the years to come.

An early photo of a young Jimmy Simpson
Taken shortly after his arrival in Banff.

While looking for a lost child in Laggan in the fall of 1896, Jimmy had his first encounter with the infamous Wild Bill Peyto. Bill was camping in the elk meadow on the south side of the Bow River, where the Lake Louise campground is today. Jimmy later recalled the event.

> *Peering inside the tent, I saw a man lying on his blankets, his head on his open palms, a rifle on his left side and a wicked looking revolver near his right hand. Very black as to the hair, with deep sunken blue eyes he pictured my ideal man that I'd dreamed of as a kid and here he was in the flesh. He was just in from a prospecting trip and the cuts on his chin showed he had*

shaved with his hunting knife, and not too well at that, but it all fitted the man himself. A look around the tent showed saddles and cooking pots and a heap of copper samples that to me resembled gold or some precious metal and I was thrilled.

Fate had brought him into the presence of E.W. "Bill" Peyto, a man who Jimmy would later describe as his hero and one who "I was determined to emulate or die in the attempt." (Hart, E.J. 1991)

Carl Rungius often used Jimmy Simpson as a model for his paintings as he did in this case. Here Jimmy Simpson leads his pack train across the Saskatchewan River at Saskatchewan Crossing.

For the next year or so, Jim tried his hand at a number of jobs. After working on the railroad, he drifted to California and New Mexico. He journeyed on to Victoria, where he signed on as a deckhand on a seal hunting boat. None of this was to his liking, however, and by late spring he headed back to Banff, where he got a job with Tom Wilson as an apprentice guide and camp cook. Here Wild Bill Peyto, Ralph Edwards, Bob Campbell, and Tom Lusk all tutored him at one time or another on the ways of the trail. During the winters he ran a trap-line, sometimes alone and sometimes with his friend and partner, Fred Ballard.

A FAMILIAR FIGURE IN A FAMILIAR SETTING: Bruno Engler photographed Jimmy Simpson near his Num-Ti-Jah Lodge at Bow Lake recently. Jimmy calls that piece of furniture he's sitting on his "Rocky Mountain Chippendale."

A photo of Jimmy Simpson taken by Bruno Engler
It was published in the *Craig and Canyon* in August of 1970 and saved over the years by my friend Phil Williams.

A watercolor by Jimmy Simpson owned by Phil Williams who graciously allowed me to scan it and publish it in this book.

Jimmy Simpson's Num-Ti-Jah Lodge at Bow Lake
A painting by Catharine Whyte

In 1898, Jimmy Simpson turned twenty-one and inherited a large sum of money from his family estate in England. This bought him saddles, packing gear, and horses and while he continued to pack for Tom Wilson, he also began developing his own clientele. Mary Schaffer, James Outram, and the noted wildlife artist Carl Rungius were regular clients. He also packed for the annual camps of the Alpine Club of Canada and guided for Sir Edward Whymper in 1901, 1903, and 1904. In 1903 he bought a lot in Banff near Wild Bill Peyto's property on the Bow River and built corrals and a residence as his base of his operations.

Trapping in the winter, Jimmy soon earned a reputation for speed and endurance on snowshoes. The Stoney Indians gave him the name "Nashan-esen", meaning "wolverine go quick." Jimmy was particularly attracted to the Bow Lake-Wilcox Pass area and ran a regular trapline there. In 1905 and 1906, he packed and guided for A. O. Wheeler, who was doing a topographical survey of the boundary between Alberta and British Columbia.

In 1911, Jimmy bought part of Tom Wilson's packing and outfitting business, when Tom had decided to focus on ranching and raising horses at Kootenay Plains. Next to the Brewster boys, Jimmy Simpson became Banff's most sought-after guide. The following year he met Willimina "Billie" Reid, a lovely highland lass from Ashistiel, Scotland. After an ardent courtship, that lasted some four years, they were wed on January 31st 1916, in Calgary. The couple made Banff their home and raised their three children there.

As young adults, their two girls, Margaret and Mary became world-class figure skaters, successfully touring the United States. Often dressed in red "Mountie" costumes, they were the headliners of the touring company. At New York's Madison Square Gardens, the audience went wild for the two sisters from Banff. The noted architect Walter Painter and his wife wrote:

> *The girls had them on their feet hollering for more. They were the idols of the Garden. Saturday night the "Mountie" act literally stopped the show and when after three or four curtain calls the announcer started the next number the crowd drowned him out and insisted on an encore from the girls. For spectacular skating they are tops.*

Simpson's son, Jimmy Jr., was more like his father and enjoyed working with him, handling horses, and going on pack trips. Jimmy and Billie lived in Banff until 1937, when Jimmy started construction on his famous Num-ti-jah Lodge on the shore of Bow Lake. "Num-Tti-Jah" is the Stoney Indian word for the pine marten, the animal Jimmy trapped as a young man when he first came to the area. Jimmy had many battles with the National Parks Service over the years, mostly relating to his guiding activities and the building of Num-Ti-Jah Lodge. He didn't have much use for bureaucrats—especially those from Ottawa. Some of his run-ins with government officials are documented in E. J. Hart's book, *Jimmy Simpson, Legend of the Rockies.*

In later years, Jimmy turned his hand to writing and storytelling as had his old boss, Tom Wilson. Outdoor magazines published several of his articles, enhancing interest in his guiding business.

A winter scene painted by Jimmy Simpson

Old Billy
A painting by Carl Rungius

"Lord of the High Country"
A painting of a grizzly bear by Carl Rungius

The great outdoorsman and artist Carl Runius
1869–1959

Num-ti-jah Lodge built by Jimmy Simpson on the banks of Bow Lake. He and a few helpers started construction of this amazing structure in 1937. Jimmy did all the framing himself with simple hand tools.

Jimmy Simpson framing his Num-ti-jah Lodge in 1937.

The Simpson Sisters posing on Bow Glacier
Jimmy's daughters were superb figure skaters and they "wowed" the crowd at
Madison Square Gardens in New York when they skated for the Ice Capades.

Bow Lake and the Bow Glacier
This is the view from in front of Bow Lodge.

In order to promote his business, Jimmy and Billie frequently visited New York: attending sportsman's shows, giving lectures and slide presentations, and visiting clients. One such client was the great western artist, **Carl Rungius.** Over a period of forty years, from 1910 until the 1950's, Jimmy took Carl on painting and hunting trips in the Rockies. They became good friends and Jimmy persuaded Carl to purchase a home in Banff, which became Rungius' Canadian headquarters until 1958. Carl's last visit to Banff was in 1957 but Jimmy and Billie often visited him and corresponded with him until his death in October of 1959.

During their years of friendship, Rungius encouraged Jimmy to try his hand at painting and gave him some lessons in using watercolours. Jimmy eventually became a very good artist in his own right and during his last years he produced some excellent watercolor paintings that he sold at Num-Ti-Jah Lodge during the tourist season. His paintings frequently featured Bow Lake and the Crowfoot Glacier, which he could look out upon from his lodge.

Apart from his own work, Jimmy amassed a large art collection, as his clients often traded art as part payment for his guiding services in the Rockies. His collection, which included many of Rungius' works became one of the finest private collections in western Canada. Some of it was acquired by the Glenbow Museum in 1958 and other works were donated to the Whyte Museum of the Canadian Rockies in Banff.

On September 2nd, 1968, Jimmy's beloved wife Billie died in the Banff Springs Hospital. Her ashes were spread in a secret spot in a meadow that she loved, overlooking Bow Lake. On October 30, 1972, Justin James MacCartney Simpson, the last of the original mountain men of the Rockies, died in Banff, passing over the "Great Divide" at ninety-five years of age. He too was cremated and his ashes were spread with Billie's above Bow Lake.

On August 8th, 1974 on what would have been his ninety-seventh birthday, Parks Canada held a special ceremony at Bow Lake and the Canadian Committee on Geographical Names broke a rule of not naming mountains after people. The mountain to the right of the lodge was officially dedicated to Jimmy to pay tribute to this a man "whose life reflected the rugged spirit of the Canadian Rockies".

Chapter 3

Early Visitors to the Rockies

The completion of the railway by the CPR in 1885 brought visitors to the Rockies from around the world. The early trains had dining cars and cooking cars, but when they reached the mountains, they had to be left behind to lighten the trains as much as possible for the steep grades of the high passes. This necessitated the building of hotels to feed the passengers at stops along the way. The CPR had already built elaborate hotels in Winnipeg, Regina, Calgary, and Vancouver. They also built smaller ones in the mountains of British Columbia at Revelstoke, Kamloops, Shuswap, and North Bend (Boston Bar).

In 1886 the CPR built the first hotel in the Rockies, **Mt. Stephen House** at Field, British Columbia at the base of Mt. Stephen. The following year **Glacier House** was completed near the summit of Rogers Pass. Beginning as a modest establishment, with a small dining room and six guest rooms, it soon became a mecca for mountaineers and hikers from Britain, Europe, and the USA. It was in operation for the driving of the Last Spike in November of 1887 but soon it was expanded to become an elegant hotel boasting ninety rooms, manicured grounds, fountains, and a billiard room. For the convenience of the guests the CPR built a rail spur from the station on the main line to the doors of the hotel.

The Banff Springs Hotel opened in 1888 and a small chalet was built on the shores of Lake Louise in 1890. After the first chalet at Lake Louise burned down in 1893 a second one opened in 1894. Since then there have been many additions and expansions to Chateau Lake Louise. All these hotels in the Rockies hosted adventurers, mountaineers, naturalists, painters, photographers, and hikers from around the world.

James Joseph McArthur – Surveyor and Mountaineering Pioneer

James Joseph McArthur, a surveyor for the Dominion Land Survey, was the first to ascend a peak in the Rockies higher than ten thousand feet. This was accomplished on September 9th, 1887, with the successful climb of Mt. Stephen, which towers over the little town of Field. Born in Aylmer, Quebec in 1856, McArthur surveyed the land on either side of the CPR railroad line from Canmore to Revelstoke. To carry out his surveying duties he had to climb to the summits of the strategic peaks to take photographs and make elevation measurements.

MacArthur also made first ascents of Mt. Odaray in 1887, Mt. Rundle in 1888, Mt. Aylmer in 1889 and Mt. Bourgeau in 1890, Mt. Owen in 1892 and Mt. Burgess in 1892. This was a remarkable record, considering the lack of modern mountaineering equipment, clothing, and footwear. He was Canada's first true mountaineer. Others before him might have scrambled up the odd peak but James McArthur was a climber. A mountain pass, a peak, and one of the most beautiful lakes in the Rockies (near Lake O'Hara) are all named in his honour.

James Joseph McArthur

The first to climb a peak above 10,000 feet in the Canadian Rockies, James McArthur and his assistant Tom Riley climbed Mt. Stephen on September 9, 1887. He also made first ascents of Mt. Odaray in 1887, Mt. Rundle in 1888, and Mt. Aylmer in 1889 (He named this mountain after his birthplace in Quebec). He also climbed Mt. Bourgeau in 1890, and Mt. Owen and Mt. Burgess in 1892. Lake McArthur near Lake O'Hara is named after him as is McArthur Pass and Mt. McArthur.

McArthur first climbed Mt. Stephen with his intrepid assistant **Tom Riley.** Without the assistance of ropes or crampons they lugged heavy photographic and surveying instruments to the summit. Chic Scott's book *Pushing the Limits* (2000) contains McArthur's account of the ascent.

> *Foot by foot we worked our way, cutting steps with our alpenstocks, and in time we reached the ledge of rock and looked down into the perilous slope. A slip on this glare surface meant death, and how we were to get down again caused us no little anxiety. Crawling*

along dangerous ledges and up steep narrow gorges, we pushed our way, expecting at every turn that one of the perpendicular walls would finally stop us with its impassable front. At last we reached the top of what we has judged from below to be the highest point of the mountain. We were not a little disheartened to see looming ahead of us another wall several hundred feet high. We moved along the broken ridge and when almost at the foot of the wall, we came to a deep chasm, which was the top of the ice gorge up which we had already cut our way.

The distance across was about three feet, and immediately opposite raised the perpendicular face from a narrow ledge. Leaving our alpenstocks behind, we stepped across and with face to the wall moved along the ledge to a slanting rift up which we clambered, our entire weight sometimes dependent on the first joints of our fingers. After a perilous climb of about one hundred feet we reached a debris-covered slope leading to the top of the ridge.... The top of this ridge was like a much broken wall, in some places not more than three feet wide and descending in perpendicular sides, sometimes forty feet, to the steep slopes of the ridge. It required all our nerve to crawl about one-eighth of a mile along the top of those half balanced masses to the highest point on Mt. Stephen.]

Reverend William Spotswood Green and Reverend Henry Swanzy

In July of 1888, two clergymen from Britain, Reverend William Spotswood Green and Reverend Henry Swanzy arrived at Glacier House, at Rogers Pass. Their mission was to map the area around Rogers Pass and to make first ascents of as many of the virgin peaks as they could. They are remembered for being the first to introduce mountaineering to the Canadian Rockies at Rogers Pass. Their exploits made Glacier House a focal point for mountaineers from around the world.

In 1890, Green wrote *"Among the Selkirk Glaciers".recounting their* mountaineering adventures of 1888. The book, which contained pen and ink sketches of the prominent peaks and the first detailed map of the area, quickly became a bible for the mountaineers and adventurers that came to the area to climb and explore.

To get started, Green and Swanzy first climbed Glacier Crest and took photos and measurements from the summit. They then attempted Mt. Sir Donald via the south ridge. Green describes the main peak of Sir Donald as being "as inaccessible a piece of rock as any climber could wish to see." Next they explored the Illecillewaet Icefield, where they were prevented from descending to the Geikie Glacier by a large number of crevasses. They travelled over Asulkan Pass to the Lord River Valley, where they camped at Glacier Circle and made a small mountain tent their base.

The Reverend William Spotswood Green

A pen and ink sketch illustrating Green and Swanzy on the final snow pitch on the way to the summit of Mount Bonney. From Green's book *Among the Selkirk Glaciers*.

Their major achievement that summer was the ascent of Mt. Bonney at the head of Loop Creek. They first attempted the mountain from the northeast via Lily Glacier but decided against this route. The next day they attempted the northwest ridge by way of the Bonney Glacier. In *Among the Selkirk Glaciers* Green describes the climb:

Every move needed the greatest possible caution...We kept the rope tight between us...he [Swanzy] holding on while I sought out fresh grips, and when he moved I made myself as secure as I could.... When they reached the top of this difficult pitch...the glance which passed from one to the other expressed the foremost thought in our minds, 'What about getting down?.

During that summer, Green and Swanzy spent most of their time camped in a rough canvas mountaineering tent. Occasionally they stayed at Glacier House where they enjoyed warm baths, wrote of their experiences, and developed their films. Green's book describes excellent mountaineering technique and is of interest for this alone. They describe belaying each other, keeping the rope tight between themselves, and the use of their alpine stocks. During their return trip to Banff and Calgary, Green and Swanzy camped on the shores of Lake Louise and were greatly impressed with Mt. Lefroy and Mt. Victoria. Green's description of making his way up to Lake Louise and seeing it for the first time is well worth quoting. It was a beautiful morning on September 3rd, 1888, and his description of the remarkable scene is not unlike that of Tom Wilson's who first saw it six years earlier.

The last word from the station agent was "Be sure whatever happens you keep to the left, for then you will meet the creek from the lake"...I was quite unprepared for the full beauty of the scene. Nothing of the kind could surpass it...At the head of the lake the great precipice of Mount Lefroy stood up in noble grandeur, a glacier sweeping round its foot came right down to the head of the lake. Half way up the cliffs another glacier occupied a shelf, and from its margin, where the ice showed a thickness of about 3000 feet, great avalanches were constantly falling to the glacier below. Above the upper glacier, the peak rose in horizontal strata, the edges of which were outlined with thin wreaths of snow, to a gently sloping blunt peak crowned with a cap of ice. The mountains closing in on either side and falling precipitously to the lake formed a suitable frame to this magnificent picture.

The lake was the deepest green-blue...and the pine forest growing actually into the water, clad the mountain sides in dense masses wherever trees could find enough earth for their roots. All this was reflected into the lake, which was barely ruffled by little puffs of wind, now striking in one place now in another, and causing the water momentarily to sparkle in the sunshine.(1890, 244-245)

Rev. William Spotswood Green and Rev. Henry Swanzy on Mt. Bonney in August of 1888.

Pen and ink sketch of Lake Louise
by Rev. William Spotswood Green August 1888.

Carl Sulzer and Emil Huber
The two amateur Swiss climbers who were the first to climb Mt. Uto (9,610feet) and Mt. Sir Donald (10,808 feet) in 1890.

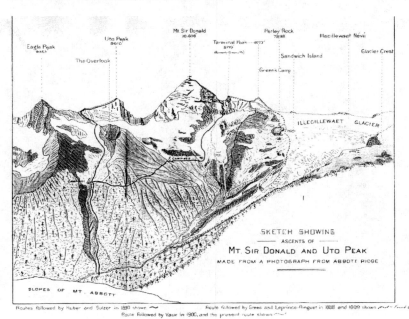

Map of Eagle Peak, Mt. Uto and Mt. Sir Donald
Drawn by A.O. Wheeler for his book *The Selkirk Range* (published 1905)

Harold Topham, Carl Sulzer and Emil Huber

The summer of 1890 was a busy one at Glacier House as mountaineers from Britain and Europe flocked to the Selkirks in hopes of achieving a first ascent. One of these was **Harold Topham**, an amateur mountaineer from Britain who, early in the climbing season of 1890, made his base at Glacier House. He explored the Asulkan Pass area and from there he proceeded to the Geikie Glacier and Mt. Fox (10,582 feet), which he climbed with his two porters, **Charlie Sinclair** and **Sam Yoes**. Next he climbed Mt. Donkin (9,704 feet) via Asulkan Pass and then he ascended Donkin Pass on the far side of the Illecillewaet Icefield. Sinclair and Yoes also acted as the porters on this climb. A few weeks later, Topham's friend **Henry Foster**, joined the threesome and again they crossed the Asulkan Pass to Glacier Circle. Following the Geikie Glacier they ascended the moraine of the Dawson Glacier and make the first ascent of Mt. Selwyn (11,023 feet), now known as Mt. Deville.

Carl Sulzer and **Emil Huber**, two amateur climbers from Switzerland, arrived at Glacier House on July 21st, 1890 and immediately set their sights on climbing Mt. Sir Donald, the "plum" of the area. Towering above the hotel at 10,818 feet, Sir Donald is even today an imposing peak – not only does it resemble the Matterhorn, it also appears to be unclimbable to most amateurs. Originally called Syndicate Peak in honour of the top executives responsible for the building of the CPR, it was later renamed in honour of Donald A. Smith, the Chairman of the Board of Directors of the CPR.

On July 23rd, 1890, Sulzer and Huber warmed up for the challenge of climbing Sir Donald by climbing Uto Peak (9,620 feet). The ascent was difficult and involved a good deal of bushwhacking, but it posed few technical problems for the two mountaineers from Switzerland. They took the trail to the Outlook and set up a temporary tent camp. They then proceeded to the Eagle-Uto col and from there they ascended Mt. Uto's sharp northwest ridge. Finding the quartzite rock of the Selkirk Mountains to be excellent for climbing, they reached the summit with few difficulties and were able to get a splendid view of Mt. Sir Donald's ferocious northwest ridge. Evaluating the prospects of climbing Mt. Sir Donald via this route, they decided to attempt the easier southwest arête.

On July 25th, Sulzer and Huber traversed across the lower slopes of Mt. Uto to the edge of the Vaux Glacier and set up another camp. The next day, the two climbers left their camp at four o'clock, "under the fading stars and morning twilight." They headed up the Vaux Glacier to the base of the Sir Donald's southwest wall and from there they climbed a steep snow couloir to the precipitous cliff bands and ledges that lead to the southwest ridge. From the ridge they proceeded to the summit and yodelled and yelled "Hurrah for the Swiss Alpine Club into the blue sky." (Wheeler 1905).

During their stay at Glacier House that summer, Huber teamed up with Topham and Foster and crossed over Asulkan Pass once again. They camped in the spot where Topham had stayed a few weeks previous and named it "Glacier Circle". From their camp the trio proceeded up the Beaver River and climbed Mt. Sugarloaf (10,742 feet) via the northeast ridge. Following this ascent they climbed Mt. Purity

(10,457 feet) by crossing Donkin Pass to Mitre Creek below Bishop Glacier. From the west end of the Bishops Group they followed a stream up to Black Glacier and then they ascended the west glacier of Mt. Purity to the steep west snow slopes that lead to the summit.

While Huber, Foster, and Topham were off climbing on the far side of Glacier Circle, Carl Sulzer and Sinclair crossed to the north side of Rogers Pass and ascended to the Hermit Group. They were the first climbers to set foot on the Swiss Glacier and the Tupper Neve and they conquered Swiss Peak (10,525 feet) with little difficulty. Their descent route was via the snow couloir between Swiss and Tundra Peaks.

Dr. Charles E. Fay

Another visitor to Glacier House during the summer of 1890 was Dr. Charles E. Fay, the Dean and Professor of Modern Languages at Tuft's College in Massachusetts. He was instrumental in establishing the Appalachian Mountain Club in Boston in 1876 and served as its president in 1878 and in 1881. He was also the editor of the club's journal *Appalachia* for forty years beginning in 1876. Fay made a partial attempt to climb Mt. Sir Donald in 1890 and returned again in 1894 to successfully complete the climb. He visited the Rockies for many years and he made first ascents of Mt. Lefroy, Mt. Victoria, and Mt. Hector in the 1890's. He also had a beautiful mountain above Moraine Lake named in his honour.

Walter Wilcox and the Boys from Yale University

In 1890 the CPR built a rustic but spacious log cabin on the lakeshore, on the northwest side of Lake Louise Creek. Access to the chalet was by foot or by horse from Laggan, in the valley below. The trail from Laggan crossed the Bow River and then through the sparsely-treed meadows where Tom Wilson had once camped. From there the trail, which Wilson blazed and later improved, led to the lake. Unfortunately the first chalet burned to the ground in the summer of 1893. Until it was rebuilt, visitors to Lake Louise had to camp in tents along the shoreline.

Among the first serious tourists to visit the Rockies was an intrepid group of young adventurers and neophyte mountaineers from Yale University in Connecticut. They were led by two keen and competitive classmates named **Samuel E.S. Allen** and **Walter D. Wilcox**. Born in Philadelphia, Sam Allen graduated from Yale in 1884 – having studied anthropology and linguistics. He was an expert in languages and accents and the study of philology – the history and comparison of languages and dialects. Allen completed his Master's Degree at Yale in 1897, but shortly afterwards he began to suffer from severe chronic depression and spent the rest of his life confined in an asylum. Allen first visited the Rockies in 1891 and climbed the Devil's Thumb above Lake Agnes at Lake Louise. He spent the following summer in Switzerland where, following **Sir Edward Whymper's** classic route, he climbed the Matterhorn from the Zermatt side with a guide.

The first chalet at Lake Louise in 1890
It burnt to the ground in the spring of 1893.

The newly completed second chalet at Lake Louise in 1894

The first guests at the newly built chalet at Lake Louise in 1894. Walter Wilcox (standing with a Winchester) Seated are G.H. Warrington, Louis Frissell and Yandell Henderson. They were the first guests at the new chalet. The furniture hadn't yet arrived and they had to sleep on the floor.

Walter Dwight Wilcox was born into a monied family in Chicago, and graduated from Yale in 1883. Not having to work, Wilcox was able to indulge his many interests, which included travelling, mountaineering and establishing a mahogany plantation in Cuba.

In the Alps Wilcox learned the basics of mountaineering, and in 1890 he climbed Mt. Hood in Oregon. In 1891 he travelled to Alaska and on the return trip he visited Banff and Lake Louise for the first time, acquiring a copy of Green's new book, *Among the Selkirk Glaciers*, which he read several times. On this trip Wilcox visited Glacier House and encountered a group of mountaineers, who, he later wrote, *"who were accustomed to gather every evening around a blazing fire and read selections from Green's Among the Selkirk Glaciers just as our forefathers were wont to read a daily chapter from the Bible."* (Walter Wilcox 1941, 177)

Walter also had aspirations of writing a book himself and later in 1909 he penned the classic *The Rockies of Canada* which made him a celebrity in Banff for years. The book described his adventures in the Rockies and featured excellent descriptions and pictures of Tom Wilson and Wild Bill Peyto. His photo of Wild Bill has been used countless times in books and pamphlets and still is.

Some time after their separate 1891 trips to the Rockies, Sam Allen and Walter Wilcox met at Yale and formed a pact to return together in 1893 and spend more time in the Lake Louise area. In that year, Allen arrived in Banff first and climbed Mt. Rundle from whose summit he was able to get a spectacular view of Mt. Assiniboine. When Walter Wilcox arrived, they learned that Chalet Lake Louise had burned down, so they were forced to purchase camping equipment and tents at Wilson and Fear's Outfitting Emporium in Banff. It was here that they met Tom Wilson for the first time. Wilson spun them a few stories about his adventures and then gave them a few tips about camping in the Rockies. He recommended Paradise Valley as a good place to set up a camp in the Lake Louise area. Wilcox later described their experiences camping at Lake Louise during that summer of 1893.

> *The writer [Walter D. Wilcox] spent almost the entire summer of 1893 at Lake Louise. At the time it was a primitive and almost desolate spot. The scenery was, of course, the same as it is now, but the immediate environment of the tents in which we lived was little more than a muskeg filled with mosquitoes and tree stumps. A new chalet was being built and two or three Indians remained there all summer helping to clear the land.* **Willoughby Astley**, *the manager, was a most energetic man and very appreciative of nature's beauty and grandeur. Besides that, he was a wizard with an axe, which was well. Every time we had a heavy wind the road all the way to Laggan was blocked and for several days there was no mail, no baggage, and not much to eat. If it hadn't been for Astley's axe we might have starved. He was an expert boat-builder as well, which was a great help in crossing the lake. The only path around the lake-shore was what is generally known as a "game*

> *trail", that is a kind of side-stepping of rocks, stumps and fallen trees and leaving nature as it was before you came along. So it required about half an hour to reach the lake's end and hard work at that. Astley's boat was far better. (Walter D. Wilcox, Canadian Alpine Journal 1944-1945)*

During that summer, Wilcox and Allen hired **Enoch Wildman,** a Stoney Indian guide. Unfortunately, Enoch suffered badly from both the altitude and the cold and decided that the high mountains meadows weren't for him. Allen and Wilcox first explored the area above Lake Louise around Mt. Lefroy and Mt. Victoria. From the Plain of Six Glaciers they attempted to reach the col between Mt. Collier and the north peak of Mt. Victoria, then called Mt. Green, to honor the Reverend William Spotswood Green. They had an excellent view of Abbot Pass which Sam Allen christened the **"Death Trap."** They also observed a long broad couloir that bisects the huge north buttress of Mt. Lefroy from the lower Victoria Glacier to the scree and snow slopes above. (This same couloir represents an acceptable alternative route to the Mt. Victoria-Mt. Lefroy col in seasons when the Death Trap is unsafe because of too little snow and too many large open crevasses.) Allen and Wilcox reasoned that Abbot Pass would normally be a safe route to the col if one stayed close to the cliffs of Mt. Lefroy and avoided the avalanches coming off Mt. Victoria.

From their camp in Paradise Valley the two young men scouted out Mt. Temple and attempted to climb the massive peak from the little lake below the east ridge. (Wilcox named the lake "Lake Annette" after a girl he was sweet on, back home in Chicago.) Ascending the mountain by traversing the southeast slopes they were eventually stopped by high cliff buttresses. It was from this vantage point that they became the first white men to behold one of the most magnificent sights in the Rockies—Moraine Lake and the Valley of the Ten Peaks.

Naming the Ten Peaks

As they looked down from the slopes of Mt. Temple, Allen and Wilcox were awe-stuck by the wild beauty of Moraine Lake and the Ten Peaks. Wilcox, who thought the rubble at the south end of the lake was glacial moraine, named it "Moraine Lake." Allen, recalling his first sight of scene, wrote:

> *I stood on a great stone of the moraine where, from a slight elevation, a magnificent view of the lake lay before me, and while studying the details of this unknown and un-visited spot, spent the happiest half hour of my life.*

The lake is an exquisite blue green colour one moment, and a deep turquoise the next. It is surrounded on the northeast by the steep cliff faces of the Tower of Babel, Mt. Babel, and Mt. Little. At the south end are the imposing peaks of Mt. Allen, Mt. Turzo and Mt. Deltaform.

Being a philologist, a student of languages and dialects, Allen had engaged their Stoney Indian packers in endless conversation in an attempt to learn their language. Because of this, he and Wilcox christened most of the peaks in the Paradise Valley and Moraine Lake area with Stoney Indian names during the summers of 1893 and 1894.

The peaks in order are:
- The Tower of Babel,
- Mt. Babel (10,185 feet)
- Mt. Fay (10,622 feet), Allan called this mountain "Heejee"
- Mt. Bident (10,119 feet)
- Mt. Quadra (10,420 feet)
- Mt. Little (10,303 feet) Allen called this mountain "Nom"
- Mt. Bowlen (10,088 feet) Formerly Peak # 3, Allen named this peak "Yamnee"
- Mt. Perren (10,028 feet) Formerly Peak #4, Allen called this peak "Tonsa"
- Mt. Septa (10,018 feet) Formerly Peak #5), Allen named it "Sapta"
- Mt. Allen (10,830 feet) Allen christened this peak "Shappe" but the name was later changed to honour him.
- Mt. Tuzo (10,658 feet) – Originally named 'Sagowa' but it was later named for Miss H.L. Tuzo, who first climbed it with Christian Kaufman in 1906).
- Mt. Deltaform (11,235 feet), the highest of the set of ten peaks, was named "Saknwa" by Wilcox and Allen.
- Mt. Neptuak (10,617 feet) has the original name given by Allen
- Mt. Wenkchemna (10,411 feet). Also bears the original name as given by Allen.

Across Wenkchemna Pass, and not really considered one of the Ten Peaks, is the towering Mt. Hungabee (11,457 feet). which means "the savage one." The peaks that are now considered the official ten peaks are in order – from east to west: Fay, Little, Bowlen, Perren, Septa, Allen, Tuzo, Deltaform, Neptuak, and Wenkchemna.

At the end of the summer of 1893, Allen and Wilcox made a trip to the Selkirks and climbed around the Rogers Pass area where they made the first ascent of Eagle Peak (9,363 feet). They stayed at Glacier House and there they met **Mrs. Julia Young** who had just become the manager. Born in Montreal in 1853, she was initially hired to work at the CPR's Windsor Hotel in that city. She was soon appointed to a management position and in 1893 she was put in charge of Glacier House, a position she held until she retired in 1920. She moved to Victoria, British Columbia, where she lived in the Empress Hotel until she died on April 25th, 1925.

After their satisfying summer of discovery, Wilcox and Allen decided to return the following year with more friends, supplies, and equipment. That winter when they were not studying, they recruited additional enthusiasts and planed for the coming summer.

Moraine Lake and the Ten Peaks on a magnificent summer day.

Moraine Lake and the Ten Peaks after a late summer snow fall

1894: A New Chalet at Lake Louise

During the summer and fall of 1893 and the spring of 1894, a second two-story chalet with a large common room, an immense fireplace, and accommodation for twelve guests was built at Lake Louise. Walter Wilcox and three friends from Yale – Louis Frissell, G. H. Warrington, and Yandel Henderson – were the first guests, preceding even the furniture! In a letter dated July 11th, 1894, Henderson gives us a detailed description of the new lodge.

> *The Chalet is an oblong frame building, thirty-five feet across the front and fifty feet deep with one big sitting room or hall extending clear across the front and two bedrooms and a kitchen back of it. Upstairs are half a dozen little rooms under a long sloping roof. The walls are sealed in light yellow pine. The big room facing the lake and the mountain, and looking out to the Southwest, is sunny by day and cheerful at night when the big logs crackle and blaze in the wide brick fireplace. The furniture for the Chalet has not come yet, so I sleep in my blanket bag on a mattress on the floor. When the furniture does come, I shall have one of the little rooms upstairs. There is a cook,* **Joe Savage**, *here and the food is plain, good and abundant, so we shall make the Chalet our headquarters.* **Mr. Astley**, *has given us a rate of $12 a week including a pony and a boat."* (The Canadian Alpine Journal, 1933)

Many years later, **Yandell Henderson** wrote an account of his summer at Lake Louise.

> *There were five in our party.* **Walter D. Wilcox** *had graduated from Yale College in 1893 and had spent some weeks of that summer in the Canadian Rockies. It was his enthusiasm that persuaded the three younger members of the party to come.He wished to map the lake and its surrounding mountains and to make some ascents of some of the then virgin peaks.*
>
> **Samuel E.S. Allen** *had graduated from Yale college in 1894. He had also been at Lake Louise the previous summer. His chief interests were in ascents and in philology (the science of language). He utilised every opportunity to learn words from the Stoney Indians of this region and from these words he developed some of the names that he gave to peaks, particularly that of Mount Hungabee, the 'savage peak'.*
>
> *The other members of the party were of an age between the junior and senior years at Yale. They were* **George H. Warrington**, **Louis F. Frissell** *and my self...My chief interest in going was also adventure. I had made a boast to a classmate, backed by a bet of five dollars, that entirely by my own efforts I would bring back the skin of one of the,-then-mythical, white goats of the Rockies. My previous experience was confined to quail shooting: I had never handled a rifle. Fortunately I had been raised in Kentucky and was familiar with horses.*
>
> *It is doubtful whether any five men ever went into a pathless wilderness knowing less than we did of the supremely important subject of camp cooking. As regards mountaineering; the pages of the 'Badminton Volume on Mountaineering', read after we reached Lake Louise, were our only source of information. We read up the night before and the next morning applied our information in practice on the mountains that are in some respects the most dangerous in the world. We had hobnailed boots, ropes and ice axes. We also had that spirit of adventure that get boys into tight places and generally gets them out again.*
>
> *On reaching the water tank and tiny house which constitutes Laggan, the station at Lake Louise on July 11, 1894, we got off the train to find* **Willoughby Astley** *waiting for us.We left him to bring up our luggage in a cart and walked three miles up a rough road through the sweet-smelling woods of spruce, fir and pine. A brook ran past us all the way, making a tremendous racket: for in three miles we climbed one thousand feet. At the top we came upon the chalet with the lake stretching away in front of it between two mountains, one covered with forest and the other with enormous cliffs of bare rock. At the*

far end of the lake, and apparently reaching almost to its waters, but really a mile beyond, is the lower end of an enormous glacier. Three miles back of it, or five miles from the chalet, rises a superb, great mountain, Mt. Victoria, covered with snow and hanging glaciers (Canadian Alpine Journal, 1933)

The First Recorded Mountaineering Accident, July 12, 1894

In a letter to his parents, Yandell Henderson records one of the first mountaineering mishaps in the Rockies. It gives a rich description of the atmosphere of the early days of mountaineering in the Rockies, when everything was new.

July 12, 1894, Wilcox was anxious to get us accustomed to ice and snow, so we went up on the glacier early in the morning. We left the Chalet at 7:30 in the morning, walked to the end of the lake and up to the foot of the glacier over very rough moraine. Then we roped up and went over the ice prodding the snow-bridges across crevasses, until we reached a grand mountain, which we call Glacier Peak [Mount Lefroy] from its being almost wholly surrounded by ice. Wilcox has studied our route, which he believes is quite practical and easy once the 800-foot precipice around its bottom is surmounted. A couloir of snow piled up in a big crack more than a hundred feet wide in this precipice seemed to offer possibilities. The slope of the snow in the couloir varies from 30 to 40 degrees. In several places there are schrunds, big cigar-shaped crevasses eight to ten feet wide.

[It is not Abbot's Pass that is being described here but the big couloir cutting the massive lower cliff wall of Mt. Lefroy from the vantage point of the lower glacier. The couloir leads to the steep snow and rock bands above the main cliff and is an alternate route if the pass is in bad shape. Wilcox later described this couloir as "an ice couloir...which no Swiss guide would venture to enter. (Canadian Alpine Journal 1944-1945). In 1913, **Rudolf Aemmer** and his client Honigman anchored a fixed ladder near the top of this couloir.]

Up this snow-slope we went, Wilcox leading and cutting or kicking out steps around the schrunds. I was next on the rope about fifteen feet down and Frissell was last. We had two ice axes with us; Wilcox had one and Frissell the other. I did not realise that on a steep slope that one has to lean away from the slope, but this is not easy when one has no axe or stock. Consequently the steps were always giving away under me. Once I slide several feet, my hands and toes digging in at the snow, until, I was stopped by the rope.When we were about 600 feet up we took to the rocks beside the couloir where firm handholds gave me more confidence. Our way now was from one ledge to another and sometimes when the next ledge was higher than we could reach, we went again on the snow...Wilcox climbed up and warned me as I followed, not to touch a loose rock some three feet long and two feet thick. It was lying now just on an edge.When I reached a point about eight feet from the boulder, and where the ledge was only about two feet wide, and was starting to climb to the next ledge, I heard something slipping and looking round saw Frissell and the boulder sliding off the ledge together. Fortunately I had time to turn around and get my feet braced and the slack of the rope in hand, well out from the loop around my own body. Then the jerk came as Frissell struck the lower ledge with a good part of his six feet two inches well over the ledge.

Frissell was lying on the lower ledge, apparently in great pain, his head bleeding and his eyes shut. I continued to haul on the rope, fearful lest he should roll off. Then Wilcox, from an upper ledge called to me to go down to him while he followed.Some snow soon stopped the bleeding. We stretched him out, his head on a hat. He urged us to leave him and go on up the mountain, but of course we refused.In the course of half an hour we were able to lift him to his feet, although in spite of great effort he was unable to walk. Throughout he bore what must have been great pain with the utmost courage. looked straight down on the glacier and wondered how on earth we would ever get there. Wilcox showed excellent generalship, but the tone of his orders was far from polite. With much helping we got Frissell down a few ledges. I un-roped and Wilcox went out on the snow slope, anchored himself with his ice-axe and feet and lowered Frissell down the snow slope for the full length of sixty foot rope. Then I slid down the rope and anchored and held Frissell while Wilcox came down. I took in the slack of the rope as to stop him if he slid past me. We did this again and again, sliding around the schrunds, until we reached the foot or the couloir. There we placed Frissell on a little pile of rocks, and I put on the rope again and accompanied Wilcox down over the worst part of the glacier. From there he went toward the Chalet for help and I returned to Frissell, treading as lightly as possible over the snow-bridges now weakened by the sun.

The accident happened at mid-day, at two-o'clock, we reached the glacier, our clothes soaked with melted snow and till half-past six Frissell and I sat there on the ice on a little pile of stones to keep us off the ice, huddling close together in the effort to keep warm as puddles froze on the glacier around us. When we went on the glacier in the morning, we had left our coats and sweaters behind us. Every few minutes an avalanche came down one of those grand peaks around us and the views were glorious, but our eyes were strained toward the Chalet at the other end of the smiling lake four miles away. We determined that unless help came two hours before dark we would run the risk of a bridge giving way under our combined weight. Meanwhile we sang all the Yale songs that we could remember.

*At half past six, **Willoughby Astley**, the Chalet custodian/manager, Joe **Savage** the cook, William the talking Indian and stoical **Tom Chiniky**, heir to the chieftainship of the Stoneys, reached us. They brought two poles and a piece of canvas, and in this litter, they carried and slid Frissell down over the glacier.*

*Generally an Indian will not go on ice, yet on that night they walked bridges with perfect coolness even after one gave way and Chiniky only saved himself by holding onto the pole of the litter. The labour of carrying Frissell over the glacier and the moraine was enormous, yet Chiniky never murmured though his moccasins were in rags. Fortunately two section hands whom Wilcox sent up from the station met them two miles above the head of the lake. It was just after midnight as we reached the Chalet. **Dr. Brett** came up from Banff on a handcar and pronounced Frissell had a torn muscle. At half-past two in the morning I saddled a horse for him to ride back to Laggan. It had been a long and eventful day.*

July 15, 1894 – This place improves steadily with acquaintance. I'm beginning to get into climbing trim and to enjoy it. My rifle, a forty-five ninety, half magazine Winchester is fine and balanced much like a shotgun. Frissell took a tumble on July 12 and we thought he had cracked his hip. But it proved to be only a muscle injury and in a week or two he will be all right. I made him a crutch this morning and he hobbles around cheerfully.

Discovering Paradise Valley

Yendell Henderson's descriptive letters from the summer of 1894 describe how this determined group of adventurous students became the first white men to see and name many of the valleys, creeks, glaciers, and peaks in the Lake Louise area. Not only did they make the first ascent of Mt. Temple, they also discovered an alternative route to the Plain of Six Glaciers. They travelled from the upper Paradise Valley to the top of Mitre Pass and then down to the Lower Victoria Glacier and across the moraine to the location of the present teahouse at the Plain of Six Glaciers. The return to Paradise Valley provided an excellent glissade down the long avalanche chutes from the top of Mitre Pass to the valley floor below. Following Paradise Creek back to their camp near Lake Annette the adventurers discovered a series of pools and waterfalls that they named the "Giant Steps". Here they had a refreshing bath in the icy cold pools before continuing down the trail.

(Author's Note: I have made this identical trip several times. The first time was with Robert "Bob" Sims in 1959–see picture). I have never forgotten looking down on the Horseshoe Glacier at the head of that pristine hidden valley. It was just as Wilcox and his colleagues had experienced it some sixty-five years previously. Beyond the Horseshoe Glacier rises the rugged peaks of Mt. Hungabee, Mt. Ringrose (10,762 feet), Glacier Peak (10,768 feet), and Wenhchemna Peak. In the early part of the climbing season one is able to glissade on the avalanche chutes almost to the valley floor and then walk out along Paradise Creek past the Giant Steps to the trail to Lake Louise. The boys from Yale named this valley well–it truly is as close to paradise as we'll see on this earth.)

Looking down on Paradise Valley from the top of Mitre Pass

Henderson's letters also describe how they named Saddle Peak, Sheol Peak, and Shoel Valley, as well as the Beehive above Lake Agnes. They explored Paradise Valley from every direction and were the first white men to climb up and over Sentinel Pass into Larch Valley. Allen named it Sentinel Pass because the pinnacle of rock at the summit resembles a man on guard-duty. Sentinel Pass has an elevation of nine thousand feet and from the col, Mt. Temple (11,621 feet) can be ascended. From Larch Valley, Wilcox and his colleagues looked down into the Valley of the Ten Peaks and into what they christened "Desolation Valley."

> *(August 8, 1894) From the top we looked down into a wild valley that we now call "Desolation Valley" bounded on the further side by what Allen calls the "Unnamed range" because it represents a blank space on the map. It is a wall of sheer rock some 2,000 feet high and several miles long without a break. Its top is jagged with sharp rock and snow peaks, and at its foot is a big glacier which half fills the valley and supplies water to many little lakes among the enormous rock piles of old moraines.*

From Larch Valley they passed along the lower slopes of Pinnacle Mountain (10,060 feet) and Eiffel Peak (10,116 feet). Their original route is now called the Eiffel Lake Trail. They then hiked over Wastach Pass into the end of Paradise Valley and back to their camp near Lake Annette. A momentous day of hiking, as they were the first white men to hike through the area, with no trails to follow.

The first campers in Paradise Valley – Walter Wilcox's camp in 1894. Mt. Hungabee and Ringrose Peak are in the background. Note the modern mountaineering tent of the day

The Giant Steps in Paradise Valley
They were named by Walter Wilcox

Mount Temple (11,636 feet) from Saddle Back Peak
This picture was taken by Walter Wilcox in 1894

Sam Allen looking toward Opabin Pass with his back toward Lake O'Hara
This picture was taken by Walter Wilcox in 1894

Mount Lefroy from the trail to the Plain of Six Glaciers
The Mitre is on the left and Mitre Pass is just to the left of Mitre Peak.

Lake Agnes covered with ice in the early spring. To the upper left of the picture is "The Devil's Thumb, the next peak is "The Needles" (One can see the "eye of the needle"). Mt. White is in the center of the picture and the "Amphitheater" connects Mt. White to Mt. Niblock (not shown)

In a letter of July 19th, 1894, Henderson made an interesting comment: *"A few days ago Sir William Van Horne, President of the Canadian Pacific Railway, and a party of railroad officials were here. He is the most powerful man in Canada."*

Early Mountaineering Technique

Henderson's letter of July 25, 1894, provides a vivid description of the mountaineering technique of the day.

> *July 25, 1894 As regards snow slopes I was pretty nervous the first time I was on one, but I have found that they are far easier and safer than grass or rock. You either kick out steps or dig or cut them with the axe. In descending, providing there are no schrunds and the bottom is all right, you glissade, that is you hold your legs stiff with the toes bent down and slide. You check your speed by digging your heels or axe into the snow. It is great sport. The first time I tried it my feet were continually sliding out from under me, but in snow a fall doesn't hurt as it does on rocks; it only makes you wet, and in this air you can't take cold.*

Tomorrow we go up the big glacier to have a look at one of the snow peaks at its upper end. The moraine at the foot is enormous: dirt, small rocks and boulders twenty feet thick piled in the wildest confusion with a big milky stream breaking out of it. We go roped together about fifteen feet apart. When we come to a crevasse the first man finds a place where it is bridged with snow. He pokes the shaft of his ice-axe into it to find out whether it is firm and then crosses, the next man keeping the rope taut meanwhile.

In the annals of mountaineering in the Rockies, these five young men from Yale were indeed remarkable. During the summer of 1894, Wilcox, Allan, Henderson, Frissell, and Warrington climbed, explored, and named the valleys, as well as most of the major peaks, glaciers, and lakes in the Lake Louise area, from Mt. St. Piran on the west to Moraine Lake and the Ten Peaks on the east. They did it in a nonchalant and unassuming manner and without modern equipment such as lightweight tents, sleeping bags, gortex clothing, expensive boots or freeze-dried food.

The Climb of Mt. Temple (11,636 feet)

In early August, 1894, Samuel Allen and George Warrington joined Wilcox, Henderson, and Frissell at Lake Louise. With the help of a Stoney Indian packer named Enoch Wildman, they moved from the comfort of the chalet at Lake Louise to a tent camp in Paradise Valley near Lake Annette.

In his book *The Rockies of Canada*, Wilcox tells of the cold they endured, the first few nights in their Paradise Valley camp:

Dawn came at long last and then for the first time we could get a good idea of our surroundings. Across the lake [Lake Annette] the precipices of Mt. Temple rose vertically to a great height and a waterfall made a great leap from some unknown source and fell not less than 1,000 feet into the lake on whose shores we had spent such an uncomfortable night. Patches of snow here and there left over from the last winter indicated our altitude.

While we had suffered during the night almost to the limit of endurance, poor Enoch's fate had been much worse, with nothing but a horse blanket over him, so he asked our permission to return to Lake Louise for the following night. "No grass for pony here," he said, "too cold me; no like it me." So after he had promised to return on the afternoon of the second day, "sun so high," he said pointing to where it would be at three o'clock, we gave him permission to return to more comfortable quarters."

Allen and Henderson made their way up Sentinel Pass on August 15th, and descended into Larch Valley. It was here that they got their first unforgetable view of Mt. Quadra, the Fay Glacier and the Ten Peaks.

> *With dark storm clouds drifting overhead and snowing falling on*
> *the peaks it was an awe inspiring sight.*

The next day Allen, Wilcox, and Frissell (who had recovered from his fall on Mt. Lefroy) made a first ascent of Mt. Aberdeen (10, 350 feet) from the Paradise Valley side. It was called Hazel Peak then and the climb was an easy scramble up the southwest scree and cliff bands. This outing was a warm up for their climb of Mt. Temple, which Allen and Wilcox had explored the year before.

At four o'clock on August 17th, Allen, Wilcox, and Frissell had a quick bite to eat and then they left their camp at Lake Annette. Their plan was to climb Mt. Temple – the highest mountain in Banff National Park. By nine-o'clock they were at the top of Sentinel Pass and after a brief second breakfast, they followed the easy scree slopes and cliff bands up the southeast ridge directly up from the top of Sentinel Pass. They found the going to be rather straightforward and avoided several buttresses by traversing to the right as they continued to scramble up. Staying on the ridge, or just to the right of it, they reached the upper snowcap by eleven o'clock. The final snow ridge that led to the summit presented few difficulties but they exercised extra care there and avoided the large cornices on the final summit ridge.

It was a glorious summer day and the temperature at the chalet at Lake Louise was recorded at seventy-seven degrees Fahrenheit. The hikers reached the summit at noon and enjoyed an unparalleled view. Despite some haze, they were able to see Mt. Assiniboine to the east and Mt. Sir Donald to the west. "Many a hearty cheer rent the air" as the three celebrated their achievement from the lofty, snow-capped summit.

Early Visitors to Lake O'Hara

In the summer of 1887, James J. McArthur became the first white man to visit Lake O'Hara. Following Cataract Brook to its source, he marvelled at the wild beauty of the emerald-coloured lake and the lacy Seven Veils Falls that tumble into its waters at the distant southeast end. Making camp in a clearing at the base of Mt. Wiwaxy, where the lake flows into a lively brook (almost exactly on the spot occupied by the present day Warden's cabin), he was rewarded with a remarkable view of the lake and the falls. This site became known as Sargent's Point in honour of the renowned painter that captured the breath-taking scene on canvass. The next morning McArthur ascended the Odaray Plateau and made the first ascent of Mt. Odaray (10,165 feet). The following day he visited the magnificent cliff bounded lake that bears his name to this day.

Two days after climbing Mt. Temple with Walter Wilcox and Louis Frissell, Sam Allen, and **Yule Carryer,** a Stoney Indian guide who also was attending university in eastern Canada, explored the well-used game trail along Cataract Brook from Wapta Lake. Following the tumbling creek to its source, Allan became the second white man to camp beside Lake O'Hara. The next morning they made their way around the lake and then they climbed above Seven Veils Falls into a large natural amphitheatre, formed by the imposing cliffs of Mt. Yukness, Glacier Peak, Mt. Lefroy, Mt. Victoria and Mt. Huber. There they discovered Lake Oesa (Ice). From Lake Oesa they made their way up steep scree and tallis slopes to the col between Mt. Lefroy and Mt. Victoria – where a stone mountaineering hut, named in remembrance of Phil Abbot stands today.

Lake O'Hara in the summer sun with the Seven Veils Falls in the background
This photo was taken from Sargent's Point in front of Grassi's cabin.

A painting of Lake O'Hara by Duncan M. Crockford

Abbot Pass–"The Death Trap"
The cliffs of Mt. Lefroy rise up from the lower glacier on the left, while those of Mt. Victoria are on the right. (Left to Right) Betty Perks, Gigi Granger & Roger Patillo.

Looking down the Death Trap the steep, ice-covered slopes of Mt. Lefroy rose some fifteen hundred feet above them. To their left, the equally precipitous snow and ice cliffs of Mt. Victoria rose a similar height. Acknowledging their limits, Allen and Carryer wisely chose not to climb the frightening bands of ice and rock presented by Mt. Lefroy. Instead they made their way down the Death Trap to the lower Victoria Glacier. They kept to the right and close to the perpendicular cliffs of the northeast buttress of Mt. Lefroy and descended hastily. Reaching the lower glacier they skirted the perpendicular cliffs that seem to rise out of the glacier and then climbed up the steep snow and ice slopes that lead to the col between Mitre Peak and Mt. Aberdeen.

From the top of this col they descended down to the head of Paradise Valley and followed the stream past the Giant Steps to their camp near Lake Annette. It was the first recorded trek from Lake O'Hara to the Plain of Six Glaciers, and the first recorded descent of the Death Trap.

This adventure was the last of the serious mountaineering activities of the 1894 season. The boys from Yale had accomplished a lot that summer. They were a remarkable group of young men who shared a common spirit of adventure and exploration, and they put their stamp on the Canadian Rockies forever.

As the group from Yale were preparing to leave Lake Louise for the season, Wilcox and Allen met **Dr. Charles Fay** and told him about the abundance of virgin peaks and the spectacular climbing in the area. Fay decided that he would bring the Appalachian Mountain Club to Lake Louise the following year for their annual mountain excursion.

Winter comes to the Rockies in 1894

After his friends departed for the East Walter Wilcox remained on the Lake Louise chalet, writing his book and exploring the area. He described the coming of winter to Lake Louise.

> *A few days later the various members of our party, one by one, bade farewell to the beautiful region of Lake Louise with its pleasant associations. I remained there five or six weeks longer until winter commenced in earnest and drove everyone away. During the first week of October I made a final visit to Paradise Valley with Mr. Astley, the manager of the chalet, in order to bring back our tent and the camping utensils. Snow covered the ground in the shady parts of the woods, even at the entrance to the valley. The stream had fallen so much that its rocky bed proved the best route up the valley, especially for the horse ...*

> *A few days later I went up to Lake Agnes to hunt for mountain goats, which frequent this place in great numbers. The snow was two feet deep. The lake was already nearly covered with ice, and I was compelled to seek shelter behind a cliff against the bitter cold wind, driving particles of hail and snow against my face. It*

was useless to prolong the contest longer. Winter had resumed her iron sway in the boreal regions and high altitudes, and in a few weeks Lake Louise too would begin to freeze, and no longer present its endless change of ripple and calm, light and shadow, or the reflected images of rocks and trees and distant mountains. (Walter D. Wilcox, 1898)

The Summer of 1895

The summer of 1895 was also a busy one in the Canadian Rockies. Walter Wilcox was back and he made Tom Wilson's corral his first stop to catch up on the latest news. Wilcox was an important client as he had many friends and connections in the eastern U.S.A. who were also interested in climbing and exploring in the Rockies.

Tom told Walter that he was organizing a trip to take **Robert Barrett,** a Chicago paper manufacturer, and his friend **J. Porter** to Mt. Assiniboine via a route he and Barrett had blazed in 1893. This route followed Healy Creek and then went up and over Simpson Pass. Tom had appointed **Ralph Edwards** as the lead guide with **Wild Bill Peyto** as second in command. Wilcox wasted no time in convincing first Wilson, and then Barrett, that he should go along as well. They were off and well down the trail before Sam Allen arrived in Banff.

On the second day out, Ralph Edwards lost his axe and had to backtrack to find it. He left Wild Bill in charge of the party. Bill took right over and led the group safely to the base of Mt. Assiniboine and helped them set up their camp. He then went back to find Edwards, who had lost his way and returned to Banff. When Edwards and Peyto made it back to the Mt. Assiniboine camp they guided the group around the base of the great mountain. This was an exhausting "forty-eight hour trip covering fifty-one miles of the toughest country imaginable." As they were returning to their base camp, who should they meet but Sam Allen and **Dr. Howard Smith** who had engaged the services of **Joe Barker,** another of Tom Wilson's guides. Allen was annoyed that Wilcox had not waited for him in Banff and not wanting to be outdone, he hired his own guide and outfit to explore the area.

Wilcox, Barrett, and Porter, together with their guides Peyto and Edwards, returned to Banff by way of Vermillion Pass and arrived in town on August 4, having spent some twenty-nine days on the trail.

With Wilcox eager for another trip, Tom Wilson suggested that he explore the area around the Waputik Icefield, where the Bow and Mistaya Rivers have their origins. Tom was familiar with the area, having passed through it in 1882 while helping Major Rogers find the best route for the railway. He had also guided **Calverley** and **Brearley** there in 1887 and packed supplies through the area for the Topographical Survey a few years later. Wilcox was enchanted with the idea and convinced Tom to let Wild Bill Peyto be his guide. Their pack train, consisting of five horses, a cook, two dogs, Wild Bill and Wilcox, left Banff on August 6th, 1895. In Camping in the Canadian Rockies (1898, 170) Wilcox described their procession;

Peyto, as packer, always rode in the saddle, for the dignity of his office never allows a packer to walk, and besides, from their physical elevation on a horse's back they can better discern the trail. A venerable Indian steed, long-legged and lean, but most useful in fording streams, was Peyto's saddle horse [Chinquay]. The bell-mare followed next, led by a head rope. The other horses followed in single file, and never allowed the sound of the bell to get out of hearing.

Wilcox and Peyto became good friends on this trip and they had some great fishing and hunting adventures along the way. They caught many fat trout in Bow Lake, including a large rainbow that measured twenty-three inches. They also enjoyed excellent fishing in the Waterfowl Lakes, Hector Lake, and Peyto Lake. Bill was an excellent shot and Wilcox later wrote: "Many a time when on the trail I have seen him suddenly take his six-shooter and fire into a tall tree, whereupon a grouse would come tumbling down, with his neck severed, or his head knocked off by the bullet." [1898, 214)

The trip took twenty-three days and covered more than one hundred and seventy-five miles. On their return to Banff, they followed Little Pipestone Creek to Johnson Creek behind the Sawback Range. They then proceeded over Edith Pass to Forty Mile Creek and followed it into Banff.

The Appalachian Mountain Club Arrives

The **Appalachian Mountain Club (AMC)** made their first excursion to the Rockies in the summer of 1895. The group numbered some twenty people – most of who were women. Most members of the group were content with simple climbs around the Lake Louise area, but **Professor Charles Fay, Philip Abbot, and Charles Thompson** looked for greater challenges. Their first order of business was to seek out Tom Wilson for information, guidance, and advice. After much discussion they decided to attempt a first ascent of Mt. Hector. Phil Abbot wrote of their planning:

Our first step was to get a hold of Wilson, the best guide and outfitter for that region, and to hold a council of war. Many plans were proposed but none hit our fancy. Finally, for about the tenth time since he joined us, Thompson brought forth his fixed idea. Mt. Hector had never been climbed; better still it had been attempted without success; and it was high, because the Canadian surveyors, when they turned back, had already reached 10,400 feet. It further appeared that Wilson himself had been with that party; and said he believed the peak could be climbed. He also told us of an enormous snowfield lying to the

west of Hector on the main watershed, and stretching away to
the north for fifty miles, which was absolutely unexplored. (The
First Ascent of Mt. Hector, Canadian Rockies, 1896, p.2)

After a difficult approach march that included fording swollen rivers and
constantly battling mosquitoes, the team of Charles Fay, Phil Abbot, and Charles
Thompson made the first ascent of Mt. Hector (11,135 feet). They were especially
proud of themselves as they accomplished their feat without the aid of professional
guides.

Wilcox Explores beyond Bow Pass

In the summer of 1896, **Walter Wilcox** decided to explore the territory north of
Bow Pass in search of Mt. Hooker and Mt. Brown, which were reported to be in
the vicinity of Athabasca Pass. With him was **Robert Barrett,** with whom he had
explored the Mt. Assiniboine area the previous summer. **Fred Stephens** and **Tom
Lusk** were their guides for this trip and **Art Arnold** was the cook.

David Douglas, the Scottish botanist who had travelled over Athabasca Pass
in 1827, reported that Mt. Hooker and Mt. Brown stood between 16,000 and 17,000
feet high. This would have made them the highest mountains in Canada. In 1893,
Arthur P. Coleman, a Professor of Geology at the University of Toronto, his
brother **L.Q. Coleman,** a rancher from Morley, and Professor **L.B. Stewart,** also
from the University of Toronto, made their way to the two legendary peaks via the
Red Deer River Valley. They ascended Mt. Brown and were surprised to find that it
was only 9,156 feet [This is not an uncommon mistake, for when a peak dominates
its surroundings it seems much taller than it actually is. The Matterhorn at Zermatt,
Switzerland, is an example of such an illusion and Mt. Assiniboine and Mt. Hector
are examples in the Rockies.]

Wilcox's route to the legendary peaks followed the Bow River to the junction
of the Mistaya River, which they then followed to Saskatchewan Crossing and the
North Fork of the Saskatchewan River. The North Fork was then followed to Wilcox
Pass, where the adventurers caught sight of the impressive glaciers of **Mt. Athabasca**
and **Mt. Andromeda**, as well as and the massive tongue of the Columbia Icefields.
From Wilcox Pass they proceeded over **Sunwapta Pass** to **Fortress Lake**, where
they climbed a peak and established that Mt. Hooker was only 10,500 feet high.
While Wilcox and his party were climbing, guides Tom Lusk and Fred Stevens
remained at the base camp and built a raft, which they used to explore the lake and
catch some fine rainbow trout.

On the return trip to Laggan, the group divided, Barrett and Tom Lusk explored
the **Molar Pass** area and then they followed the Pipestone River to the Bow River
Valley at Laggan. Wilcox, Fred Stephens, and Art Arnold made their way directly
to Laggan via the familiar Bow River route. When they arrived at Laggan they
learned that **Philip Abbot** had been killed in a fall on Mt. Lefroy.

An Early Tragedy: The First Recorded Mountaineering Death in the Rockies

Philip Stanley Abbot graduated from Harvard Law School in 1893 and was an active member of the Appalachian Mountain Club (AMC). He had climbed in England, Wales, California, and Alaska and had conquered several notable peaks in the Alps. Reputed to be one of the finest mountaineers in North America, his presence among the relatively inexperienced AMC climbers was a great asset.

Twenty AMC members had visited Lake Louise in the summer of 1895, climbing some minor peaks and doing some serious hiking in the area. **Charles Fay, Philip Abbot** and **Charles Thompson** had made a first ascent of Mt. Hector, and later they had examined Mt. Lefroy, Mt. Victoria, and the Death Trap from the slopes of Mt. Colliers at the Plain of Six Glaciers. The following summer, a much smaller group returned, intend on attempting some major ascents.

Fay, Thompson, and Abbot and a colleague, George Little, were fit and raring to go when they arrived at Glacier House in mid July. The four climbers warmed up by hiking in the Rogers Pass area and then over Asulkan Pass to Glacier Circle, where they practiced snow and ice-climbing techniques. Returning to Glacier House, they climbed Mt. Avalanche and Eagle Peak. Their most notable conquest, however, was their first ascent of Mt. Rogers (10,546 feet). Phil Abbot, George Little, and Charles Thompson accomplished this using a route that crossed the Hermit and Rogers glaciers.

After these successes in the Glacier House area, the Appalachian group took the train to Banff where they sought out Tom Wilson, asking him for advice as to the best route up Mt. Lefroy. They also arranged for Tom to pack them up the Bow River Valley to the Balfour Glacier so they could climb Mt. Balfour (10,721 feet). Tom agreed to meet them for this trip at the Lake Louise chalet on the morning of August 4th, after they had climbed Mt. Lefroy. He promised to bring a string of pack ponies, a wrangler, and a cook with him.

The AMC members were enthusiastically confident when they checked in to the chalet at Lake Louise on August 2nd. After unpacking their bags and getting their gear in order, they hiked up to Lake Agnes. It was a perfect afternoon and the weather for the next day looked promising.

Up and dressed at four o'clock, the following morning Fay, Little, Abbot, and Thompson had a hearty breakfast of flapjacks, eggs, and bacon. By five-thirty they were on the trail to the end of the lake. It was a cloudless morning and they made good progress. By seven thirty they were at the Plain of Six Glaciers and hiking down the moraine to the lower Victoria Glacier and the entrance to the Death Trap. There was a good snow in the pass that year and travel over the crevassed lower glacier went quickly. They were roped in two pairs, Fay and Little on one rope and Abbot and Thompson on the other. Abbot and Thompson led the way and kept relatively close to the imposing cliffs of Mt. Lefroy in order to avoid the constant avalanches and ice falling from the upper slopes of Mt. Victoria. They were able to move quickly up the pass and had no difficulty crossing the *bergschrund,* as a substantial snow bridge spanned it that year. Reaching the col between Mt. Lefroy and Mt. Victoria (the present site of the Abbot Pass hut) just before noon, they stopped for lunch and discarded their heavy packs and jackets. They already had accomplished a "first" – the first known ascent of the Death Trap from the Plain of Six Glaciers.

From their vantage point on the col the climbers were not only able to look down to Lake Oesa and Lake O'Hara, but they could also study possible routes up Mt. Lefroy and Mt. Victoria. This was the same col that Sam Allen and Yule Carryer had crossed over on their journey from Lake O'Hara to Lake Louise in 1893.

The imposing cliffs of Mt. Lefroy presented an erratic combination of precipitous, ice-filled gullies, large sections of snow and glare ice, and random outcroppings of rotten limestone rock. [The rock in the Rockies is different from the solid quartzite of the Selkirks. It is generally weathered limestone that presents unstable and unreliable handholds and footholds.] As they packed up their lunch, Abbot confidently assured his comrades: *"The peak is ours!"* (Always a bad omen!)

Proceeding up the alternating bands of snow, crumbling rock outcroppings, and ice slopes with prudent caution, the party spent considerable time zigzagging upward and cutting steps as they ascended. They were all on one rope and it took them an inordinate amount of time to cut steps, belay each other, and negotiate the rotten rock bands. It was almost five thirty when the four climbers neared the summit.

With one rock pitch to go, Abbot, who had led the entire way, asked the others to unrope while he negotiated the last short, rock pitch leading to the summit. Almost immediately afterwards, Little, and then Thompson and Fay, saw Abbot falling backward past them. They watched in horrified disbelief as he struck the back of his head on the rocks at the base of the steep ice slope below them. He then did a grotesque flip in the air and tumbled like a rag doll over and over, down the steep slope. His limp body tangled itself in the rope as it bounced off the lower cliff bands and the icy slopes.

The three men were paralysed with shock and terror at the sight. In addition, they had no rope to assist them in descending to their mortally-injured comrade. With only their ice axes for support, they slowly made their way down to Abbot, who lay in a battered heap below them. Fay later wrote a harrowing account of their descent to the motionless body of their comrade and their subsequent night on the col.

> We began our descent with ice-axes only, each responsible for his own safety. Our ample footsteps were now a priceless safeguard. On the treacherous rock slopes we could secure a tolerable substitute for seven feet of rope by attaching two ice-axes together by their straps, a wholly inadequate resource for this dangerous passage. Thus for three hours and until the beautiful sunset glow had faded on the high arête of Mt. Lefroy, we worked our slow way downward. At length we stood beside the motionless form that all this time had laid in full view.
>
> To our surprise life was not yet extinct. The fatal wound in the back of his head, evidently received in the short initial fall of perhaps twenty feet, was the only grievous outward mark, and

the autopsy proved that not a limb was broken. A faint murmur, that my imagination interpreted as a recognition of our presence and an expression of gratitude that we had at least escaped from peril, alone broke the silence of a brief moment, and then we three bared our heads in the twilight, believing that his generous spirit was already passing. But a moment later the faint breathing was resumed.

If living, then of course we would bear him down with us; difficult as the labor would be. We now at least had the ropes, and with their aid such a task did not seem impossible. To tarry in this spot was at all events out of the question. With tender hands, having first disentangled the ropes, we raised him, and began the dreary descent; but we had scarcely reached the brink of the little cliff, when he again ceased to breathe. Not satisfied with this evidence, we tested pulse and heart. That all was over in the mortal life for our loved companion was subject to no manner of doubt.

The Death Trap–Abbot Pass
Mt. Lefroy is on the left and Mt. Victoria is on the right. Avalanches swoop down the precipitous slopes of both peaks into the "Death Trap". On August 3, 1896 Phil Abbot fell from a spot near the summit of Mt. Lefroy.

Broken-hearted, the three men left Abbot's body in a safe and secure spot and attempted to get down to the col where they planned to spend a long, sad night grieving for their comrade. It was approaching 10:00 p.m. and raining heavily, when they finally reached the col. None of them had a warm jacket or a sweater, as they had cached them that morning when they had left for the final assault on the mountain. Feeling confident, and that "the peak was already theirs", they didn't plan on needing extra clothing until they scampered down in the mid afternoon.

Philip Abbot. On August 3, 1896 Abbot became the first mountaineering fatality in the Canadian Rockies when he fell to his death from near the summit of Mt. Lefroy.

Now it was raining heavily and they couldn't find their warm cloths. In addition they had no hot drinks to lift their spirits. With their nerves shattered, they spent a miserable night huddled together to keep warm in the storm.

At first light they proceeded down the Death Trap to the Plain of Six Glaciers and back to the chalet at the head of Lake Louise. The next day, a rescue party led by Tom Wilson, retrieved Abbot's body. Fay described that long lonely night huddled at the col between Mt. Lefroy and Mt. Victoria as follows:

> *The seriousness of the task we had assumed as a matter of course at once became evident. To lower the lifeless body down this short precipice was a labour involving a large risk for three persons. Only with competent aid and by long daylight could it be brought from its lofty resting-place to the chalet we had left so hopefully that morning. Twilight was deepening into dusk as we decided to leave it here and descend as far as possible before darkness should prevent further advance. By the dim reflection from the sky and the snow we could faintly discern our upward footsteps in certain places; in others merely divining them. The general course, avoiding dangerous precipices on our left, we could make out without difficulty. We reached without mishap the top of the rock-strewn promontory, but by a strange misfortune all three of us forgot that it was near this point, and not in the pass itself, that we had left our rucksacks with food and our only stimulant ...together with an extra sweater—an oversight we had occasion bitterly to repent. Not until we reached the col, and failed to find our belongings, did the truth dawn upon us, and a return in the darkness failed to bring the seeker to the desired spot.*

Assembled again at the pass – it was now 10:30 p.m. – we accepted the decree that we should spend the remainder of the night ... The bare rock of the lowest point of the pass, upon which we now found ourselves, was at least preferable to the snow for a couch, so we lay down upon it face downward. Soon however, the rising breeze drawing freshly over the col from the north [the Plain of Six Glaciers] made us long for some shelter from its chill. The cairn would offer slight defence and up to it we hastened. Seating ourselves in its lee one close before the other, each held the one in front of him in a close embrace to utilize, so far as possible, our bodily warmth. Often we would lightly pound ourselves, or one another, to increase the sluggish circulation... Our condition became somewhat worse toward morning, when the sky became over cast and flakes of fine snow began to sift over us, the forerunners of a storm, the severity of which was fortunately delayed for some hours. The night wore on but slowly. Occasionally one or another would doze for a quarter or half an hour, then waking, consult the watch and congratulate himself on his happy fortune. By 4:15 a.m. it was light enough, despite the cloudiness, for one to move about, and only too gladly I proceeded to overcome my numbness by recovering the rucksacks. Strengthened for the decent by the welcome food – we had eaten nothing since noon of the day before – we set out at five o'clock, and reached the chalet at 9:30 a.m. in the midst of a rainstorm. (Appalachia Vol. VIII, 1896-1898)

According to plan, Tom Wilson, along with a wrangler and a cook, arrived at the Lake Louise chalet just before nine o'clock on the morning of August 4th. They had four pack ponies and some riding horses for Abbot, Thompson, Little, and Fay to use on their trip to the Waputik Icefield. Tom was tying the horses to the hitching post beside the chalet when the three demoralized and rain-soaked climbers arrived with the news of Abbot's death. Fay, Thompson and Little related the tragic events of the previous day as they huddled near the bone-warming woodstove in the common room of the chalet and drank the steaming coffee that Astley and Tom had liberally laced with brandy. Warmed from without and from within, they related the ghastly details of Abbot's fall and told of their cold and rainy night on the col between Mt. Victoria and Mt. Lefroy.

Joe Savage, the congenial cook at the chalet, served the hungry climbers a mountain of pancakes, together with bacon, eggs, elk sausage, toast and marmalade. A short time later, Wilson, Astley, Little, Fay and Thompson left for the Plain of Six Glaciers to retrieve Abbot's body. Reaching the Victoria-Lefroy col a two thirty in the afternoon, they encountered a summer snow squall that slowed their progress. It was not until four o'clock that they were able to get to Abbot's body. They carried it down to the col where they wrapped it in a canvass sack and slid it down the Death Trap. It was almost dark by the time they arrived at the lower Victoria Glacier.

Tom Wilson resting in Abbot Pass while recovering the body of Phil Abbot.
L to R. Tom Wilson, George T. Little, Willoughby Astley (Chalet Manager),
and Prof. Charles Fay

Exhausted, they left the body beside the cliffs of Mt. Lefroy and made their way
back to the chalet by lantern light. The next morning, Tom Wilson led six labourers
from the CPR back to the Plain of Six Glaciers. They carried Abbot's remains to
the end of the lake, where manager Astley waited with a rowboat to ferry the body
back to the chalet. It was then taken by train to Banff for an autopsy to be performed
by Dr. Brett.

The Reverend James Outram offered an account and an analyses of the tragedy in
his book *In the Heart of the Rockies* published 1905,

> *On August 3, 1896, the chalet was left behind at 6:15 – a somewhat
> noticeably late hour in view of the distance and the difficulties
> that lay before the party. In an hour and a quarter the glacier was
> reached, and seventy-five minutes later they roped up opposite
> the familiar couloir. Soon they turned the shoulder of Mount*

Lefroy and entered on the new ground of the magnificent gorge dividing that mountain from Mount Victoria.

The usual thunders of frequent avalanches greeted their ears, and the superb cascades of powdered ice and drifting snow were at their best. With but a single brief halt they pressed toward the narrow V-shaped nick at the head of the long snow slopes that rise steadily to the level of the cliff walls which form the confines of the glacier below.

Not till 11:50, however, did they gain the longed-for crest, and turned to scan the massive mountain-side, whose ice-crowned pinnacle still towered 2000 feet above the pass. Almost immediately the joyful exclamation came from Mr. Abbot's lips, "The peak is ours!"

Outram quotes from Fay's account of the climb and notes that the last words that Abbot uttered as he told his comrades to unrope so he could proceed upward in a rotten gully leading to the summit arête were: "I have a good lead here." Outram then proceeds to analyse the possible cause of the tragedy:

The cause of the accident remains a mystery. Whether a slip occurred, or the climber trusted a mass of rock which suddenly gave way, or was struck by a falling stone, cannot be determined. The intense rottenness of the Rocky Mountain quartzite lends strong probability to the view that a hold may have proved treacherous.

Abbot's caution was proverbial amongst his comrades, though combined with an enthusiastic boldness, and a slip is the least likely of the three contingencies. The strange neglect to coil the rope is quite inexplicable to any experienced mountaineer, and the trail of its nearly 120 feet and liability to catch on the numerous projections and jerk the climber backward in a critical position, suggests another possible explanation of the fatal fall.

The lesson taught at so terrible a cost has not been in vain. The enthusiastic love that Abbot had for Nature's noblest works has been transplanted by his death to our hearts. The craft he so delighted in has gained adherents through his memory; whilst at the same time the awful shock of accident, occurring to a most skilful and habitually cautious mountaineer, has proved a valuable and perhaps much needed warning, lest undue familiarity, a moments want of thought or care or adequate testing of conditions, should involve not one life only but very likely several.

Though the poor shattered body lies in the peaceful shelter of a New England tomb, the spirit of Philip Abbot lives again in many of those who knew him not, as well as those who had the privilege of intercourse and friendship with a rare personality; and his true monument is not within the lowland precincts of Mt. Auburn, but—standing majestically among the crags and glaciers he loved so well—the splendid peak of MOUNT LEFROY. (1905, 115-123)

Quite naturally, the AMC group cancelled their trip to Mt. Balfour and the members, still in shock, returned to their homes in Massachusetts. Walter Wilcox, who had just returned from Sunwapta Pass, arrived at the Lake Louise chalet a few days after Abbot's death and was on hand later for the inquest in Banff. Walter bid a sad goodbye to Professor Fay and his colleagues at the Banff station and then he and Tom Wilson made plans to pack into Lake O'Hara.

The first act of the first Canadian Rockies mountaineering fatality concluded with the inquest. The second act of the drama would unfold the following year. The summer of 1896 would always be remembered in the Rockies.

1897—A Professional Guide Comes To The Rockies and Mt. Lefroy Is Conquered

Abbot's tragic and dramatic death caused an uproar, amplified by the fact that he was from a wealthy and influential New England family. His parents seemed intent on fixing the blame for their son's death elsewhere, focusing on the CPR. They contended that the railway was somehow negligent in failing to have professional mountaineering guides available at Lake Louise and Glacier House. The controversy received extensive media coverage and drew in some politicians. For a time, there was even talk of banning the sport of mountaineering.

In all of the debate, scant attention was paid to the fact that Abbot was a victim of his own rashness and bad judgement as he had decided to unrope from his climbing companions. It is perhaps this omission that prompted Otram's comments, previously quoted.

That winter plans were underway in New England, to "avenge" young Abbot's death by launching a full assault on Mt. Lefroy the following season. Abbot's father asked Professor Charles Fay to organize a new attempt on the mountain to prove that his son had chosen the right route. Fay proposed that the best international climbers be invited, under the auspices of the Appalachian Mountain Club, to climb the peak on August 3rd, 1897—the first anniversary of Philip's death. The senior Abbot was delighted with these plans and agreed to help finance the expedition.

Professor Fay first invited the Alpine Club of London to send representatives to the expedition and was pleasantly surprised when **Professor Harold B. Dixon,** who had climbed with Abbot in the Alps and in the Lake District in England, agreed to participate. His acceptance was followed by that of **Dr. Norman Collie**—one of the best-known mountaineers in Britain at the time. Collie had accompanied **A.F. Mummery** and **Geoffrey Hastings** on an expedition to the Himalayas in 1896. The party climbed to an elevation of twenty thousand feet (higher than anyone had ever climbed before) on the towering Nanga Parbat. Tragically Mummery was lost when trying to cross Diama Pass.

Other climbers joined the party and on August 1st, 1897, the group assembled at Lake Louise. In addition to Dixon and Collie, the members included: **Charles Fay, A. Michael, Reverend Charles L. Noyes, Herschel C. Parker, J. R. Vanderlip** and **Charles S. Thompson** from the AMC. The group also had a "ringer" with them in **Peter Sarbach**, a Swiss guide from Saint Niklaus, Switzerland. With his participation in this ascent, Sarbach became the first professional Swiss guide to climb in the Canadian Rockies. Coincidentally he had guided young Abbot up the Matterhorn from Zermatt, two years previous.

The group limbered up that day by taking a pleasant hike up to Lake Agnes. Later that evening they swapped stories in front of the chalet's open fireplace with Willoughby Astley. The next day they hiked to the Plain of Six Glaciers to look over the Death Trap and plan how they would climb Mt. Lefroy. They decided on the route taken by Fay, Abbot, and Thompson the previous year, and then they returned to the chalet for a delicious meal of moose steaks prepared by chef, Joe Savage. After supper they checked their gear, packed, and repacked their rucksacks, and turned in early to be well rested for the following day's climb.

On August 3rd, after a "loggers breakfast" the assault team left the chalet at four thirty. The predawn was a clear and crisp as the party of climbers rowed down the lake in silence. By the time they landed at the end of the lake, it was getting light and there wasn't a cloud in the sky. At the Plain of Six Glaciers, Dixon and Collie stared in awe at the towering, glacier-clad peaks of Mt. Aberdeen, the Castle Crags, the Mitre, Mt. Lefroy, and Mt. Victoria. Proceeding cautiously, they ascended the Death Trap and by eight thirty were standing on the col between Mt. Lefroy and Mt. Victoria. As they studied the steep slopes of Mt. Lefroy, Fay and Thompson pointed out the details of the route they had taken the previous year with Phillip Abbot.

There was a lot of snow on Mt. Lefroy and Mt. Victoria during the 1897 season, and they chose a route with a series of two long switchbacks bearing initially up and to the left of the col and then back to the right, and finally back to the final summit. By nine o'clock they had finished a second breakfast and were roped into three separate groups. Sarbach took the lead and the group moved surely and quickly up the steep slopes of alternating snow and rock bands. The snow conditions were as close to perfect as one could ask for – not too hard and not too soft. They were able to kick firm steps all the way to the summit which was reached by eleven o'clock, with no real difficulty. They then build a cairn and Fay led the group in a prayer for the soul of Philip Abbot. Following this, they enjoyed a lunch of cheese, elk sausage, bannock bread, kippers and dried pemmican and marvelled at the matchless view in all directions. [I've found that food always tastes better at the summit of a hard won peak].

The group started the descent of the mountain at twelve fifteen, following in the steps they had kicked on the way up. The snow remained in excellent condition and the men were able to reach the col in just eighty minutes. The descent down the Death Trap was uneventful and the party was able to glissade for long stretches. They decided to name the pass in honour of their fallen comrade.

Mt. Lefroy had put up a valiant fight turning back Walter Wilcox and his colleagues in 1894 and the Appalachian team in 1896, before submitting in 1897.

Since then it has remained one of the most dangerous and unpredictable peaks in the Rockies.

The First Ascent of Mount Victoria

Two days later, on August 5th, 1897, Sarbach led Fay, Michael and Collie back up Abbot Pass to the col between Mt. Lefroy and Mt. Victoria. This time they tackled the demanding slopes of Mt. Victoria.

The party kept to the left as they ascended in two roped teams to the top of South Peak. Sarbach had Fay as his rope-mate and Collie teamed up with Michael. From South Peak they proceeded down the steep, snow-covered ridge to the "Sickle" where they were impressed with the knife-edged ridge that falls away for thousands of feet on either side. Carefully belaying each other along the way, they finally reached the summit of Centre Peak at eleven thirty.

The return route followed the line of their ascent and the group was safely down to the col by three o'clock. Arriving back at the chalet in time for supper, they enjoyed a dinner of roast venison and bear spare ribs. Sarbach broke out a bottle of Schnapps for the occasion and Professor Dixon passed around his bottle of Bristol Cream sherry to toast the success of their expedition.

Collie, Dixon, and Baker–The Climbers From England

On August 7th, a few days after the successful ascents of Lefroy and Victoria, G. P. Baker, a friend of Collie and Dixon from the Alpine Club (London) met them at the Lake Louise chalet. The next day, guided by **Wild Bill Peyto,** they followed Charles Fay, Charles Thompson, Herschel Parker, and others of the AMC up the Bow River Valley to the Waputik Icefield in search of Mt. Balfour. Bushwhacking through dense fallen timber, muskeg, swollen streams, and pine forests–along what Peyto called a "trail"–was a real education for the gentlemen from England. Their horses sank up to their bellies in endless swamps and muskegs along the route and they were almost eaten alive by mosquitoes. At one point they became separated from the main group and got lost, causing Wild Bill to backtrack and look for them. The next day they reached Bow Lake and the following day they explored Mt. Balfour, Mt. Gordon, and the expansive Waputik Icefield.

While climbing Mt. Gordon (10,346 feet), Thompson fell head first into a crevasse and had to be rescued by Collie. This delay spoiled their plans to climb Mt. Balfour, but from the summit of Mt. Gordon they were able to view the impressive Waputik Icefields as well as the massive Freshfield Icefield. Shimmering tantalizingly in the distance were Howse Peak (10,800 feet), Mt. Chephren (10,715 feet), Mt. Freshfield (10,945 feet), Mt. Forbes (11,902 feet), and Mt. Outram (10,670 feet). Further away was the towering Mt. Bryce (11,507 feet). It was an amazing sight – one that Collie and Dixon never forgot.

Members of the Appalachian Mountain Club who avenged Abbot's death by making the first ascent of Mt. Lefroy on August 3, 1897–the 1st anniversary of Abbot's death in 1896. From Left to right are: Charles Thompson, Charles Fay, Chalet Lake Louise manager Willoughby Anstey, (not on the climb) H. B. Dixon (seated), Arthur Michael, Reverend Charles Noyes, L. R. Vanderlip (top) J.N. Collie (with a pipe), Herschel Parker, and the great Swiss guide Peter Sarbach.

Peter Sarbach
The first professional Swiss guide to climb in the Canadian Rockies. Sarbach led members of the Appalachian Mountain Club to a first ascent on Mt. Lefroy on August 3rd, 1897. Two days later he led Professor Charles Fay, Art Michael and Norman Collie to a first ascent of Mt. Victoria.

Professor Charles Fay
Pioneer climber in the Canadian Rockies

Mount Victoria

The author on the summit ridge of Mt.Victoria–July, 1962
There was a lot of snow that season.

A Daring Rescue

In a book co-authored with Hugh Stutfield (*Climbs and Explorations in the Canadian Rockies*, Longmans Green & Co. London, 1903) Collie describes the rescue of Charles Thompson from the crevasse near Mt. Gordon. It is a fascinating account of early mountaineering in the Rockies.

It was near the top of the second peak that Thompson very nearly ended his mountaineering experiences. Not far from this second summit a huge crevasse partially covered with snow had to be crossed. All the party had passed over but Thompson, who unfortunately broke through and at once disappeared headlong into the great crack that ran perpendicularly down into the depths of the glacier. Those of the party who were still on the first peak saw their friend gesticulating in the far distance, but did not take much notice until Sarbach [Peter Sarbach the Swiss guide] drew attention to the fact that there were only four people instead of five to be seen: someone therefore must have fallen down a crevasse. A race across the almost level snow then took place, Sarbach being easily first. Although Thompson was too far down to be seen, he could be heard calling for help and saying that, although he was not hurt, he would be extremely grateful to us if we would make haste and extricate him from the awkward position he was in, for he could not move and was almost upside down, jammed between the two opposing sides of the crevasse.

It was obvious that every second was of importance: a stirrup was made in the rope, and Collie, being the lightest member of the party – and, withal, unmarried – was told to put his foot into it, whilst he was also carefully roped around the waist. Then he was pushed over the edge of the abyss, and swung in mid air.

To quote his description: I was lowered into the gaping hole. On one side the ice fell sheer, on the other it was rather undercut, but again bulged outwards about eighteen feet below the surface, making the crevasse at that point not much more than two feet wide. Then it widened again, and went and went down into dim twilight. It was not till I had descended sixty feet, almost the whole available length of an eighty foot rope, that at last I became tightly wedged between the two walls of the crevasse, and absolutely incapable of moving my body. My feet were close to Thompson's, but his head was further away, and about three feet lower than his heels. Face downwards, and covered with fallen snow, he could not see me. But after he had explained that it was entirely his own fault that he was there, I told him we would have him out in no time. At the moment, I must say that I hardly expected to be able to accomplish anything. For, jammed between two slippery walls of ice, and only able to move my arms, cudgel my brains as I would, I could not think what was to be done.

I shouted for another rope. When it came down I managed to throw one end to Thompson's left hand, which was waved about, till he caught it. But, when pulled, it merely dragged out of his hand. Then with some difficulty I managed to tie a noose on the rope by putting both arms above my head. With this I lassoed that poor pathetic arm which was the only part of Thompson that could be seen. Then came the tug-of- war. If he refused to move, I could do nothing more to help him; moreover I was afraid that at any moment he might faint. If that had occurred I do not believe he could have been got out at all, for the force of the fall had jammed him down further than it was possible to follow. Slowly the rope tightened, as it was cautiously pulled by those above. I could hear my heart thumping in the ghastly stillness of the place, but at last Thompson began to shift, and after some short time he was pulled into an upright position by my side. To get a rope round his body was of course hopeless. Partly by wriggling and pulling on my own rope I so shifted that by straining one arm over my head I could get my two hands together, and then tied the best and tightest jamming knot I could think of round his arm, just above his elbow. A shout to the rest of the party, and Thompson went rapidly upwards till he disappeared round the bulge of ice forty feet or more above. I can well remember the feeling of dread that came over me lest the rope should slip or his arm give way under the strain, and he should come thundering down on the top of me; but he got out all right, and a moment later I followed.

Most marvelously no bones had been broken, but how any one could have fallen as he did without being instantaneously killed will always remain a mystery.... We were both of us nearly frozen and wet to the skin, for ice-cold water was slowly dripping the whole time on to us; and in my desire to be as little encumbered as possible, I had gone down into the crevasse very scantily clad in a flannel shirt and knickerbockers. (1903)

Collie and Barker Explore the Mount Forbes Area.

After Thompson's rescue, the AMC group returned to Lake Louise and departed for Banff and points east. **Collie, Baker,** and **Sarbach,** remained behind and on August 10th, left for Bow Pass and the Freshfield Icefield with **Wild Bill Peyto,** packer **Lou Richardson** and cook **Charlie Black.** They made their way up the lower ramparts of Mt. Freshfield, but were turned back by a violent storm that featured plenty of thunder and lightning. Looking north from the slopes of Mt. Freshfield they got a good view of Mt. Columbia (12,294 feet) some thirty miles away.

On the way back to Field the group explored the base of Mt. Forbes and then Wild Bill led them through heavy snow over Howse Pass and then the rugged Amiskwi Pass to the Kicking Horse River. This was the first recorded crossing of Amiskwi Pass, and Bill and Lou had to cut through miles of deadfall and blow-downs. By the time they reached Field, they were exhausted. Collie and Baker recuperated for a few days at Mount Stephen House before returning to England. Another season of adventure in the Rockies had come to an end.

Did Professor Jean Habel Discover the Yoho Valley?

Professor Jean Habel, a professor of mathematics, was born in Berlin in the 1830's. A member of the German-Austrian Alpine Club, he first visited the Canadian Rockies in 1896. In Banff, he spent a considerable time at Tom Wilson's corral learning all he could about the area. He then went to Lake Louise where he talked with **Walter Wilcox** and his colleagues. While travelling on the train from Laggan to Field, he caught a glimpse of the intriguing Mt. des Poilus and the Wapta Icefield. He was captivated by the mysterious, white, pyramid-shaped mountain, far in the distance and christened it "Hidden Peak". He resolved to return the following summer and explore the area and perhaps even climb the enticing peak.

The following summer, Habel arrived at Mount Stephen House, where he had arranged with Tom Wilson to have an outfit and guides ready to take him on his search for his hidden mountain. For this campaign Tom had assigned **Ralph Edwards** as the guide, **Fred Stephens** as the packer, and **Frank Wellman** as the cook.

The party made its way from Mount Stephen House to Emerald Lake on the overcast morning of July 15th, following the trail that Wilson had blazed the year before. He set up camp near the lake and the next morning the party he left Emerald Lake in a steady downpour and made their way over Burgess Pass and then over Yoho Pass, high above the Yoho Valley. [This was probably the first party to ever to cross over Yoho Pass and to camp at Yoho Lake.] Habel spotted Takakkaw Falls far in the distance, across the valley, and was probably among the first white men ever to see this magnificent sight. Although Tom Wilson claimed that it was he who had discovered the great falls some years earlier and vociferously disputed Habel's claim.

On July 22nd, 1897 as the little group became the first to descend to the Yoho Valley. They then camped at the base of Takakkaw Falls and then journeyed to the head of the Yoho Valley and on to the Wapta and Yoho Icefields, In doing so they were the first to discover Laughing Falls, and Twin Falls, and the seldom seen Diableret Falls near the tongue of the Yoho Glacier.

Deciding that Mt Balfour would make an excellent climb, Habel and Edwards, together with the reluctant Fred Stephens, roped up and proceeded to cross the icefield toward the distant peak. The climb was going smoothly until the burley Fred Stephens attempted to cross a snow bridge that appeared to be solid. It wasn't, and as it gave-way under Steven's considerable weight, he disappeared into a gaping crevasse. Somehow Edwards and the slightly-built professor Habel managed to haul a freezing and thoroughly frightened Fred Stephens out of the icy abyss. Since the weather showed no sign of improving, the party gingerly made their way down the Yoho Valley to Takakkaw Falls and then out to the Kicking Horse River Valley. [For a detailed account of Habel's trip into the Yoho Valley, read Ralph Edward's book "*The Trail to the Charmed Land*"].

Later, Habel claimed to have discovered Emerald Lake, the Yoho Valley, and Takakkaw Falls. On hearing this, an incensed Tom Wilson, did his best to refute these claims. Tom maintained that he had first ventured to Emerald Lake shortly after finding Lake Louise, while working for the CPR survey crew and guiding Major Rogers through the Kicking Horse Canyon. Wilson also vociferously asserted that in late August of 1882, while prospecting with his Stoney Indian friend Eddy Hunter, he had explored the Yoho Valley and was probably the first white man to see Takakkaw Falls, Laughing Falls, and Twin Falls. He finally told of how a few years earlier, he had tried to interest Professor Fay and the Appalachian Club in the area as a climbing destination.

> In 1895 I tried to get some members of the Appalachian Club to explore and write it up. In 1896, I cut and cleared out the old Indian trail from Field to the crossing of Emerald Creek, and from there, I cut a trail to the lake and along the North side to the Gravel Flats at the East-end … then in July of 1897, I got Jean Habel to go into the Yoho, to photograph it and write it up". [Quoted by E.J. Hart, Diamond Hitch, 1979, p.36]

In a letter written to J.B. Larkin, Commissioner of Dominion Parks in the 1920's, Tom wrote:

> Jean Habel did not discover the Yoho Valley any more than he discovered the CPR station at Field. I prospected the Yoho Valley in 1882, and in 1885 and the Habel Party saw my cuttings. In 1897 in order to get the CPR interested in this region, I got the German Professor to go in and take photos and write it up in a magazine. I gave him three men and seven head of horses, provisions, tents etc. all for $7.00 per day and it cost me $11.50 per day, cash. Then the damn German took all the credit [Hart, E.J. 1979, 36-37]

Ralph Edwards, who worked for Tom Wilson, and who guided Professor Habel over Yoho Pass and down into the Yoho Valley in 1897, suggests that Habel's was the first group ever to explore the area and to camp at the base of Takakkaw Falls. They also were the first to blaze a trail from Takakkaw Falls down the Yoho River out to Kicking Horse Flats, east of Field., so Habel has a legitimate claim,

The magnificent peak that captured Habel's interest and imagination was later named in his honour. Years later, the politicians in Ottawa renamed it "Mont des Poilus" (10,371 feet).

In Search of Mounts Hooker and Brown – 1898

1898 was the year of the great Klondike Gold Rush, but rather than dreaming of Klondike gold, **Norman Collie** dreamed of the lofty, virgin peaks beyond Mt. Forbes. He returned with climbing companions **Hugh Stutfield** and **Hermann Woolley** in the early summer and immediately consulted Tom Wilson as to the feasibility of their plans. They arranged for **Bill Peyto** to guide them, as he had impressed Collie greatly with his skill and determination the year before.

The party left Laggan on July 31st with packers **Bill Vavasour** and **Roy Douglas**, cook **Bill Byers**, thirteen horses, and three dogs. They followed the route that Wilson had laid out for them – up the Pipestone River to the Siffleur River, then down the Siffleur River to the North Saskatchewan. From the Saskatchewan River Crossing they headed north to Sunwapta Pass and the Wilcox Meadows that overlook the magnificent Mt. Athabasca (11,452 feet) and the equally impressive, Mt. Andromeda (11,300 feet). The trip took them nineteen days.

On the bright, clear morning of August 20th, Collie and Woolley became the first to climb Mt. Athabaska, ascending the northeast ridge. From the summit, the view of the immense icefields was spectacular. Two towering giants immediately caught their attention. One they named Mt. Bryce (11,507 feet) in honour of Sir James Bryce. The other they thought to be Mt. Hooker, but it was actually Mt. Columbia some 12, 294 feet above sea level.

From the summit of Mt. Athabasca, the pair traversed to the northwest ridge and descended to the north glacier, and then they returned to their camp. Two days later, Collie, Stutfield, and Woolley spent the night high on the right bank of the north glacier and got an early three o'clock start for the massive peak to the north.

> *The day was warm and sultry, making us all tired, but for several hours we tramped across this almost level ice-sea towards the goal of our ambition – that great glacier-clad, chisel-headed peak…but the peak we were walking towards was farther off than we imagined, for it lay on the opposite shore of this frozen ocean. It did not look as if it would be difficult to climb, but finally we had to give up.*

On the way back to camp, the group ascended the relatively easy slopes of Mt. Snow Dome (11, 340 feet). They then crossed Wilcox Pass and entered the Upper Sunwapta Valley, where they climbed Diadem Peak (9,615 feet). From this summit they got a great view of Mt. Alberta (11,874 feet), which towered above the icefields with precipitous, black cliffs rising up on three sides from the snow and ice at its base. They discussed climbing this impressive peak, but their supplies were running low so they decided to leave it for another day. Returning to the junction of the North Saskatchewan and the Siffleur rivers, Wild Bill was unable to locate their cache of food there. Following a long delay and considerable cussing and carrying on by Wild Bill, he eventually found it and they ate a hefty meal before returning to Laggan.

The meadows above Twin Falls
Mont des Poilus (10,371 ft) is in the background

Mt. Athabaska (11,452 ft.) first climbed in 1898 by J. Norman Collie and H. Woolley after being guided to the mountain by Bill Peyto.

Fay and Curtis Climb Mt. Niles in August of 1898

Professor Charles Fay and **R.F. Curtis** had also returned to the Rockies in 1898 and set their sights on climbing the still unconquered Mt. Balfour, at the edge of the Waputik Icefield. They too preferred climbing virgin peaks more than they fancied moiling for gold in the Klondike. Fay and his colleagues from the AMC had explored the area the previous summer. After seeking out Tom Wilson's advice, Fay decided to approach the mountain from the south by gaining the icefall at the head of Sherbrook Valley. Tom assigned **Bob Campbell** to pack Fay and Curtis to the base of the mountain via a new trail that passed by Sherbrook Lake.

The party left Laggan for Hector Station (at Wapta) on a railway handcar early in the morning of August 2nd. From there they hiked to Sherbrook Creek, at the edge of Wapta Lake and worked their way upstream to Sherbrook Lake. They then bushwhacked up to the head of the valley and traversed along the edge of the Waputik Icefield to the base of Mt. Niles where they camped for the night. Mt. Balfour was still almost four miles away across the relatively flat glacier and snow neve.

The next morning promised to be a beautiful, cloudless day. It was very hot, however, and the party didn't get an early start. After a leisurely breakfast they started off at nine-thirty, by which time it was getting warm. Under the intense August sun the snow became very soft and as they crossed the glacier on the way to Mt. Balfour they began to sink up to their knees. The portly Curtis frequently sank up to his waist and soon became hopelessly fatigued. Exhausted, he declined the opportunity to go further, but urged his colleagues to press on.

While ascending a rather easy arête on the north side of Mt. Balfour Fay dropped his ice axe into a crevasse. By the time he had retrieved it they both decided to call it a day. After a brief snack, they headed back across the glacier to their camp.

After resting a day and taking some pictures, Campbell and Fay rose early on the morning of August 5th, and climbed Mt. Niles (9,752 feet) with little difficulty. The next day they returned to Laggan following the route they had taken on the way in.

The First Trip from Lake Louise to Lake O'Hara via Abbot Pass

After arriving back at Laggan, Fay and Curtis stayed at the Lake Louise chalet for a few days, where they did some hiking and modest scrambling around the lake. Fay then decided that they would attempt cross Abbot Pass to Lake O'Hara. **Sam Allan** and **Yule Carryer,** a Stoney Indian porter, had made the trip from Lake O'Hara to Lake Louise in 1893, but no one had actually completed it in the other direction. Tom Wilson didn't have a guide to spare at that time and so young **Jimmy Brewster,** who was a working at the chalet as a pot-washer and looking after the horses in his spare time, was pressed into action.

The three left the chalet at first light on August 8th, and rowed to the end of the lake. Fay had been to the col of Abbot Pass on at least four occasions and had even spent a cold and rainy night there on August 3rd, 1896 – the day Phil Abbot perished. He knew the route well and led the party to the Plain of Six Glaciers and then down the moraine to the lower Victoria Glacier. Jim Brewster had never been to the Plain of Six Glaciers before. He had little climbing experience and had never used a rope or an ice axe, but this did not daunt his enthusiasm. Fay later said that Jim's youthful agility and bravado more than made up for his inexperience.

The party roped up, with Fay leading and Curtis in the middle. Travelling over good, hard snow, and then over a thick snow bridge crossing the bergschrund, they reached the summit of Abbot Pass by ten-thirty. It was a beautiful morning – warm and cloudless – and from the top of the pass they could look down on Lake Oesa and Lake O'Hara.

It was the second time that Fay had returned to Abbot Pass since his colleague Philip Abbot had been killed. As he reflected on the events of the tragedy and looked up at the treacherous, gleaming bands of ice, rock, and snow on the precipitous slopes of Mt. Lefroy, he felt a shiver go through him.

The descent from the summit of Abbot Pass to Lake Oesa, presented few difficulties, but they stayed roped as they guided the corpulent R. F. Curtis down the scree slopes to Lake Oesa, which was completely free of ice. They couldn't help but marvel at the incredible beauty of the spot as they paused and drank in both the water and the scenery.

From Lake Oesa they made their way to the cliffs at the Seven Sisters Falls above Lake O'Hara and found a goat trail leading to the lake itself. Fay and Curtis enthused at the beauty of the lake as it sparkled and shimmered with alternating shades of green and blue in the warmth of the late afternoon sun.

Making their way around the south side of the lake, they camped at Sargent's

Point, where the lake empties into Cataract Brook. The next morning the men hiked along Cataract Brook to Hector Station (at Wapta) where they caught a train to Laggan. Bidding farewell to Jim Brewster they carried on to Banff. It was Jim Brewster's first experience guiding, but it wouldn't be his last.

Young Jim Brewster on one of his first guiding trips.
He's descending Abbot Pass on the Lake O'Hara side with Professor Charles Fay and R. F. Curtis in 1898. Charles Fay probably took this picture.

The Climbing of Mt. Balfour—1898

On July 30th, **Reverend Harry P. Nichols**, **Reverend Charles L. Noyes**, **Charles S. Thompson** and **George M. Weed** left Laggan with **Ralph Edwards** as their guide on their way to conquer Mt. Balfour (10,741 feet) a. The group had travelled on the train from eastern Canada with Fay and Curtis to Laggan, but they parted company when they arrived. They immediately consulted with **Tom Wilson**, who suggested that they proceed by way of the Pipestone River and then over Dolomite Pass to Bow Lake. After drawing them a sketch of the landmarks to look for along their way and wishing them well, he assigned **Ralph Edwards** to guide them.

The group arrived at Bow Lake in record time, making the first known crossing of Dolomite Pass. While camped at Bow Lake, they climbed some minor peaks around the Bow Glacier. They then moved on to Hector Lake where they prepared for the ascent of Mt. Balfour.

On August 11th, Noyes, Thompson, and Weed left camp at first light and after a long trek across the glacier they reached the summit in the afternoon at four o'clock. Noyes described the climb as requiring "tact, agility and care", but they found it to be neither difficult nor dangerous.

J. Norman Collie and H. E. Stutfield taking a rest on the trail to Sunwapta Pass. (1898)

Other Early Climbers

Other early climbers in the Rockies and visitors to the chalet at Lake Louise prior to 1907 included **Mary Schaffer, George, William, and Mary Vaux**, the **Reverend George Kinney** (who later made an early attempt on Mt. Robson), **Herschel Parker**, and the University of Toronto professors, **A.P. Coleman and L.B. Stewart. Arthur O. Wheeler,** an early explorer, master surveyor, and founder of the Alpine Club of Canada, also spent many nights at the chalet.

The Reverends A.M. Gordon and S.H. Gray both made early climbs of Mt. Lefroy, and **W.S. Jackson** made one of the first ascents of Mt. Temple. **S.H. Baker** climbed Mt. Wilcox, Mt. Wapta, and Cascade Mountain as well as Howse Peak, Bow Peak and Mt Yoho.

The remarkable **Miss G.E. Benham** of London, England was one of the best women to ever climb in Canada. Before coming to Canada, she had many ascents in the Alps including Mont Blanc, Monte Rosa, the Matterhorn, the Weisshorn, and the Jungfrau. In the Rockies she conquered Victoria, Lefroy, Temple, Balfour, Assiniboine, Fay, and Gordon. While in the Selkirks she climbed Sir Donald, Dawson, Bonney, Rogers and the Swiss Peaks. Benham possessed excellent strength and stamina and was not intimidated by exposed heights.

Her first ascent of Mt. Fay, with guide **Christian Kaufmann,** caused great controversy and cost Kauffman his job. It was felt that Kaufmann had purposely deceived **Professor Fay** and slipped away with Miss Benham to capture the first ascent of the mountain that had unofficially been promised to the good professor. When Edward and Ernest Feuz learned of what Kaufmann had done they were furious. They marched into the Chateau manager's office and demanded that Kaufmann be fired. Soon after this he was paid out and "sent down the road".

H.C. Parker frequently visited the chalet at Lake Louise and made first ascents of Mt. Hungabee and Mt. Deltaform with Hans and Christian Kaufmann. He was an experienced climber and, successfully ascended Mt. Goodsir, Mt. Biddle, Mt. Lefroy, Mt. Victoria, Mt. Temple, Mt. Stephen, Mt. Dawson, Mt. Gordon, and Mt. Sir Donald. In the United States he climbed Mt. Rainier, Mt. Shasta and Mt. Hood. In the Swiss Alps he scaled Mont Blanc and the Matterhorn.

The popular **Miss H.L. Tuzo** from Surrey, England, was also a welcome guest at Lake Louise and climbed Mt. Victoria, Mt. Collier, and Mt. Tuzo (the seventh of the Ten Peaks) with guide **Christian Kaufmann.** In the Selkirks she climbed Sir Donald, Bonney, Rogers, Afton, the Swiss Peaks and Eagle Peak with guides **Edward Feuz Sr. and Christian Haesler.**

Val A. Fynn was a remarkable climber and an early member of the Alpine Club of Canada. He was a regular at Chateau Lake Louise for many years. He made many first ascents and discovered new routes in the Rockies. He specialized in face climbs and had an impressive record in Europe as well as in Canada. In 1909 he made the first ascent of Mt. Ringrose. He was the first to climb the northwest ridge of Mt. Sir Donald and in 1911 he traversed the Matterhorn. In 1917 he climbed both Mt. Lefroy and Mt. Victoria in one long day with Rudolf Aemmer. That season he also made the second ascent of Mt. Louis with Edward Feuz Jr. He was a regular at the Alpine Club camps and served as an unofficial guide. Although he climbed regularly with guides Rudolf Aemmer and Edward Feuz Jr., he also did many climbs without a guide. He was also a frequent contributor to the Alpine Club Journal.

All these personalities visited the Rockies and made their historic climbs prior to 1907.

Valere A. Fynn
An excellent climber, an early visitor to the Rockies, and a frequent contributor to the *Alpine Club Journal*.

Mrs E. Evelyn Berens of Kent, England On August 3rd, 1901 she became the first woman to climb Mt. Sir Donald at Rogers Pass. Her guides were Edward Feuz and Karl Schluneggar.

Chapter 4

Swiss Guides of the Rockies

No book about the Canadian Rockies would be complete without considerable time being devoted to the Feuz family. It is an understatement to suggest that this family of mountaineering guides, particularly Edward, Ernest, and Walter were an integral part of the history of Canadian mountaineering. They were legends in their own time and major celebrities at Lake Louise for many years. Much respected by their peers and the early pioneers of the area, they introduced and fostered proper mountaineering practices and guiding standards in the Canadian Rockies. Their presence in the Rockies spanned a period from 1899 until 1985 when Walter, the last of the brothers, passed away in Golden, British Columbia.

I was fortunate to have climbed with them on numerous occasions. Many evenings, over a bottle of wine or two in their chalet near the Chateau Lake Louise, I'd encourage them to tell me about their early adventurous days in the Rockies, when they were young men among the virgin, snow-capped peaks. In the dim, lantern-lit, log chalet, filled with the sweet aroma of the "Amphora" or "Sail" pipe tobacco they always smoked, I'd jot down notes as they reminisced.

Professional Guides Introduced to the Rockies

Realising that the Rockies presented world-class mountaineering opportunities and that they had excellent facilities to accommodate climbers at Banff, Lake Louise, Field, Yoho, and Glacier, the CPR decided to capitalize on the opportunity by encouraging tourists and mountaineers from all over the world to visit the mountains of western Canada. Under the direction of Basil Gardom, the CPR construction crews built many mountain trails and shelters for the convenience and enjoyment of hotel guests. At Glacier House in the Selkirk mountains broad trails were built to Avalanche Crest, the Asulkan Valley, the Abbot/Afton Crest, the Sir Donald loop, the Hermit range and Mt. Rogers, and to the Nakamu Caves. Most of these trails still exist as they were originally laid out and constructed—complete with authentic, European-style stone bridges. At Field and Yoho, crews built trails around Mount Stephen House, the Natural Bridge, Emerald Lake, the Yoho Valley and Twin Falls. At Lake Louise, trails were built to Saddle Back Mountain (where there was once a teahouse), Paradise Valley, Lake Agnes, the Plain of Six Glaciers, and Ross Lake. Along the way shelters were constructed at the best vantage points for spectacular views.

In the late 1880s and early 1890s, amateur hikers and mountaineers tackled the trails and the peaks unassisted by professional guides. Walter Wilcox and his colleagues from Yale, and Professor Fay and his fellow climbers in the Appalachian

Mountain Club along with some English enthusiasts were among the first explore the area.

But it was Phil Abbot's death on Mt. Lefroy on August 3rd, 1896 that set in motion a series of events that would transform climbing in the Canadian Rockies. As is often the case after a tragedy takes place there were those who look for someone to blame. Despite the fact that Phil Abbot was an experienced mountaineer (he had climbed in the Alps and the previous year he had climbed Mt. Rogers in the Selkirks and Mt. Hector in the Rockies) it was suggested that the CPR somehow negligent in not having professional mountaineering guides available to assist serious climbers and to ensure the safety of the foolhardy. Those who sought to keep the controversy alive overlooked the fact that Abbot had unroped and was the victim of his own misadventure. Some politicians and other wags even suggested that the sport of mountaineering be banned.

To deal with these pressures the CPR began to explore how they could hire professional guides. They naturally looked to Switzerland and to Interlaken and Zermatt as this was the Mecca for mountaineering at the turn of the 20th century.

Peter Sarbach – the First Professional Guide in the Rockies

The first of the Swiss guide came to the Rockies in 1897. **Peter Sarbach** from St. Niklaus, Switzerland was engaged by **Norman Collie** and **Professor Harold Dixon** to climb with them and **Professor Charles Fay** in an attempt to conquer Mt. Lefroy and avenge Philip Abbot's death. (Coincidentally, Sarbach had been Abbot's guide in the Alps in 1892 and had guided him up the impressive Matterhorn and the challenging Wiesshorn.)

Born in 1844 in St. Niklaus, in the shadow of the Matterhorn near the historic village of Zermatt, Sarbach was just twenty years old when he participated as a porter in one of Sir Edward Whymper's several attempts to climb the Matterhorn. He was fifty-three years of age when he first came to Canada. He quickly showed what an experienced mountain guide could contribute to climbing in the Rockies. On August 3rd, 1897, he led the first party to reach the summit of Mt. Lefroy. Two days later, he guided Collie, Fay, and Michael to a first ascent of Mt. Victoria. Following this he accompanied Collie and Dixon, and the AMC to the Waputik Icefield where he led a party in a first ascent of Mt. Gordon The group then proceeded to Howse Pass/Mistaya River area where Sarbach guided Collie and Baker up a peak that was named in his honour, Mt Sarbach (10, 260 feet.). St. Nicholas Peak (9,616 feet.) on the edge of the Wapta Icefield above Bow Lake was also named in his honour.

Peter Sarbach returned to Switzerland in the fall of 1897 and never returned to Canada. He continued to guide in the Alps for many years and died in 1930 at the age of eighty-six.

Fuez and Haesler Begin a Dynasty

The aftermath of the death of Phil Abbot in 1897, and the urging of several influential clients, such as the Vaux family and Charles Fay of the AMC, convinced the CPR that they should have professional guides available to ensure the safety of aspiring amateur mountaineers who were coming to Banff, Lake Louise, Field and Glacier House in increasing numbers. In 1898, through the offices of Cooks Travel Services in Interlaken, Switzerland, **Edouard (Edward) Feuz Sr.,** the chief guide of the district, was approached with an offer to go to Canada and set up a guiding program in the Rockies and in the Selkirks. After the details were worked out, Edward agreed to give it a try and in the spring of 1899, he left for Canada with his friend and colleague, Christian Haesler Sr. They went directly to Glacier House where they guided for the summer. This was the advent of Swiss guiding services in the Rockies. In all of the eighty-six years that followed – from 1899, until Walter, the last of the original Feuz brothers, died in 1985 – the Swiss guides never lost a client – although there were a few close calls.

During his brief time in Canada, Edward Sr. spent most of his time at Glacier House making Mt. Sir Donald his speciality. On this magnificent peak the senior Feuz developed many new routes. He also guided clients to first ascents of Mt. Sifton, Mt. Swanzy, Mt. Macoun, Mt. Hermit, Fleming Peak, and the first traverse of Mt. Avalanche.

Each fall, the Swiss guides returned to Interlaken to be with their families for the winter. Edouard Feuz Sr. crossed the Atlantic and the vast Canadian prairies some twenty-six times before he retired in 1911. He continued to climb in the Alps and guided at Interlaken until he was seventy years of age. He died in his beloved Interlaken on June 12th, 1944 at the age of eighty-five.

Christian Haesler Sr. returned to Interlaken in 1910 and stayed there for eight years until his wife died. He returned to Golden in 1918 to live with his son Christian Jr. and died there in 1924. During their first season at Glacier House, Edouard Feuz Sr. and Christian Haesler Sr. guided at Banff, Lake Louise, Field, and Rogers Pass.

In 1899 Professor Charles E. Fay, writing for the mountaineering journal *Appalachia* (Vol. IX 1899-01 P259), described his first introduction to the two guides from Interlaken.

> *I reached Glacier on the 3rd of August 1899. I believe I may assert with no immodesty that my advent was a source of unmixed pleasure to at least two of the varied company gathered on the platform to witness the event of the evening, the arrival of "No. 1" – as the westbound, overland train is commonly designated. I refer to the two unique-looking, bronze-faced men who, religious in the performance of their duty, paced the platform during these important half hours in hob-nailed shoes, pipe in mouth, and otherwise attired in regulation Swiss guides clothing. No pair of twin brothers were more nearly duplicates in raiment; no two guides ever more effectively supplemented one another in excellencies than did Christian Haesler and Edward Feuz of Interlaken. Glad they were, for they were longing for more enterprising labours than these promenade at the train station.*

In 1900, on the recommendation of Edouard Feuz Sr., the guides **Friedrich Michel, Jacob Muller and Karl Schluneggar** were hired to work at Glacier House in 1901. **Christian Bohren**, born in 1865 at Grindelwald, Switzerland, also came to Canada to guide for the CPR. He was stationed at Field and on August 31, 1901 he and **Christian Haesler Sr.** guided **James Outram** to a first ascent of the impressive Mt. Assiniboine.

Edward's oldest son, **Edward Jr.** came to Glacier House for the 1903 season and his second son **Ernest,** and his nephew **Rudolf Aemmer** arrived in 1909. After the CPR established the Swiss Village of Edelweiss near Golden in 1912, most of the guides and their families made this their permanent home and remained in Golden throughout the winters. The Feuz brothers were often employed at Chateau Lake Louise and at Lake O'Hara Lodge to cut and store ice from the lake for use in the summers, to shovel snow from the roof of the hotel, and to act as general caretakers.

Of the six traditional Swiss style houses built on the steep hillside above Golden, only four were permanently occupied. Rudolf Aemmer occupied the top left chalet, while the top right one was occupied by Walter Feuz, (It had been Edward's until 1915). The lower left chalet was Ernest's, and the centre one was Christian Haesler's.
The two on the right were usually empty or reserved for guests. These chalets remain a landmark in the Golden area. The wives of the guides did not like the location of the chalets, as it was a long walk into Golden to get groceries and other supplies and the children had a long way to walk to school. They also felt isolated from the community.

From 1900 until 1905, **Christian Haesler Sr.** was stationed at Mount Stephen House in Field during the climbing season, together with **Fritz Michel**, the **Kaufmann brothers, Hans and Christian**.

Edward Feuz Jr. was nineteen when he arrived at Glacier House in 1903 and he guided in the Rockies until he retired in 1949. He obtained his guiding licence in Grindelwald in 1908 and by 1930 he had over fifty first ascents of peaks over ten thousand feet. to his credit in Canada. His many regular clients included, Roy Thorington, Howard Palmer, Lillian Gest, J.W. Hickson, Katie Gardiner, and John Linn, the pianist at Chateau Lake Louise.

In 1912, Lake Louise became the headquarters for Fritz Michel, Christian and Hans Kaufmann, Christian Bohren, Christian Jorimann, Gottfried Feuz and Christian Haesler Jr. In 1917, Mount Stephen House at Field was closed and the guides there were transferred to Glacier House and to Lake Louise. In 1920, the guide's chalet was built at Lake Louise and Christian Haesler Jr. and Ernest Feuz were transferred there for the 1926 season.

Ernest   Emil   Suzanna   E. Feuz   Ed Jr.   Ida Emma   Frieda

    Walter   Werner   Clara

The Feuz Family
This Photo was taken in Interlaken in 1903

Edouard Feuz Sr. and Christian Haesler Sr.
Taken at Glacier House in 1899 by Mary Vaux

Edouard Feuz Sr. was born in Lauterbrunnen in 1859. He earned his guiding license in Switzerland in 1881 and began guiding at Glacier House in 1899. In 1911 he and his wife Suzanna returned to Switzerland and retired in Interlaken.

Christian Haesler Sr. was born in Gsteigwiler, Switzerland in 1857. He guided in Canada until 1910 when he returned to his home village in Switzerland. In 1919 his wife Emma died and he returned to Golden to live near his son Christian Jr. who was working as a guide for the CPR. He died in Golden in 1924 and is interned in the Golden Cemetery.

Early Swiss Guides
Back row – Peter Schlunegger , Jacob Muller and Hans Kaufmann
Front Row – Peter Kaufmann, Christian Kaufmann and Edward Feuz

Swiss Guides at Glacier House
Edward Feuz, Friedrich Michel, Jacob Muller and Karl Schlunegger

Edward Feuz Sr.

A rare photo of Edward Feuz Sr. It was printed in the article "The Ascent of Mt. Macoun", by Rev. J.C. Herdman in the Canadian Alpine Journal of 1907. He can be considered as the "Father of Mountaineering" in Canada for he and his sons nurtured, fostered and developed the tradition of mountaineering in the Rockies and the Selkirks. He came to Canada in 1899 with his life-long friend and fellow climber Christian Haesler Sr. and established a dynasty. This photo of Edward was taken in his beloved Interlaken in 1931. He died in Interlaken on June 12, 1944.

Building Abbot Pass Hut

In 1922, Edward Feuz Jr. and his brothers, along with Rudolf Aemmer and Christian Haesler Jr., proposed that an alpine hut be built at Abbot pass on the col between Mt. Victoria and Mt. Lefroy. The idea was approved and work began in August of that year. The guides assisted CPR Construction Superintendent, **Basil Gardom,** in the construction. At 9,598 feet the Abbot Pass Hut was the highest alpine cabin in North America for many years.

Jimmy Brewster's horses and mules were used to pack the cement, timbers, and supplies up Abbot Pass as far as the bergschund. From there the supplies were winched up to the top with a cable and a windless. By October the construction was completed. When one sees this solid stone building, one is struck by the enormity of the task. In early 1923, the Swiss guides packed up all the blankets, furniture, and kitchen gear to the hut from the end of the trail and climbers officially opened it for use in June.

I've stayed at Abbot Hut on many occasions over the years and always enjoyed the warmth of the thick, red Hudson Bay blankets that were once kept in a trunk upstairs. Strangely though, I've never slept well in that high cabin. As I mentioned in my book *Lake Louise at its Best*, I've frequently been awakened by what sounded like someone attempting to get in the door or tapping at the windows. Strange sounds, like someone calling or coming up the pass from below, have disturbed my sleep. Perhaps they are the spirits of Abbot and Geddes, each of whom fell to their deaths from the treacherous cliffs of Mt. Lefroy and died from their plunge of more than 1,500 feet to the glacier below. Or maybe they are the spirits of the three Mexican women and their hapless guide, who missed the route on Mt. Victoria, slipped on the steep, icy slopes and fell two thousand feet to their deaths on July 30, 1952. Then again, it may have been the spirit of the unfortunate climber who perished after a fall into a crevasse near the top of Abbot Pass – not far from the cabin door. Perhaps if I hadn't known of so many tragedies that occurred near that wind-swept, desolate cabin, I would have slept more soundly.

The Plain of Six Glaciers Teahouse

In 1924, Edward Feuz Jr. planned to build a Swiss-style log chalet at the Plain of Six Glaciers. The CPR Hotel Department took over the concession however, and under the direction of Basil Gardom, a construction team built a two story stone building was built in 1926. In addition, three frame cabins for sleeping. Mrs. Edward Feuz Jr. managed this teahouse for many summers, attending to the needs of the many climbers and hikers in the area. In later years it was taken over by Irene Stanfield and following Irene, B.J. Mills and Pat Denholm (Turner) became the proprietors. For the past forty-five years Joy Kimball has managed the teahouse. (See picture Page 4)

Glacier House Burns to the Ground

The doors of Glacier House closed for the last time on September 15th, 1924 and it burned to the ground the following spring. For thirty-eight years it had served mountain climbers and hikers, but with the advent of the automobile, and the hotel's subsequent inaccessibility by highway, the clientele dwindled. The only access to the hotel prior to the building of the Rogers Pass highway in the early 1960s was by rail, and few travelled by rail after the automobile became popular. When Glacier House closed, so did the Nakamu Caves. After that, only serious climbers journeyed to Glacier. They arrived by train and pitched their tents near the grounds where the magnificent hotel had once stood. In 1941 the Alpine Club of Canada built the A.O. Wheeler Hut, not far from where the hotel once stood. Until the road went through, those who travelled in and out of the area by train were the only ones to use it.

For many years after the hotel closed, the Swiss guides and their families returned to the area both to climb and to harvest the large blueberries and blackberries that grew under Avalanche Crest – just above the old snow sheds of the railway. The fruit they picked was put in jars and enjoyed by their families all winter long. Berries still thrive around the Rogers Pass area but the many grizzlies and black bears that frequent the area also seek after them. This often makes a berry-picking excursion a memorable event!

As the area presents excellent mountaineering challenges, the Swiss guides returned each year with their clients to climb Mt. Sir Donald, Mt. Uto, Mt. Rogers, Mt. Tupper, Mt. Bonney, and the Swiss Peaks. They also maintained the Hermit Hut as well as the hut at Glacier Circle.

After Glacier House burned, Edward Feuz Jr., and his brothers, Ernest and Walter, were stationed at Lake Louise where they lived in the new Swiss chalet during the summer months. Some years they stayed throughout the winter as caretakers at Chateau Lake Louise and were often pressed into action to shovel snow off the roof of the hotel when it got dangerously high and heavy. They also helped cut ice from the lake and pack it in sawdust to be stored until the summer. They were on hand to fight the great fire that destroyed much of the Chateau on July 3rd, 1924 and they helped Basil Gardom build the teahouses at Lake Agnes and the Plain of Six Glaciers as well as the Abbot Pass Hut, and the Swiss guides chalet near the Chateau.

The three Feuz brothers followed in their father's footsteps and became some of the most successful and prominent guides ever to climb in the Canadian Rockies. They were small in stature – not much over five feet tall – but somehow they seemed taller than that. Soft-spoken, they were tough and wiry with handsome features. Dapper in appearance, they usually dressed in white shirts, ties, grey Swiss tweed jackets, wool or leather knickers, and grey wool knee stockings. They seldom climbed without their Tyrolean hats and they loved their large, curved Peterson pipes which they would smoke on mountain summits or in the evenings in their chalet.

Edward Jr., Ernest and Walter guided clients on well over a thousand climbs, many of them first ascents. Edward Jr. alone had over one hundred first ascents in forty-one years of climbing in the Selkirks and the Rockies. Ernest had well over fifty and Walter had twenty-two in fourteen years. The brothers admitted that they lost track of the number of times they climbed the regular route on Mt. Victoria, Mt. Lefroy, Mt. Temple, Mt. Hungabee, Mt. Huber, Mt. Odaray, Mt. Sir Donald, the Swiss Peaks and Mt. Rogers. Their skill and judgment was remarkable and in all their years of guiding they never lost a client or sustained a serious injury – although Edward Jr. almost lost his own life when buried by an avalanche in Abbot Pass, and Nick Morant was almost killed by a grizzly bear near Sherbrook Lake.

After 1942, Walter became a caretaker at Lake O'Hara and later the boatman at Lake Louise. Although he suffered from vertigo in his later years he cheerfully looked after the rental, maintenance, and repair of the canoes at the Chateau. His habit of using binoculars to watch for climbers on Mt. Victoria enabled him in 1954 to alert rescuers that four members of the Mexican climbing party had fallen to their deaths. Brother Ernest, with Harry Green, led the rescue effort to get the survivors down safely.

A pack-train taking supplies part way up Abbot Pass
to build the hut in 1922

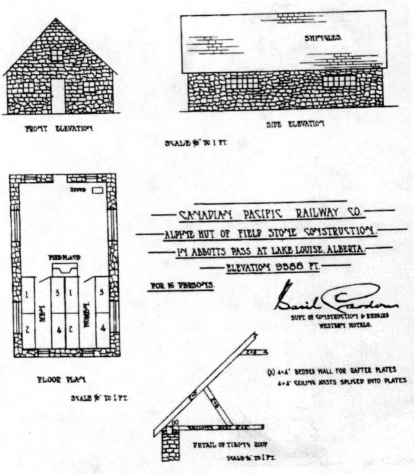

The original plans for the Abbot Hut signed by Basil Gardom

Abbot Hut

Situated on the col between Mt. Victoria and Mt. Lefroy, this hut was built in 1922 by the Basil Gardom (Superintendent of Construction-Western Region of the CPR) and the Swiss guides.

Abbot Pass Hut

In 1922, Edward Feuz and his brothers Ernest and Walter, together with their cousin, Rudolf Aemmer and brother-in-law Christian Haesler assisted Basil Gardom (the Western Superintendent of Construction for the CPR), with the construction of the Abbot Pass Hut at the col between Mt. Victoria and Mt. Lefroy. Situated some 9,598 feet above sea level, it was the highest alpine cabin in North America.

Work was begun in August 1922 and was completed in October of that year. The Brewster's supplied the horses and mules that were used to pack the cement, timbers and supplies up Abbot Pass, as far as the big bergschrund. From there, it was winched up to the top by cable and a windless. Two Italian stonemasons from Banff assisted in the construction and when you see this solid stone, mountain hut, you're struck by the wonderful workmanship with which it was built. In early 1923, all the blankets, furniture and kitchen gear were packed up from the end of the trail by the Swiss guides. It was officially opened for use in June of 1923.

Basil Gardom – Master Builder of the CPR

Basil Gardom was without doubt the master builder of the CPR. He was the Western Region Superintendent of Construction for the railroad for many years. Among other achievements, he was instrumental in rebuilding the wing on the Chateau after the Great Fire of 1924. He also built all the teahouses and mountain huts around Lake Louise, the staff residences, the new wing on the Banff Springs Hotel, a large addition to the Empress Hotel, and the Crystal Gardens in Victoria.

Born in Leamington, England, Basil met Gabrielle Gwladys Bell from Swansea, Wales while on assignment at Lake Louise in the early 1920's. Gabrielle was working at the Chateau at the time and in due course they fell in love and were married. Their son Garde was born on July 17, 1924.

Basil and Gabrielle lost all their belongings in the Great Fire of July 3, 1924 but they never made a claim for any damages. They were richly compensated in another way however, for two weeks later their son was born. Young Garde was the first white baby to spend the winter at the Chateau and probably the youngest trail rider ever to ride from Lake Louise to Moraine Lake when at two years of age he did so with his parents – riding in the saddle in front of his father.

Garde B. Gardom went on to become a prominent lawyer, a Q.C. and a much loved Lieutenant Governor of the great province of British Columbia.

Basil and Gabriella loved Lake Louise and the Chateau and visited it often throughout their lives. Upon their death, their ashes were scattered in the poppy fields at the front of the hotel which look out upon Mt. Victoria and the magnificent lake that meant so much to them both.

Edward Jr. and Ernest climbed well into their senior years. Ernest was in his seventy-second year when he led Phyllis Hart and C.C. Cameron a staff member of Deer Lodge, up Mt. Hungabee in 1961. A year later at age seventy-three, I accompanied him up the same mountain in mid-August. One of his regular clients was set to go with us but he took sick that morning and remained in the Elizabeth Parker Hut while the two of us made the climb. We had a fine day together and it was a special treat for me to have Ernest all to myself. We moved along quickly and it took us just three and a half hours from the top of Opabin Pass to the summit. Ernest was in fine form that day and told me many stories of the experiences he'd had in the mountains. I remember that he spoke with great affection and admiration about Conrad Kain and Walter Perren. He also told me of his climbs with Georgia Englehard, Katie Gardiner, Lillian Gest, Harry Green, and Val Fynn.

On his eightieth birthday, in 1964, Edward Feuz Jr. led some clients up Mt. Temple and was later featured in *Ripley's Believe It Or Not*. He had over one hundred first ascents to his credit, seventy of which were over ten thousand feet. At the age of eighty-two, Edward was featured in a television special as he led a group of climbers over Abbot Pass from Lake Louise to Lake O'Hara – an amazing feat for a man of that age.

Climbing with these phenomenal legends and sitting on the tops of many peaks with them holds precious memories for me. The brothers were in their mid-to-late seventies then and I'd listen carefully as they'd look out over a sea of peaks and talk of their climbing experiences. Sometimes Ernest would lean back, a pipe in his mouth, and gaze out over the snow-capped peaks with a wistful, almost melancholy, look in his soft, brown eyes. I knew that it was a special time that would not come again and I tried to savour every moment – still it went by all too quickly.

The Swiss Guides
Ernest Feuz, Rudolph Aemmer, Edward Feuz Jr., Christian & Walter Feuz

The Swiss Chalet at Lake Louise
A home for the Swiss guides at Lake Louise was built in 1920 by the guides themselves, under the direction of Basil Gardom the Superintendent of Construction (Western Region) of the CPR.

Walter Feuz is at the top of the stairs on the left and on the right is Christian Haesler. Rudolf Aemmer is walking down the stairs with a new rope to meet Georgia Englehard who looks like she's dressed for the evening concert in the lobby of the Chateau.

Ernest died in Golden on May 14th, 1966 at the age of seventy-seven. He had officially guided from 1909 until 1960 in the employ of the CPR but he also climbed well after that with his friends, just for the joy of it. At the Glacier Camp in July of 1947, Ernest was elected an Honorary Life Member of the Alpine Club of Canada. In recognition of his "unselfish services and friendship towards the Club," the club presented him with an illuminated life membership certificate.

Harry Green wrote Ernest's obituary for the 1967 *Alpine Club Journal*, *remembering him as a friend.*

> *Ernest was my companion on many wonderful days in the mountains. On the high hills, when time permitted, he loved to pause for a while and enjoy the beauty all around us. Ernest will live in the memories of all who climbed with him as a gallant mountaineer and friend and as one to whom are owed countless happy days in the mountains. (P 133)*

Edward Jr. climbed and guided in Canada from 1903 until 1980. His last ascent was the Tower of Babel in the summer of 1980. He passed away on April 13th, 1981 at the age of ninety-six, and his ashes were scattered over the mountains he loved. His obituary appeared in the 1982 edition of the *Canadian Alpine Journal*:

> *Edward was an important figure in Canadian mountaineering history and a chat with him was always of great interest to*

a mountaineer. I was greatly impressed with his skill and personality – to watch him cut steps up frozen snow, as fast as a party could walk, was an education – Guides now are a different breed and we shall not see Edward's like again. Respected and admired by all who knew him, he left his mark for all time on the Canadian mountain scene."(P 44)

Walter joined his brothers in passing over the "Great Divide" in 1984, at the age of ninety. With his death came the end of the golden age of mountaineering in the Rockies. Both Ernest and Walter were buried in the little cemetery in Golden not far from the Columbia River, the Kicking Horse River canyon, and the Selkirk Mountains overlooking the rugged peaks of the Purcell Range. This spot is just about half way between Lake Louise and Rogers Pass in the Selkirks Range. Buried near them are their colleagues, Christian Haesler Sr. and his son Christian Jr.

Learning the Mountain Pace[4]

John Linn, the much loved pianist at Chateau Lake Louise, and Phyllis Hart, the teletype operator, were long-time friends of Ernest and Edward Feuz, and enjoyed many exciting climbs with the brothers. When I knew them in the late 19560s and 1960's, they'd take some strenuous hikes, but they usually wouldn't climb without Ernest. Every so often they'd say: "Roger, Ernest is coming tomorrow from Golden. We're going to do the Needles and the Devil's Thumb with him. Can you come with us?"

Could I come? Opportunities to climb with Ernest could not be missed and even then I appreciated his legendary stature. That evening, if I were the Night Houseman at the Chateau, I'd get the lobby, front offices, and stairs cleaned and vacuumed in record time. This would enable me to collapse onto a ballroom couch for a good night's sleep and be ready to go early the following morning. If I weren't the Night Houseman, I'd trade shifts with whoever was, so I'd be free the next day.

Ernest, with his well-used climbing rope over one shoulder and across his chest, would appear early and ready to climb in his grey wool knickers and knee-high stockings. He always carried his ice axe in his left hand, leading the way with his slow, regular, never-stopping, mountain pace. John would follow behind him, then Phyllis, and I would bring up the rear. Up we'd go to Mirror Lake with slow deliberate strides and then on up to the Lake Agnes teahouse. The first time I went climbing with Ernest, John, and Phyllis, I thought I'd impress them with my strength and stamina. With great speed I pressed on ahead of them, past the Fairview ladies residence and up the trail. It wasn't long before I was winded and had to rest while I waited for them to catch up. In a few moments, Ernest and the others appeared, moving ever onward with slow, steady, short steps – carefully placing one boot ahead of the other on the trail.

---

4 An early version of this story was told in my first book, *Lake Louise at its Best*

Ernest Feuz and Georgia Englehard sitting on the porch of the Swiss guides chalet at Lake Louise

Ernest Feuz and Georgia Englehard nearing the summit of Mt. Victoria. Lake Louise is in the background.

The Swiss Chalets at Eidelwiess near Golden
These chalets are still standing. They were build by the C.P.R. as homes for the Swiss guides in 1912. These pictures were taken in 2000.

Mount Stephen House at Field

Glacier House at Rogers Pass -1910

Ernest didn't say a word as he passed and didn't break his pace. John and Phyllis followed dutifully as they proceeded onward and upward without comment. I fell in behind, but soon I felt rested and stepped up the pace and passed them a second time, giving it my all up the trail. Again I became winded, and this time my thighs and calf-muscles were burning. I also had a pain in my side and had to stop to rest again, feeling like a real fool. In a few minutes, Ernest, Phyllis and John appeared still plodding along with slow, carefully-placed steps. Again they passed me, and again no one spoke a word.

Unbelievably this scenario repeated itself once more before they reached Mirror Lake ahead of me. Exhausted, I finally caught up to where they had stopped to admire the lake and the waterfall tumbling down from Lake Agnes, which was just above us. Collapsing on a stump nearby I tried to catch my breath. Ernest, John and Phyllis however talked easily and seemed hardly puffed.

Suddenly Ernest turned and addressed me – almost sharply. "You charge up da hill like crazy pack-horse!" he scolded. "You make your feet do all the vork and you look like old voman puffing and panting, red in da face each time ve pass you again. Now I show you da mountain pace. You not forget! Follow me!"

Sheepishly I followed him to the left of the lake and up the steep trail leading to the top of the waterfall, while John and Phyllis took the trail to the right. As the trail began to steepen, he stopped and said, "Now I vant you to follow me slowly and valk in my foot steps. Don't charge ahead. Take each step slowly, carefully, and don't valk on your toes or pushing off vit da foot. Place da boot flat on the ground and let da tigh muscle do da vork. Lean into da trail and place da one foot flat ahead of da udder. Try to get da rhythm. Vatch me now and follow. Ve go up for tea!"

Dutifully, I followed Ernest's example as he slowly proceeded up the trail. I tried to concentrate on each step and to place each foot flat on the trail as he suggested, rather than pressing forward on the balls of my feet. This time I let my thighs do the work, as I followed Ernest's slow deliberate steps. Before I knew it, we were at the top of the trail and on the flat slabs of rock at the top of the waterfall, across from the teahouse. Waiting, Phyllis and John smiled and waved at us from the porch where they sat.

Then Ernest reached out and shook my hand. As he did so, he looked carefully into my eyes and smiled briefly as the edges of his own dark brown eyes wrinkled ever so slightly. "You vill be good climber if you listen and come mit me sometimes. I show you what you need to know. I call you at hotel when I have place on da rope for you; it cost you nutting. Now, vee have da tea."

We proceeded to the teahouse, stepping over the little bridge that crossed the outlet stream of Lake Agnes and joined John and Phyllis. Sitting on the porch, we enjoyed "da tea" and looked out over the broad Bow River Valley and the hazy Pipestone Range far below. I sat to the side of our group so I wouldn't interfere with their conversation, yet I could still listen as they talked.

Irene Stanfield was the manager of the Lake Agnes teahouse at that time, and she welcomed John, Phyllis, and Ernest with warm hugs. With her white apron on and her hair pulled back, Irene scurried about as busily as the ground squirrels on the porch and the rocks nearby. She chattered on about how the season had been and inquired as to how things were down below at the Chateau. Then we were off again. We hiked along the cobalt-blue Lake Agnes and then on to the end of the lake and up the switchbacks to the Big Beehive and the Devil's Thumb col, where there is a lovely alpine meadow and larch trees. On the way up the switchbacks, I followed Phyllis and practiced the mountain pace, staying in line, and not charging ahead again. I had learned my lesson.

Ernest roped up in the little alpine meadow at the top of the Big Beehive so that we could practice carrying the coils of rope before we started the actual climb. He showed me the knots he tied and then had me practice them. We turned right and proceeded through the alpine meadow to the Devil's Thumb and then across to the Needles, taking turns standing above the "Eye of the Needle". Ernest belayed us up the steeper pitches, stopping at intervals to teach me how and when to belay. Then he led us to the top where we took off our packs and had lunch. Ernest never un-roped on the top of a mountain and always cautioned people to sit still. He had once seen an inexperienced hiker un-rope, take a step back while taking a photograph, and fall from the summit to the punishing rocks below. Apparently he never walked too well after that mishap.

I also learned that whether snow and ice was expected or not, Ernest always carried his ice axe with him. Even on flat trails and mountains such as the Needles in the late summer, where no snow was likely to be found, Ernest has his ice axe. I asked him about this one afternoon and he told me that it was his "third leg." He didn't want to wait until there was an emergency to use it, but preferred that it become a part of him, ready at any time. With a twinkle in his eye he said: "I can always use it to fight off da bear if I have to, or to open can of 'uice!". From that time on, I always carried an ice axe, even on simple hikes to the Plain of Six Glaciers.

After lunch, Ernest knocked out his pipe and re-filled it with some fresh Sail tobacco. He lit it, took a few puffs, and began to point out different peaks in the distance as he told stories about them. Sitting behind John and Phyllis, I listened intently as they quietly discussed whether Mt. Assiniboine – far in the distance – had more snow on it than usual. They commented on the condition of the Mitre and mused as to whether Abbot Pass would be easy or difficult to negotiate that season. This quiet half-hour was one of the most memorable times I ever spent in the mountains. I knew even then that I needed to remember every word, every sound, and every detail of my time with Ernest.

Since then, I've taught many new hikers and climbers the mountain pace, just as Ernest taught me. Still today, as I hike along a trail and am passed by some young buck charging up the slope in sneakers – or worse, a new pair of boots, I'm reminded of Ernest. I can almost hear him mutter "Crazy pack-horse! once again. In a few minutes, sure enough, I pass the panting, red-faced youth as he sits gasping beside the trail. Somehow, he looks a bit like I did when I was young and eager, too many years ago. Some things never change.

During the summer of 2002, I took three of my sons on the short hike up to Lake Agnes. The boys were aged nine, thirteen, and sixteen. As usual, I started out using the slow mountain pace that Ernest had taught me so many years ago. Joel, the nine-year-old, followed me and stayed close as we moved slowly upward. The thirteen and sixteen-year-olds sprinted ahead, burning up the trail with youthful enthusiasm. Before we reached the quarter-way mark, we caught up to with the two speedsters. I didn't say a word as I passed them. Soon the two passed us again, but we caught up to them by the half-way point where the trail switches back to the right. They were panting with their shirts off and wanted me to carry their discarded clothes in the pack I carried. Joel and I just kept on going, never altering our pace.

We were passed once again, but by the time we reached Mirror Lake the two sprinters were exhausted. One was lying down beside the lake and the other was lounging on a large log. They wanted to go back, and complained that I hadn't truthfully told them how long and strenuous the hike would be!

As I looked at the pathetic pair with amusement, I couldn't help but recall Ernest muttering long ago: *"Crazy pack-horses!"*. I could almost hear him chuckle as he looked down from on high. Somehow I felt that he was very close to us at that moment.

Other Notable Swiss Guides

Other guides from Switzerland who came to the Rockies from the Interlaken area included: **Hans, Peter,** and **Christian Kaufman, Peter Schlunegger, Jacob Muller, Rudolf Aemmer,** and **Christian Haesler Jr.** They each returned to Switzerland after spending many years guiding clients for the CPR.

Christian Haesler Jr

Christian Haesler Jr. obtained his Swiss guide's licence in 1912 and came out to Golden that year. On his arrival he married Rosa Feuz, the daughter of Rudolf Feuz. That year Walter Feuz also came to Golden from Interlaken. (Photograph on page 218 shows their arrival in Golden.)

The CPR first stationed Christian Haesler Jr. at Field and then he was transferred to Glacier House, where he stayed until it closed in 1924. Christian knew every peak and route in the Selkirks and frequently climbed with Ernest Feuz. Together they maintained the Hermit Hut and the Glacier Circle Hut, taking many climbing parties there. He eventually transferred to Lake Louise and Miss Lillian Gest became one of his regular clients. She climbed with him each year from 1932 until his death in October of 1940. In 1933, he made the first traverse of the South Tower of Mt. Goodsir, from north to south, with Katie Gardiner, Lillian Gest, and his younger brother Walter. They then ascended the demanding North Tower.

Together with Edward and Ernest Feuz and Conrad Kain, Christian was a regular guide at the Alpine Club summer camps. Sadly the last years of his life were not happy ones as misfortune fell upon him in the form of a series of tragedies. In 1937, he broke his ankle coming down from Mt. Stephen. Shortly afterwards his son Bill was accidentally killed in the basement of their home while experimenting with a home chemistry set. In September of 1939, Christian and Nick Morrant, the well-known Banff photographer, were hiking above Sherbrook

Lake when they were attacked by a grizzly bear. Both men were badly mauled and Haesler's recovery in the Banff hospital took several months. Shortly after his discharge, his wife became ill and died. These tragedies devastated Christian and he passed away in Banff in October, 1940. Lillian Gest wrote Christian's obituary for the *Alpine Club Journal*:

> *During the summer of 1940, Chris made a valiant attempt to pull himself together and to regain his strength. He continually exercised his wounded arm to develop the muscles again and refused to let his misfortunes over-whelm him. His friends hoped and believed he would succeed but realized that his death was probably a welcome release from the cruel fates which seemed to pursue him. (1940 p.231-234)*

Rudolf Aemmer

Rudolf Aemmer received his Swiss guides licence in 1907 and came to Canada to guide for the CPR in 1909. He went straight to Lake Louise where he remained until his retirement in 1949 at the age of sixty-five. At the end of the 1911 climbing season, he and Ernest Feuz returned for a brief visit to Interlaken. While there, Rudolf, Ernest, Christian Haesler Jr., all married pretty frauleins. They returned to Canada in the late spring of 1912 bringing their wives with them and young Walter Feuz, who went to work at Glacier House as a bellboy.

At Lake Louise, Rudolf lived with the other Swiss guides in the chalet that the CPR built for them in 1920. The next year, he was instrumental in the rescue of Mrs. Stone from Mt. Eon near Mt. Assiniboine. Rudolf's account of that rescue, which he recounted to George Stephen, was published in The Canadian Alpine Journal of 1963.

The Rescue of Mrs. Stone–1921 As told by Rudolf Aemmer

Dr. Stone fell Sunday at about 6 p.m. He was unroped to get further on. His wife called up to ask how he was doing and he replied.'This must be the top; I can't see any more.' A few minutes later he fell past her and she, shocked, spent the night right where she was at the bottom of the summit chimney.

The next day, she climbed down past the snow in search for her husband's body. Failing to find it she spent Monday night on the mountain. The next day, she continued down, but did not traverse along the ledge that would have brought her to an easy decent. Instead she got down to another ledge by "roping off", but found it was a dead end. She had no strength to climb up again, but she made an attempt by piling up stones to try to reach a hold. She remained on that very ledge until the following Sunday morning.

Thursday evening at Chateau Lake Louise, the manager, Mr. Evans, told me that the RCMP commanded me to go to Banff, as there had been an accident. I drove in the truck with Warden Phillips over the unfinished road and spent the night in Banff at the barracks. The next day, Phillips, Bill Peyto and the RCMP man and I rode by horse – in one day – to Assiniboine camp.

Saturday we went over Wonder Pass on foot, past Marvel Lake and up Marvel Pass. Here we found the Stone's camp. We searched the contents and came across a written report by Messrs. Lindsay and Wakefield a year earlier, stating that they had attempted the north ridge of Eon and had failed. I figured that since he had his wife with him, Dr. Stone would not try this difficult route. So we pushed on around to the south side and bivouacked at the tree line for the night. We had no blankets or tents. We just lay down.

Sunday morning, I studied that mountain from the south side and found a ledge. We climbed along this ledge to the ridge to get a better look at the mountain. I was just bringing down the binoculars when I heard a scream. (Mrs. Stone later told me that she did not see us but kept shouting in case someone was near). Right away I spotted her with the glasses, in her trapped position. We climbed along the ledge above her and found her rope where she had rappelled. I roped down to her on my rope and when Mrs. Stone saw me she said: 'Oh Rudolf, I knew you would come.'

The men above pulled Mrs. Stone up to the ledge as I guided her feet into the footholds. Mrs. Stone was too weak to walk after seven days of exposure with no food or water, so I carried her in a rope sling on my back for four hours, down to the tree-line. The others helped as much as possible but they were not used to climbing mountains.

We made Mrs. Stone as comfortable as possible at the tree-line, using the canvass stretchers as a lean-to and feeding her sugary tea. Dr. Bell soon arrived to take over as far as Mrs. Stone was concerned. Next day, Bill Peyto and I spent the day tracing all the couloirs and gullies, with water running under the snow, without finding Dr. Stone's body. Tuesday we tried again, but the changing weather forced us down. I told Bill, 'It's no use risking our own lives.' We know Dr. Stone is dead,' for Mrs. Stone had told us what she knew of his direction of fall.

By now, Mrs. Stone had recovered sufficiently to be transported back to Banff by stretcher, and we took three days getting her there. I later returned with three others (Ernest Feuz and Conrad Kain) and we recovered Dr. Stone's body. (George Stephen "Memories of a Guide" p.103-108)

Rudolf was handsome in a rugged way, and this brought him parts in several movies that were shot at Lake Louise. In particular he played John Barrymore's double in the acclaimed *"Eternal Love"* also staring Camilla Horn.

In 1922, Rudolf assisted in the building of the Swiss-style stone hut at the top of Abbot's Pass. He lived at the Chateau and in Golden until he retired. Returning to his beloved Interlaken in 1950, Rudolf lived happily there until his death in the summer of 1973. Much loved and admired by his many clients, friends, and colleagues he made a great contribution to the Swiss guiding tradition in the Rockies. Even today I get letters from older former staff members of the Chateau remarking on how much they admired Rudolf and telling of the fun they had with him, both at the Chateau and on the trail.

The arrival of the Swiss guides and their brides in Golden in July of 1912
(From Left to Right)–Elise Feuz, Walter Feuz, Ernest Feuz, Rosa Haesler,
Christian Haesler Jr., Clara Aemmer, Rudolf Aemmer, and Joanna Heimann

Ernest Feuz and Rudolf Aemmer

A photo taken in 1930 by Nick Morant. Rudolf's good looks landed him a part in the movie "Eternal Love" filmed on the Victoria Glacier. Rudolf acted as a double for John Barrymore.

Rudolf Aemmer and John Barrymore (left)

Taken while filming "Eternal Love" in 1928 and sent to Rudolf with best wishes from John Barrymore.

Camilla Horn the leading lady of "Eternal Love"
Filmed in 1928 at Lake Louise.

One of the last pictures taken of Rudolf Aemmer
Taken by Nick Morant "The Gentleman Photographer of the CPR"

Ernest Feuz at a cabin at Lake O'Hara

How the Guides Were *Really* Treated!

A perceptive writer, probably a Swiss guide, wrote about how the early Swiss guides were treated by their clients:

> *Swiss Guides—they haul them up the cliffs, lower them down precipices, place their hands and feet where they should go, soothe their ruffled feelings, carry their paraphernalia and cheerfully assume responsibility for life and death; then, just before reaching the summit, they stand to one side, take off their hats and say, "After you, Sir", You step on the summit, and according to mountaineering etiquette, have made a first ascent or otherwise, that is blazoned forth far and wide.*

Conrad Kain made a similar observation after his first experience guiding for the Alpine Club in O'Hara and the Yoho Valley.

> *At the end of the Alpine Club tour I saw the Canadian tourists have the same attitude as some of the Europeans: In the valley the guide is soon forgotten. In the mountains and in camp he is "dear friend!" None of the thirty people thought about me. A Swiss guide there said to me: "They won't trouble themselves any more about you. I know the Alpine Club all right: in the valley or the dining room they would rather be guideless. (Thorington, 1935)*

A bronze statue at Lake Louise in tribute to the Swiss guides of the Rockies

Edward Feuz Jr. 1915
Photo taken by Byron Harmon

Walter Feuz
Like his brothers Walter was an excellent climber and guide. He also served as the "Boatman" at Chateau Lake Louise for many years and was the last of his brothers to pass away. His death in 1984 brought an end the "Golden Age" of mountaineering in the Canadian Rockies. (Photo taken by Nick Morant).

The graves of Ernest and Walter Feuz and Christian Haesler Jr.
in the cemetery in Golden BC.

Ernest Feuz "The Gentleman Guide of the Rockies"
This photo was taken by Nick Morant. It was one of the last taken of Ernest before his death in Golden, on May 14, 1966. Of the three brothers, Ernest was my favourite. There was a softness and a vulnerability about him that is hard to describe.

Chapter 5

The Saga of Sir Edward Whymper:
The Prince of Mountaineers

Introduction

At the turn of the twentieth century Sir Edward Whymper "The Prince of Mountaineers" (as he was referred to by the press of the time) was the most famous mountaineer of his day. He had conquered the famous Matterhorn" near Zermatt, Switzerland, on July 14th, 1863, and he had impressive credentials as a mountaineer, explorer, and researcher. The CPR decided that he was just the man to promote its railway and chain of luxury hotels in the Rockies, so in 1901 they hired him to hike and climb in the Rockies and then write about his experiences in popular magazines.

Accordingly, Whymper visited the Canadian Rockies in 1901, 1903, 1905, and in 1909. He hiked, climbed, and became acquainted with the early Rockies as well as the early guides, packers. His remarkably detailed journals of this time were recently discovered stored away in the Scott Institute in Cambridge, England, and they are riveting. Simply entitled *Diaries of Trips to Canada,* they shed much light on the early personalities of the Rockies as well as, many interesting observations and anecdotes. He succeeded in promoting the area as a desirable destination for climbers, hikers, adventurers, and visitors from around the world. He also named many of the peaks in the Yoho Valley and had some dramatic run-ins with Wild Bill Peyto, Tom Wilson, and several of the Swiss guides – not to mention the managers of the Banff Springs Hotel, Chateau Lake Louise, Mt. Stephen House at Field, and Glacier House at Roger's Pass. His life story is a remarkable one.

Who was Sir Edward Whymper?

Edward Whymper was born in London on April 27th, 1840, the son of an artist-engraver who distinguished himself as an illustrator of books and became a member of the Royal Society of Painters in Water Colours. Young Edward went into his father's business when he finished grade school and become an apprentice. He quickly gained an excellent reputation in his own right until photographic methods of illustrating replaced the older methods. Edward was also an excellent wood carver and engraver and a talented artist in watercolours. It was his ability as an artist and illustrator that first took him to the Swiss Alps to make drawings for the second edition of the book *Peaks, Passes and Glaciers,* a book published by the English Alpine Club.

One of the peaks on his list to draw was the unconquered Mont Pelvoux (12,973 feet) in the French Alps. It was believed to be the highest peak in the Dauphine Alps and in 1860, **Professor Bonney** and other members of the English Alpine Club planned to climb it. They made an attempt but bad weather prevailed and the project had to be abandoned.

The next season the twenty-one-year old Whymper returned to the area and with a guide made the first ascent of the mountain. From the top of Mt. Pelvoux he spotted an even higher virgin peak, Point des Ecrins (13,462 feet) and he soon added this impressive peak to his conquests, climbing it with guides Michel Croz and Christian Almer. During the next four years Whymper climbed extensively in the Alps and made numerous first ascents. However, the crowning achievement of this period, and indeed of his whole life, was the first ascent of the Matterhorn (14,800 feet). It was an achievement clouded in a controversy that dogged Whymper for the remainder of his life.

The Conquest of the Matterhorn

Mountaineering as an art was in its infancy when Whymper conquered the Matterhorn. Before then, the mountain had held climbers in awe. In his classic *The Alps* Arnald Lunn wrote of the allure and the fear of the Matterhorn.

> *The history of mountaineering contains nothing more dramatic than the epic of the Matterhorn. There is no mountain, which appeals so readily to the imagination. Its unique form has drawn poetic rhapsodies from the most prosaic....The first view of the Matterhorn, and the moment when the last step is taken on the final crest, are two moments which the mountaineer never forgets. ...The great mountain remained unconquered mainly because it inspired in the hearts of the bravest guides a despairing belief in its inaccessibility. (1914, p.147)*

Whymper wrote of the hold that the mountain exerted on the local population.

> *The superstitious natives in the surrounding valleys (many of whom firmly believed it to be not only the highest mountain in the Alps, but in the world) spoke of a ruined city on the summit wherein the spirits dwelt; and if you laughed they gravely shook their heads, told you to look yourself to see the castle and walls, and warned one against a rash approach, lest the infuriated demons from the impregnable heights might hurl down vengeance for one's derision.*

The first serious attempt on the legendary mountain took place in 1858 when three natives of Breuil, the little Italian village at the foot of the Matterhorn, met at the chalet of Avouil. The three were **Jean Jacques Carrel** (the leader), **Jean Antoine Carrel**, and **Aime Gorrett**. Jean Jacques Carrel was a hunter and a good mountaineer. Jean Antoine was also a good mountaineer but he was described as being difficult to control – a good leader but a poor follower. Gorrett was a young and inexperienced youth of twenty. Leaving for their climb without proper provisions or gear, they mistook the way, and then amused themselves by throwing rocks off a cliff. When they reached the spot known now as Tete du Lion (12,215 feet), they looked up at the final summit ridge and decided they'd claim their prize some other day.

In 1860, **Alfred, Charles,** and **Sanbach Parker** of Liverpool, England attempted to climb the great mountain by way of the east face that rises above the village of Zermatt. The three brothers were determined and enthusiastic but they were poorly prepared. Lack of time prevented them from climbing above twelve thousand feet. In the same year, another party consisting of the English climbers **Vaughan Hawkins** and **Professor Tyndall,** with guides **J.J. Carrel** and **Bennen,** attempted the mountain from the Italian side and reached a height of thirteen thousand feet before being turned back. All of the early attempts were via the Italian ridge. Later events would prove that the first serious attempt up the eastern face would be successful.

In 1861, Edward Whymper returned to the Alps with two goals in mind. He intended to be the first to climb both the Matterhorn and the Wieshorn, the two premier mountains of the Alps. When he arrived at Chatillon, he learned that Tyndall had already climbed the Wieshorn and was on his way to Breuil to conquer the Matterhorn. The race for the lofty peak had begun in earnest.

The Matterhorn from the North-East (Zermatt side). The route of the first ascent is marked as is the spot where Douglas Hadow slipped.

The Matterhorn from the North (Zermatt) side. Note the gentle slope of the Northeast ridge, making it nothing more than a challenging scramble as far as the shoulder (S). "A" is the Swiss summit and "B" is the Italian summit.

The Matterhorn–Northwest (Italian side). Points B, C, D, show the great Italian South-West ridge. B is the Italian summit and C is the point where Tyndall turned back on his last attempt.

Whymper raced to Breuil and arrived there on August 28th, along with an Oberland guide. He unsuccessfully tried to hire **Jean Antoine Carrel** but there was a minor dispute and Whymper was left to find another local guide. One guide after another declined the opportunity to climb with Whymper so he decided to tackle the mountain with only his Oberland guide. As night fell, they bunked in a cowshed. The next morning proved unsuitable for climbing and the attempt was abandoned.

Attempt after attempt was made from both the Italian and Swiss sides of the mountain, but the great monarch of the Alps continued to stand unconquered. In the three years that followed, Whymper set out on six different occasions to climb the mountain. On one occasion he climbed alone and unaided higher than any of his competitors, to a height of thirteen thousand five hundred feet. It was a much heralded accomplishment.

Whymper's archrival Tyndall was also making repeated assaults on the mountain, each ending in failure, just when success seemed assured. Finally Tyndall hired the great Swiss guide Bennen, and a Valaisian guide named **Walter Anton.** He also hired the two of the Carrel brothers to act as porters and seemed poised to claim victory.

Whymper countered by hiring the other two Carrel brothers **Jean-Antoine** and **Caesar Carrel,** as his guides, and prepared an ascent by the popular Italian ridge. The next morning Whymper was told that a flag had been seen on the summit, a claim that proved to be false. Tyndall's attempt had failed some two hundred feet short of the summit. (Whymper later claimed that Tyndall was at least 800 ft. below the summit when he quit).

Upon his return, Tyndall complained bitterly that his guides had robbed him of sure success. Apparently the Carrels were hired in the subordinate capacity as porters, and when appealed to for their opinion as to the route, they retorted: "*We are porters not guides.*" The Carrels had always believed that the Matterhorn should be climbed from the Italian side with an Italian guide leading. Tyndall's chief guide on this attempt was Bennen, a Swiss national and the Carrels weren't eager to cooperate.

In 1863, the elite of the Italian mountaineering fraternity met in Turin and founded the Italian Alpine Club. They all agreed that the honour of conquering the Matterhorn should go to an Italian and that the route should be via the Italian ridge. The champion they chose for the ascent was **Felice Giordano**.

Edward Whymper and his guide Carrel made another attempt on the big mountain in 1863, but were turned back by bad weather. No attempts were made in 1864, but the Italians continued to plan for their ascent. Felice Giordano and **Quintino Sella,** both university professors and scientists met secretly with Whymper's guide Jean Antoine Carrel to obtain his support for their cause. Carrel was proud of his Italian heritage and preferred to lead an Italian to the summit rather than an Englishman, especially since it had been an English climbing party that had robbed the Italians of the honour of conquering Monte Viso, the "prince of Piedmontese peaks."

In 1865, the twenty-five-year old Whymper returned once again to the Matterhorn. After an attempt to climb the great couloir on the Italian side to the Furggen ridge with the guides **Michel Croz** and **Christian Almer** had to be abandoned, he decided to focus his attention on the Swiss face. He soon discovered that the eastern face of the Matterhorn was a fraud. From Riffel, and from Zermatt, the face appears to be almost perpendicular. However when viewed from the Zmutt glacier, it is not nearly as imposing. The average angle of the slope as far as "The Shoulder," at the fourteen thousand feet, is approximately thirty degrees. From there to the summit the angle steepens considerably but it is never more than fifty degrees.

On July 8th, 1865, Whymper met with Jean Antoine Carrel in Breuil and outlined his plan to attempt the climb of the Matterhorn from the Swiss side above Zermatt. After listening to the details, Carrel announced that he had been previously engaged by a "family of distinction" in the valley of Aosta. The family was none other than Whymper's Italian rival Felice Giordano. Carrel left Whymper and met up with Giordano and five handpicked men, who were reputed to be the best guides in the valley. Their expedition was cloaked in secrecy and the ropes and the provisions were quietly taken to Avouil—a tiny remote village close to the Matterhorn. In a letter to Quintino Sella, Giordano wrote of Whymper's presence:

> *I have tried to keep everything secret; but that fellow, whose life seems to depend on the Matterhorn, is here suspiciously prying into everything. I have taken all the competent men away from him; and yet he is so enamoured of the mountain that he may go with others and make a scene. He is here in this hotel, and I try to avoid speaking to him.*

On July 10th, Whymper learned that he had been duped. He was furious and loudly complained that he had been "bamboozled and humbugged," but it was too late. The Italian party had already started for the Matterhorn, taking a large store of supplies and provisions with them. But then, just when all seemed lost, Whymper's luck changed. Giordano and his colleagues proceeded at a leisurely pace mistakenly thinking that they had foiled Whymper's attempt to make a run for the summit. They thought they had the mountain all to themselves and they didn't count on the young Englishman's determination or a sudden change in the tides of fortune.

The next morning a climbing party arrived in Breuil, led by **Lord Francis Douglas,** who had just made the second ascent of the Gabelhorn and the first ascent of the Zinal. They had come from Zermatt across the Theodule. Douglas was young, inexperienced, and rather ambitious and he quickly decided to join forces with Whymper for an assault of the Swiss face of the prized Matterhorn. They returned to Zermatt the next day, where more good fortune shone upon Whymper. **Reverend Charles Hudson**, a well-known mountaineer had just arrived in Zermatt with the famous guide **Michel Croz** for an assault on the unclimbed giant.

After a few introductions, and a round or two of brandy, the two parties decided to join forces. Hudson insisted on taking along his companion, a nineteen-year-old Harrow graduate named **Douglas Hadow**. Whymper had some misgivings about this, but on being assured by Hudson that Hadow had climbed Mont Blanc and was quite capable, he agreed to take him along. **Old Peter Taugwalder**, who was Lord Douglas' personal guide, brought along his son **Young Peter** to act as a porter. And so, on the cloudless morning of July 13th, the hastily assembled team left Zermatt at five thirty for the climb of their lives.

Edward Whymper
This picture was taken in 1865 the year he became the first to climb the Matterhorn He was twenty-five years of age at the time.

Michel A, Croz
The great guide lost his life on the Matterhorn

Douglas Hadow
He was a nineteen-year-old, inexperienced climber who should never have been taken on the climb. He made it to the summit and can be numbered among those who made the first ascent of the Matterhorn, but his slip on the descent cost the party dearly. .

Reverend Charles Hudson
He was thirty-seven when he fell to his death from the Matterhorn

Lord Francis Douglas
He also perished on the Matterhorn. His brother was the Marquis of Queensberry who established the rules for the manly art of boxing.

Old Peter Taugwalder of Zermatt
One of the three that survived the tragedy on the descent of the Matterhorn.
A dark cloud of suspicion followed him for the rest of his life. Did he cut the
rope when Hadow slipped and fell?

Young Peter Taugwalder of Zermatt
Young Peter also survived to tell the tale of what happened on the Matterhorn
when four of the party fell to their deaths.

The party moved quickly and efficiently and arrived at the base of the peak at eleven thirty. Once on the great eastern face, they were astonished to find that places that had looked entirely impractical from the Riffel side were "so easy that they could run about." Just after noon they pitched the tent in a safe place at the eleven thousand foot level and Michel Croz and Young Peter Taugwalder went ahead to explore the route. They returned at three o'clock and excitedly reported that there was no major difficulty ahead. They could proceed to the summit on the morrow and return.

Just before dawn on Friday, July 14th, the climbing party left for the summit *"The whole of the great eastern slope was now revealed, rising for three thousand feet like a huge natural staircase."* The way was relatively easy, and for the most part a rope was not required. Hudson led some of the time and at other times Whymper took the lead. Soon they arrived at a snow ridge known as "The Shoulder," just five hundred feet below the summit. From there they angled a bit to the right and onto the north face. Whymper later reported that this traverse proved a little more difficult, but that the general angle of the slope was not more than forty degrees.

Here Hadow's lack of experience became evident, as he required *"a certain amount of assistance."* The spot did not prove too difficult however, and a long stride around a rather awkward corner brought them to the snow ridge once more. The summit of the Matterhorn was now a mere two hundred feet of easy snow slope away. Victory was assured. Still Whymper was not convinced that they would be the first to reach the top. The Italians had left four days earlier. Was it possible that they had been there ahead of them?

Again in Whymper's own words:

> *The slope eased off; at length we could be detached; and Croz and I, dashing away, ran a neck-and-neck race which ended in a dead heat. At 1:40 p.m. the world was at our feet, and the Matterhorn was conquered.*

Much to their surprise and elation no footsteps were to be found anywhere on the summit snow. When Whymper walked to the Italian side of the peak and looked down, there on the ridge far below was the Italian party. Whymper and Croz yelled, and yelled once again, and then tossed a few rock slabs down to attract the attention of the Italians. Whether the Italian party actually saw Whymper and Croz on the top of the summit or imagined that they were the "devils" of the mountain is unknown, but according to Whymper, they turned and fled. Later in Breuil, the dejected Italian party returned and confirmed that the old legends were true–"there were spirits on the top of the Matterhorn. We saw them themselves and they hurled stones down on us."

Croz planted a tent pole in the virgin snow of the peak and attached his red climbing shirt to it as a banner for all to see. "A poor flag," wrote Whymper, "but it was seen everywhere." He was magnanimous in his victory however, and some time later when reflecting on the climb and his old rival Carrel, he wrote:

> *Still, I would that the leader of the other party could have stood with us at that moment, for our victorious shouts conveyed to*

him the disappointment of a lifetime. He was the man, of all those who attempted the ascent of the Matterhorn, who most deserved to be first upon its summit. He was the first to doubt its inaccessibility; and he was the only man who persisted in believing that its ascent would be accomplished. It was the aim of his life to make the ascent from the side of Italy, for the honour of his native valley. For a time, he had the game in his hands; he played it as he thought best; but he made a false move, and he lost it. (E. Whymper Diaries).

Carrel later confirmed that he had indeed seen Whymper on the summit.

The Disastrous Descent

After an hour on the peak, the victorious party prepared for the descent – always the most difficult part of any climb. It is accepted mountaineering practice that the most experienced members of a climbing group should be the last ones to descend. In this case, the last climber should have been Michel Croz. But for some reason, Croz led the descent followed by Hadow, Hudson, and Douglas. When Whymper went back to put their names in a bottle at the summit, Croz started down with Hadow, Hudson and Lord Douglas in that order, tied together on his stout climbing rope. Whymper, rushing back from the summit, then tied onto the rope shared by the Taugwalders. Old Peter then followed in the first party's footsteps, A few minutes later, Lord Douglas asked Old Peter to attach himself to their rope, as he felt that he would be unable to hold his colleagues if one or more happened to fall. Old Peter did so with a weakened rope, not much bigger than a clothesline. Now each member of the group was attached to the others. Croz then continued, leading the descent down to The Shoulder.

At about three o'clock they reached The Shoulder, where Michel Croz laid his axe aside and faced the rock wall in order to give Hadow greater security. He placed the inexperienced climber's feet one by one into their proper positions, but as he turned around to advance another few steps, Hadow slipped; falling against Croz and knocking his feet out from under him. There was a startled exclamation from Croz as he and Hadow fell downward and over the edge of the precipice. The next moment Reverend Hudson and Lord Douglas were jerked from their positions and dragged over the cliff by the weight of Hadow and Croz. Seeing the disaster unfold, Old Peter Taugwalder and Whymper planted themselves as firmly as they could on the rocks and waited for the weight of the four hurling bodies to hit them. The jerk of the rope was fierce but Old Peter and Whymper were able to hold on for an instant. Then the rope which was no bigger than a cloths-line, snapped very close to Old Peter's ample waist.

For the next few fleeting seconds, as if in slow motion they watched in horror as their comrades slid downwards on their backs – spreading out their hands in a vain attempt to save themselves. Then, one by one, they disappeared over the precipice, falling to the Matterhorngletscher (glacier) some four thousand feet below.

The Matterhorn in all her summer glory.
This photo was taken on July 14, 1986 on the 121ˢᵗ anniversary of Whymper's first ascent.

At this point Whymper was tied between the two Taugwalders, who were "crying like children". Young Peter was the highest on the mountain. Petrified with fear and crying uncontrollably, he refused to move further. After much coaxing and assurance, he cautiously descended to where Whymper and Old Peter waited. After assessing their predicament, Whymper assumed the leadership position and tied himself to the end of the rope. It was while he was doing so that he noticed that the rope that Old Peter Taugwalder had tied himself to Lord Douglas with was quite inferior and certainly the weakest of the three ropes that they had brought. This fact was the basis for much speculation in the days and years to come.

For more than two hours after the accident, Whymper expected that the Taugwalders would also fall, but at six thirty they finally reached the snow shoulder. It was here that the three distressed climbers witnessed a strange apparition in the form of an enormous arc of light that rose up to them from the valley below. Whymper described this phenomenon in his book *Scrambles Amongst the Alps* as follows:

> *Pale, colourless and noiselessly, but perfectly sharp and defined, except where it was lost in the clouds, this unearthly apparition seemed like a vision from another world; and, almost appalled, we watched with amazement the gradual development of two vast crosses, one on either side. If the Taugwalders had not been the first to perceive it, I should have doubted my senses. It was a fearful and wonderful sight; unique in my experience, and impressive beyond description, coming at such a moment.*

Apparition on the Matterhorn
A rendering of the apparition that appeared to Whymper and the Taugwalders as they descended the Matterhorn following the deaths of their comrades a few moments earlier.

Whymper dismissed this amazing sighting as a solar fogbow – a rare but not unheard-of occurrence. The Taugwalders, on the other hand, felt that it was a heavenly manifestation and this, together with Whymper's urging, gave them the courage to carry on. At the snow shoulder they gathered up the most necessary items from their camp of the previous night and headed down the mountain until darkness fell. They were then forced to spend the night on a "wretched slab, barely large enough for all three."

At daybreak the exhausted three-some descended slowly to the village of Zermatt, where they told the villagers the tragic news. The next day, Sunday, July 17th Whymper and the Reverend Canon McCormack left the village to recover the bodies. The local priest threatened excommunication for any guide who missed Mass to accompany them but some guides from other valleys assisted in the search. At eight thirty they found the remains of Hudson, Croz, and Hadow.

Croz and Hadow were lying next to each other on the snow and Hudson was about one hundred and fifty feet away. The bodies had been stripped almost naked during the fall and were barely recognizable. Croz was missing the top of his head and was identified only by his beard and a rosary cross imbedded in his jaw. Their boots lay next to them together with other personal belongings. Save for a single coat sleeve, a boot, a belt and a pair of gloves, no trace of Lord Douglas was ever found. (Fleming 2000 P 278-279)

The tragedy shocked the mountaineering community as well as the general public. For more than five weeks, not a day passed without an article or letter appearing in the newspapers. Many criticized the sport of mountaineering, speculating about the cause of the accident and who was at fault. There were rumours that either Whymper or Old Peter Taugwalder had actually cut the rope with the jackknife that each mountaineer always carried. For three weeks Whymper kept his silence and then he finally gave a restrained account of the accident. The villagers of Zermatt however, persisted in their belief that either Whymper or Old Peter had actually cut the rope.

Why Did This Tragedy Happen?

Over the years, many have speculated as to how and why this tragedy took place. Now after reading between the lines of many accounts and trying to imagine myself as a member of that ill-fated party, I offer the reader my own views on the events of that infamous descent of the Matterhorn.

The Selection of the Group

There can be no doubt that the decision to include the untested Hadow in the climbing party was the biggest single mistake. He was young and inexperienced, and as the climb played out he proved to be dangerously tense and inept at his first encounter with difficult climbing and exposure. This was demonstrated on the ascent when the party manoeuvred around The Shoulder. This section of the climb presents an elementary bit of climbing and later in his account of the accident, Whymper felt compelled to remark that: "Hadow's lack of experience became evident and he required a certain amount of assistance." In the end it was his inopportune 'slip' near the top of 'The Shoulder' that started the disaster."

Why did they take Hadow?

Whymper was desperate – he probably would have agreed to take the devil himself at that point. He was driven to be the first man to summit the great mountain – England depended on him. In addition he felt that he had been *"bamboozled and humbugged"* by Carrel, Giordano, and the rest of the Italians who had conspired to "fix" all the competent guides in the area so that none would be available to him, or be "otherwise occupied", when he needed one most.

By July 12th, Carrel and the Italian party had been on the mountain for two days. Whymper was now frantic. If Lord Francis Douglas had not happened into Breuil, all would have been lost. He still harboured a glimmer of hope, and so he and Lord Douglas left immediately for Zermatt to stage a last-minute assault. They'd be three days behind the Italians, but perhaps they could win the race after all.

After a hurried trip over the pass from Breuil to Zermatt, Whymper was intent on putting together a party to tackle the Swiss side. Fortuitously he found that Reverend Charles Hudson, a countryman and a mountaineer of some reputation, had just arrived in Zermatt with the respected guide, Michel Croz. "Perhaps," Whymper no doubt thought, "I can still win the race for the Matterhorn."

When he heard of young Whymper's quest, Hudson agreed to join him, but he demanded that his protégé, the nineteen-year-old Douglas Hadow, go along with them. As proof of his young friend's abilities, Hudson offered the story that Hadow had climbed Mont Blanc in "jig time". Whymper, now almost beside himself agreed to take Hadow along. This, I submit, was the most critical mistake leading to their undoing.

Who was Old Peter Taugwalder?

In the area surrounding Zermatt, Old Peter Taugwalder was neither well regarded as a mountaineer, nor as a human being. He was described as being a "somewhat coarse, dirty, old beggar." Perhaps that's why the covert plans of Giordano and Carrel didn't include him as one of the guides that would be "otherwise engaged". They may have felt that Old Peter and his son were not worth worrying about. Lord Douglas may not have known any better when he hired Old Peter, and had not really planned to tackle the Matterhorn anyway. It seems that the Taugwalders and Michel Croz were the only guides available.

Old Peter also had a reputation for being crafty and self-serving when he felt another climber might falter and cause an accident. A story was told of one expedition he was on with some inexperienced climbers. While descending a long steep slope of bare rock from the top of Tete Blanche, he took the off the rope attaching himself to the rest of the party. It was speculated that Taugwalder knew that if one of them slipped, which was a distinct possibility, he would be able to choose whether to hold on or to let go. When his actions were discovered, he was told to tie back onto the rope at once. This he did reluctantly, but after the climb the story got around and few trusted him thereafter. Some went so far as to suggest that Whymper should have checked to see how far Old Peter's fingers were from the break in the rope.

Speculation had it that scheming Old Peter Taugwalder had sized up the situation on the ascent and had noticed that Hadow was the weak link. Old Peter didn't want to be anywhere near Hadow on the way down and probably convinced Michel Croz to lead the descent, with Hadow next in line, so he could assist the inexperienced climber from below. He may have suggested that he, his son Young Peter, and Whymper, who Croz respected as a competent climber, would be the last to come down. They would be the anchors to hold everyone in the event of a slip by the lower members of the party. By rights, Old Peter should have been the first to descend – leaving Croz and Whymper to belay the rest of the party.

It is further conjectured that the reason Old Peter didn't initially attach himself to the main group was that he suspected trouble. Being on a separate rope with his son and Edward Whymper would assure his personal safety. He planned to use his own rope for the occasion and even though it was somewhat worn and frayed, it would have been perfectly suitable for a strong party of three. When asked by Lord Douglas to tie on to the main rope to provide added safety for those below, Old Peter reluctantly agreed – but he did so with a grossly inferior and well used rope that was described as being "not much bigger than a clothesline". These details came out in the inquest and some of the villagers gossiped that Taugwalder might have even weakened the rope between himself and the main party with his trusty pocket knife to ensure that if the main party fell, the thin and weakened rope would break before it pulled himself, his son, and Whymper off the mountain.

After the accident, Whymper noted that the Taugwalders seemed more concerned about who would pay their wages, as Lord Douglas was undoubtedly dead. The Taugwalders were also notable by their absence in the efforts to recover the bodies. Shortly after the incident Old Peter left Switzerland for America and returned only a short time before his death.

The Order of Descent

As previously mentioned it is customary in mountaineering for the weakest members of a party to descend first and for the strongest members to descend last. This way, if an inexperienced member slips, he can be easily arrested and held from above, before he falls too far and gains momentum. In the event of a slip, a novice climber usually slides but a few feet before being held from above by the alert, stronger members. If the weaker member comes down last and slips, he either bowls the rest of the party down, or he flies past them at such a rate that it is almost impossible to hold the climber when he hits the end of the rope. If two or three climbers start sliding together with great momentum there is no hope of holding them on a steep slope.

Old Peter undoubtedly had this figured out before the descent ever started. That's why he didn't lead on the way down and convinced Croz to do so on the pretext of being needed to help young Hadow. It was also a motivating factor in not tying on to the main party. He finally tied on to the others when asked to do so by Lord Douglas, who must have anticipated trouble from below as well. Old Peter's comrades in Zermatt persisted in the belief that he had cut the rope – if not during the sudden event, then beforehand in anticipation of the impending disaster.

All this speculation was never proven at the inquest, but Old Peter Taugwalder quickly left town and Whymper carried the burden of guilt and remorse with him for the rest of his life. He blamed himself for not being more meticulous in checking the ropes before the descent began – something that all seasoned mountaineers do as a matter of course.

Many years later, in 1921, it was revealed that: "the rope used on the Matterhorn in 1865 had indeed been effectively cut". This revelation came from Dr. G. F. Browne, the late Bishop of Bristol, to whom Whymper had reportedly gone to for support and advice following the tragedy. Sir Martin Conway, President of the Alpine Club, a close colleague of Browne's, later announced that: "two or three strands of the rope might have been severed beforehand without anyone knowing". (Fleming 2000, 341-342) Whymper undoubtedly related these facts to the Reverend Browne but for some unknown reason he chose not to reveal them to anyone else – even on his death bed.

The question that arises is: Who cut the rope thus weakening it so that it would break when a serious strain was placed upon it? The evidence, in my opinion, points directly at Old Peter Taugwalder, as it was not far from his fingers that the rope between he and Lord Douglas broke when the four lower climbers fell. Had Whymper committed the foul deed, Old Peter would have been pulled off the mountain with the rest and the rope would have broken leaving just Whymper and Young Peter on the high cliffs of the Matterhorn. In addition, Old Peter had been reluctant to tie on to the rope attached to the four lower climbers and only did so upon Lord Douglas' demand. This was not the first time that crafty Old Peter Taugwalder has sought to protect himself when in a tight spot with inexperienced climbers. Why Whymper did not reveal these facts at the inquest, or in later writings and lectures, has long remained a mystery. Perhaps he blamed himself for not checking the ropes before he tied on to it above Old Peter. And perhaps it was not in his nature to point the finger of blame toward another – even if he knew that person was largely responsible for the tragedy.

Life After the Matterhorn

After the Matterhorn tragedy Whymper led expeditions to Greenland in 1867 and again in 1872. There he discovered that the interior of the great island was a plateau of snow-covered ice. From these journeys he brought back an amazing collection of stone-age fossils, which greatly impressed the Royal Geographic Society.

In 1880, Whymper also led a scientific expedition to the high Andes of Equador and made observations on the effects of low atmospheric pressure on the human body. There he made at least twelve high climbs over fifteen thousand feet–most of them first ascents. He also climbed Chimborazo (20,545 feet) twice and spent twenty-four hours on the summit of Cotopaxi (19,613 feet) – the highest volcano in the world. For these expeditions he was given the Gold Medal of the Royal Geographical Society and knighted as a member of the Order of St. Maurice and St. Lazare. He also wrote a number of books, among which were: *Scrambles Among the Alps* in 1871 and *A Journey Among The Great Andes of Equador in 1881.*

The Lion of the Matterhorn comes to Canada

In 1901, at the urging of the CPR, Sir Edward Whymper, then sixty-two years of age, made his first trip to the Canadian Rockies with four hand-picked guides – Christian Klucker, Joseph Bossonney, Christian Kaufmann, and Joseph Pollinger. The dispatches announced that the "conqueror of the Matterhorn" was on his way to conquer Mt. Assiniboine, the "Matterhorn of the Canadian Rockies," which had eluded climber's boots on its summit, despite some earnest early attempts.

Whymper's success in the Rockies was limited. Some said it was a complete fiasco from start to finish, and the source great frustration to him personally. Despite ongoing exasperation with his guides and just about everyone else he met, Whymper did manage to climb several peaks. These included Mt. Habel, now called Mont des Poilus (10,600 feet), Mt. Collie (10,500 feet), Trolltinder (9,600 feet), Isolated Peak (9,300 feet), Mt. Balfour (10, 741 feet), and Mt. Wapta. His guides also climbed The Mitre near the Plain of Six Glaciers at Lake Louise. It had been lamented that Whymper had not left a record of his experiences in the Canadian Rockies, but recently his journals were discovered at the little known, Scott Polar Institute in Cambridge, England. They make riveting reading and provide unique insight into the character and personality of the man. The following excerpts chronicle Whymper's experiences in the Rockies. The journals are simply entitled: *Diaries of Trips to Canada*"

Whymper's Journeys in 1901

Early in 1901, Sir Edward Whymper engaged **Christian Klucker** of Sils, Engadin, **Joseph Pollinger** of St. Nicolas (the home of Peter Sarabach), **Joseph Bossonney** of Chamonix, and **Christian Kaufmann** of Grindelwald, and directed them to meet him in Geneva, Switzerland, on May 11th, **Henry Kindig**, an agent for the CPR looked after them, paid their bills at the Hotel de la Poste and got tickets for them to travel to London. Whymper saw the four guides through the customs at London Bridge station and took them by cab to DeKeyser's Royal Hotel at Blackfriars. He stayed with them there until the morning of May 16th. He noted that: "Klucker said they were bored by the grandeur of this Hotel." This is the first inkling we get that things were not about to go well.

While staying in London, Mr. W. E. Davidson and other members of the Alpine Club showed hospitality to the guides on several occasions and Mr. Baker, European Manager of the CPR, took them all to lunch. On May 23rd, they journeyed from London to Liverpool and boarded the ocean liner *Australasian*. In his journal, Whymper notes the effective way that the ship's captain had of "smoking out the emigrants" that refused to get up in the morning. The captain carried large numbers of emigrants on his ships – sometimes as many as fourteen hundred.

> *They were very lazy, and it took much trouble to make them turn out and go on deck. This was overcome by taking a heated shovel*

into the cabins with some ground pepper on it, which fumed and produced violent sneezing. He said that if they once had experience with the pepper it was never necessary to use it again. It sufficed to show the shovel, and there was a general helter skelter.

During the trip, a concert was held in the second-class saloon that lasted over two hours. The guides entered into the merrymaking with great enthusiasm – Klucker sang a solo and Bossonney took part in a French song. [Here we get an indication that the guides were a fun-loving group who loved a party.] On Sunday June 2nd, they sailed down the St. Lawrence River from Quebec to Montreal where **G.W. Franklyn** took them to the Place Viger Hotel for the night and Whymper walked about Montreal for more than an hour before turning in. The next morning Franklyn, who would be Whymper's assistant during his time in Canada, escorted them to Windsor Station in downtown Montreal, where they would catch their train for the West.

Things got off to a bad start at the station as there were only two births available on the sleeping car, one for Whymper and one for Franklyn. The four guides would have to travel in the Colonial Car. They then learned that the train would not leave for another two days.

They finally left Montreal on Thursday June 5th, and all went reasonably well until it stopped at a small station somewhere in northern Ontario. With just ten minutes before the train was to depart, Whymper discovered that the guides' sleeping car had been taken off the train with all their bedding. He insisted that the Station Master put four mattresses and pillows on board before the train pulled out of the station. He then tried to get some blankets from the remaining sleeping car porter, but he had no success. In desperation, he sent a telegram to Brandon, Manitoba, requesting that blankets be put on the train there. When the train arrived in Brandon, they learned that the telegram had not yet arrived. Furthermore there were no blankets to be had, as all the stores were closed. The guides were totally miffed, as Whymper's entry reveals.

Had unpleasantness with Klucker about this, who spoke very rudely and expressed himself as thoroughly discontented with the accommodation, offered him....In consequence, I declined to take supper with them this evening. Sat up until 1 a.m. to see one of Strathcona's Horse get out of the train at Moosomin. He gave me a card of introduction to Mr. William Peyto, who he said had returned to Banff [from the Boer War].

When the train arrived in Moose Jaw on Saturday morning, Whymper was finally able to buy some blankets. The train arrived in Banff at five thirty on Sunday morning, June 9th. Given the fact that the train was a steam locomotive it made remarkable time – taking only four days to travel from Montreal to Banff. The entire trip from London had taken only seventeen days.

Sir Edward Whymper in his prime.
This picture was taken in 1901, just before he left for the Canadian Rockies.

Whymper's Guides of 1901
Left to Right—Christian Kaufmann, Joseph Pollinger, Christian Klucker, Joseph Bossonney. They were a fun-loving group but they considered themselves to be professional mountaineering guides not porters, cooks, and camp lackies. This did not go over well with Sir Edward who felt that they should pitch in and help with all the chores associated with his expedition.

It was raining in Banff when Whymper arrived and the group took a tally-ho coach to the Banff Springs Hotel. Whymper had thirty-eight pieces of luggage with him and it took a second wagon to carry everything from the station to the hotel. Hearing that he had arrived, **Wild Bill Peyto** dropped in to meet Sir Edward and after a rather long discussion, he agreed to guide Whymper and his entourage for $2.50 per day. Whymper then called on **Mr. Norman Sanson,** the meteorological observer at Banff, who agreed to receive and read his barometer at stated hours. Sir Edward then presented manager Matthews with a Jubilee photo of Queen Victoria and one of himself. The next day Whymper assisted the guides in setting up four tents on the tennis court of the Hotel to make sure that they were in good condition. During this operation, a sudden rainstorm passed over soaking everything. Later that morning Whymper and Klucker went to the museum to see Norman Sanson about checking the barometers. This entry gives us some insight into Whymper's crotchety moods:

> *Arrived there about 11 a.m., but it [the Banff Museum] was closed and we could not get in. After kicking and knocking at the front door, went round to the rear, and kicked and knocked at three other doors. No one came, and there was no sound, except of a barking dog. It appeared to me that we must wait....Then I took to knocking and kicking again, and at 12:15 sounds of feet*

*were heard within, and presently Mr. Sanson appeared clad in a
dressing gown and no trousers, having apparently, and I think
evidently, just got up. His manner was very peculiar...Tom Wilson
called after lunch-time, and asked me to visit him, and I did so in
the afternoon. His place is close to the large bridge over the Bow.
He showed a number of photos of the Rockies, most of which were
uninteresting or bad. Peyto called in the afternoon.*

Robert E. (Bob) Campbell's account of Whymper's first days in Banff paints
rather a different picture. Campbell was one of Tom Wilson's packers and heard the
story from Tom himself. He tells of it in his book *I Would Do It Again, (1959).*

*For a man who had traveled so much, Whymper was strangely
ignorant of people. To him North Americans were of the lesser
breeds, and he proceeded to act accordingly. Arriving in Banff
in the early morning (on Sunday June 9th, 1901) he succeeded in
antagonizing the dining-room help before finishing his breakfast.*

*His manner of addressing them was obnoxious. By the time he
had finished his name was an anathema. Then he went in search
of the manager. Their conversation went like this:*

You know this chap Wilson?" Whymper said curtly.

"Do you mean Tom Wilson?"

*"I do not know what he is called. The chap that has the horses for
transporting people into the mountains."*

"Oh yes, I know him quite well."

"You will have him at my rooms at three this afternoon".

With that the great man turned on his heel and went off.

*Mr. Matthews was not used to such brusqueness. He looked at his
office staff. His clerks smiled. There was no telephone in Banff
except to the station. So Matthews sent a boy to find Tom and tell
him that Mr. Whymper wanted to see him at 3 p.m. The message
was delivered.*

*Tom Wilson was the type who never owned, or needed to own,
a watch. A squint over his shoulder, and he would hit the time
within fifteen minutes. Minutes were inconsequential to him. He
counted time by days and months. Only when catching a train
did minutes count, but he was never late. So early that afternoon
he walked up to the hotel, where he stood chatting with the guests
till he thought it was time to report. A bellboy escorted him to
Whymper's room and announced him.*

*On the table stood a small clock showing the time was 2:55 p.m.,
the great man was walking up and down the room with a long-*

stemmed pipe in one hand and a glass of Scotch and soda in the other. Without preliminaries he said that his instructions were for three. Tom was thunderstruck. He was a man slow to wrath, but in all his years in dealing with tourists he had never met with such preemptory usage. He turned to leave the room, but was stopped by Whymper telling him he would show him his luggage. Tom's only thought was to find some reasonable excuse for telling the old boy where to go.

Arriving in the baggage room, Tom saw a stack of boxes, all stamped E.W. There were twenty-nine pieces, each 40x16x16 inches, and put together with three-inch nails countersunk in the wood. Did Mr. Whymper propose to take all these boxes into the mountains? "What do you think I brought them here for? I do not propose to have my goods pillaged"

That was the opening Tom was looking for. The Irish blood of his ancestors boiled over. Pillage! He wanted Mr. Whymper, and anybody like him, to know that neither he nor his men were thieves. For years he had been taking guests into the hills and never in all those years had anyone ever hinted at dishonesty on the part of him or his men. As far as he was concerned, Whymper could go plumb to hell and get someone else to outfit him.

Manager Matthews was now desperate to find someone to take Whymper to the Yoho valley. He appealed to Tom to think of a solution and Tom (never at a loss when there was a problem to be addressed) suggested his old friend Bill Peyto might take on the chore. Wild Bill had just returned from the Boer War and wanted to get into the outfitting business on his own. Matthews asked him to come to the hotel as soon as possible. That afternoon, Wild Bill started his own guiding business with some horses and equipment borrowed from Wilson. His first client was the irascible Sir Edward Whymper.

On Tuesday, June 11th, Whymper wrote:

Mr. A. O. Wheeler of the Topographical Survey staff made himself known, asked to see my tents, and tendered assistance. Asked him to get the Laggan sheets of the Survey for me. Went with him to meet Douglas, the Superintendent of the Rocky Mountains Park, who was polite, and offered to do various things for me.

More hints of Whymper's trouble with his guides are revealed in his June 14th, entry:

The four guides had been directed last night to come to my room this morning a little before 6 but they did not. After waiting for 1½ hours, I sent a boy to stir them up, and he came back saying that they had gone for a walk! I then asked Matthew (the Manager) to let me have young Kaufmann and he did so, and said that my men were only just getting up!! On my return from Tunnel Mountain I

*was told another story, namely that they had risen at 6, and had
waited half an hour for me. I cannot tell which story is true.*

On Saturday, June 15th, the friction between Whymper and the four guides
boiled to the surface.

*When walking home to the Hotel, apparently all on good terms
with each other, Kluckner suddenly burst out in a violent
harangue, which was illogical and at times incoherent; from
which it appeared that he and the others considered themselves
very much aggrieved at various things. He used the word
"chicaneries" several times. After we had our dinners, I invited
them into the depot, to state their grievances in a calmer manner.
It appeared that ... they felt they were guides, not porters and
they had not agreed to do that description of work... On this
occasion Klucker's behavior was the worst of the lot, and he made
no attempt to explain or apologize for "chicaneries". Joseph
Pollinger's manner was the best of the lot. To bed at 11 p.m.*

The next day the guides climbed the west ridge of Mt. Cascade and found a
bottle in a cairn on the summit. It contained a piece of paper with the names of
Norman Collie and **Fred Stephens** on it, with the date September 10th, 1900.

On June 17th, Whymper ordered a good supply of whiskey and beer and arranged
to have it sent to Laggan. The next day he and his four guides boarded the train and
got off at Castle Mountain siding. Whymper later complained that the train hadn't
stopped long enough for them to get all of their luggage and supplies off. **Wild Bill
Peyto** and **Jack Sinclair** left Banff at six fifty the same day with seven packhorses
and met the group at their Castle camp. They then proceeded to the summit of
Vermillion Pass where they set up another camp.

Later that week Whymper complained in his journal that he had slept very
little for the past two nights, because of the encroachment of Bossonney. Whymper
occupied a tent with Klucker and Bossonney while Franklyn, Pollinger and
Kaufmann occupied the other tent. "Peyto and Sinclair preferred to dwell in a tent
that they have extemporized" Whymper noted.

Klucker and Kaufmann explored the base of Mt. Ball on June 20 while
Pollinger and Bossonney explored the mountains to the north. Peyto and Franklyn
went to search for game and fish and brought back six small trout that Whymper
sarcastically estimated weighed just over a pound in all. Four days later Whymper
sent Wild Bill Peyto back to Banff to get more supplies and another bottle of
Scotch whiskey.

On June 27th, Sir Edward had another dust-up with Klucker and described it as a
"very disagreeable experience". It disturbed Whymper to such a degree that he wrote
a letter to the other three guides.

Dear Joseph, Kaufmann and Bossonney,

*You saw this morning a regrettable incident with M. le Guide
Chef, but you do not know what occurred before it took place,*

and I therefore write this letter to you, in order that you may understand.

It was seen yesterday that the summit of Mt. Ball is farther away than had been supposed, and it was arranged last night between the Guide Chef and myself that we would all go off this morning at 5 to examine it more closely, if the weather was fine. It was arranged that the same things as yesterday should be carried along. Mons. De Bossonney was to carry the provisions. I asked M. DeBossonney to show me what was left of them yesterday, and as I saw that there was no meat & no bread, I told him to get what he needed from Mr. Franklyn. This morning I looked again at the bag and found that there was no meat & no bread in it. If we had gone away like that there would have been scarcely anything to eat. M. de Bossonney told me that Mr. Franklyn had gone to bed before he could get the things from him; and I told M. de Bossonney that in that case he should have spoke to me so that I might have given the necessary orders. (I take this opportunity to say to you all that when it is decided to start early next morning everything must be prepared on the night before. If this is not done, we shall always start out late.) M. le Guide Chef came up while I was speaking to M. de Bossonney, and said several times that "the fault was not with M. de Bossonney." I asked him to say whose fault it was, and he did not answer me. He said that I was always finding fault with M. de Bossonney. I contradict that absolutely, but I take this opportunity to say that if either he or any of you do not execute the orders I give, it will be necessary for me to speak.

You perhaps do not understand the meaning of these words in English. I cannot and will not permit anyone to use such language to me. There has been no "cheating" or "roguery" on my part to anyone of you, and I can only suppose that M. le Guide Chef does not understand the offensive and impertinent nature of the words he used. I desire to make our journey a pleasant one, but it cannot be a pleasant one if such language as this is used between us, and I therefore take this opportunity to say that it must not be used.

On June 29th, Whymper wrote from their Vermillion Camp:

Instructed my people to camp at once as I feared rain and snow but Pollinger and Kaufmann sulked and did nothing, and said they wanted food. They did nothing, however towards preparing it, and when it was ready I observed how hungry they were by going off fishing, without partaking of it.

On July 1st, Whymper and company left the Vermillion area and headed back the Bow River – stopping for the night near the Eldon station. After arriving and turning the animals loose to browse, Wild Bill and Sinclair disappeared for awhile, ostensibly to search for the trail and to prepare it for the next day.

July 2nd began on another sour note, as Klucker had forgotten to set the thermometer needle to take the minimum temperature for the previous night. After much berating, the group finally got underway – following the steep trail that Peyto and Sinclair had blazed the night before. They reached the banks of the Bow River at ten thirty on comparatively open ground. It was raining heavily by then and persisted until four o'clock. When it subsided the group left at top speed for Laggan, some ten miles away. They reached Laggan in three-and-a-half hours and Whymper tried to telephone the chalet from the station. Much to his annoyance the phone wouldn't work and so they had to wait for two hours until a conveyance came down to meet the No.1 train.

It was on this date at Laggan that Whymper renamed the days of the week: *Stormday, Rainday, Mistday, Hailday, Thunderday, Snowday and Sleetday.* He also remarked that the mosquitoes were unendurable when they get into one's armpits and the small of one's back.

That evening Whymper settled up his accounts with Wild Bill.

According to the terms of our agreement of June 17, I owe you, up to and including July 3rd, the sum of one hundred and sixty four dollars, namely:

For yourself, from June 10, to July 3, – 24 days at $2.50 = $60.00
For 8 horses, from June 16 to July 3, – 18 days at $4.00 = $ 72.00
For packer from June 18 to July 3, – 16 days at $2.00 = $ 32.00
Total *$164.00*

Whymper closed off his diary that day with yet another annoyance directed towards his guides:

G.W. Franklyn (photographic assistant) reported today that some of the guides had made some remarks to him, which were not of a pleasant nature.

Disgusted with the inclement weather at Lake Louise, Whymper caught the train for Banff the next day and attended to some business there. He also went to the museum to get the meteorological observations that he had commissioned Norman Sanson to take for him in his absence and then took a refreshing soak at the hot springs.

Went to the "Cave" and found it shut up, although it is supposed to be kept open until 10 p.m. Knocked up the guardian, got in, and had a bath, all alone. Very nice sandy bottom, but the water was only about 4 feet deep. The guardian said I was the first person who had bathed there this month! Of the 3 bathing places in Banff, "the Pool" is by far the best. The water is bright and in the open air, and it has in places a depth of more than 6 feet.

On July 6th, Whymper caught the train for Laggan and booked into the chalet at Lake Louise. The following day being Sunday he was up at five o'clock. and bathed in the lake. The temperature of the water was fifty five degrees at the edge and he noted with some annoyance that there was no good place for *"plunging"* [diving]. Later that morning Wild Bill Peyto and Jack Sinclair arrived with three horses to take Sir Edward and his guides up to Lake Agnes. They arrived at the lake at a noon and had lunch at the teahouse, which was then a small chalet measuring 22'x18'. Following this, they proceeded to the end of Lake Agnes, and made camp. [There was a small teahouse at Lake Agnes in 1901].

Whymper noted that: *At 2:30 the 4 guides left with their things. They had not been gone 7 minutes before I saw them sitting down! The way they go on, or rather the way they do not go on is heartbreaking!*

Later Whymper went up a spur of Mt. St. Piran with Wild Bill.

The following day the party proceeded up to the amphitheatre at the long col between Mt. Whyte and Mt. Niblock. Whymper wrote:

> The rock everywhere was rotten. The snow, though not in very bad condition was not in a good state, and the route taken (for which the guides were responsible) was somewhat at risk from avalanches of the recently fallen snow, which poured down like water. ... Kaufmann and I alone remained on the col. It took some time levelling off a place for the tents, as the ground was rough and everywhere covered with debris. About 5:30 p.m. a violent wind arose, snow and hail fell, and there was thunder and lightning. Snow continued to fall on and off throughout the evening, and the atmosphere looked about as bad as it could. Kaufmann worked hard and was cheerful.

On July 10th, Klucker, Bossonney and Pollinger left the chalet at Lake Louise at two thirty in the morning and arrived at the camp on the col between Mt. Whyte and Mt. Niblock at seven o'clock. After breakfast, Whymper dispatched his guides to climb Mt. Whyte. They reached the top at nine forty and stayed on the summit for about an hour.

On Sunday, July 14th, Whymper returned to Banff on the train, but this excursion was not without its frustrations as well.

> I asked **Mr. Howard** [the manager of the Lake Louise chalet] to telephone to Laggan to say that I was coming down to take the freight train, and asked him to have the horses ready at once. This was done, and I gave the driver half a dollar to go quickly. We arrived at Laggan station just as the train went out of it, the conductor deciding that he would not wait. The Station Master told me that he had told the conductor I was coming. I consequently had to wait 4 hours at Laggan to take the No. 2 train."

In Banff, Whymper sent a telegram to Franklyn to tell Klucker that Pollinger and Kaufmann should go up The Mitre, a small, but demanding little peak, situated between Mt. Lefroy and Mt. Aberdeen. The following day July 15th, he sent Franklyn a second telegram telling him that he was returning to Lake Louise by train but when he arrived at the Laggan station, there was no one to meet him. Whymper noted in disgust that the telegram was not handed to Franklyn until thirteen hours after he had arrived at Laggan.

At seven o'clock the following morning, Whymper spoke to Klucker and found that he had not received the telegram instructing him to join Pollinger and Kaufmann in climbing The Mitre. The dispatch was later found in the pocket of Mr. Howard. Again, Whymper was highly miffed that Howard had kept the telegram for twelve hours without delivering it.

Two days later, Whymper decided to leave Lake Louise and go to Stephen House at Field. He then discovered that the only way to get to Field with his twenty-eight pieces of luggage was on the No. 1 train, which was eight to nine hours late. He sent his luggage down to Laggan in two trips during the day and waited for the summons to go down to the station. He reported that the mosquitoes were so bad in the hotel that is was difficult to rest, or do any serious work. He asked for his bill on several occasions during the course of the day without being able to get it. At five thirty he reported that manager Howard was distinctly intoxicated! Here is Whymper's account of his attempts to get down to the station.

> *Everything was ready and our baggage was waiting for a conveyance. I waited and waited, and a little before 8:00 p.m. began to press the waiter both for the bill and for the conveyance. The bill was at last given to me, and I at once saw that the addition was wrong to the extent of 10 dollars. This was corrected, but I did not notice until after the bill was paid that one item was too much by more than 50 dollars. I discovered this in the train after the account was paid.*

> *The waiter said that the conveyance would make only one trip. I pointed out that there was time to make two trips before the arrival of the train, that the conveyance could not possibly take our six selves and six other persons on one trip, and claimed priority on the grounds that our departure had been notified a day beforehand, and that we had been waiting for the conveyance all afternoon. The waiter replied that Mr. Howard's orders were that the conveyance was only to make one trip and that preference was to be given to the other passengers over my guides. On hearing this I asked to see Mr. Howard, and was told that I could not see him, as he was in bed (the best place for him, in his then condition). I then insisted that the waiter should go to Mr. Howard to obtain his order for the conveyance to be placed at my disposal, and got for reply that the conveyance would hold six persons, and that there were four riding ponies, and that we six and the other six persons must shift for ourselves as best we could. I called Franklyn to hear the astonishing message. The end of it was that Franklyn and Klucker were obliged to walk, the three guides rode the ponies and carried the instruments, and I alone rode in the*

*conveyance. We waited at the Laggan station more than 1½ hours, before the train arrived–more than sufficient time for a second trip. Got to Field at midnight and was politely received by **Miss Mollison** who was up and to her work."*

This vignette seems to typify the frustration that Whymper experienced throughout his trips to Canada. He had a superior, condescending manner about him, and was used to those around him acquiescing to his whims and idiosyncrasies. In the Canada frontier where men were judged more for their actions than a stuffed-shirt reputation, such attitudes and demands didn't go down too well. Men like Tom Wilson, Wild Bill Peyto, Bob Campbell and managers Howard and Matthew weren't impressed, and they didn't mince any words in telling him so.

Whymper also continued to have trouble with his guides. This was because he expected them to always be at his beck and call–attending to his whims and commands and acting like porters and bearers. They, on the other hand, were professional mountaineering guides from the Alps, where porters and apprentice guides carried the heavy loads, set up the camps and did the cooking and clean-up duties. Mountaineering guides, safely guided their clients up and down the mountains. They weren't expected to be beasts of burden, cooks, or pot washers. This is why Whymper had so much trouble with them from the beginning to the end.

On July 20th, Whymper and his four guides visited the fossil beds on Mt. Stephen during the afternoon. The trail up Mt. Stephen began just behind the hotel and the fossil beds were found on the slopes facing southwest about two thousand five hundred feet above Field. The next day **Professor Charles Fay**, the **Reverend James Outram**, and **Professor Scattergood** arrived at Stephen House after attempting to climb Mt. Chancellor and Mt. Goodsir.

On July 22nd, Whymper told Wild Bill Peyto and **Jack Sinclair** to take eight large boxes of supplies as far as possible into the Yoho Valley and return on the 24th to take in the remainder. Instead of advancing into the valley they stopped at Emerald col.

[At this time, hikers went into the Yoho Valley via Emerald Lake and then over Emerald col (Yoho Pass) above Emerald Lake. The trail down the Yoho River from Takakkaw Falls to the Kicking Horse River, which Whymper later christened "Tom Wilson Pass." was not established then. Professor **Jean Habel** and **Ralph Edwards** were actually the first to descend this route from Takakkaw Falls to the Kicking Horse Valley in 1896. It was a rough trip involving a lot of work to negotiate it with their horses. The full story of this trip is told in Ralph Edwards book *"The Trail to the Charmed Land"*.]

Later that afternoon, **Miss Mollison** asked Whymper if he could give up one of his rooms to accommodate a lady who had arrived unannounced. Whymper agreed and gave away the room that Pollinger and Kaufmann were staying in. He left it up to Klucker to tell them that they'd have to sleep in a first class sleeping car on the siding near the hotel. They didn't like this arrangement and Klucker was elected to complain to Whymper and to inform him that they absolutely refused to sleep in the car.

The next day, Whymper and his guides hiked to the base of Cathedral Mountain and got a splendid view down the Yoho Valley. From this vantage point they could see Mont des Poilus (then called Mt. Habel), the massive Yoho glacier, and the Wapta Icefield. It was a very hot morning and Whymper's thermometer registered just over one hundred degrees Fahrenheit in the sun at eleven o'clock. Pollinger and Kaufmann sulked most of the morning and refused to eat their breakfast. The next day, Whymper noted that: "The four guides loafed almost all day long, this being the second successive day on which Kaufmann and Pollinger had done nothing."

On July 24th, Peyto took two more loads to the camp he had set up at Yoho Lake. Whymper sent all four guides with him to carry the instruments, noting in his journal that he was "glad to get them out of the way."

Wild Bill and Kaufman returned to Field the next day and Bill reported that he was feeling ill. In addition, two of his horses were sick and would have to be taken back to Banff. Bill thought that he was coming down with the same affliction that had laid him low while he was in South Africa fighting in the Boer War. Whymper was unsympathetic to Bill's pleadings however, and sent him back to the Yoho camp with the remaining load. He himself left Field at two thirty with Franklyn and Kaufman. They walked to Emerald Lake and then went on to the camp just over Emerald Pass. He noted that the newly- constructed trail into Emerald Lake was little better than a swamp in many places.

The next morning he described in his journal the beauty of the site that Peyto had selected for their camp.

> The water in both these lakes is very clear, and of a fine green color. The surroundings are pleasant. The trees are symmetrical, and in some instances large and handsome. A small chalet at the top of the pass, on the margin of the lake would be a great convenience and would facilitate the visits of tourists to the Yoho Valley. It would be a refuge in bad weather, and a residence in fine. Both lakes are adapted to swimming.

> The effect of the continued bad weather on all of my men is very depressing. Instead of being roused by my example (I am always at work), the more I do the less they seem inclined to do. We went to bed at 10 last night and I roused at 6, and set to work writing notes, and attending to things in general. Klucker and Bossonney (in my tent) were quite aware that I was at work, but they would not stir until I compelled them at 7:10. Kaufmann turned out at 8:10; Franklyn at 8:30, and Pollinger at 8:45, but only to eat the breakfast which had been prepared for them, after which, they passed the entire morning in doing nothing except smoking and talking, and the afternoon in the same manner.

Whymper neglects to mention a famous confrontation he had with Wild Bill earlier that morning, later told by Bob Campbell in his book, *I Would Do It Again*.

Peyto and his friend Jack Sinclair pulled out early in the morning going via Emerald Lake. Later the same day [July 26ᵗʰ] Whymper and his guides left, but were to travel via Burgess Pass. The usual procedure for the pack-train work was to eat a hearty breakfast, travel for approximately seven hours, and then make camp, have a snack, and then have a big dinner. We seldom bothered packing a lunch with us, and to stop and make a fire only delayed things; it was hard to keep the horses from rolling on their packs. But Whymper and his guides took a lunch prepared for them at the hotel.

Bill and Jack expected their guests to arrive if not before them, surely soon after. But they were disappointed. They pitched camp and then waited. But their guests failed to appear. Night came on and the boys lit a great fire to guide the party. They fired their rifles, they yelled themselves hoarse; still no arrival. They sat up all night trying in every way to help their friends for it seemed evident they had lost their way. It was all in vain. Morning came and they switched the bright fire to a smoky one, piling on wet and green wood.

Meanwhile they were very hungry. What were they to do? They must have food, and the food was packed in those big boxes. They had no screwdrivers. They tried to determine which of them contained the food. Imagination then played them tricks. They tried smelling for the ones with the bacon. They were sure they had the right ones. They tried using their axe for a screwdriver, but the screws were countersunk. Bill tried a beautiful camp knife he had brought from South Africa, and broke the end off it. Jack tried the same stunt, with the same result. They were thinking so much about their hunger that things got worse. Bill got desperate and made the air blue with his language. He tried prying the lid off. It split. Now he was in trouble, the box instead of holding the bacon had scores of two ounce bottles with large mouths, packed in like eggs in an egg case. He might as well be hanged for a sheep as a lamb, so he selected another box, only to find it had other stuff than bacon. A third was broken into, and now they had food.

Meanwhile the mountaineers had started to climb Mt. Field and found a bed of fossils with which they loaded their rucksacks. Hours were spent in pursuit of trilobites, etc. While there, why not climb Mt. Wapta? They did. But after traveling the length of that mountain they ran into a precipice that even the Swiss could not navigate. They had to turn back. Strangers in a strange land, without any trails to follow, and in thick forest, to which they were unaccustomed. Hungry and without knowledge of where they were, they made a fire and spent the night bemoaning their fate, with Whymper railing at them for getting lost. Morning came. Two of them climbed the mountain to try and ascertain their whereabouts and far in the distance they spied smoke, but their pals were in a thick bush with no way to see them. They descended to rejoin their party. Now hungry and very tied, they had to climb the mountain again and travel to the camp miles away.

You would think that any man so tired and hungry would have some sympathy with his packers—but not Whymper. When he arrived he flew at the boys, accusing them of pillage. It seemed he could think of no other word. Peyto went wild. Wigs were on the green. It was all that Jack Sinclair could do to keep him from attacking his client. From that minute, hatred burned between them. Only Jack's constant reminders about the money they were owed, kept Bill from pulling out."

Sunday, July 28, dawned a beautiful morning but Whymper continued to have his troubles. He wrote:

I called Klucker and Bossonney to turn out at 5:30 a.m., but they did not show any disposition to get up, although the morning was fine. All the others of course were asleep, and would have gone on until some one brought them breakfast. When I came back Peyto was lying down covered up in a tent. I was told that he vomited. He complained of a bad headache. Gave Sinclair quinine, arrowroot and chlorodyne for him.

The following day found Peyto feeling much better but later that morning he had another fiery confrontation with Whymper. Whymper's diary describes his side of the story and Peyto's side of the events was told in his:

Fully expected to have to go down to Field to bring up medical assistance for Peyto, and help to replace him, but in the morning he declared himself well enough to go out, and he went off to continue trail making, and Sinclair, Klucker, Kaufman & Pollinger soon after him. Bossonney remained in camp. While comparing the measuring lines almost a hundred yards from our camp, I thought I heard a noise, and looking in the direction of the camp saw Peyto overhauling the box No. 2 with cookery tines. On going towards him to ask what he wanted, & how he was, he commenced cursing and swearing in a way, which settled his future with me. He vowed that he had not seen Klucker, Pollinger or Kaufmann, and that they had done no work on the trail. He declared that he had finished the trail himself. On being asked why he came back at 4 o'clock there was another outburst. His manner and words were altogether outrageous."

Wild Bill's version of the events replicates the essential details of the story, but from a different perspective.

I feel like I've been boiling in Satan's own cauldron and am only just beginning to feel human again tonight. The last few days are only a blur, but Jack told me the details, and they are not pretty. He (Jack Sinclair) fed me copious amounts of Whymper's quinine and chlorodyne and that got me through the worst of it.

Despite feeling weak this morning, I went out to do my best to help clear the trail. In the afternoon when I came back to the camp I went to one of the boxes containing cooking supplies to get something and while doing so Whymper came up and asked in his usual tone what I was doing trying to get into one of his boxes. That was too much given my recent troubles and I lost my temper, giving him a good dose of trail language. When he asked where the Swiss guides were I answered that I had finished clearing the trail myself and that they were probably sleeping somewhere in the bush, as usual. Then the feathers really flew and I decided right there that I had to find some way of getting away before I ended up breaking his bloody English neck. [Told by E.J. Hart in his book "Ain't it Hell–Bill Peyto's Mountain Journal" 1995]

The next day, Wild Bill and Jack Sinclair packed the camp further up the Yoho Valley but Whymper complained that Peyto had simply "dumped" the loads down where he pleased and therefore, he was forced to camp at that spot. Peyto then accused Whymper of taking advantage of his good nature and swindling him. Much perturbed, Bill left the camp and headed for Banff for a few days. The next morning Whymper and the guides hiked from their camp in the Little Yoho Valley and climbed Mt. Kerr (9,394 feet) and Mt. Marpole (9,832 feet). Pollinger wanted to name Mt. Kerr after himself and Kaufmann had named Mt. Marpole after himself, but Whymper renamed the peaks "Kerr" and "Marpole," after two executives in the CPR who happened to be his benefactors, and entered them on his map.

On the morning of August 1ˢᵗ, Wild Bill and Jack Sinclair arrived in camp bringing eight boxes from the Emerald summit camp to the their camp high up in the Yoho Valley. Whymper reported that Wild Bill was "as surly as he had been latterly, and it was difficult to avoid an explosion." Later that morning Whymper spotted Pollinger and Kaufmann on the summit of Isolated Peak (9,234 feet) with his telescope. They made a large stone man or cairn that could be seen from their camp.

Checking his supplies Whymper found that he only had ten pounds of bacon left. As Peyto had packed in more that ninety pounds the week before, he wondered how it was being consumed so quickly.

While these various matters were being attended to I had also to carry on a discussion with Peyto, who seemed to desire to provoke an explosion. He cursed and swore, and behaved outrageously. I tried to get at his grievances, if there were any, but failed to uncover them. He asked if I would mind making up his account to the end of July, and if I would let Sinclair take 2 horses to Banff. He would be back in three days!!! The last part of the evening was passed pleasantly enough, all around the campfire chatting. I conjectured that the sudden change in Peyto's demeanor might have been due to something that Sinclair might have said to him. Sinclair had heard all the abuse and oaths, which had been lavished upon me, and how I had maintained calm, and told him plainly to his face that he must not swear at me, and was damaging himself in the way in which he was going on.

The following Friday it was decided that Bossonney, who had been sick for a few days, should be taken down to Field to see a doctor. Wild Bill announced that he himself would do this and then he planned to proceed to Banff with what Whymper called: "his two 'nominally' sick horses."

Whymper wrote:

I overheard Peyto say to Sinclair before he went away – "Perhaps I shall not come back at all, but I will send you a good man, who knows the way to the Ice River." I was in my tent, and he did not know that I was there. Nothing of the sort was said to me.

The next day Whymper and the guides returned to Field via Emerald Pass and arranged for Tom Wilson to dispatch **Tom Martin** to assist them, as Wild Bill Peyto refused to have anything more to do with him. He also made the acquaintance of the **Reverend James Outram**.

A few days later, **Tom Wilson** and wranglers **Bob Campbell** and **Tom Martin** accompanied Whymper, Outram, and Klucker to Emerald Lake and then over Emerald Pass to the camp that Whymper had established in the Upper Yoho Valley. [This camp was actually in the Little Yoho Valley.] It seems that Tom and Whymper made up their differences, for now he had the highest of admiration for Tom. Whymper thought so much of Wilson that he named the Yoho Valley from Takakkaw Falls to the Kicking Horse River, "Wilson's Valley." Later he named Mt. Wilson (10,648 feet) after Tom.

On reaching camp, Whymper noted that Pollinger and Kaufmann had done nothing while he had been away in Field. Bossonney stayed in Field, still feeling too sick for any strenuous activity. That night, Whymper had another dust-up with his guides but he neglected to mention it in his journal. Bob Campbell did record the story and it appeared in his book *I Would Do It Again*.

Not being used to camping duties, the Swiss guides were unprepared, and the result was confusion. Everybody tried to help at each bit of work. They started a fire and each contributed his share. Soon they had a bonfire rather than a small cook fire.

Klucker, the oldest of the guides, was to do the cooking. He cut a pan full of bacon and in trying to fry it let it drop in the flames. He then tried to make a wooden handle by tying a piece of green willow to the handle with a bit of cord. The flames burnt the cord and that pan full ended up in the fire. By that time Tom had our afternoon lunch ready, and we three were sitting eating and listening to our new friends talking in German. We did not know a word of that tongue nor did we need to. From the tone of their conversation we knew they weren't having a prayer meeting. Suddenly Whymper's right flew out, connecting with Klucker's jaw, and the Swiss hit the dust. In a jiffy it looked as if the whole four of them were going to take a hand in the fray. We yelled at them to stop, and they did. I told Whymper he shouldn't do that. He glared at me and reminded me that I had insisted that he run his own camp, and he would thank me to mind my own affairs and he would mind his. When you know that you have the upper hand you can afford to be cool.

"That is just what I propose to do," I said. "I presume that you know something of the authority and duties of a Justice of the Peace in England?"

"Quite," he retorted. "What has that got to do with it?"

"Quite a lot. You have committed an assault. I am a J.P."

His face went blank. Used to seeing all the trappings of a court in England, it was hard for him to realize that before him stood a young fellow still in his twenties, his feet covered with moccasins, pants much the worse for wear, a buckskin shirt thrown open and an old black hat containing sundry holes, his thumbs shoved under a belt from which hung a gun on one side and a sheath knife on the other—embodying all the majesty of British Law. His face not only betokened surprise but doubt. It was Tom who broke the silence. "That's right Mr. Whymper, Bob is a J.P.," he said. Whymper was flabbergasted. After a moment's silence he asked, "Well what do you propose to do?" I replied that I hoped that I would not have to do anything more than to suggest that he apologize to his guide for hitting him.

Loss of face before one of his servants was a bitter pill. But he might be treated to a more bitter one if he refused. Walking over to his guide, he reached out his hand and made some remark in German.

The four Swiss smiled. I gather that the apology was not only ample but accepted. I waved the Swiss to go to our camp and told Tom Martin to give them something to eat. Turning to Whymper I told him I would bring him his afternoon tea. That done I returned to the job of cleaning the fool hens [he had shot several earlier in the day]. Dan helped the Swiss to get their camp in shape, Tom busied himself building bannocks, and the conqueror of the Matterhorn took a walk, no doubt communing with himself on the mentality of Canadians. We had a good dinner that night, fried chicken (fool hen), with Swift's bacon, hot buns, jam and tea. The guides and we boys ate together, while Whymper ate his half chicken in his own tent.

The following day, they left camp early and proceeded down the Yoho Valley to Field. Whymper wrote: *This days work was the best hitherto accomplished, we went from our camp in the Upper Yoho Valley to Field, and our success was very much due to Wilson, whose knowledge of the trails in the West was of service."*

A few days later Whymper noted that: *"At the end of the afternoon, 17 goats were noticed on the slopes of the mountain that I call the 'Whaleback'. Pollinger and Bossonney went out with their guns, fired ten or eleven shots and did nothing."*

Outram, Kaufmann, and Pollinger climbed the second Emerald Peak on August 13th, and the next morning all four guides, together with Whymper and Outram, climbed Isolated Peak. It was a beautiful day and Whymper commented upon it in his journal: *"This was the finest day we have had so far. The sky was cloudless; the heat considerable in the sun—was not oppressive, and there was a light wind, which made things pleasant."*

August 15th was another magnificent day in the high Rockies and the group ascended Habel's Hidden Peak (now called Mont des Polius). The view from the summit was spectacular and Whymper described it in glowingly poetic terms:

The bewildering immensity of an almost boundless horizon, with range after range, endless groups, and multitudes of isolated mountains, enormous forests and lakes, and winding streams, rendered it difficult to fix one's attention on any single object, and, if for a moment it was arrested, in the next one it was wandering away over the huge cliffs and precipices, the vast waste of titanic, shattered rocks, and the glaciers plunging down into the valleys below, merging with the glittering snows above.

The party left their camp in the Little Yoho Valley the next day and made their way down into the Yoho Valley. They passed Laughing Falls and came within six hundred yards of the Great Falls (Takakkaw). Whymper noted with disgust that: *"In the short distance between the camps, Kaufmann and Pollinger sat down six times to rest, without once consulting me!"*

The next day they returned to the head of the Yoho Valley and passed Twin Falls on the way. At this point Whymper and Peyto got into another of their ongoing arguments as Whymper wanted to camp at the end of the glacier but Peyto wanted to camp at a spot just beyond Twin Falls.

Twin Falls tumbling into the upper Yoho Valley. The large rock between the two falls appears to have a face on it. Some have suggested a likeness to that of Sir Edward Whymper. The Twin Falls Chalet is visible at the lower right of the picture.

Takakkaw Falls tumbling into the Yoho Valley. This spectacular falls is fed by the massive Daly Glacier and the Waputik Icefields

I protested that we wanted to go to the end of the glacier, and not to stop there, and he behaved as usual, swore at me, and was impudent and impertinent. ...After more discussion, it seemed to us, however, that the place where Peyto had stopped was more desirable than any place nearer the glacier and we decided to go back to it. [This was a rare admission by Whymper.]

On August 18th, James Outram ascended to the top of Twin Falls and climbed Yoho Peak (9,056 feet). The next day, Whymper and Outram left camp at sunrise with Klucker, Pollinger, and Kaufmann and climbed Mt. Collie (10,325 ft.). Kaufmann led the group the whole way from the glacier to the summit. The ease with which they accomplished the climb led Pollinger to remark:"I thinks to go up these mountains is quite foolish!"

While they were gone, Wild Bill came into the camp and commandeered four bottles of beer and a jar of pickles. This nettled Whymper no end when he heard of it and he commented upon it in his journal.

Two days, later Whymper left camp at seven thirty with Outram, Klucker, Kaufmann, and Pollinger and climbed Mt. Trolltinderne (9,670 feet). But even before they left for the climb, there was another flare-up between Whymper and Pollinger. Whymper wrote: There was a violent explosion from Pollinger, who declared that he was a guide not a porter, etc. etc. I did not say much to him beyond telling him, before the rest, that he did not understand his position.

Outram with Pollinger and Kaufmann were on the trail by six o'clock the next morning and negotiated a pass to Lower Bow Lake. Whymper named this pass "Balfour Pass." From Bow Lake they planned to journey to Laggan and catch the train for Field. Whymper then set about organizing the moving of the camp back to Takakkaw Falls, but Wild Bill decided to return to Emerald Lake via Summit Lake. This upset Whymper greatly, as he had planned to take photos of Takakkaw Falls. They arrived back at Mount Stephen House in the early evening as did Outram, Kaufmann, and Pollinger.

The next morning, Wild Bill arrived at Mount Stephen House and was paid $617.85 for his services. Here is Whymper's account of their parting:

Peyto came in at 10:30. While unloading was taking place, he kept quiet; but when he came to be paid he resumed his insolent manner. I said nothing about his not having come in last night, my desire to pay him off and get rid of him as soon as possible. He threatened me with legal proceedings, and I told him that if that was his intention, I would adjourn payment until they were over. Ultimately he sobered down somewhat, and I paid him what he was owed.

Mr. Jean Habel came in today from a 2 month journey to the north of my district [The Yoho Valley] and spoke of having had fine weather nearly all the time.

Some days later, Outram climbed Cathedral Mountain with Klucker and Bossonney. That same day Whymper planned to go up Mt. Stephen with Kaufmann and Pollinger to take measurements, but they refused to carry anything and demanded that he hire porters to carry the instruments and packs. Whymper was unable to find any porters in Field and so the climb was abandoned. This was the beginning of an outright revolt by the four guides, and Kaufmann was nominated to be their chief spokesman and negotiator. In his diary Whymper detailed the conditions that Kaufmann set for himself and his colleagues if they were to remain with him until the end of September.

> ...*Kaufmann said that he would remain until September 30 on the following conditions:*
>
> *-He be paid 20 franc a day for the whole of the period up to the return to Montreal.*
> *-From Montreal to Grindelwald he was to be paid 10 francs a day, instead of the 8 francs according to our contract.*
> *-If Haesler and Bohren left before the 30th, he was to leave also, but yet was to be paid up to and including the 30th of September*
>
> *He said that the C.P.R. paid the others 20 francs a day from arrival at Montreal until return to Montreal, and 10 franc a day for all the rest of the time. If sent back earlier they would be paid as up to the 30th of September. He said that Haesler would confirm this, and I said that I should like to hear what Haesler had to say before arriving at a decision. The greater part of the day was occupied by these discussions.*

Early the next morning Christian Haesler called Whymper and confirmed what Kaufmann had said the day before. Later that morning, Whymper wired **Mr. Robert Kerr** of the CPR to send him the money for the guides. Kerr had previously agreed to pay all of Whymper's expenses while in Canada. This was part of the deal to have Whymper come from England to promote the Rockies and the CPR hotels. In gratitude Whymper, named Mt. Kerr for his benefactor.

Sir Edward left Field by train with Tom Wilson and the four guides on August 29th and got off at the Leanchoil station, near the present site of the Chancelor Camp Ground, between Field and Golden. Bob Campbell made camp near the station and Whymper remarked in his diary that it was a beautiful night, with a magnificent full moon. The next morning they crossed the Kicking Horse River at daybreak and headed for the entrance to the Ice River valley which runs between Mt. Clawson, Mt. Chancellor and Mt. Vaux on the west, and Mt. Mollison and the Goodsir Peaks on the east.

The following morning, they crossed the Kicking Horse River at Hoodoo Creek and continued along a shaded forest trail to the junction of the Ice and the Beaverfoot rivers. Crossing the Ice River, they turned to the left and followed the trail past the Goodsirs and the Hanbury Glacier. They finally made their camp at the head of the valley and Whymper noted:

The Ice River at our camp was a moderately large mountain torrent, about 35 to 40 feet across, flowing swiftly. Although its water was not clear, it had scarcely the look of water issuing from glaciers. I saw some small fish in it near our camp and at the side of the trail numerous black current bushes.

The first two days of September were quite rainy, so Bob Campbell went off fishing and returned later that afternoon with fifteen trout weighing ten-and-a- half pounds in total. While hiking up the Ice River valley the other members of the party met a prospector who claimed to have found a zinc deposit and some sodalite.

Whymper continued to have trouble with his guides in the Ice River camp. On September 3rd, he and the guides left their camp and made a bivouac camp in a little valley leading up to the south side of the Goodsir Peaks. The guides refused to carry anything so Whymper was forced to hire a prospector to carry his supplies and cameras up from the main trail. At this point the weather worsened and the guides were anything but pleased at the prospect of spending the night at the bivouac camp. That night it rained, hailed, and blew and the next day it started snowing. The guides, who had had enough, informed Whymper that they were going back to the main camp at the head of the Ice River valley. They told Whymper that if the weather improved they would return for him the following morning. Whymper was thus left to fend for himself and spent a miserable time alone. He wrote the following account in his journal:

I saw the four guides meet Campbell, and then turn back, so I was left alone, and soon perceived that there was work cut out for me. At 12:45 p.m. it commenced snowing steadily again and continued to do so until 12 at night. No firewood had been left me – and no water. The nearest water was too far away to go to under the prevailing conditions, and I had to melt snow. Dry wood for firing was speedily put out of sight by the snow, and was difficult to get. "You've got plenty of food," one of the men had said satirically as he was going off, and so there was, but it was mostly tinned stuff, and I had no can opener. ...The greater part of the night was spent keeping up the fire – which must be neither too big nor too little. I kept the fire going until nearly midnight, and then used up all the stuff except a few dry twigs reserved for the morning.

The next morning, Kaufman, Bossonney and Pollinger returned to the bivouac camp just after sunrise, as promised, and retrieved Whymper who by this time was feeling cranky and miserable. They packed up quickly and headed down to the Ice River Camp where they discovered that Tom Wilson and Tom Martin had come to help pack them out. Whymper noted that Wilson gave the four guides a "good rating" for leaving him alone in the bivouac camp the previous night. The next day, they left the head of the Ice River Valley and made it all the way back to Field by seven o'clock. The return trip took them just over eleven hours.

At Field, Whymper settled up his accounts with his four reluctant guides and they boarded the No. 2 train bound for Montreal that very afternoon. In his journal Whymper noted: *"Kaufmann and Pollinger behaved decently, and shook hands as the train was leaving. The other two put themselves out of sight."*

Of the four guides who came to the Rockies with Whymper in 1901, only Christian Kaufmann returned. He and his bother **Hans** returned to Canada for many years. They worked for the CPR and were much respected as guides who made many first ascents. Unfortunately, Christian was fired as a guide by the CPR in 1904 when he was accused of "pulling a fast one" on poor professor Charles Fay, by guiding Miss G.E.Benham to the first ascent of Mt. Fay. Everyone knew that this peak, above Moraine Lake, had been unofficially reserved for the professor.

Whymper stayed in Field for a few more days, busying himself packing his specimens of insects and fossils found on Mt. Stephen and in the Burgess shale deposits. He even captured a young eagle near Banff and kept it in a cage all summer. On Friday, September 13th, he boarded the train for Glacier House and arrived there that evening. The following day, he wired Kerr of the CPR and advised him that he had engaged Tom Wilson until the end of the season. He stated that Wilson was: *"worth more than all of four guides who have just gone back."*

Sir Edward left Glacier house on the eight o'clock train Sunday morning and went to Banff, where he got a new cage for his eagle. Franklyn then took it to Vancouver where it was left in the menagerie of the public park – probably Stanley Park.

On Friday, September 20th, Sir Edward left for Emerald Lake in the horse carriage with Reverend James Outram and guides Christian Haesler, and Christian Bohren, with plans to climb Mt. Wapta. At that time there was a small chalet at Emerald Lake with a canvas roof that Whymper referred to as "the Shack." It rained heavily while they were at Emerald Lake and Whymper commented: *"The noise of the rain on the canvas roof, and the mice running about, kept me awake pretty well throughout the night. To scare the mice, at 10 p.m., I lighted a candle and kept it going until day break."*

While at Emerald Lake, he was told that there were plans to build a small hotel on a promontory opposite the shack, so he looked over the site. Being an expert in most matters, he commented on the proposed location for the hotel. "It appeared to me that it would be an inferior site to the existing one. It would be less in the sun, would not give so good a view of Mt. Burgess, and the composition of the view in general is inferior."

On Sunday, September 29 the **Duke of York,** the **Governor General, Lord Minto,** and **Prime Minister Sir Wilfred Laurier** arrived at Field with an entourage on two trains. Whymper's described of the big event as follows:

> No one seemed to get out or even look out of the first train, and no cheer arose from the assembled multitude of about 200 persons. When the second train (conveying the Duke of York and his suite) arrived there was not a single Cheer; though when they departed

there was a faint one. The Duke and most of the persons in his train alighted. He came into the Hotel and walked about it, but seemed to take a very slight interest in the scenery. I kept out of the way. Outram got in their way and was rewarded by being allowed to talk to them. I could not fail to see that the members of the Duke's suite paid him very little attention."

On Sunday, October 6th Whymper left for another trip to the Ice River valley with Tom Martin and Bob Campbell. They reached the mid-point of the Ice River valley on the 10th and set up a camp, where Whymper stayed and puttered about until the beginning of November. They prospected for minerals, and hiked about but didn't attempt any climbs. Whymper stayed at Mt. Stephen House until December 26th, and then left by train for Montreal, from where he took a steam ship for England. Whymper described Christmas at Field in 1901as follows:

Two large Christmas trees were established in the new front of the Hotel for the benefit of the children at Field, who went away laden with dolls and sweet stuff. The last thing before they departed was the singing of "Praise God From Whom All Blessings Flow".

The Climbing of Mt. Assiniboine

While Whymper was in the Ice River valley, the Reverend James Outram was preparing to climb Mt. Assiniboine. Outram's plans for the climb took shape while he was with Whymper in the Little Yoho Valley. At that time, Wild Bill Peyto had come to Whymper's camp with the news that **Walter Wilcox** and **Henry Bryant**, along with guides **Edouard Feuz Sr.** and **Friedrich Michel**, had attempted to climb Mt. Assiniboine and managed to ascend to within one thousand feet of the summit. Peyto proposed that Outram round up a couple of mountaineering guides and meet him in Banff near the end of August. He promised to pack them to the mountain in record time.

On August 31st, Outram, along with **Christian Haesler Sr.** and **Christian Bohren,** met Wild Bill in Banff. They left bright and early the following day and took a short cut across the Sunshine Meadows. They then proceeded up and over Citadel Pass to Lake Magog and the Assiniboine meadows, where they made camp.

At sunrise the next day they left for Mt. Assiniboine. Making good progress, they soon reached the second col that joins the western spur of Mt. Assiniboine with Mt. Sturdee and saw that the route not excessively difficult. Unfortunately the weather changed and heavy clouds and a steady drizzle moved in. Despite this, they continued up to the south ridge that overlooks the spectacular east face of the mountain – building cairns as they went to mark the route for their return. Finally, in near whiteout conditions, and with darkness setting in, they were forced to retreat. The next morning dawned clear and cool, so Outram and the determined guides left camp at six o'clock. Knowing the route, they quickly reached the base of the southwest face, and after an uneventful ascent, they reached the summit just before noon. At 2 o'clock they began their descent via the north ridge that overlooks Magog Lake. This went well and by six o'clock they were eating their supper. Not only was Outram's party the first to conquer the "Matterhorn of the Rockies," they were also the first to traverse the mountain.

The Reverend James Outram
He was a remarkable climber and made first ascents on some of the loftiest peaks in the Canadian Rockies including Mt. Assiniboine

Christian Bohren

Born in Grindelwald in 1865 Christian Bohren came to Canada to work for just one year. On August 31, 1901 he and fellow guide Christian Haesler Sr. accompanied the Reverend James Outram to the summit of Mt. Assiniboine. They were taken into the peak by Wild Bill Peyto, whose idea it was that they should rush to the peak to be the first to climb it. An attempt to climb the mountain by the Americans Walter Wilcox and Henry Bryant, guided by Edouard Feuz Sr. and Friedrich Michel, almost succeeded a few weeks earlier.

1903 – Whymper Returns to the Rockies

In July 1903 Sir Edward Whymper arrived back in Canada. He spent a few days in Montreal discussing his plans for the summer season with **G. McNichol** and **Robert Kerr** of the CPR. Whymper proposed to walk along the CPR line from Kananaskis, Alberta to Yale, British Columbia. Kerr and McNichol suggested that he change his plans and explore throughout the Lake Louise and the Valley of the Ten Peaks areas and then move to the Field and Yoho areas where new trails were needed. He was also asked to look for suitable locations for roads over which motor-carriages could travel with tourists. Kerr made it known to Whymper that the total sum to be expended for the season was not to exceed two-thousand dollars and that a full report of his summer's campaign should be published in a leading American magazine.

In his inimitable fashion, Whymper replied that the season was now far too advanced for him to change his plans to walk from Kananaskis to Yale. Instead he proposed to carry on with his plans, and accommodate Kerr and McNichol's request later in the season.

On the morning of July 8th, Whymper left Windsor Station in Montreal and rode in *"The Bombay"* sleeping car, all the way to Field – arriving late in the evening of July 12th. At the hotel he met **Professor Charles Fay**, who was getting ready for another season of climbing.

The following day, Whymper made arrangements with **Bob Campbell,** who was now **Tom Wilson's** partner in the outfitting and packing business, to hire **Harry Taltrie** to assist him for the summer, as he had not brought guides or porters with him. His experiences during the summer of 1901 had taught him a lesson.

With Taltrie, Whymper walked to the Natural Bridge along a new road that had been constructed the previous fall and spring. He noted that a shelter, sufficient to accommodate ten people, had been built a few yards away from the western side of the Natural Bridge.

At Emerald Lake, Whymper reported that the new hotel was at the southern end of the lake. It was approached via a bridge that was several hundred feet long and built on pilings. Beside the hotel were several other buildings, namely an icehouse, a boathouse, and a servant's house. The charge for a boat or a canoe was twenty-five cents an hour and a single room at the hotel cost three dollars a day. Whymper recommended that:

- The tall trees close to the hotel be cleared to prevent damage to the buildings, in case of forest fires of high winds.
- A trail or rustic path be built around the eastern side of the Lake so that visitors could walk a circuit, and
- The guides stationed there be required to maintain the trails. He noted that while he was there, "C. Bohren was doing nothing except loaf, or amuse himself on the lake in a boat."

Back in Field on July 17th, Sir Edward met **Fay** and **H. C. Parker** who had just made the first ascent of Mt. Goodsir with guides **Christian Haesler** and **Christian Kaufmann**. Later that week, Whymper made a few suggestions about how the Swiss guides should occupy their time.

I noticed again as I had done in 1901, that a great part (if not the greater part) of their time is spent in idleness. This is not good for anyone and I suggest that they might be usefully employed in clearing out old trails and making new ones. The guides who have already been in the Rocky Mountains for several seasons could, I have no doubt, suggest places where new trails would be useful and I would encourage them to make the suggestions, and compel them to execute the work.

A Walk Through The Rockies

Whymper commenced his historic walk of the CPR rail line from Kananaskis, Alberta to Yale, British Columbia on August 6th, 1903 at the age of sixty-three. While at Kananaskis, he reported on an example of Rocky Mountain dentistry:

"There was a man with a decayed tooth and Mr. Loder after exhaustive trials with pairs of pincers, pliers and other instruments, finally took a hammer and iron chisel and effected the purpose."

Leaving Kananaskis just before eight o'clock Whymper walked twenty-eight miles and arrived at the Banff Springs Hotel at nine o'clock that evening. He reported crossing seven bridges on his way to Canmore and stopped at the Canmore Hotel for lunch. He remarked that although his day's walk was only twenty-eight miles, he felt somewhat tired. The first part of the hike was very bad and he only averaged about two miles per hour.

The next day, Whymper left Banff at six thirty, noting that it was a "heavenly morning, sunny, with a light breeze and cool." Walking twenty-four miles that day he remarked, *"I am never tired of gazing at the clear, green waters of the Bow. A single glance at it is refreshing. From Kananaskis to two miles beyond Laggan (where the rail and the river separate) I followed the course of this river for sixty three miles."*

That night Whymper slept in a tent by the section house at Eldon but he ate his meal in the station. When he awoke the next morning, the ground was white with frost. He left Eldon at six o'clock and headed for Laggan. While passing the Valley of the Ten Peaks and Mt. Temple, he remarked on the beauty of Mt. Temple, writing, *"Mt. Deltaform, although inferior in elevation to Temple, is more attractive to the mountaineer. It has a tower at its summit with sheer walls 200 feet or so high, which are perhaps insurmountable."*

Arriving at Laggan at ten forty-five he wired up to Chateau at Lake Louise for a bottle of beer which the manager sent down to him with his compliments. He then went to Mrs. Black's boarding house for a rest and a bite to eat. Leaving Laggan at one o'clock he walked steadily to the summit of the pass and reached the Hector station near Wapta Lake at two thirty. From there he walked down to the large bridge crossing the Kicking Horse River and then on to Field. That day he walked a total of twenty seven miles.

On Sunday August 9th, Whymper reported that he had "slept like a top" and after attending a church service at the hotel, he resumed his journey. It was overcast and rainy and Sir Edward noted:

> *The rain held off until beyond Ottertail. It then looked so very thundery that I stopped at the Sawmill one mile further on, as there was no house or other refuge between there and Leanchoil. Shortly after I stopped there was a heavy rainfall, accompanied by thunder and lightning, and other rainstorms followed at intervals. I waited 2½ hours and this rendered it impossible for me to walk beyond Leanchoil this night. When the rain appeared likely to cease, I started for Leanchoil, and actually arrived there with only a slight sprinkling. I got in at 7:30 p.m., and was well received at the Section House by the Swede. Very heavy rain, accompanied by thunder and lightning, occurred at 8:40 p.m.*

Whymper walked a total of fourteen miles that day and closed his journal that evening with the following observation.

> *Although there are some very picturesque points on the line between Field and Leanchoil, the scenery is not equal to that on the Bow, which as a river, is more attractive than the Kicking Horse, the water of the former being a clear green and the latter being turbid.*

Despite a cold and cloudy morning, Whymper hiked the twenty miles from Leanchoil to Golden and walked over three new bridges crossing the Kicking Horse River. About one-and-one-half miles east of Palliser, he came upon what he called: "the worst piece of line I had seen on the railway. An embankment was giving way. Sixteen or more sleepers had subsided, and in several places the rails were supported by only one sleeper instead of two." Eleven hours after starting his day's journey he checked into the Kootenay House, which was just opposite the railroad station.

The next morning, Whymper walked from Golden to Donald a distance of nineteen miles. On this leg of the trip he passed the Blaeberry River and noted that it was a large stream, with deep, fast running, water. He surmised correctly that it drained a large watershed.

On this section Whymper injured his left leg and foot.

> *The little toe which had been sore inside, had had cold cream applied to it several times, and did not give much trouble, but the base of the big toe felt as if it had had a bruise or a sprain, and the pain constantly increased as the day advanced. On arrival, I could scarcely hobble. I kept the foot (which was puffed and inflamed) in cold water for an hour, had it rubbed over with liniment, and went to bed, hardly having eaten all throughout the day.*

From Donald, he caught a freight train for Beavermouth and booked into the hotel where he tried to look after his swollen foot. The next morning the foot was worse – very hot, swollen, red, and throbbing strongly even when not touching anything. As his foot grew worse, he rested for a day or so at the hotel.

It was raining heavily on Friday, August 14th, and so Whymper caught the train to Glacier. **Mrs. Young** met him at the station and escorted him to Glacier House, where **Dr. Schaffer**, a hotel guest from Philadelphia, examined his foot and prescribed the application of sugar of lead. The next day he was able to hobble around a bit, and in his journal we glimpse a demonstration of his never-give-in spirit.

After lunch, I waddled up the path (which is a good one) at the back of the hotel as far as the point where it divides; the left hand branch being marked "To the Glacier", and the right hand one marked "Road to the Asulkan Glacier and Fish Creek Valley.

Later that day he met a man who imparted a valuable bit of information to him which he carefully recorded in his journal:

An intoxicated man in Vancouver said to him that the way to prevent drunkenness was to take a tablespoon of olive oil every morning. After that he added that one might drink all day and yet would never become drunk.

While at Glacier House Whymper learned that **Sir James Hector's** son had been killed in an accident and was to be buried in Revelstoke. He attended the funeral with Mrs. Young and a contingent from Glacier House.

By August 20th, Whymper's foot was beginning to feel better and he returned by train to where he had interrupted his trek. Starting out at eight thirty the next morning, he walked eleven miles to Beavermouth. During that leg of the trip Whymper describes coming upon a strange cemetery about a mile west of Donald, which he called "The City of the Dead."

A considerable number of internments have been made, dating back from the early eighties. Many of the graves are those of infants and children. It probably went hard for youngsters in those times – very few people of advanced age. One of the most recent, marked by a pure white marble slab, is to Albert B. Masters, of Kentville, Kings County, Nova Scotia, who was accidentally killed by an engine near Glacier on June 17, 1893.

Two days later Whymper left Beavermouth at seven o'clock and walked twenty-four miles to Glacier House. It was one of the most interesting days of his journey. He crossed thirty-six bridges between Beavermouth and Glacier, including "Stoney" the loftiest one on the line. Two of the bridges were more than nineteen hundred feet long and one was over twenty-two hundred feet long. He passed through twenty snow sheds, ascended eighteen hundred feet, and descended two hundred feet. At Bear Creek, he bathed his sore left foot in the cold water of the creek as he ate his lunch. Reaching Roger's Pass station at six o'clock, he then hiked the four miles to Glacier House in just one hour. Unfortunately there was no room for him at the hotel, so he slept on a mattress in the barbershop.

Leaving Glacier House early in the morning of Sunday, August 23rd, Whymper walked twenty-two miles to Albert Canyon. While proceeding along the Illecillewaet River, the torrent was so noisy that he didn't hear a train approaching from behind until almost the last moment. He was forced to leap to the side to avoid the speeding locomotive. None-the-less he arrived at Illecillewaet station at five o'clock and after a light snack, he left immediately for Albert Canyon – arriving there just as it became dark. Whymper amusingly reported that at Illecillewaet there was a hotel named the Windsor Hotel, undoubtedly named after the famous Windsor Hotel in Montreal.

It rained heavily that night and the next day, but Whymper was up early and on the trail to inspect Albert Canyon and the hot springs. He enjoyed the natural mineral waters of the springs and left Albert Canyon at eleven twenty. He then marched twenty-two miles to Revelstoke, arriving cold and wet just before eight o'clock. Staying at the Revelstoke Hotel, Whymper was greatly annoyed that it was too late for a meal, as the chef had gone home. The manager finally found some mutton and ham but nothing more. The next morning, Whymper reported in his diary that he had spent a miserable night, as there were numerous trains shunting about throughout the night, and this kept him awake. He told the CPR officials that the positioning of the hotel was much too close to the tracks and therefore it was most unsuitable.

On August 25 Whymper walked the twenty-seven miles from Revelstoke to Griffin Lake. It was dark and the raining when he arrived at Griffin Lake but he was up early the next morning and had a bracing swim in the lake. In his journal he suggested that a hotel or a chalet be built on one of the lake's promontories.

Leaving Griffin Lake at nine-thirty he arrived at Craigellachie at one thirty and had lunch. It was a hot day and he departed for Sicamous at two-twenty. Amazingly, he arrived at the Sicamous Hotel at ten-thirty, having hiked another twenty-seven miles. The manager of the hotel was **F.W. Padmore**, who Whymper described as being "*very kind and sociable*". He commented that the Sicamous Hotel was almost hanging over the lake. "*The rooms are good and so was the food. The windows are protected by wire netting to prevent the ingress of mosquitoes.*"

Resting there for the next two days, Sir Edward enjoyed the surroundings near Shuswap Lake and described this lake as being a combination of Lake Windermere, in the Lake District of England, and Lake Lugano, in Switzerland. For a diversion he hiked over to Mara Lake and back.

On Saturday, August 29th, Whymper left Sicamous and hiked nineteen miles to Salmon Arm, where he enjoyed a refreshing dip in the lake. He walked sixteen miles the following day to Notch Hill and slept in the Section House that night. Again he complained of poor sleep due to the constant noise of seven trains and the ticking of the telegraph.

On August 31st, Whymper walked five miles to Ross station – near Shuswap and the next day he hiked seventeen more miles from Ross to Ducks, stopping for lunch and a swim in the Thompson River. Arriving in Kamloops in the late afternoon of September 2nd, he stayed at the Grand Hotel, although he noted in his journal that it really wasn't very "grand".

The next day he left Kamloops just before eight o'clock. on a fine, bright morning and walked twenty-five miles to Savanna, where he stayed at Ferguson's

Lake View Hotel. The following day he hiked another twenty-two miles from Savanna to Ashcroft and the next day he walked the twenty six miles to Spences Bridge in the rain.

On September 6th, Whymper marched briskly for twenty-two miles and arrived at the Globe Hotel in Lytton at six-thirty. The next morning he was almost run down by Locamotive 374, while crossing a long bridge. A few miles from Lytton, he observed native Indians fishing for salmon and drying them in front of fires on the shore. He walked to Chaumox that day and the following day, he reached North Bend, where the CPR had constructed an impressive hotel similar to the one in Field. The manager of the hotel turned out to be **Mrs. Mollison**, the former manageress of Mount Stephen House. Also present was Mrs. Mollison's dog, "Mac" who had made friends which Whymper two years previous in Field. In his diary he also commented on the lavish flowers around the hotel–geraniums, gladiolas, and blue-edging nemophilia.

The final twenty-six miles to Yale, was completed in heavy rain on September 9th. Ironically there was no time to celebrate his success. He had just twenty minutes for a quick bath and change of clothes before boarding train No. 2 heading east for Field. Whymper arrived at Field at 10 o'clock the following evening.

By any standard, Whymper's walk on a rough rail line across the Rockies and British Columbia, (over five-hundred miles), was a remarkable feat. No one could ever suggest that he lacked the stamina, the grit and the determination to see a task through to the end. Taking just over a month, this sixty-three-year-old mountaineer averaged twenty-six miles a day in good weather. He passed through thirty-six tunnels, walked through fifty-three snow sheds, and passed over four-hundred-and-fifty-six bridges. His journal indicates that there was not a dull mile over the entire route.

After tending to some business in Field, Whymper left for the Crow's Nest Pass and the site of the Frank Slide in the southern Rockies. Just a few months earlier, on April 29th, 1903 Turtle Mountain broke apart and buried the town of Frank in the valley below. He also visited the southern British Columbia towns of Michel, Sparwood, Fernie, Elko, and Cranbrook. On September 27th, he left Cranbrook for Kootenay Landing by rail and traveled to Nelson on a lake steamer. He then took a train to Mt. Robson junction and from there to Montreal. On October 12th, he left for New York, via the Delaware and Hudson Railway, and a few days later, he departed by ship for England.

The summer of 1903 was a demanding one for Whymper, but once again he proved to be a remarkable personality. His iron will and his indomitable spirit was consistent with some of the great Victorian heroes of the day – his peers would have expected nothing less.

Whymper returned to Canada in 1904. He left England on June 14th and landed in Quebec City on June 25th. The next day he left for Montreal, where he once again booked into the Windsor Hotel. Leaving Montreal on the "Canadian" on June 30th, he arrived in Field on July 4th. His old friend Tom Wilson met him at Banff and rode with him to Field, catching up on the latest news.

Whymper, now sixty-four, was not particularly active that summer. He made excursions to Emerald Lake and to his old camp at Emerald Summit. On July 22nd he travelled to Fort Macleod, Frank, and the Crows Nest Pass area. Tom Wilson accompanied him on this trip as well and Christian Haesler and Christian Michel joined them at the Summit Hotel in Frank. They managed to climb Crow's Nest Mountain which an enthusiastic newspaper writer described as a "*majestic dome that overlooks the entire valley of the Crow's Nest Summit.*" The writer described the feat as one that had "*hitherto been believed to be among the things impossible.*"

Whymper did no further climbing that season. After poking around the Crow's Nest Pass area for a few days, he returned to Field and early on August 13th, he left Field and spent a few days in Banff, and Calgary. He then departed for Montreal where he caught a steamer bound for England.

Whymper made another visit to the Rockies in 1905 but his journal reveals no details. His last visit was in 1909, when he was the guest-of-honour at the Alpine Club of Canada camp that was held at Lake O'Hara. Despite being sixty-nine-years old, he walked the eight miles along Cataract Brook from Hector Station at Wapta Lake to Lake O'Hara. **Elizabeth Parker** reported that: "his countenance was dour, and I did not once see him smile. His health was not good and he stayed in the camp for only three days."

Sir Edward Passes Away

Sir Edward Whymper died, surrounded by his beloved mountains in Chamonix, France on September 16th, 1911. Seventy-two-years old and in poor health, he checked into a hotel on September 10th. That evening he confided in his friends that night that he was not feeling well and that it was doubtful if he would see his beloved mountains again. He then went to bed with a bottle of his favorite Scotch and in the morning a friend from Chamonix found him dead in his bed.

According to an English newspaper, Whymper was haunted with the memory of his comrades falling to their deaths on the Matterhorn. Just before he left for Chamonix, he had confided to a friend that:

> *I am seventy-two years of age and I am finished. Every night, I see my comrades of the Matterhorn slipping on their backs, their arms outstretched, one after the other, in perfect order at equal distances – Croz, the guide first; Hadow, then Hudson, and lastly Douglas. Yes I shall always see them slipping in order on their backs with their hands turned back, and I shall never see Zermatt again, where I spent my most ardent hours, nor my Matterhorn."(The Journal, Alpine Club of Canada, 1911),*

Sir Edward Whymper was truly a remarkable personality. He was a lonely, brooding man with an iron will, an indomitable spirit, and the determination of the famous

British bulldog. No matter what the odds he would see a task through to the end. His accomplishments were many:

- He was well regarded as an engraver and carver.
- He was an excellent writer and authored a number of books.
- He was a superb mountaineer with a remarkable number of first ascents to his credit in the Alps, the Andes, and the Rockies.
- At sixty-one years of age he pioneered and laid out many of the trails in the Yoho Valley and climbed and named several of the peaks in the Rockies.
- At sixty-three years of age he walked over five hundred miles along the CPR rail line from Kananaskis Falls, Alberta, to Yale, British Columbia in less than a month—averaging more than 25 miles per day in all types of weather.
- In the employ of the CPR, he provided excellent publicity and awareness of the Rockies and the railroad – writing numerous magazine articles of his travels.
- He was a meticulous amateur scientist. His studies the effects of high altitude in the Andes at the Equator earned him a gold medal from the Royal Geographical Society.
- In 1867 and 1872 he explored Greenland and the great icecap that covers the interior of that country.

Like all of us, Whymper had his shortcomings, but these do not detract from his strengths and accomplishments. He liked a good drink or two of Scotch whiskey after a hard day on the trail as Bob Campbell, writing in *I Would Do It Again*, reveals.

Never have I known such a man. When out on the trail his daily allowance was a bottle of House of Commons Scotch and ten pints of ale. And don't forget that the whiskey was pre-war stuff when Scotch was Scotch, not the anemic stuff you now pay up to $6.00 for. Yet I have never seen him under the influence of liquor. Many think this is impossible, nevertheless it is true. What he drank around the hotel no one can guess. I have never been in his rooms when I saw him farther from a Scotch and soda than the length of his arm. His dinners were well set. He ate at a table by himself and always had the same waiter, who knew exactly what drinks he wanted. With his fish and soup it was a pint of sauterne. His meats were washed down by a pint of St. Julien. His dessert was always MacLaren's cheese and soda biscuits, and with this he sipped a pint of Mumm's. He invariably spent two hours at dinner. Often after that he would send for his drinking pal, the CPR trainmaster, and they would have a pint of champagne. Then he would escort his friend down three flights of stairs to the railway platform and conduct him to his home, and return to the hotel as brisk as a teenager going on a date. His room was on the third floor of the hotel and there was *no elevator. Up those stairs he would go, and never need a hand laid on the banister. Often he would finish the day by writing a scientific treatise for the English journals. But he never drank his whiskey neat; it was always either diluted with water or soda water, preferably the later.*

Whymper did not suffer fools gladly. He possessed a superior intellect and this made him appear pedantic, aloof, and insensitive. He set high standards for himself and others, and he hated to see idleness of any sort when there was a job to be done, a trail to clear, or a mountain to climb. He felt that the Swiss guides in Canada were spoiled and lazy for when they were not climbing, they sat around, smoking their pipes, and in Whymper's words, "generally loafed about". Little wonder that he was not popular with the Swiss guides at Lake Louise and at Field.

Sir Edward Whymper and Dr. James Hector at Glacier House in 1903

Sir Edward Whymper – the old warrior in his last years
April 27, 1840 – September 16, 1912

Whymper was not a student of the "human relations" school of management. He was a hard taskmaster, but he never asked others to do what he wasn't prepared to do himself. He had a strong work ethic, characteristic of the Victorian era. His disappointment with the behaviour and attitude of his Swiss guides (Kaufmann, Pollinger, Bossoney and Klucker) seems to have been justified. He also hated to see people idly "sitting around and lazing about" when he thought they could be working. Initially he got off on the wrong foot with Tom Wilson, but he grew to respect and admire Tom and it seems that the feelings were mutual. They became good friends and corresponded with each other until Whymper's death.

Little things relating to basic efficiencies, such as trains being late, messages and telegrams not being delivered, people not doing what they had promised to do, or being short-changed on services and money, nettled him immensely. Many commentators have chosen to focus upon Whymper's weaknesses and foibles by recounting humorous events and episodes. In doing so they unfairly malign his good name and sterling reputation. Some consider it great sport to find some small quirk in a great person's character and then blow it out of all proportion by recounting things that should remain discretely unsaid or confidential. Some examples are the exaggerated, and mostly unsubstantiated, stories of Whymper's amorous adventures chasing chambermaids, and the occasional female guest, in the hallways of Mount Stephen House in Field.

In 1906 the Alpine Club of Canada held it's first annual, summer camp in the Little Yoho Valley, close to where Whymper had made his camps in 1901and 1903. The Stanley Mitchell Hut was also built very close to the same spot. There can be no doubt that Sir Edward Whymper left his mark upon this valley, and over the years on misty, moon-lit nights, some have told of seeing his brooding, ghostly figure walking the trails along the Whaleback, the Little Yoho Valley, and the Twin Falls outlook. He was an exceptional personality, cast out of the mold of the great explorers of the Victorian era. A valiant pioneer in the sport of mountaineering, he was a legend in the Alps, the Andes, and the Canadian Rockies. He truly was the "Lion of the Matterhorn" and the "Prince of Mountaineers." May he roam in peace among those great, unclimbed peaks and alpine meadows in the Great Beyond.

The Quarter Way House that once stood just off the trail along Lake Louise. Sadly it was never reconstructed after it fell into disrepair in the 1960's.

Chapter 6

A.O. Wheeler and the Alpine Club of Canada

The Early Years

Arthur Oliver Wheeler's contribution to the sport of mountaineering in Canada is inestimable. He was another giant among the many pioneers and legendary personalities of the Rockies. His work as a Commissioner on the Boundary Commission, deciding the boundary between Alberta and British Columbia, and his surveying of the Selkirks and the CPR right-of-way through the Rockies established his reputation as perhaps the greatest land surveyor this country has ever known. His dedication in establishing, nurturing, and promoting the Alpine Club of Canada, often at his own expense, gained him an international reputation and the gratitude of all those who have seriously hiked and climbed in the Rockies and the Selkirks. **Esther Fraser's** excellent book *Wheeler*, published in 1978, describes his rich and adventure-filled life. Many of the details that follow are taken from that treatise.

By the time Arthur Oliver Wheeler was born, his family had lost a good deal of its fortune. Josephine Helsham, Arthur's mother was a well-educated young woman with a fine Irish lilt to her soprano voice. She was fluent in German and French, could read Italian, and had a good grounding in history and the classics. On October 28th, 1857 Josephine married Captain Edward Oliver Wheeler at St. George's Church, in Hanover Square in London, England. Shortly after the couple moved to Dublin and on May 1st, 1860, their son Arthur was born.

Young Arthur went to grammar school in Dublin and Ballinasloe, County Gallway and when he was fourteen years old he entered the distinguished Dulwich College in London. Fraser describes it as:

A distinguished old school, with an emphasis on "playing the game", devotion to duty, sports and Kingsley's "muscular Christianity" – it was one of those institutions whose object was to produce elite young gentlemen with a serious approach to life's work, trained for the universities, professions, and civil service. In the last three decades of the nineteenth century these schools were caught up in the enthusiasm of Imperialism and students were strongly motivated by a "mission to Empire". Graduates with this moral fervour did like Arthur Wheeler – they made significant contributions as civil servants in Queen Victoria's Empire (Wheeler, 1978)

In 1876, Wheeler's parents suffered more financial reversals and had to sell many of their possessions and migrate to Canada. They set sail with six children and one very much on the way. Reaching Ottawa on May 14th, 1876, they took some rooms in a Sparks Street hotel. The next day little Josephine Wheeler was born.

Captain Wheeler eventually got a job as the harbour master at Collingwood, Ontario, on Georgian Bay, where he and his family rented a large house. Here Arthur, then sixteen years of age, learned to paddle a canoe and discovered the ways of the forests, the lakes, and streams of the Muskoka-Georgian Bay wilderness. In the spring of 1876 he met the noted land surveyor, **Lauchlan Alexander Hamilton**, and became his apprentice. Soon he determined to become a surveyor himself. To qualify as a Dominion Surveyor Arthur had to master the first six books of Euclid and demonstrate his knowledge of plane and spherical geometry, trigonometry, astronomy, geology, plotting and map-making. He also had to learn how to the keep field note books and demonstrate the use of instruments in actual surveying experience.

In the spring of 1877, Wheeler. became an apprentice to the well-known land surveyor **Elihu Stewart,** and worked north of the Great Lakes in the Algoma area. There he had more wilderness experiences and learned the joys of blackflies and mosquitoes. He slept out in a tent all spring and summer and returned in the fall to continue his studies. Later he described the summer of 1877 as one of his toughest in the outdoors, but it prepared him well for the role he would later play in the Canadian Rockies.

In 1878, Elihu Stewart won a contract to survey the native Indian reserves near Prince Albert, Saskatchewan and eighteen-year-old Arthur Wheeler accompanied him. The survey party crossed Lake Superior to Duluth and travelled by rail through the United States to Moorehead, Minnesota. There they took a paddle-wheel steamboat up the Red River to Winnipeg, where they acquired Red River carts and loaded them with equipment, food, and supplies, and camping essentials. They then headed northwest across the waving grasslands of the prairies. Since their budget didn't include saddle horses, they walked the whole six-hundred-mile trip, passing through Portage La Prairie and Brandon on their way to Fort Ellice. From there they travelled up to the Qu'Appelle River Valley to Fort Qu'Appelle, where the North West Mounted Police had established a fort the year before. From there they continued northwest to the Great Salt Plain and then on to Prince Albert, where the Saskatchewan River splits into the North and South branches.

During that summer of adventure, Wheeler became familiar with the rolling prairies and the western woodlands. He also learned how to live off the land, how to negotiate with the Indians of the plains, and how carry out his surveying duties under extreme field conditions. It was an experience that moulded and shaped the eighteen-year-old and prepared him for the rigours of being a field surveyor in the wild mountains of Alberta and British Columbia. It also built great stamina, toughness, and above all, character. In the fall he returned to Collingwood and resumed his studies, which seemed like child's play to him in comparison to the hardships that he had endured on the trail that summer.

In 1872, Prime Minister Sir John A. MacDonald started planning for the great transcontinental railway. To get an idea of what challenges such an endeavour would face, he sent Sir Sandford Fleming across the country. With Fleming on that historic trip was a botanist, **Professor John Macoun**, who would play a large role in Wheeler's life in the years to come.

In 1881, Arthur Wheeler qualified as an Ontario Land Surveyor and two years later as a Manitoba and Dominion Land Surveyor. During this time he worked surveying the CPR right-of-way through the prairies. When he returned from the field in 1882, the tracks of the new railroad had reached just beyond Regina.

In 1882, Wheeler again worked on the prairies, but this time for George Ryley of Collingwood who has recently become a surveyor for the Department of the Interior. He worked along the U.S. border from Fort Dufferin to the Cypress Hills. As the winter on the prairies approached, he left for Ottawa and was promoted to the position of Third Class Clerk, in the Department of the Interior. There he began to study a revolutionary new technique of surveying with a camera and soon became one of the most competent surveyors in the country with this new methodology.

In January 1883, young Wheeler moved to Ottawa to work with the Department of the Interior as a Third Class Clerk. Within a few weeks he was transferred to the office of the Surveyor General of Canada. There he worked under Dr. Edouard Deville, who was experimenting with the use of cameras as surveying tools. He taught Arthur everything he knew.

In Ottawa, Wheeler joined some outdoor clubs and made a few excursions into the Laurentians. He loved canoeing, skating, riding, and snowshoeing and he spent as much time as he could outdoors. While in Ottawa he met many influential people and cultivated acquaintances that would prove to be valuable to him in the future. He also became a part of the social circuit and in so doing, met Professor John Macoun's two winsome daughters, Minnie and Clara. He enjoyed Minnie's sparkling company, but he was smitten by the lovely Clara.

In 1885 word of the Northwest Rebellion in the Red River country reached the East and Wheeler was one of the first to join Middleton's militia as a surveyor with the Intelligence Corps. He and his fellow recruits endured basic training at Fort Qu'Appelle and then journeyed on to Duck Lake and Batoche. He saw service at Fort Pitt, Fort Carlton and Loon Lake, as General Middleton and his troops put the run on Big Bear and the Cree allies of Louis Riel and Gabriel Dumont.

Later Wheeler made many uncomplimentary comments regarding Middelton and his lack of organisational ability – calling him a "damned fool" and noting that the inept general's brain was "incapable of formulating any plan whatsoever." Having put down the rebellion more through good luck, than through good management, Middleton's troops returned to the East as conquering heroes. Wheeler rejoined the Department of the Interior as a surveyor and continued his friendship with the Macoun girls.

On June 6th, 1888, Arthur Wheeler married Clara Macoun at St. Andrew's Presbyterian Church in Ottawa and two years later Clara gave birth to their only child, a son Edward Oliver Wheeler (later known as Oliver).

Shortly after this, Wheeler. decided to go into private practice in New Westminster, British Columbia. On the train trip to the west, Wheeler first saw the Rockies. The family settled in New Westminster and Wheeler found work surveying timber licences for the provincial Department of the Interior at Revelstoke, Salmon Arm, Shushwap, Pitt Lake, the Stave River Valley, and Garabaldi Park.

In January, 1894, Wheeler gave up his private practice and joined the Federal

Ministry of the Interior, where he was appointed to the Topographical Survey Branch. He surveyed south of Calgary, Alberta, along Jumping Pond Creek, the Elbow River, Fish Creek, the Sheep and Highwood rivers, Willow Creek, the Oldman River, Pincher Creek, and down along the American. border. He also surveyed near Waterton and along the Little Bow, the Belly, the St. Mary's, and the Milk rivers. On all these trips Wheeler and his crew lived in tents in the field. Occasionally his father-in-law, Professor Macoun, joined him to study the flora and fauna of the area.

In January of 1898, the Wheelers built a home in Calgary and he continued his surveying activities in southern Alberta. In 1901 Arthur was commissioned to do a photo-topographical survey of the Selkirk Range. He established his headquarters at the Glacier House Hotel and quickly made friends with **Mrs. Young**, the manager. During one of his trips to Banff, he met **Sir Edward Whymper,** visiting him at the Banff Springs Hotel and inspecting his equipment. Whymper must have been impressed with Wheeler because he mentions the occasion in his journal.

Beginning his work at Glacier House, Wheeler found that in order to take photos and carry out his survey work, he needed some assistance with climbing the rugged Selkirk mountain peaks. He initially engaged the Swiss guides, **Edouard Feuz Sr**. and **Christian Haesler Sr**. to train him on travel on the high glaciers and snowfields. Some of the guides later became his life-long friends but others resented what they saw as his brash, forceful attitude. After two or three times out with the Swiss guides, he confidently dismissed them and proclaimed that he and his men were "quite their equals" on rock climbs. Occasionally he hired a guide or two for exceedingly difficult trips but for the most part he and his team worked on their own.

Some Swiss guides felt that they must accompany anyone who ventured off the beaten trail onto a mountain or a glacier, and they resented it when Wheeler guided himself and his survey team up the peaks and glaciers around Glacier House and journeyed deep into the Selkirk Range. The Swiss guides were used to doing relatively short, one or two-day trips, using the hotel as their base. Wheeler, however, would stay out for weeks at a time, sleeping in alpine meadows and among rocky crags as he carried out his surveys. He was a man used to living in the outdoors and the mountains environment simply represented a few additional challenges.

Wheeler was a fast learner with a lot of common sense and out-doors savvy and he quickly became experienced in the high country and learned how fickle the mountain weather can be. One of the more challenging peaks Wheeler and his team climbed was Mt. Sir Donald (10, 808 ft.). On the day of the ascent, he left Glacier House with two guides at two o'clock. in the moonlight and returned at ten o'clock that evening. The summit of Mt. Sir Donald was later used as a camera station for his spectacular panoramic photos of the surrounding peaks.

In 1903, Wheeler was appointed as a topographer with the Department of the Interior and given the task of surveying the railroad right-of-way through the Rockies. He began in the Lake Louise area and surveyed north along the Bow River to Bow Lake. That summer, his survey crew established 57 camera stations on peaks at Bow Lake, Moraine Lake, and Sherbrook Lake. Other camera stations were set up in Consolation Valley, Paradise Valley and at Lake Louise. That winter the Wheelers celebrated Christmas at Glacier House, helping **Mrs. Young** decorate the dining room and rotunda of the hotel. Never one to sit around for too long, Wheeler. explored some of the glaciers in the area on snowshoes and took some winter photos of the mountains near the summit of Asulkan Pass.

Mrs. Julia Mary Young
Mrs. Young managed Glacier House from 1893 to 1920. Various writers who stayed at Glacier House, including Walter Wilcox, A.O. Wheeler, Sir Edward Whymper, and Charles Fay referred to her often in their writings.

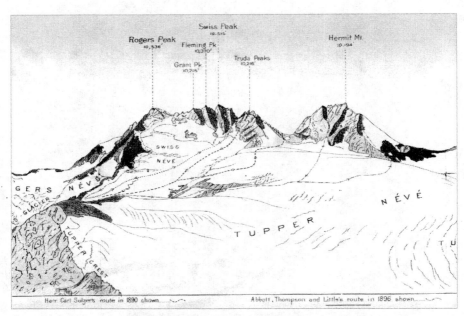

Map of the Mt. Rogers, the Swiss Peaks, and Mt. Hermit
Drawn by A.O. Wheeler for his book *The Selkirk Range* (published 1905)

Glacier House all decked out for Victoria Day

Glacier House at its peak

The Pacific Express at Glacier B.C. in 1903.
Note the snowplough on the steam engine.

All that remains of the glory that was Glacier House
Photo taken in July 2002.

In 1904, Wheeler's surveying work took him to the Pipestone Valley, Lake O'Hara, Lake McArthur, Emerald Lake and the Yoho Valley. In 1905, he published his monumental study entitled *The Selkirk Range of British Columbia* – an outstanding work, containing an impressive array of maps and pictures of the major peaks and glaciers. The book covered all aspects of the Selkirks – the flora and fauna, the wildlife, the history, and the topography. One section, "Mountaineering in the Selkirks", particularly interested climbers as it contained detailed maps and drawings showing early routes up Mt. Uto, Mt. Sir Donald, Mt. Rogers, the Swiss Peaks, and Mt. Bonney., as well as photos of many of the early climbers. The book is still treasure. The quality of the work, the meticulous attention to detail, and the care with which all aspects of the mountain range are examined made it the "bible" of the Selkirk Mountains for years. The book is a reflection of the man himself.

In May 1905, Wheeler was asked to be a guest speaker at the annual meeting of the Appalachian Mountain Club of Boston. He and his wife Clara were the guests of **Professor Charles Fay**, the avid mountaineer and annual summer visitor to the Rockies. In the course of his work Wheeler had come to know most of the enthusiastic mountaineers and young adventurers who annually visited Banff, Lake Louise, Field, and Glacier. He met **Walter Wilcox, Edward Whymper** and his four Swiss guides, **Norman Collie, James Outram, Mary Shaffer**, and many other climbers who were systematically climbing the best peaks in the area. He also knew and occasionally employed **Tom Wilson, Wild Bill Peyto, Jimmy Simpson, Conrad Kain, the Feuz brothers, Curly Phillips, Ray Legasse, Ulysses LaCasse** and **Bob Bapti** as guides, outfitters, and packers. He also took **Byron Harmon** with him on a number of his expeditions to photograph scenery.

The Founding of the Alpine Club of Canada (ACC)

During one of Wheeler's visits with Professor Charles Fay, a proposal was made to start an alpine club to promote and teach climbing in the Rockies. He and Fay decided that a North American Alpine Club should be formed with a Canadian Branch centred in Banff. To whip up some enthusiasm, Wheeler wrote a letter proposing the idea and had it published in the major newspapers across Canada. Within days, he received a fiery response that was published in the *Manitoba Free Press*. The feisty **Mrs. Elizabeth Parker** chastised Wheeler for being unpatriotic because he had not proposed a purely Canadian alpine club. Wheeler challenged her to help him to raise support for such a club and Parker accepted, on the condition that the club would be independent and completely Canadian.

Elizabeth Parker was a reporter for the *Manitoba Free Press,* who wrote a regular column and book reviews. Her editor, J. W. Dafoe, reluctantly embraced the idea of a Canadian alpine club and allowed her to promote the undertaking in his newspaper. Wheeler and Parker then wrote letters to every influential Canadian they could think of, asking them if they would be in favour of forming an independent Canadian alpine club, or a branch of an American alpine club. There was overwhelming support for an independent Canadian club. This galvanized

Wheeler and Parker into action and by March of 1906, the Alpine Club of Canada (ACC) had been formed with seventy-five charter members. *"Nothing, since the formation of the Lord Strathcona Horse, has so appealed to the Canadian feelings for Empire,"* observed Wheeler.

Wheeler immediately moved his family to Banff where he set up his new office. His unmarried sister Kathleen soon joined them and worked in the office of the new club. Wheeler convinced the head of the Western Division of the CPR that the club was an excellent idea, and then persuaded the executive to provide twenty free return train tickets to Winnipeg for the inaugural meeting.

The first meeting of the Alpine Club of Canada was held on March 27th, 1906 in Winnipeg. The twenty-seven delegates elected A.O. Wheeler as their founding president and Mrs. Elizabeth Parker as the inaugural secretary. Parker remained an enthusiastic and dedicated spokesman for the ACC for the rest of her life, serving as the editor of the Alpine Club Journal until her death in 1944. She attended most of the annual summer camps, but never climbed much higher than the alpine meadows just above the tree line.

The founding members of the Alpine Club of Canada
This picture was taken outside the Winnipeg, YMCA during the inaugural meeting in 1906. Elizabeth Parker is in the front row with a climbing rope over her shoulder. A.O. Wheeler is to the left of her. Jim Brewster is to the far right in the front row.

Sir Sandford Fleming was nominated as Honorary President of the club and the members agreed to convene the first annual ACC summer camp in the Little Yoho Valley later that year. Wheeler used his influence and brashness, to obtain grants from the provincial and federal governments for the new endeavour. The Department of the Interior gave Wheeler and his survey crew time off, with pay, to organize and attend the historic event. The CPR allowed the Swiss guides to attend, and provided cooks from their chalets and hotels. They also provided half-price fares to club members travelling to the camp. The North West Mounted Police at Banff and Calgary loaned tents and camp equipment, and Tom Wilson and Jimmy Simpson provided free pack-train services. Wheeler also invited representatives from the major newspapers to attend, as well as representatives from alpine clubs from around the world.

Elizabeth Parker 1856-1944
This picture was taken in 1938.

The founders of the Alpine Club of Canada from Banff
Taken in Banff in 1906 - Back Row (L –R) unknown, Tom Martin, A.O. Wheeler, Tom Wilson, unknown, Bob Campbell. Front Row (L-R) Dan Campbell, unknown, Syd Baker, unknown, unknown.

The organizing and the logistical skills required for such an undertaking were considerable, but Wheeler, Kathleen, and Elizabeth Parker were up to the task – handling all the details with military precision. Thirty to forty tents had to be set up at the site in the Little Yoho Valley, and hundreds of pounds of food and provisions had to be packed into the camp. Each day, the enthusiastic attendees devoured eighty loaves of bread, fifteen sides of bacon, four hams, and innumerable tins of canned stew, jam, and butter. They also drank gallons of coffee, tea, and hot chocolate. Church services were held on Sundays, and each night there was a large community campfire for singsongs. Byron Harmon showed up and assumed the position of official camp photographer. Those wishing to climb were required to sign out and had to be accompanied by a camp guide. The camp lasted for one week and it was an outstanding success.

The men who attended arrived in tweeds and Derby hats. The women came in floor-length skirts and large feminine hats. They were all greatly impressed by the grandeur of the surrounding peaks and the incredible wild beauty of Emerald Lake. Attendees hiked up to Yoho Pass, and along the Whaleback trail to the Little Yoho. From the high-line trail they could view the massive Waputick Icefield and Yoho Glaciers, and to their right and across the valley, they could catch sight of the magnificent Takakkaw Falls, tumbling thousands of feet to the valley below. They could also roam the lush alpine meadows of the Little Yoho Valley at the base of Mt. President and Mt. Vice-President. These mountains were among the graduating climbs for those who chose more serious mountaineering adventures. Edouard Feuz, his son Edward Jr, and Christian Haesler were on hand to teach the basics of mountaineering and to ensure that everyone returned safely. The season came to a successful end when Wheeler convinced Sir Sandford Fleming to write an article for the inaugural edition of the Canadian Alpine Journal.

In the following year, 1907 the ACC held their summer camp in Paradise Valley, and one-hundred-and-fifty members hiked and climbed at Lake Louise, Lake O'Hara and Moraine Lake. Preparing for that camp required another Herculean effort of cutting and clearing trails, building a campsite, and packing in tents, equipment, and food supplies. The ACC was off to an excellent start and Wheeler was delighted.

Wheeler spent the winter of 1907 in England. While visiting his cousin Dr. Hugh Helsham, they decided to go to the Alps to climb the Ulrichshorn. They were in a party of nine, with two guides, and all was going well until the final pitch. They all roped up at this point but Sir. Henry Bergne, a member of the English Alpine Club, disdainfully declined to do so. Within minutes he slipped and plunged to his death. Needless to say the climb was abandoned. Wheeler was considerably shaken by this mishap and from then on, he always insisted that members of his climbing parties be suitably roped.

In 1908, the Alpine Club Camp was held at Rogers Pass and Wheeler saw to it that Sir William Cornelius Van Horne was sent a special invitation. Van Horne graciously declined to attend, but sent his heart-felt regrets in a personal letter to Wheeler. Sadly, an unfortunately tragedy on the second day marred this third annual camp.

An Early Mountaineering Tragedy

Young Oliver Wheeler was just eighteen years old at the time of the ACC camp at Rogers Pass. On the second day of the camp he was given the responsibility of leading his first party up the rather easy slopes of Mt. Avalanche. **P. D. McTavish** and the **Reverend A.M. Gordon,** both reputed to be experienced climbers, were in the group, as was the English alpinist **G.E. Howard.** The climb was not a difficult one but young Wheeler asked the two women of the group to wait above while he descended a moderately steep snow slope. In her book Wheeler, Esther Fraser gives an account of what happened next.

> *He had just started down when one of the women shouted: "Look out, I'm coming!" Full of confidence and exhilaration, she began to run, lost her footing and, with increasing velocity, shot past him. Reacting instantly, he reached out to grab her. She was inches beyond his reach. In a split second she fell over a precipice. She was dead when her horrified companions reached her.*

> A thorough examination of the scene of the tragedy and an inquest concluded that: 'the calamity was not through any fault or negligence of any person in the party. Very especially we express the greatest confidence in the guide, Mr. Oliver Wheeler, one of our experienced guides who was leading the party most carefully. Very wisely, as soon as the rescue team arrived, the party asked Oliver to lead them to the summit to demonstrate their trust in him." (1978, 72)

The first annual Alpine Club camp in the Little Yoho Valley – 1906.
Elizabeth Parker and A.O. Wheeler are at the flagpole in front of the dining tent.

The first graduates of the 1906 ACC camp.
A young Edward Feuz Jr. is the guide seated in the front lower left of the photo.
The photo was taken by Byron Harmon – a founding member of the Club.

Many of the basic tenants of safe mountaineering were ignored and they culminated in this tragedy.

    1) Young Wheeler was an inexperienced lad of eighteen and should never have been leading the party with inexperienced climbers in the group.

    2) All members of the party should have been roped. The fact that they weren't was a fatal mistake.

    3) The so-called "experienced" climber from England should have known

better, and so should Gordon and McTavish. Even on the simplest of climbs, on rock or snow, all members of the party should be roped. If nothing else it can be instructive for new climbers to get some experience handling and managing the rope, learning basic techniques, and becoming aware of the dangers inherent in mountaineering.

The Alpine Club camp at Laughing Falls 1906
Check out the attire worn by the ladies. Elzabeth Parker is seated at the table in the foreground. Tom Wilson is astride a fine steed in the background.

A full report of the tragedy appeared in the 1908 Alpine Club Journal, and in an attempt to exonerate his son, A.O. Wheeler wrote: *Even the Swiss guides at Glacier, who are models of precaution, stated that none would have dreamed of using a rope on the ground where the accident happened.*

Personally I doubt this. The Swiss guides that I knew (Edward Feuz Jr., and his brothers Ernest, and Walter) always roped up novices before the real climb began, as it gave them an opportunity to teach the proper handling of the rope before it was needed. It makes no sense to have to show someone how to use and handle a rope or an ice axe in a dangerous situation when lives depend on it. Better to do it before hand, in order to provide some familiarity and some practice with the equipment, before an emergency occurs.

The Annual Meeting of the ACC, held at the camp on July 10th, passed a number of resolutions were passed:

1. Condolences were sent to the parents of Miss Hatch.
2. Oliver Wheeler was exonerated: "*We express our conviction that the calamity was not through any fault or negligence of any person in the party. Very especially we express the greatest confidence in the guide, Mr. Oliver Wheeler, one of our experienced guides, who was leading his party most*

carefully. This was remarked upon by different members of the party, before the accident occurred."

3. Official telegraphic accounts were forwarded to the leading newspapers, in both the east and the west to avoid sensational accounts being printed.

4. The camp program would carry on as planned.

As an expression of confidence in young Oliver Wheeler, the members of the original party, save for Miss Parslow, asked him to again lead them up the mountain, which he did.

Women Climbers on Mt. Burgess at the first Alpine Club Camp of 1906.
Check out the climbing apparel worn by the ladies

Women Climbers at the first annual Alpine Club Camp in 1906
They are descending the President Glacier. Note that the women are wearing skirts. They are carefully roped and in good mountaineering and guiding practice, they are leading the descent.

This was the second mountaineering death to take place in the Canadian Rockies–the first being Phil Abbot. To some degree, A.O. Wheeler defused what could have been a devastating blow, both to himself and his son, and to the fledgling club. Sadly this is the last time that the Alpine Club mentioned Miss Helen Hatch. A memorial plaque, an annual bursary financed by the club, or a room named in her honour in the A.O. Wheeler hut at Rogers Pass, might have been a suitable gesture. Perhaps it is not too late to have a bronze plaque remembering Miss Hatch and her unfortunate death placed in the front room of the A.O. Wheeler Hut that is situated in the shadow of the mountain on which she perished.

A similar accident took place in 1881 when Major Rogers and some native Indians climbed Mt. Avalanche above Roger's Pass. On the descent, no one was roped and one of the Indians took a spill. He couldn't self-arrest and was badly injured when he crashed into the punishing rocks that waited for him far below. He apparently never walked too well after that incident.

A Permanent Clubhouse in Banff

1909 was an eventful year for Wheeler and the ACC. They opened a new clubhouse in Banff and a successful camp was held in the meadows at Lake O'Hara. A large contingent of English climbers and several members of the British Association for the Advancement of Science accepted the invitations that Wheeler personally sent to them. **Frank Oliver,** the Minister of the Interior, who was somewhat jealous of Wheeler's extensive circle of influential friends in high places in Canada, England and the United States, selfishly instructed the Surveyor General to deny Wheeler and his assistants time off to attend the camp. In response to Oliver's edict, the major newspapers in the country indignantly took Wheeler's side, emphasising the role of the ACC in promoting Canada and the Rockies. In the end Oliver backed down and gave Wheeler, and his assistants, permission to attend the annual camp. But Frank Oliver didn't forget the episode.

Wheeler, who never met an influential person he didn't like, had the ability to meet people, and quickly gain their confidence and support. Without this the ACC would have withered on the vine within a year or two. Instead Wheeler fashioned it into the premier club in Canada, with patrons and supporters from among the highest echelons in the country. Anyone who was influential, from **Lord Strachcona** to **Sir Sandford Fleming** to **William Cornelius Van Horn,** was asked to become a member, or an honorary member, of the new of the new Alpine Club of Canada. It's no wonder that Frank Oliver and his minions were jealous of Wheeler and nervous about his increasing influence and status.

Meanwhile, Wheeler had a busy spring and early summer supervising the building if a new clubhouse on the slopes of Sulphur Mountain in Banff and making all the arrangements for the summer camp at Lake O'Hara. The clubhouse was a marvellous addition to the ACC, as it provided a base from which to operate and to receive the nearly 200 guests who came from around the world for the opening ceremonies. It had a large veranda, a library, a large meeting room, a massive fireplace, and some offices. Sleeping quarters were in tent-covered buildings next door.

In the spring of 1910, Wheeler was busy with the finishing of the clubhouse and preparing for another annual summer camp. His plans hit an obstacle when Frank Oliver again issued instructions through the Surveyor General that there would be no provision for Wheeler and his assistants to do Alpine Club work that season. Wheeler, who by then was fifty years old, reacted by resigning in disgust after close to thirty years of work with the Department. When this news was made public, letters of complaint were sent to twenty-one of the principal newspapers in Canada. At the annual meeting that summer, members appointed A. O. Wheeler as the first permanent director of the Canadian Alpine at the highest salary the club could afford.

The summer camp was held at Lake O'Hara and featured sixty bell tents set up in the meadows near the present site of the Elizabeth Parker Hut. Over two hundred people attended the camp for a week of climbing, hiking, and camaraderie. **Jimmy Simpson** packed in the supplies following the old trail along Cataract Brook, and Wheeler hired a young Austrian guide by the name of **Conrad Kain** to assist the CPR's Swiss guides with aspiring climbers.

Later in the fall of 1910, with funding from the Alpine Club assured, Wheeler continued with his demanding surveying and exploration activities. He took **Dr. Tom G. Longstaff**, a noted mountaineer from Britain along with him. They met in Golden where **Conrad Kain,** two packers, and **Byron Harmon,** the pioneer nature photographer from Banff, were waiting to join them. They left on Captain Armstrong's stern-wheeler and manoeuvred down the mighty Columbia River to Spillimacheen Landing.

Here a packtrain met them and they followed a trail up Bugaboo Creek for fifteen miles and then bushwhacked above the timberline. Wheeler and Conrad Kain carried the survey equipment to altitudes of between seven and nine thousand feet as they beheld a panorama of "magnificent snow-crests, innumerable glaciers, rock spires, snow peaks, a galaxy of snow, ice and rock." For the first time, white men were gazing upon the Bugaboos. Fifty years later, these mountains would become an immensely popular mountaineering and skiing destination. The group returned to Spillimacheen on October 1st and Kain complained that he couldn't sleep well in his bed at home with it sheets and blankets, as it was too soft and too comfortable!

The Saga of Mount Robson – Who climbed it first?

After Wheeler resigned from the Department of the Interior, he proposed an expedition to the Mt. Robson area under the auspices of the ACC. The Grand Trunk Pacific Railway, the predecessor of the Canadian National Railroad, (CNR) hoped to run its line through the Yellowhead Pass west of Jasper and they badly needed survey information. Wheeler proposed doing a thorough exploration of the Mt. Robson area, as he knew from **James McEvoy's** work of 1898 that the mountain was probably the highest in the Canadian Rockies.

In 1907 Wheeler had heard of how the **Reverend George B. Kinney** and the **Coleman Brothers** had made a heroic attempt to climb the Mt. Robson, but they were foiled by bad weather. They were also thwarted in their attempt the following year. They planned to try a third attempt in 1909, but Kinney heard that some foreigners were planning an assault on the mighty peak.

There was no time to rally the Colemans so Reverend Kinney hurried to Jasper with all due haste. There he met **Curly Phillips,** a young wrangler and drifter. He convinced young Phillips to join him for the adventure of his life. Curly agreed, and in cowboy boots and without an ice axe, he doggedly followed Kinney up the mountain. On the way down, they met the British mountaineering team of **Mumm, Hastings,** and **Amery** and proudly announced that they had just conquered the peak. **Inderbinen**, Mumm's guide, examined Mt. Robson from a distance and reckoned that the summit would be theirs in just eight hours. He was wrong, and when the experienced team, who had climbed throughout Europe and in the Himalayas, missed death from an avalanche by inches, they retreated in defeat.

Moving quickly, Wheeler proposed a comprehensive survey of the area and attempted to muster support for the project wherever he could. He enlisted the sponsorship of the British Geological Society and contacted **Dr. Charles Walcot**t of the Smithsonian Institute. He also contacted **Ned Hollister** of the National Museum. He then let the government of British Columbia know that he was available to survey the Mt. Robson area. In typical Wheeler fashion, he didn't bother to consult with the bureaucrats of the day. He simply called on the Lieutenant Governor, the Premier, the Surveyor General, and the Minister of Public Works. He also suggested that his work could include surveying and placing boundary monuments along the boundary between B.C. and Alberta. As might be expected, the provincial bureaucrats were less than overjoyed, but knowing of Wheeler's friends in high places, they reluctantly acquiesced and gave him nominal support.

While awaiting word as to the feasibility of the Robson expedition, Wheeler secured some surveying work in the Bella Coola area for a dam at Tetachuck Lake. By the time he wrote his report for the annual Canadian Alpine Journal, he was able to announce that the funding had been confirmed and the expedition to climb Mt. Robson was "a go."

The expedition got off to a good start and in the late spring of 1911, Wheeler sent his main pack train to Yellowhead Pass under the leadership of **Curly Phillips**. Wheeler arrived at Phillip's camp a few days later with **Fred Stevens, Conrad Kain,** the **Reverend George Kinney,** and **Byron Harmon**.

They followed Resplendent Creek and eventually caught their first glimpse of Mt. Robson:

> As we topped the crest, the whole wonderful panorama came
> into view. At our feet flowed the Robson Glacier. Across the wide
> river of ice ...the great massif of Mount Robson, rising supreme
> above all other peaks. White against the sky of perfect blue, it
> seemed to belong to a world other than our own. Ethereal snowy
> Mount Resplendent, crowned with immense sculptured cornices:
> the splendid sharp conical peak of Mount Whitehorn. it was the
> most stupendous alpine scene I had ever gazed upon, setting the
> blood coursing through the veins as fast as a torrent, with the pure

joy of being alive – and there. There was no doubt about it: these peaks will provide excellent work when we hold our annual camp at the summit of Robson Pass.

They continued with their survey and photographic work and in early August they camped near the base of Mt. Robson. They climbed a small mountain to view the Robson Glacier and from there Conrad Kain picked out what he felt would be the best line of attack for the ascent – the route attempted by Mumm and his party in 1909. As they studied the mountain, Kinney pointed out the route of his climb with Phillips in 1909. Conrad desperately wanted to climb the mountain right then and there, but Wheeler wanted to save it so it could be climbed during an ACC summer climbing camp.

Kain was thoroughly frustrated at Wheeler's desire to save not only Mt. Robson, but also all the surrounding peaks, for the Alpine Club climbing camp the following season. He could not hold himself back any longer and early one afternoon he headed out on his own to climb the 11,000 foot Mt. Whitehorn. He ran into a bad storm with heavy thunder and lightning, but he kept going and eventually gained the virgin summit where he built a small cairn in which he deposited a small metal match box with "N. Hollister" scratched on the side. In the matchbox he placed a piece of paper with his name and the date on it.

It was late when he started his decent and pitch dark by the time he reached the glacier. Reluctant to spend a miserable night in the open, he headed across the treacherous glacier with only the constant lightning flashes to illuminate the huge gaping crevasses. He reported later that he yodelled with delight when he reached the rocks. Exhausted, he made his way back to camp in the pouring rain just before daybreak. Later Conrad admitted that it was one of the craziest and most foolhardy things that he had ever done. A few days later he and Byron Harmon stole away and made the first ascent of Mt. Resplendent. (11,240 feet) Wheeler was furious when he found out, but there was little that he could do about it after the fact.

Near the end of August, the last sections of the work in the Mt. Robson area were finished, so the party completed the first circuit of the mountain. They returned to Jasper and then proceeded to Maligne Lake. Wheeler was greatly impressed with the surroundings and recommended that the boundary of Jasper Park be extended to include the Maligne Lake area. He then selected a site for a chalet near the lake.

It was a perfect afternoon when I came to the Lake. In its setting of towering peaks, forests of golden-green and dark blue-green spruce it was incomparable climbs enabled the Lake to be mapped with a fair degree of accuracy. And the vistas from the heights! Then narrow far-reaching valleys of the Sunwapta and Whirlpool; barely discernible, noble Mount Columbia rising from its massive icefield; "the gigantic fangs" of the Tonquin Valley- all called the explorer with no uncertain voice.(Fraser, p.94)

The Alpine Club of Canada Club House in Banff 1910

The Assembly Room in the Club House

Arthur Oliver Wheeler at the 1913 annual Alpine Club camp

A.O. Wheeler addressing the 1910 annual Alpine Club Camp at Lake O'Hara.
The group is assembled on almost the exact spot where the Elizabeth Parker
Hut is now.

During this trip **Byron Harmon** took some remarkable photos of Mt. Robson, the Jasper area, and Maligne Lake. This further established his reputation as a leading outdoor photographer. He then joined Conrad Kain, the Reverend George Kinney, and Curly Phillips on the trip from Jasper to Lake Louise. It was mid-September and snowing regularly when the little group set out for Lake Louise. The intrepid adventurers had to negotiate high mountain passes with snow several feet deep. This required amazing stamina and determination from both man and beast. It also made for some remarkable photographic opportunities, and Byron Harmon was able to take many outstanding pictures that are still sold today, over ninety years later. These were indeed "great days in the Rockies".

The little pack train made the one-hundred-and-twenty-mile trip back to Laggan in just eleven days. The route they followed eventually became the Banff–Jasper Highway.

Later that fall, Wheeler went on a lecture tour to promote the work of the ACC and to lobby the Province of British Columbia to create Mount Robson Provincial Park, which it did. Wheeler's articles and Harmon's pictures appeared in several American and European journals and magazines creating great interest in the area. It was a good year and Wheeler had strengthened his reputation as a man for the mountains.

Near the end of the season, Wheeler received word that the Reverend Kinney and Curly Phillips had not actually reached the summit of Mt. Robson on their climb of 1909. Apparently a storm had turned them back short of the summit, and they had had to retreat, narrowly escaping death, as they descended the treacherous slopes in the storm.

The origins of this story are not clear. Some say that the truth leaked out while Kinney, Kain, Phillips, and Harmon made their trip back to Laggan from Jasper. Others speculated that Curly spilled the beans to Conrad Kain sometime during the winter they spent trapping together in the Jasper and Yellowhead Pass areas. Still others speculated that Wheeler paid someone to get Curly liquored up and then convinced him that he and Kinney hadn't reached the summit after all. Whatever the source, the news got out and it gave Wheeler the opportunity he'd been waiting for to put the ACC on the map. Under the auspices of the club, he quickly put together a strong Canadian team and began soliciting funds for the Mt. Robson summer climbing camp of 1913.

In the spring of 1913, Wheeler was appointed as the British Columbia representative on the three-member Inter-provincial Boundary Commission. He was also employed to survey and map the Alberta-British Columbia border, which allowed him to continue his leadership position in the Alpine Club of Canada.

The first camp of the Alpine Club of Canada in 1913 was held below the crags of Mount Cathedral in the Kicking Horse Valley. When the general camp was finished, Wheeler and his assistants rushed to Mt. Robson to set up the climbing camp for the assault on the summit. Some sixty-nine eager club members spent two memorable weeks at the foot of Mt. Robson at Kinney Lake. Some also camped further up the mountain at Berg Lake. It was a fifteen-mile hike to the camp along the trail that

Phillips and Kinney had blazed in 1911, but no one complained in the magnificence of the surroundings.

Arthur Oliver Wheeler – Lion of the Rockies

On the evening of July 30th, Conrad Kain guided **W. W. Foster** and **A. H. McCarthy** to the high moraine on the route that he had studied from a distance two years earlier. A testimony to Conrad Kain's remarkable stamina was the fact that he had climbed Mt. Resplendent earlier that day and didn't even return to camp before joining Foster and MacCarthy for the climb of Mt. Robson.

After a quick breakfast at four o'clock, they started up the glacier toward the mountain's massive cliffs. Conrad led his team ever upward over ice slopes, sheer cliffs, snow-ridges, and overhanging cornices, with long icicles glittering in the sun. On the ferocious summit ridge, high in the heavens, Conrad cut steps as if inspired. Suddenly, he turned to his "Herren" and, in one of the most famous utterances in Canadian mountaineering history, declared, *Gentlemen, that's as far as I can take you.* They had reached the summit of the highest peak in the Rockies and they had done it under the auspices of the ACC.

Donald "Curly" Phillips

Reverend George Kinney

The party descended by another route, making the first traverse of the massive peak. Conrad knew that they would have to spend the night on the mountain, and so he tried to get his clients down as low as possible to avoid the bone-chilling cold of the higher altitude. At ten o'clock, they stopped on an exposed ledge for the night. Conrad then built a small rock wall to protect his clients from the wind and to provide some psychological comfort from the abyss below. Then he tied his "Herren" to a rock and together they spent a long, cold, but clear and peaceful night on the mountain.

When the sun reached them at six thirty the following morning, Conrad discovered that both MacCarthy and Foster were painfully snow-blind. He applied cold poultices to their eyes until they were able to open them, and then he led them step by step down to safety. At five o'clock, they reached the main camp where Elizabeth Parker and Wheeler welcomed them as conquering heroes in the name of the ACC. It was a remarkable achievement and one that made Conrad Kain the undisputed premier mountaineering guide in the Rockies.

It is said that while MacCarthy and Foster were describing their climb around the campfire, Curly Phillips, who was in the camp and listening intently, went up to Foster and said, *"We didn't get up that last dome."* When asked by Elizabeth

Parker how high the dome was, he is reported to have said, *"Between sixty and seventy feet."*

The mountaineering world had found it hard to believe that a man of the cloth and a cowboy in high-heeled riding boots, who had never climbed a mountain before, could have conquered the Monarch of the Rockies without a professional guide or even an ice-axe. In fact they didn't want to believe it. Wheeler and Conrad Kain had studied the mountain carefully in 1911 and critically looked over the route that Kinney said he and Curly had followed. Later in the Canadian Alpine Journal, Wheeler wrote that in his opinion:

> *The route looked impossible, the great wonder is that they returned alive. Kinney took a desperate last chance and succeeded. He has been criticised rather severely by practical mountaineers for taking on so extremely dangerous a climb with a companion who had had no previous experience.*

Some others suggested that Wheeler and the climbing elite of the day rigged the whole affair. They contended that the Reverend Kinney and Curly Phillips were "jobbed" out of their first ascent of the great mountain. Wheeler was accused of orchestrating the whole thing and encouraging someone to ply poor Curly with some cheap whiskey and then put words in his mouth. For many it doesn't matter much. The feat of Kinney and Phillips was perhaps more miraculous than that of Kain, McCarthy, and Foster. They had no trails, no support group, and no seasoned professional guide to take them to summit.

The controversy raged for years, and Wheeler and the ACC were maligned for manipulating Phillips into recanting of his achievement. Conrad Kain was interviewed two years after his 1913 ascent, and he magnanimously acknowledged the achievement of Phillips and Kinney. In the 1915 edition of the Canadian Alpine Journal he testified:

They deserve more credit than we. Though they did not reach the highest point in 1909, they had many more obstacles to overcome than we. Mt. Robson is one of the most beautiful mountains in the Rockies and certainly the most difficult one. In all my years of mountaineering, in different countries Mt. Robson is one of the most dangerous expeditions I have ever made.

Reverend Kinney returned to the ministry and after forty years of service he retired with his wife to Victoria, British Columbia. In his later years he began to resent that he was not given the credit for conquering Mt. Robson. His brother-in-law even got into the act, with some well-chosen pronouncements, crediting Kinney and Phillips with the ascent.

Paddy Sherman, in his book *The Cloudwalkers,* reported that some fifty years later, Reverend Kinney finally conceded that he was probably mistaken, and was actually "a few feet short of the summit". In *Wheeler (1978)* Esther Fraser assumed that Curly Phillips' statements about their climb were true and she was delighted that Reverend Kinney had finally revealed the truth.

Finally after fifty years of controversy, Kinney's summit register and flag were found by a group of avid climbers from the Harvard Mountaineering Club. Their discovery finally settled the matter. In late July of 1959, a party of climbers from Harvard was ascending the steep south face (the northwest bowl) below Emperor Ridge at its western corner. They were near the beginning of the ice gendarmes about a thousand feet below the skyline of the ridge when Craig Merrihue of Berkley California, spotted an old rusty can with a red flag sticking out of it in a natural cairn. It was a Canadian flag and there was a folded message, wrapped inside it. Carefully unfolding the note, Merrihue discovered that it was George Kinney's account of his climb some fifty years earlier.

Mt. Robson (Yuh-hai-has-kun) (12,972 ft.)
The tallest peak in the Canadian Rockies – Photo by Phyllis Munday.

Conrad Kain (left), Albert MacCarthy, William Foster (right).
The first to conquer Mt. Robson on July 31, 1913.

Curly Phillips with A. O. Wheeler on the Alpine Club-Smithsonian Expedition to Mount Robson in 1911

The Reverend George R. B. Kinney

The Harvard group was initially disappointed with the implications of their discovery because they too had always believed that Kinney and Phillips should have been given credit for the first ascent of Mt. Robson. They found the can, the flag and the note well below the summit, and well below the severe difficulties that lay ahead. A chill ran up Merrihue's spine when he realized that the note had been written exactly fifty years earlier, to the day.

When he returned home to Harvard, Merrihue wrote to Reverend Kinney. The letter described Merrihue's climb and told of how he had found the flag, and the note that had been left in a bottle by Kinney himself. The letter was recently published by Muriel Poulton Dunford in her book *North River: The Story of British Columbia's North Thompson Valley and the Yellowhead Highway.*

> *Dear Mr. Kinney*
>
> *I have just returned from an attempt of the Northeast ridge (the so-called Emperor Ridge) of Mt. Robson, on which attempt my party reached a point about 200 feet from the summit, before being forced to turn back due to dangerous snow conditions and bad weather.*
>
> *On the descent from this attempt, I crossed a small broken rock outcrop on the west face, where I found the remnants of a tin can containing a Canadian flag, in which was wrapped a small corked glass bottle bearing a note, signed by you and Curly Phillips and dated July 27, 1909. The note itself was wet, somewhat faded, and disintegrating. However it was possible to make out the script, which read more or less as follows:*
>
>> *'I have come in with a five horse train from Edmonton to capture this summet(sic) for the club. I am an active member of the Canadian Alpine Club.*
>>
>> *George Kinney Donald Phillips July 27, 1909*
>
> *The outcrop was at about 12,000 ft. The can completely disintegrated on touch, but the flag was in good condition except for two small rust spots where the tin can had decomposed. With your permission, I would like to send these items to the Canadian Alpine Club, for perpetration (sic) in their collection of important historical items, as these should certainly be preserved. Judging from the extent of decomposition of the tin can at the time I discovered it, I doubt that the flag would have lasted much longer on the mountain.*
>
> *Incidentally, in view of the difficulty of the mountain by this route, and the many hazards and hardships experienced by our own party, we were all in agreement that your early attempt on this mountain*

was among the most noteworthy in mountaineering history.

I am most anxious to hear from you about this, in particular about whether I may forward the flag and note to the ACC.

Yours truly,
Craig Merrihue,
American Alpine Club

This remarkable evidence confirmed Curly's story and Reverend Kinney's confession of the truth before he died. It also vindicated Arthur Oliver Wheeler, whom many had maligned in their eagerness to discredit both him and the Alpine Club of Canada. Wheeler was a man of honour and integrity, and would not have discredited Kinney and Phillips, unless he had serious doubts about their claims. In the end, his judgement and assessment of their story of the climb proved correct. The credit for the first ascent of Mt. Robson rightfully goes to Conrad Kain, William Foster, and Albert MacCarthy. It also goes to A.O. Wheeler, who organized the expedition, arranged for the financing, and was the driving force behind it. (Dunford, pp 148-156)

Craig Merrihue of the Harvard Mountaineering Club in July 1959 with the flag that George Kinney and Curly Phillips left in a natural cairn well below the summit of Mt. Robson in 1909.

Clara Wheeler

Miss Emmeline Savatard

The Elizabeth Parker Hut in the Lake O'Hara Meadows

Miss Elizabeth Parker 1856–1944

Co-founder of the Alpine Club of Canada and its first secretary. She was later voted the Honorary Secretary of the Club. She helped A. O. Wheeler with his book The Selkirk Mountains and she was the editor of the annual Alpine Club Journal from its inaugural issue in 1908 issue until a year or two before her death. She should have received an Order of Canada but was never given one.

One of the last pictures taken of A.O. Wheeler
Taken in the meadows of Lake O'Hara, just behind the Elizabeth Parker Hut.
"The Grand Old Man of the Mountains"

The A.O. Wheeler Hut at Rogers Pass.
It was dedicated in 1941. (Photo taken 2002)

The graves of A.O. Wheeler and his first wife Clara (right), and his second wife Emmeline Savatard (left) in the Banff Cemetery. (Photo taken 2002)

The Later Years

Wheeler continued his boundary survey work and continued to be a tireless promoter of the ACC. He also encouraged the CPR and the Canadian government to build chalets at Yoho, Lake O'Hara, and Moraine Lake. In 1914 the annual ACC camp was held at Takkakaw Falls and the Upper Yoho Valley. It was a sombre event, as World War I had broken out. The next year, the camp was held in Ptarmigan Valley, but the attendance was very small.

In 1916 while working on the Freshfield Glacier for the Boundary Survey, Wheeler fell into a gaping crevasse. His men rescued him before any real damage was done, but the experience shook him up considerably. That year, the annual ACC summer camp was held again in Paradise Valley and in Consolation Valley. That same year Wheeler launched a business adventure, *Mt. Assiniboine Walking and Riding Tours*. He planned trails and campsites with proper facilities and in some places he had small huts built. As the years passed, he was kept busy with his surveying activities, promoting the ACC, and arranging the summer climbing camps. The Walking Tours were not the financial success that he hoped they would be.

Wheeler's beloved wife Clara died on August 23, 1923, and was buried in the quiet little cemetery in Banff. Just over a year later Wheeler. married **Miss Emmeline Savatard**, who had been the girl Friday of the Alpine Club for twenty years.

In 1925, Wheeler chaired a special committee of the ACC to mount an expedition to climb Mt. Logan. The expedition was a great success and **Lambert** and **MacCarthy** made the first ascent of Canada's highest mountain. A year later Wheeler sold his interests the Mt. Assiniboine enterprise to **Erling Strom** and later that summer, at the Tonquin Valley ACC summer camp, he delivered his last address as the Director of the Club. After that he continued to attend the annual camps and made occasional excursions with Emmeline to Oregon and California. During this time he was increasingly asked to write the obituaries for the *Canadian Alpine Journal*, as no one knew the early pioneers of the Rockies more intimately than he. **Professor Charles Fay** died in 1931, **Tom Wilson** in 1933, **Professor Coleman** in 1938, **Mary Schaffer-Warren** in 1939, and **Byron Harmon** passed away in 1942. Wheeler eulogized each of them in the *Canadian Alpine Journal*. It must have been hard on the "old mountaineer to say his final goodbyes to his friends and comrades, as he remembered them in their prime – when they were strong, fit, and vital, as was he.

In 1941 A.O. Wheeler was eighty-one-years of age and the annual camp was held at Rogers Pass. He addressed the general meeting, wearing his familiar alpine cape and hat. Later the "A.O. Wheeler Hut" was built and dedicated to his memory. In 1942, he visited Moraine Lake and Lake Louise for the last time and visited with old friends Edward, Ernest, and Walter Feuz, and Rudolf Aemmer.

In the fall of 1943, word came that Elizabeth Parker, his life-long friend and the co-founder of the ACC, had passed away on October 26th, The following March he too passed away in Banff. Funeral services were held at St. Georges in the Pines, and he was buried wearing his Tyrolean cape. His casket was draped in the colours that he had used to design the crest of the Alpine Club of Canada–green for the earth, grey for the rocks, and white for the snow. Crowning the casket were his ice axe, his climbing rope, and his Tyrolean hat.

He truly was "the Lion of the Canadian Rockies".

The crest of the Alpine Club of Canada, as designed by A.O. Wheeler

Chapter 7

More Exceptional Personalities

Conrad Kain (1883–1934) Mountain Guide Extraordinaire

Conrad Kain was perhaps the greatest mountaineer ever to climb and guide in the Canadian Rockies. His accomplishments were monumental. In New Zealand he had 30 first ascents in the Southern Alps and in Canada, more than 60 in the Rockies, the Selkirks and the Purcell ranges. These include the three highest peaks of the Canadian Rockies.

Kain was born in the Austrian village of Nasswald, near Vienna, on August 10th, 1883. His father, a coal-miner, died in 1892, leaving behind a large family. As Conrad was the eldest child, he had to leave school at fourteen years of age to work in a quarry where he developed his climbing skills. In 1904 he became a mountain guide and successfully led parties up some of the most difficult peaks in the French, German, Austrian, and Italian Alps. In late 1908 he went to Vienna to study English, and while there he was encouraged to go to Canada.

In *Where the Clouds Can Go* we read Kain's insightful account of leaving home and travelling to Banff.

> *The day of departure was May 29th. 1908. During the last days in Vienna a travel-fever came over me: it is not easy to part with my many good friends in the mountains. To those who were dearest to me I went last of all. With some I had to hold back tightly lest I reveal emotion. At nine o'clock, on the evening of Pentecost Saturday, the train left Northwest Station. My baggage consisted of a large travelling bag, a chest, a rucksack and two ice-axes. Just before the time of departure Dr. Beryl and his family arrived. There were only a few minutes during which we could look back at the beautifully illuminated city of Vienna, but they were unforgettable, for I had only one thing in mind: I am going now on a long journey, who knows when I shall return.*
>
> *The fever of travel was burning in me. On the third of June, in the afternoon we left the Hotel Cecil [in London] and went by train to Liverpool. At Liverpool we spent the night in the Station Hotel. At last I was at the port and on-board the "Empress of Britain". As there were no more cabins to be had, I was taken down to the bottom of the ship. That didn't please me very much: but, to be sure, it would only be for eight days. Just at dusk the last bit of land was still to be seen, and so I said with the English people:*

"Farewell sweet home – if I have good fortune I shall see you once more!" (J. M. Thorington, 1935, p.203)

The above sentiments provide some insight as to the type of personality that Kain was. His description of his train ride from Quebec to Banff is also most revealing.

Conrad Kain
Taken in Banff in 1910 on his arrival from Europe

George Kinney, Conrad Kain and Curly Phillips huddled around a smudge fire while on the trail with A.O. Wheeler. The "smudge" kept the pesky mosquitoes away, thus ensuring a pleasant night around the campfire—it was a bit tough on the eyes and the lungs though.

On June 11th, 1909 we landed in Quebec, Canada's oldest port. It was a right comfortable feeling to be on firm ground once more, although I had never been seasick. About eight o'clock the train started for the Wild West. There are seats for groups of four persons, and a de-mountable table in the middle. Then there is a shelf to be pulled down and used as a bed for two people and for the other two, the seats are used. Good drinking water is at hand and there is a good stove in every car, on which one can cook little things. The employees of the Canadian Pacific are very kindly, and it does not at all agree with what I have heard of foreigners being handled like cattle.

On the first few days en route from Quebec to Winnipeg, one doesn't see much of fertile Canada – nothing but bushes and rocks. For half a day at a time, there is not a house or human habitation. Before reaching Winnipeg it becomes more interesting. Winnipeg is a large city and for a long time it was the point of departure for the West. It is said that eighteen languages are spoken there. The prairies begin at Winnipeg.

As far as the eye can see there is nothing but fields, all the way through Manitoba. It is said to be the best province for growing wheat. The region is too flat for me and the broad plain hurts my eyes.

On the afternoon of June 16th, 1909, I arrived in Calgary, where the Canadian Alpine Club has its headquarters. Calgary is a sprouting city in western Alberta. All nationalities are to be found here, and Germans are well represented. I saw a "Chinaman" for the first time. Near the city there are even Indians – Stonies. Calgary is an Indian word, meaning "slow moving water." The city is situated in the foothills of the Rockies. I looked at the snow-covered peaks with longing! (Thorington, 1935, p.208)

Conrad, now twenty-six years of age, made his way to Banff where he tried to get work as a guide with the CPR. This was unsuccessful, as the CPR was only hiring Swiss guides from Interlaken. A. O. Wheeler, of the Canadian Alpine Club hired him a few days later, and put him to work getting the recently completed clubhouse and grounds ready for the summer season. Wheeler then sent him to the annual ACC camp at Lake O'Hara to help set it up and act as a climbing guide. This was the beginning of Kain's long and rich career, as one of the premier mountaineering guides in Canada.

On July 20th, we left Banff, to put up the big summer camp, at Lake O'Hara. **Mr. Fynn**, *[Val Fynn] was very kind to me and explained many English words. We went westward by train to Hector (the first station in British Columbia.) There, A. O. Wheeler waited for us with horses. There was no hotel at Hector so two tents were put up and lunch was prepared. The horses were then packed and we started off. Our packer was Clausen Otto, a woodsman through and through. We went through swamp, over stones and windfall, tiresome for man and beast. At evening we reached Lake O'Hara, really a magnificent lake. Surrounded by fir trees and mossy ground: the lovely mountains surrounding it are all from ten to eleven thousand feet high, the colour of the lake being from the clearest green to the deepest blue.*

The next day was vacation, which we wished to devote to the ascent of Odaray. I was the first to awaken and when I opened up the tent saw to my astonishment—snow! We had breakfast, smoked a pipe and things got better. So we started off and after twenty minutes reached the edge of the woods, continuing to the glacier. We took the precaution to use the rope and took a steep little snow slope that leads to the ridge. It was easy, except for the last part—which is somewhat brittle. We took a long rest on the summit and enjoyed the view. .... Soon we were back in camp again, had a good lunch and then we walked to Lake O'Hara, where we met the Swiss guide, Edward Feuz, with a party. They had been on Mt. Odaray, but only on the south peak. The Swiss were very reserved toward me: he spoke only a few words and those in English. I had my own thoughts about it. (J.M. Thorington, 1935, p 214)

For the next week Conrad helped set up fifty or sixty tents for the Alpine Club summer camp. The following Sunday was a day of rest and so Conrad decided to climb Mt. Victoria alone.

Past Lake O'Hara and a lovely waterfalls I followed the little brook to Lake Oesa: it is renowned as being a frozen lake, open for only four to six weeks of the year. Suddenly the thunder of avalanche! An avalanche fell right into the lake. That was something to see! I continued over the scree to Abbot Pass, between Mts. Lefroy and Victoria. This pass is well known in Canadian climbing circles for there on August 3, 1896, occurred the first accident in the Rockies: a Mr. Abbot fell on the slopes of Mt. Lefroy and was killed. I ascended Mt. Victoria in a short time, as I discovered old tracks. It is one of the finest tours in the Rockies and may be compared with Swiss climbs. The view of the famous Lake Louise and the chalet is exceptionally beautiful.

*During my descent I met the Swiss guide **Aemmer** with another man, who was in the mountains for the first time. They descended the "Death Trap" so called on account of the avalanche danger. I returned to camp by my same route and went to the two little lakes near Lake O'Hara that I had seen from the summit of Mt. Victoria. Oh what a lovely picture, unforgettable and indescribable! A bit of forest separates the two lakes. One is deep blue—the other is light green, hemmed in by candlestick firs. Countless moss flowers grew on the bank. I thought at the moment of my old mountain friends at home, those who love flowers so much. It was like a dream, and I am not sure but that I dreamed it all. That evening the first guests arrived, about fifty people and we had our first big campfire.*

Conrad Kain after the first ascent of Mt. Robson on July 31, 1913

Conrad Kain on the Ice-Wall of Mount Robson 1924

Mt Robson from Berg Lake
(Photo by H. Pollard)

The following day we made the first tour of Mt. Huber—Mr. Fynn, three men from Calgary and I. Where the climbing begins, we fixed a rope for the parties following. First we attempted to reach the summit from the right but the bergschrund forced us back. So we went to the left, over a rather steep ice-slope, cut big steps, after which it went easily to the top. About six o'clock in the evening we were back in camp and were receiving congratulations. The place was full of tourists (mostly women). There were three Swiss guides there, which the C.P.R. had loaned for several weeks to make excursions in the vicinity of the camp. Later in the evening by the campfire, I became acquainted with the famous trapper Jimmy Simpson. (Thorington, 1935, p 216)

The next day Conrad led another group up Mt. Huber (11,051 feet). His account reveals some of the initial animosity that existed between the Swiss guides and the Austrian newcomer.

Again a group for Mt. Huber. It was a frosty morning and when we were climbing through a gully from O'Hara and reached the pass between Wiwaxy and Mt. Huber, it began to storm and snow. Everyone turned back. Only Mr. Fynn, who also led a party and I with three women and a man, waited in the shelter of the rocks for better weather. I promised sunshine and told amusing stories of climbing from my experiences as guide, so that the people would not loose their courage and desire for the ascent. We waited in the cold, and at last, a blue patch appeared in the sky! For a few minutes the sun appeared though the fog. Right above the pass some easy climbing begins. But the rocks were very cold and progress was slow. Mr. Fynn had to turn back with his party because one of the ladies had almost frozen her fingers. I would have had to as well if I had not fortunately brought several extra pairs of gloves for my women. Now we came to the glacier, which we ascended diagonally, then over a short ice-ridge to a wall of rock, a step that interrupts the glacier, then over the glacier again to the col between Mt. Victorian and Mt. Huber. The weather changed in the meantime, but as the ladies knew we were the only ones out of fifty-five people who had not given up,.they were full of joy and desire to reach the summit, despite the obstacle presented by the unfavourable weather. I told them not to be dismayed by the fog, and that if a wind did not arise we would attain the peak without trouble. In this fashion we kept up their confidence and courage.

Without difficulty we reached the ice-slope, now covered with fresh snow. This was the only really dangerous place of the whole excursion. I was obliged to improve the old steps which we had made several days ago but without further incident we reached the summit of Mt. Huber. For a few minutes of our halt we had a good view down to the camp.

While descending the risky spots on the ice-slope a wind sprang-up and away went our good steps in the snow. That was not pleasant for me, for as guide I could not go first in descending and my tourists were all beginners. I put the strongest woman in front. Slowly and with great care we went down step by step. A single mishap would have been fatal, for I could not anchor myself. I breathed easier when the last woman descended over the bergschrund.

As we approached camp everyone came toward us, more than one hundred people with the Club President Mr. Wheeler at their head. Mr. Wheeler offered me his hand and said: "I thank you, Conrad. Now you have your witnesses, and I see that it is just as Dr. P. wrote to me about you, that Conrad never stops until he has completed his task." As he finished his speech, the younger men lifted me on their shoulders and carried me to the camp-fire, with fearful shouting of "Hip-Hip-Hurrah" and singing "He's a jolly good fellow". Naturally the ladies were given a thunderous "Hurrah."

The Swiss guides present in camp did not enter into the felicitations. When I entered the sleeping tent, one said to me rather scornfully in his dialect: that he thought such a trip was stupidity and that in his home no one went out in such weather. I replied: "If I had not met with bigger storms in Switzerland, I would not be able to say very much about the dangers of the mountains "When he replied: "Oh. What do you know about Switzerland? I became angry, hunted for my guide's book and threw it to him. He read it and discovered the truth of my assertions. He approached me pleasantly: "Don't be angry! You look much too young, and one can hardly believe that you have travelled so much." We shook hands and were then friends. (Thorington, 1935, p.217-218)

Conrad Kain went on to become one of the great guides in the area and over the years, he and the Swiss guides grew to respect one another's abilities. After the Alpine Club assignment at Lake O'Hara, Conrad went to the Selkirks and made solo climbs of Mt. Avalanche, Mt. Abbot and Mt. Sir Donald.

Glacier house was overflowing with tourists and travellers in July and August of 1909. As there were no parties to guide during the next days, I climbed Mount Sir Donald—considered to be the most difficult peak in the Selkirks. The guides had told me much about it. But I found no difficulties at all, although naturally it is different if one is guiding people. The view from the summit is magnificent. Unnumbered peaks and glaciers spread before the eyes. With a good glass one could easily count more than a thousand peaks. (J. M. Thorington, 1935, p.230)

From Roger's Pass, Conrad journeyed to Revelstoke and while there he was much impressed with the salmon that came that far up the river from the ocean.

Salmon come up to Revelstoke. It sounds unbelievable to one who has never seen so many fish, to hear that one actually cannot see the bottom of the brook because of their numbers!" One sees hundreds of fishermen on the shores, mostly Indians. The fish are caught in all possible ways and manners, and then smoked, also canned and shipped to all countries. (J. M. Thorington, 1935, p.231)

Conrad spent his first winter in Canada at Fort Saskatchewan near Edmonton, learning the secrets of trapping and how to survive in a harsh climate. When spring came in 1910 he went back to Banff and again worked for A.O. Wheeler and the Alpine Club of Canada. During May, June, and early July he helped set up the Club's summer camp in the Yoho Valley and then went to the climbing camp in the Consolation Valley. That summer he climbed Mt. Fay, Mt. Bident, Mt. Temple, and Eiffel Peak. He then went to Bow Lake, the Waputik snowfield, and back to the Yoho Valley with **Dr. T. Longstaff** and a party that included **Mary Vaux, Byron Harmon,** and **Fred Bell**. On August 30th, he accompanied Dr. Longstaff to the Purcell Range that lies between the Rockies and the Selkirks. Byron Harmon went with them and was delighted to catch his first glimpse of the Bugaboo Mountains.

In 1911, Conrad was on Wheeler's expedition to the Mt. Robson area. **Byron Harmon, Bill Peyto, Curly Phillips, Jimmy Simpson, Bob Bapti,** and **Ulysse La Casse** were all on this trip. It was on this expedition that Conrad, much to Wheeler's annoyance, climbed Mt. Resplendent with Byron Harmon and then he climbed Mt. Whitehorn alone.

During the winters of 1911 and 1912, Conrad trapped marten, wolverines, and wild cats with **Donald (Curly) Phillips**. In August of 1913, Kain, along with W.W. Foster and A.H. McCarthy, were the first team to climb Mt. Robson, the highest peak in the Canadian Rockies, and one of the most difficult, because of its sheer size, its technical difficulties, and unpredictability of the weather. The ascent took place a few days before Kain's thirtieth birthday.

During the descent the team spent the night on the mountain, returning to camp on August 1st, after having spent some thirty hours on the climb. During the most difficult part of the attempt, Conrad cut more than five hundred steps and MacCarthy is reported to have said: "*Conrad, if it not too dangerous for you cutting steps, then don't worry about us. We'll trust you and fortune.*" Conrad had an exceptional ability to inspire confidence and courage in those he guided on some of the most difficult climbs in the Rockies and Phyllis Munday, the first woman to climb Mt. Robson, often commented on this.

On August 10th, **A. H. McCarthy, B. S. Darling** and Conrad set out to climb Mt. Robson from the southwest. The team got to the 12,500 foot level, but they were turned back by a vicious storm. Years later, Conrad wrote about his many experiences on Mt Robson.

> *I have ascended Mt. Robson several times and my verdict is that it is long and offers many problems to the leader. No matter from what side it is climbed there are dangerous sections, even under the best conditions. He who hires himself out for such a climb earns his pay, and the amateur who can lead to the summit is in my opinion a full-fledged mountaineer.*

During the last part of 1913, Conrad journeyed to the Southern Alps of New Zealand, where he recorded more that thirty first ascents, including Mt. Conrad, which was named after him. In Canada, Mt. Kain and Nasswald Peak in the Rockies, and Birthday Peak in the Purcells, are all named in his honour.

In 1916, during the Healy Creek ACC camp, Kain and A. H. McCarthy made the first ascent of Mt. Louis, the sheer rock spire just west of Banff. The brief comment that Conrad made to MacCarthy as they returned from climbing the pinnacle reflects the imposing nature of this intimidating spire:

> *Upon reaching the edge of the timber east of Mt. Edith, we stopped and looked back at our mountain, and Conrad spoke volumes when he said: "Ye Gods Mr. McCarthy, just look at that: They never will believe we climbed it." (Thorington, 1935, p.369)*

Conrad always considered Mt. Louis to be one of his most difficult ascents. Another was the descent of the east face of Monument Peak on the North Fork of Toby Creek in the Purcells. Several years later Conrad pointed out the route to a prospector, who remarked: *"Say, you are either a fool or a dog-gone liar!"*

In August of 1916, Kain and McCarthy were the first climbers to visit the Bugaboo area, where the peaks are on a par with the best in the Alps. This area was reached in two days from Spillimacheen in the Columbia Valley. Conrad wrote of the difficulty. "It was pioneer work, and the loftiest mountains were the attraction; but these, unlike the highest summits of many groups, were needles to test one's mettle." Conrad and McCarthy did first ascents of Howser Spire and Bugaboo Spire which Conrad rated as his most difficult Canadian ascent and certainly as difficult and as interesting as any he had encountered in the Alps. On this trip Conrad had the opportunity to inspect and assess Snow Patch, which at that time was simply named Spire No. 2.

> *With sheer cliffs on all sides, it is the most picturesque of all and rises some 2000 ft. above the glacier. After carefully searching with powerful binoculars, I have come to the conclusion that it will prove very hard to conquer. Since then I have had the opportunity to study the peak from different angles and have not*

> *changed my opinion. I feel inclined to prophesy that this peak will be the most difficult ascent in the Canadian Alps." (Thorington, 1935, p.372)*

💐

Reflecting on over thirty years of climbing and guiding Conrad summed up what he felt were the essential features of any good mountaineering guide:

> *It was in the early days of my career as a guide that I learned that the leader on any climb must hold the confidence of the party. This is not always simple. Having thirty climbing seasons to look back on, I could write columns on the subject. To mention a few of the points a guide should bear in mind will not be amiss. First he should never show fear. Second he should be courteous to all, and always give special attention to the weakest member in the party. Third he should be witty, and able to make up a white-lie if necessary, on short notice and tell it in a convincing manner, fourth he should know when and how to show authority; and when the situation demands it he should be able to give a good scolding to whomsoever deserves it." (Thorington, 1935, p 375)*

In June of 1917 Conrad married Henriquito Ferreira. After their marriage, they settled down on a farm at Wilmer in the Columbia Valley, where they raised mink, martens and chinchilla rabbits. In July, Conrad was back in the Rockies and guided Mr. and Mrs. McCarthy up Mt. Hungabee, the first ascent by a woman. In March of 1919 Conrad made the first winter ascent of a peak over eleven thousand feet in the Canadian Alps when he climbed Mt. Jumbo in the Purcell range on snowshoes.

In 1920, Conrad spent the whole winter alone and trapping from the North Saskatchewan and the Mistaya rivers to Lake Louise. A story is told of how Conrad managed to spend so much time alone in the wilderness without losing his mind:

> *One autumn he tossed a coin to help him decide whether to take with him a three pound volume of Victor Hugo's Les Miserables or some extra, and badly needed, food. The book won and Conrad thought that it saved him from going insane through loneliness." (Thorington, 1935, p.380).*

In July of 1921, Conrad, with **A.H. McCarthy, L. Lindsay, Edward Feuz, Rudolf Aemmer,** and **Wild Bill Peyto** assisted in rescuing **Mrs. Stone** from Mt. Eon near Mt. Assiniboine. Conrad retrieved Dr. Stone's body and assisted in bringing it back to Banff.

With his old friend **Jimmy Simpson**, Conrad guided **W.S. Ladd** and **J.M. Thorington** on an expedition to the Columbia Icefield in 1923. He wrote: "*In those days the Columbia Icefield region was considered wild and far away, having been visited by only a few climbers since it's discovery by Collie in 1898.*" Everything went smoothly and they climbed several peaks, including Mt. Castleguard (10,096 feet), the North Twin (12,085 feet, first ascent), Mt. Saskatchewan (10,964 feet, first ascent), Mt. Columbia (12,294 feet), and Mt. Athabaska (11,452 feet). On the summit of Castleguard, Thorington observed:

> *Jimmy Simpson and Conrad are lying flat on the shale, with a map spread out: There is great pointing of fingers toward distant valleys, and the remarks which come to my ears indicate that the fur-bearing animals next trapping season had best look out for themselves. The highlights of the climbing were Conrad, cutting through the little cornice of Mt. Columbia; and his care and concern during the descent of Mt. Saskatchewan, when our position became hazardous because of avalanches and wet snow. Back in Banff following that trip Ladd and Conrad achieved the third ascent of Mt. Louis. But so much damage was done to the seats of their trousers that they waited until dark before daring to reappear in the village – those were good days. Conrad was continually pointing out the features of the country, helping with the packing, keeping us in an uproar with his stories and making himself generally useful. Here he had cached his traps; there he had spent a cold night in the snow – dreaming of a warm fire. For those that took part, this journey stands out in memory as one of the happiest and most successful ever made in the Canadian mountains. (Thorington, 1935, pp 385-386)*

In 1924, J.M. Thorington engaged Conrad for an expedition to Athabaska Pass. Thorington wanted to climb Mt. Alberta, Mt. Hooker, and Mt. Robson. He also hoped to climb Mt. Resplendent, Mt. Whitehorn, and Mt. Longstaff. While climbing Mt. Hooker (10,782 feet), the group came into some danger because of falling rock:

> *We were all struck but luckily without damage. Conrad, calmly said 'Gentlemen, we must move a little to one side,' and relieved the tension. We quickly got out of range, just in time to avoid a heavy bombardment of larger boulders that came banging down over our intended path. We realized that in Conrad's cool leadership, in emergency, we had seen one of the finer things produced by mountaineering art. (Thorington, 1935, pp 385-386)*

In July 1924, Conrad guided **Phyllis Munday** up Mt. Robson – the first woman to conquer it. Conrad made two successful trips up to the summit of Mt. Robson that year in just three days. Following this he guided a group into the Tonquin Valley for a first ascent of Simon Peak (10,899 feet.).

> *Conrad was in great form that evening, and treated us with tales of startling adventure: snake-collecting in Egypt, sheep-herding in Australia, gold washing in the Northwest, wanderings in the South Seas, hunting in the Siberian Altai. The most beautiful place in the world, he believes, is the island of Madeira; there he would like to spend a little of his old age before retiring to a cottage in the Tyrol. Slowly rose the moon; not in solemn*

grandeur, but rather with full face smiling, as if in sympathy with our merriment. A wind from the Tonquin Pass was gently moving the pine-tops; there was a tinkling of bell as our horses wandered across the meadows." (Thorington, 1935, p.388)

Thorington comments further on the joy of having Conrad along on a trip:

Kain was a voluminous reader on many subjects and had a vivid curiosity concerning human nature. No one in the Northwest could tell a better story. With laughter and vivid expression ever at the surface, Conrad was inclined to think the world an amusing place and treated it accordingly. He styled himself a "baloney peddler," meaning that he had the "gift of the gab". It was dangerous, especially in mixed company, to press him for a tale. A wild look of delight would come over him and he was quite apt to cut loose with a narrative bringing blushes to all within hearing distance. He did not like to be forced. But, given his own time, there was an almost oriental facility in his story telling, and the last of the thousand-and-one nights would not have ended the spark of mischief in his eye, the gay mimicry in his voice, and the subtle gesturing of his hand. When Conrad Kain and Jimmy Simpson were together, one began where the other left off. (J. M. Thorington, Where the Clouds Can Go, 1935, p.415).

Early in 1933, Conrad's wife of sixteen years died in Cranbrook, B.C. following an operation. Conrad missed her terribly. He climbed occasionally that year with old friends and clients such as Dr. Thorington and his wife and H. S. Kingman. In 1933 he climbed Mt. Lefroy and on his fiftieth birthday he climbed Mt. Louis. He also climbed Pigeon Spire in the Bugaboos and Mt. Conrad, the highest peak in the in the Bobbie Burns group. This was the last climb he ever made.

On September 20th, 1934, Conrad wrote to his friend J.M.T. Wilmer:

Now I am home picking apples, harvesting the vegetables & fixing things up for the all too long winter, then I will go hunting, and after that I might go visiting to the Okanagan Valley, as at times I get so damenable lonely. I miss my old Sweetheart more than ever. I beg you to send a copy of "'The Glittering Mountains of Canada" to Miss Amelia Malek. And please send her a picture of 'Snowpatch from the South' and write on it 'The Mountain the Conrad Could Not Climb.'

On February 2nd, 1934, Conrad died suddenly from a severe case of encephalitis lethargia. He was buried next to his wife in the Cranbrook cemetery. The news of his death was a great blow to all who knew and admired him. Jimmy Simpson wrote:

He gave the best of his life to the ACC and the Dominion Gov't under A.O. Wheeler and he gave every ounce of his best at all times. He would die for you if need be, quicker that most men think of living. No matter what his creed, his color or his nationality, he was measured by a man's yardstick, no other. We shall miss him. (Thorington, 1935, p.441).

J. M. Thorington eventually took Conrad's notes, journals, and manuscripts and with dedication and sensitive editing published "Where the Clouds Can Go" in 1935. He dedicated it to Conrad's mother and three friends of his youth who meant a lot to him. Anyone who loves mountains and people should read this tribute to a truly exceptional personality. Thorington's last paragraph sums up his thoughts about Conrad Kain.

> *Conrad was undoubtedly the most glamorous figure in Canadian mountaineering, and those who climbed with him know that his death separates all that went before from whatever the future may bring forth. Guides in days to come will scarcely have his great experience in travel, new ascents and trail-breaking. But he was so much more than just a guide – he was your friend, playing a part in the inspiring moments of many lives and giving more to life than he asked of it. He had no routine moments on a mountain and, if you had not employed him, he would have been climbing by himself for the pure joy and beauty of it all.*

> *"He will be missed," wrote his neighbours in the Columbia Valley, "for he was a kind and honest man." There is probably no better epitaph.*

Thorington noted that Conrad had the rare ability to inspire confidence in those whom he guided, as well as many other fine qualities.

> *On rock, in his prime, Kain was unquestionably a finished performer. On snow and ice his judgement was sound, with step-cutting unfailingly conforming to the needs of his party. The latter factor determined his use of the rope: he had no fixed procedure. Wide experience in various districts had taught him all the tricks. Even on new peaks he preferred to traverse and would cleverly find a way down, with almost unique ability in route finding on the mountain at hand.*

> *With an axe in the woods Conrad was the equal of Curly Phillips or Jim Simpson. He was a good clean cook, and handled horses with gentleness, talking to them as it they were children. His great capacity for weight carrying was constantly overtaxed. He was about five feet five inches tall, stockily built, waist narrow and shoulders broad – the torso of an athlete. His hair and moustache carried a tinge of auburn; he had high coloring and a radiant, ready smile. A short, curved pipe was his constant companion.*

> *No desire to rush up peaks or break records was to be found in Kain's makeup. He loved the varying lights and colors too much for that, and would loaf on a summit if there was a chance of*

seeing a fine sunset, even though it meant getting in late. Light, life and joy contrasting with shadow, mystery and pathos – Conrad was keenly attuned to the drama of their interplay. ... He knew well that life is not compounded soley of action he had no more important lesson to teach (1935, 444-445)

In a room of the American Alpine Club, an old ice axe hangs on the wall. The cutting edge is blunted and the wooden shaft is worn where the hand grips it far down in the step-cutting position. But it has been the silent witness of high adventure, and on it a small brass plate reads:

CONRAD KAIN (1883-1934)
GUIDE, PHILOSOPHER, FRIEND
MT. ROBSON 1913, MT. LOUIS 1916, BUGABOO SPIRE 1916

A great guide has gone, and with him something that made life infinitely gay. It is no small thing to have held so much of mirth and wonder and loveliness. "Who so touches a joy as he flies, lives in Eternity's sunrise" – If this be hero-worship make the most of it. For some of us a door was opened upon a golden world, and Time has all too quickly snatched away the key. (Thorington, 1935, p.445)

Conrad Kain on the summit of Mt. Cook in New Zealand

Conrad Kain leading four climbers from the Alpine Club of Canada to the summit of Mt. Resplendent in 1913. This photo was taken by Byron Harmon who was on the climb.

Byron Harmon – Pioneer Photographer of the Rockies

No historical account of Banff, Lake Louise, and the mountains would be complete without mention of Byron Harmon, the great pioneer photographer of the Rockies. For years the Harmony Drug Store in Banff featured a remarkable collection of enlarged black-and-white photos of mountains, native Indians, early pioneers, and climbers. These pictures were hung high, almost to the ceiling, and they stirred the viewers' imagination and curiosity, leaving you wanting to know more about the scenes and the man who took the photos.

Edward, Ernest, and Walter Feuz, and Jimmy Simpson of Num-Ti-Jah Lodge told me many stories about Byron Harmon and the trips they had made with him throughout the Rockies. Whether Byron was accompanying A.O. Wheeler to photograph the great Columbia Icefields, or serving as the "official photographer" for the Alpine Club of Canada at one of its many camps, he always carried his big box cameras with him.

The story of Byron Harmon and his remarkable portfolio of photos is loving told by his granddaughter, Carol Harmon, in the book *Great Days in the Rockies – The Photographs of Byron Harmon, 1906–1934 published in 1978*. This project preserved the work of the "Amstel Adams" of the Canadian Rockies.

Harmon was born on February 9, 1876 near Tacoma, in Washington State. He was raised by his mother on a Puget Sound Indian reservation, where she worked as a matron to support her family of three. Sadly Byron's father ran off shortly his birth and his heroic mother was left to raise the family.

Byron's early experiences with native Indians and their ways served him well as he used this knowledge all his life, whether on the trail or in his studio in Banff. From early age he was interested in photography and in the 1880s, when Kodak first came out with the first roll film, he made a primitive box camera. His early successes with film, photos, and cameras gave him the courage to open his own portrait studio in Tacoma. This enabled him to support himself and pursue his passionj for photography.

From Tacoma, Byron travelled throughout North America, eventually arriving in the Canadian Rockies. While enjoying the hot springs in Banff, he decided that the town needed a photo studio and he opened up a little shop on Banff Avenue. He soon developed a large portfolio of exceptional photographs featuring mountain peaks and lakes, wild life, and many of the local climbers and personalities around Banff. He started a successful postcard business, selling prints of more than 100 different photographs to tourists coming to town on the CPR. Whether riding, climbing, or hiking he always carried a four-by-five inch, or a five-by-seven inch still camera, a movie camera and tripod, a changing bag, extra film, and glass plate. Like all photographers, he was always looking for the "perfect light." Sometimes he'd perch on a cliff for hours, waiting for the "right" light to hit a glacier or a mountain before he would take his photos.

Harmon was a founding member of the ACC, along with A.O. Wheeler, Elizabeth Parker, Wild Bill Peyto, Tom Wilson, Reverend G. Kinney, and James Simpson. He loved being associated with the club and was named its official photographer. For years he attended the annual ACC mountaineering camps in the

Rockies and took some spectacular photos. His involvement with the Alpine Club and mountaineering fraternity put him in contact with some of the great pioneer guides and outfitters of the day and their clients.

Byron Harmon

Byron Harmon in camp during the 1911 trip with A.O. Wheeler and Conrad Kain to the Columbia Icefield, Mount Robson, Yellowhead Pass, and Maligne Lake. He was always happiest when he was on the trail with his friends.

Tom Wilson liked and admired Byron immensely, especially his easy-going, steady manner and his wry sense of humour. Conrad Kain, Edward, Ernest, and

Walter Feuz, Rudolf Aemmer, Christian Haesler, Bill Peyto, Jimmy Brewster, Curly Phillips and Jimmy Simpson were all larger-than-life characters and he photographed them, camped with them, and bushwacked through the backcountry of the Rockies with them.

> *From such men Harmon learned the secrets of mountain life; from the subtleties of the alpinist's knots and the packer's diamond hitch, to the trick of drying out wet matches in his hair. With them he formed his closest friendships – alliances that lasted long after his most active days on the trail were over."* (Harmon, 1978)

Pioneer photographer Byron Harmon 1876-1942
His pictures and post cards were remarkable and captured the spirit of the Rockies. They still sell in great numbers today.

Bow Lake and packer Bob Bapti taken by Byron Harmon in 1911
This picture is typical of Harmon's excellent photography.

In the fall of 1910, Byron went with A.O. Wheeler on a three-week trip into the Purcell range, west of the Rockies and south of the Selkirks. On this trip he discovered and photographed glaciers, mountains, and lakes never before seen by white men. One glacier Harmon discovered while exploring on his own was christened Harmon's Glacier, but later the name was changed to "Bugaboo Glacier". It, and the surrounding area, would later become one of the most spectacular skiing and climbing areas in the world.

Byron Harmon and Conrad Kain became close friends, as they shared many days on the trail and many nights by the campfire. Conrad was a favourite subject of many of Harmon's mountaineering photos.

> *Both Harmon and Kain were mirthful souls at the fireside, and the two of them together had a special ability to keep a camp in high spirits. To improve our humour, we held an Indian dance. Dr. Longstaff and the two packers put on bear hides and I the goat skin. Mr. Harmon, the photographer, was the band. His instrument—the pans, so we danced about the fire, making a terrible din.*

Ulysse LaCasse
Helping pack horses through the snow on the way back to Lagan from Jasper. This photo was taken by Byron Harmon in 1924. Ulysse became a park warden in 1931. He often served as cook on expeditions and was noted for his sense of humor.

The next summer, Harmon and Kain were together again with A.O. Wheeler and four scientists from the Smithsonian Institute. They did a three-month trip to the Columbia Icefields, the Rainbow Mountains, Jasper, and Mt. Robson.

> It was a major trip into uncharted mountain wilderness and jungle. Kain wrote; "Not incorrectly is this called the "Wild West". No houses, no roads: only Indian trails. The valley's are wet and boggy, and one often sinks to ones knees. On our first excursion we were almost buried by an avalanche, and Mr. Harmon had to photograph it at the very worst moment." (Thorington 1935)

On this historic trip Byron and Conrad Kain achieved the first ascent of the magnificent Mt. Resplendent in the Mt. Robson group. Conrad then made the first ascent of Mt. Whitehorn alone.

In 1922, Kain and Harmon packed into the Lake of the Hanging Glaciers. Byron took plenty of camera equipment along as well as thirty-six sticks of dynamite, which he loaded on one of Jimmy Simpson's packhorses. The dynamite was intended to assist Nature for a series of photos to be entitled "The Birth of an Iceberg," The story of this trip is quite humorous and reveals the type of adventures that Conrad, Jimmy Simpson, and Byron Harmon had during those great early days in the Rockies.

> Conrad went over and dug a hole in the ice and placed his dynamite, tamped it down and lighted the fuse. When he came back he remarked that something should come loose as there were

seven sticks about to let go. Harmon took a last anxious look into the view-finder. The earth shook, the air turned purple: Mother Earth agonized, and a few pounds of ice trickled off into the lake as the smoke drifted away. But, of course, that was understood. We were waiting for the aftermath, the mighty avalanche we were sure to get.

Now when Old Bill, an ornery packhorse, had been unloaded, he strolled off to browse on some tufts of green and no one gave him a second thought. When the first report of the discharge took place, Old Bill started a charge of his own. What mattered it to him if the cameras were in his line of his advance? He came down the stretch hitting on all fours, his mane flying, his nostrils dilated and flaming, his eyes holding the fire of battle. He hit Harmon first! Down went the camera and Old Bill walked up the spine of the vanquished photographer. He hit the second, third and forth cameras with sickening precision and then careered off down the Valley. And then it happened! The whole top of the mountain eased off a bit, toppled and crashed to the glacier below in the mightiest of the mighty avalanches. (Thorington, 1935–p 383).

In the summer of 1924, Harmon organised his last expedition into the mountains – a seventy-five-day, five hundred-mile trip to Jasper via the Columbia Icefields and the headwaters of the Athabaska River. The trip was a big success and Byron had a wealth of pictures to process, enlarge, and print.

Throughout his life Byron Harmon operated a studio in Banff and kept his interests in the mountains alive. He maintained close contact with his friends in the Alpine Club of Canada and was a founding member of both the Trail Riders of the Canadian Rockies, founded in 1924, and the Skyline Trail Hikers of the Canadian Rockies, organized in 1933. He maintained his friendships with Tom Wilson, Bill Peyto, Conrad Kain, A.O. Wheeler, Jimmy Simpson, and the Feuz brothers until his death. He left a remarkable legacy of photos that captured early life on the trail and the majesty of the Rockies.

During the spring of 1942, Harmon's health took a turn for the worse, largely as a result of the high blood pressure that he suffered from. He died on July 10th, 1942, and was buried not far from his good friend Tom Wilson. The site of his grave has a great view of the mountains that he gave to the world through his remarkable photographs.

Lawrence Grassi – Trail Builder of the Rockies

Andrea Lorenzo Grassi or "Grassi" as he was called by all who knew him, was born on December 20, 1890 in Falment, of Piedmont Province in Italy. He immigrated to Canada when he was twenty-one and after a year in Ontario, he moved to Hector in the heart of the Rockies where he became a "section-man" for the CPR. In late 1916 he moved to Canmore, and worked as a coal miner there for over thirty years.

Grassi was in his late sixties and still going strong when I first met him at Lake O'Hara during the summer of 1958. At the urging of Edward and Ernest Feuz, he was hired by the Warden's Service to look after the trails and meadows of that precious area. He lived in the small Warden's cabin beside the lake and registered climbers coming into the O'Hara area. Situated on Sargent's Point, the cabin had an excellent view of the Seven Veils Falls. (Sargent's Point was named after John Singer Sargent, an artist who first came to O'Hara in 1916.)

A lover of nature and the high mountain meadows, Grassi became an excellent climber and amateur guide. He never charged to guide people up the mountains he loved. It was payment enough for him to see their enjoyment and to share their enthusiasm. He also loved to build mountain trails and he spent most of his spare time doing so around Canmore, Mt. Rundle, the ACC clubhouse on Sulphur Mountain in Banff, and especially in the Lake O'Hara area.

Not a large man, he stood about five feet, four inches tall. His hair was steel grey and he always wore a battered, Stetson hat along with a thick, wool, Harris Tweed jacket and twill pants held up with suspenders. He was very soft-spoken and had a dry sense of humour. His dark eyes would twinkle with mirth when he told stories about the trouble some tourist got themselves into in the mountains. Although he walked a bit stooped over in his later years he still possessed super-human strength. He once carried a large cook-stove on his back from the main road at Wapta to Lake O'Hara and set it up in the kitchen of the Elizabeth Parker Hut – a distance of approximately nine miles. He also carried Dr. Williams of Calgary down from near the top of Mt. Bastion and along the trail for almost two miles to a rescue party, after the portly doctor slipped and badly injured his ankle.

Grassi was an excellent packer, guide, and climber in his younger days and made the first ascent of Mt. Ball, between Banff and Castle Junction. During his lifetime he made over twenty ascents of Mt. Louis near Banff and accompanied Byron Harmon on several trips into the Rockies. He also helped pack for the ACC during its annual summer camps.

Anyone who knew Lawrence Grassi will remember him building, improving, and maintaining the many trails in the Lake O'Hara region. It is still a mystery how he managed to move, lever, and position huge flat rocks and boulders into position to make perfectly placed steps and staircases up cliff-sides and through the meadows on the trails leading to Lake McArthur, the Opabin Plateau, Lake Oesa, Linda Lake, and the Morning Glory Lakes. The trail around Lake O'Hara, which winds along the shoreline, up and over Seven Veils Falls, along the lower cliffs of Mt. Huber and Mt. Wiwaxy, and then down to the shoreline again to Cataract Brook, is an amazing feat of design and construction. Grassi built it with just a pick, a pry-bar, and a shovel. His trails were without doubt the best in the Rockies and can still be seen and marvelled at today.

> All through the years Grassi has gone to Lake O'Hara and there, working alone with axe, crowbar and spade, improved old trails, built new trails and made rock walls and bridges, all of which have made hiking and climbing in that incomparable region the delight it is today. His handiwork can be recognised on every side. On the

trail to Lake Oesa, a wooden, pole ladder was the only way visitors to the Lodge who were not experienced in mountain travel could surmount one of the cliffs. Grassi replaced that ladder with a rock staircase, the steps of which are each of them one great heavy flat stone. (Canadian Alpine Journal 1977, 41-42)

Lawrence Grassi in his mid-forties on the Tower of Mount Eisenhower

Grassi in his later years as the Warden at Lake O'Hara
He's standing just outside the Elizabeth Parker Hut in the O'Hara Meadows.

Grassi taking a well deserved rest near one of his staircases leading to McArthur Pass. His trusty wheelbarrow and his pick, shovels and pry-bar were always close at hand. He was not a tall man but he had the strength of Hercules and the heart of a lion.

At the recommendation of the Swiss guides, Grassi was appointed Assistant Warden in O'Hara, where he had his own cabin. It was pure magic to be walking down a trail from a climb of Mt. Hungabee, Mt. Odaray, Mt. Wiwaxy, or Mt. Huber and see Grassi working away on the trail. He would usually have his wheelborrow, pry-bars, shovels, and a rake or two with him and he'd be putting the finishing touches on a stone staircase or a special step. I would sit down with him for a moment and he would light his pipe and eventually begin to talk about the mountains that were in our line of vision, or the trail he had just finished working on. He was a soft, gentle man that fit perfectly into the magic of Lake O'Hara. (I'm told that he was also a special friend of the "Little People" that inhabit the secret, moist glades along the gentle streams that trickle down from the Opabin Plateau and the Sheaffer Meadows. These tiny creatures make themselves visible only to those who have music in their hearts, and who love this enchanted place above all others on earth.)

On June 26th, 1970, when Grassi turned eighty years of age the ACC erected a plaque in gratitude for his unselfish and remarkable work on the trails of O'Hara. It is located at his rock staircase near the Seven Veils Falls, at the end of lake and reads:

"THIS PLAQUE IS A TRIBUTE TO
LAWRENCE GRASSI A.C.C.
"TRULY ONE OF NATURE'S GENTLEMEN"
WHO BUILT MANY TRAILS IN THE BANFF-LAKE LOUISE AREA,
INCLUDING THIS TRAIL AND THESE STEPS, SO THAT
THOSE WHO FOLLOW MIGHT MORE
EASILY ENJOY THE MOUNTAINS HE LOVES.
ERECTED IN GRATITUDE BY THE ALPINE CLUB OF CANADA
A.D. 1970"

During his rich lifetime, Grassi was awarded honorary Life Memberships in the Alpine Club of Canada, the Canadian Youth Hostels Association, and the Skyline Trail Hikers of the Canadian Rockies. All of these organizations recognized his special nature and his unselfish contribution to the Rockies he loved.

> *Utterly selfless and unassuming, he was a friend of all mountain lovers and lovers of nature and the outdoors. A born naturalist with a profound knowledge gained in the school of experience of the fauna and flora of the Rockies, he was never happier than when taking one or more of those privileged to know him along some rarely trodden trail or out for a climb. (*Canadian Alpine Journal 1977, 41–42)

Just before his death, Grassi donated a significant sum of money to the ACC. His only stipulation was that it could not be spent on anything that could become the property of the government. A commitment was given to Grassi that the funds would be used to build a hut and the Board of Management later approved the construction of a mountain cabin to be named in his honour.

Located in one of the most remote areas of the Canadian Rockies, the hut is situated just off the Clemenceau Icefield, at the southeast end of Cummins Ridge. It is the most distant hut in the ACC chain and is accessed by helicopter, ski plane, or a very long hike. The hut is a heavy-duty, high-altitude, metal-sided, Gothic arch structure with a view of some of the biggest and wildest peaks in the Rockies. The single room has a double sleeping platform for eighteen people (sixteen in winter) with tables, benches, a large kitchen area, and an oil-burning stove for heat. The mountaineering and ski touring in this area is outstanding.

After Grassi's death on February 5th, 1980, his ashes were spread above the Seven Veils Falls – not far from the bronze plaque honouring his work.

Of the many individuals I have met in my life, I'm thankful that I knew and spent many joyful hours with Lawrence Grassi along the trail and in his cabin. He always had a kettle of hot tea on and I treasured the times I spent chatting with him near the warm stove as I waited for the weather to clear. He was truly one of God's special people.

Sometimes when there is a bit of "scotch mist" hanging over Lake O'Hara and it's too wet to climb, it's good to go for a hike up and around the Opabin Valley circuit that eventually leads back to the Lake O'Hara. Even today, as you stop and admire one of Grassi's staircases, you can almost hear the "tap," "tap," "tap" of his crowbar, from just around the corner, as he works on the positioning of one of his huge rock steps. Grassi's spirit lives on in O'Hara and for those who knew him there, it always will.

The Lawrence Grassi Hut – he would have been pleased

Erling Strom: The man who introduced downhill skiing to the Rockies

On March 4th, 1928, **Erling Strom** and six "easterners" got off the train at Banff with some strange-looking downhill skis, packs, and equipment. The locals scratched their heads in incredulity, as until then skiing in the Banff area had been primarily restricted to ski jumping which Conrad Kain had introduced to the area. Conrad was known for impressing the locals with dazzling jumps on the slopes of Mt. Norquay. The wooden skis these eastern dudes carried were long, had "bear-trap" bindings, and didn't have metal edges. Strom was no stranger to downhill and alpine skiing however as he had spent most of the First World War as a commander of storm troops on skis in the Italian Alps. He was also familiar with the mountains, snow, and avalanche conditions, and backcountry survival. He later wrote about the early reactions of the Banff residents.

> *Skiing had been introduced through ski jumping, and like most other places on this continent, people had been led to think, "skiers must jump." For winter travel they had the Indian snowshoe, and even to this day one can get into heated arguments as to which of the two forms of ambulation is the more practical. (Strom 1933).*

The group of six left Banff with their skis and gear on March 5th, and travelled on a gravel road along the Bow River. Three miles west of town at Healy Creek they turned left and proceeded up the creek until they reached the snow line. There they put on their skis and climbing skins and gained altitude rapidly. As they ascended, the snow became better and better and they proceeded up Healy Creek, past Howard Douglas Creek and on to Brewster Creek, where there was an overnight cabin that had been built by A.O. Wheeler. There they made themselves comfortable for the night.

The next day they climbed over two thousand feet to the top of Brewster Pass, an elevation of eight thousand feet. From the top of the pass the party had some terrific downhill skiing all the way down to Allenby Creek. This was the first recorded ski trip over Brewster Pass. They proceeded on to Bryant Creek at the base of Gibraltar Rock and then turned west and headed for the top of Assiniboine Pass:

> We entered at this pass, which forms part of the Continental divide, one of the prettiest little valleys in the world, and one as adapted to skiing as we had hoped to find. My enthusiasm for this spot has no limit. Mount Assiniboine itself, the centre of the picture, is of all mountains, the most perfectly shaped. Almost 12,000 ft. high, it rises far above the surrounding peaks, fully deserving its nickname "The Matterhorn of Canada. (Strom, 1928)

The party stayed three weeks at the Assiniboine camp, enjoying remarkable spring weather and unbelievable snow conditions.

> We did not miss one day of skiing. And such skiing! Wide open slopes up and up in all directions, an inexhaustible number of runs, all with vertical drop of two-thousand feet or more, and all ending near camp. Enough timber right around to provide good sporty skiing on stormy days and over all the most perfect snow we had ever seen—from five to ten feet of it on the level." (Strom 1933)

The party returned to Banff, tanned and enthusiastic. The following year they arrived back in Banff with a larger group. Strom recounts that some of the locals asked if they could come up and see the skiing for themselves. Cliff White and Cyril Paris came up and left full of "enthusiasm and future plans."

With that trip, skiing quickly became popular in the Rockies. In 1930 six young men skied the two hundred-and-twenty-mile trip from Jasper to Banff for the first time. Another group skied the two hundred-and-fifty-mile return trip from Jasper to the Columbia Icefield in record time. This group had been into Assiniboine with Strom the year before and they asked him to accompany them. While on this trip they climbed Mt. Castleguard. In 1931, Strom and his party did the Jasper–Columbia Icefields–Banff ski traverse once again, and Russ Bennett and Cliff White of Banff made the first winter ascent of Mt. Snow Dome. Strom later wrote:

> Since then, many more successful trips have been made and skiing in the Canadian Rockies is now and established fact. Most of the skiing is above the timberline, with runs many miles in

length, starting near the very tops, usually finishing between open growing larch and spruce in the bottom of the valley. These runs have a vertical drop of from two to four thousand feet. Although not quite as long, they are just as steep, fast and sporty as any ski runs in the world. (Strom, 1933)

Two permanent ski camps were developed in the 1930's—one near Mt. Assiniboine and the other at Skoki across the valley from Mt. Temple near the village of Lake Louise. Assiniboine was developed, managed, and operated by Erling Strom who turned out to be a man of great vision, character, and ability. In 1933 he wrote:

Assiniboine cannot be reached in less than two days, and is no place to run out for the weekend. Inexperienced skiers should not attempt the trip alone. For this reason I have established a weekly guide (and mail) service. One of my men is to be found in Banff every Thursday. He starts out on Friday morning during the season, March and April. At Assiniboine I do the guiding myself. From time to time other camps will surely pop up. North America's best winter playground is in the making. We started something over seven years ago that no power on earth could stop today. (Strom, 1933)

The Mount Temple—Skoki Ski Area

The Mount Temple and Skoki ski facilities were operated by **James Boyce** of Banff. The Skoki Lodge was reached after a four-to-five hour trip on skis from the Lake Louise station. The skiing began at Temple Ski Lodge, which was reached by a gravel road and trail along Corral Creek. The lodge was a two-storey log building with a roaring fireplace and a magnificent view of Mt. Temple and the Lake Louise group of peaks, across the valley. Since there were no ski lifts in those days, one had to learn the old "herring-bone hump" to ascend the slopes in order to enjoy the thrill of the down-hill "shoosh".

From Temple Lodge, the trail followed Corral Creek up to Ptarmigan Lake where there was a halfway cabin with a small cooking and eating area and room for eight people to sleep. A small, tin-sided stove that glowed bright red in no time, heated the cabin so effectively that one had to open a door or window for relief. The cabin was always unlocked and available for anyone to use during the summer hiking season – as were all of the other cabins in the mountains. Unfortunately, it was also well populated with a friendly family of pack-rats that seemed to steal anything that wasn't nailed down.

From the Ptarmigan Hut, skiers and hikers proceeded over Boulder Pass and then down the other side to Skoki, where there was a large log lodge. The Post Hotel, originally known as the Lake Louise Ski Lodge, in the village of Lake Louise was the base of operations. In 1942, with the second World War preoccupying everyone, the ski operation was closed.

Ike Mills, "the mad musher of Skoki" passing Mt. Ptarmigan as he heads down from Boulder Pass on his way out to the village of Lake Louise for supplies. In the winter season Ike ran a regular service in and out of Skoki bringing in supplies, mail, and baggage for those staying at the Skoki Ski Lodge. Jimmy Simpson said that he was one of a kind.

Early downhill skiers in the Rockies
Note the crouched style. In those days there were no metal edges on the wooden skis and the bindings were called "bear traps"

The Post Hotel of the 1950's and 1960's.
It was the base of ski operations at Lake Louise and in the summer it was a popular tourist facility. **Ray Legace** and his wife Alpha operated the hotel for many years and Ray had a corral behind the hotel where he rented out saddle horses. The hotel was directly across the street from Boyle's Esso gas station and general store. Built in 1942, it was one of the largest and the most impressive buildings in the village for many years.

Skoki Ski Lodge under construction in 1936.
The original cabin was build in 1931 and this addition gave it much more room.

Mount Temple in the setting sun, viewed from the Ptarmigan Valley near the Temple Ski Lodge. Corral Creek sparkles in the foreground

The Herring-bone Hump
Before ski lifts were invented one had to master the old "Herring-bone Hump" to get to the top of a hill for the "shoosh" down. It was good for the leg and the arm muscles. It built good cardiovascular fitness and excellent stamina, but most of all … it built character.

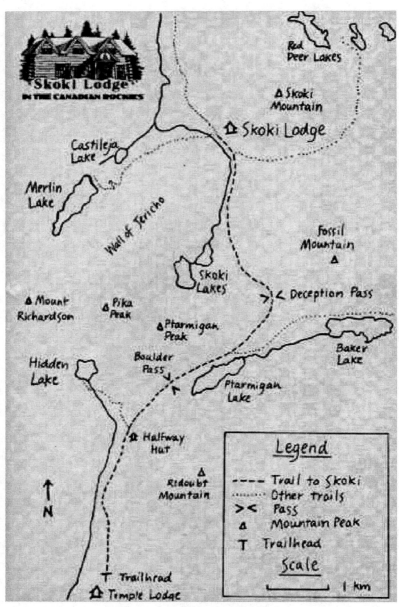

A Map of the Skoki Area

In 1947, **Sir Norman Watson**, a British Aircraft manufacturer who had made a fortune during the war, purchased the ski operations and the surrounding cabins. He also acquired the Mount Temple Ski Lodge, the Skoki Ski Lodge, and the Post Hotel. In the 1950s he developed the Whitehorn ski area and installed the first ski lift near Mount Temple Lodge. A few years later, the first gondola ski lift in the Rockies was erected on the south western slopes of Mt. Whitehorn. Today it is the world-class Lake Louise-Whitehorn ski facility.

Sadly, Sir Norman Watson never personally took charge of his holdings in Canada. *Jack McDowall* managed them for twenty-one years. Watson married for the first time at the age of seventy-nine. Sadly this proved to be a big mistake as the union was anything but a match made in heaven. Lady Watson was considerably younger than Sir Norman, and she apparently detested all things Canadian. It was rumoured that she made Sir Norman liquidate his Canadian holdings and in 1979 the Post Hotel was sold to the *Schwarz family* of Switzerland. This family has lovingly remodelled, refurbished, and redeveloped the hotel into one of the premier establishments in the country. Watson continued to visit the area annually, unaccompanied by his wife, until his death in England at the age of eighty-six. The Lake Louise ski operation was taken over and managed by a company headed by Charlie Locke in the 1990s and under his inspired leadership, the mountain has become one of the finest ski facilities in the world.

Georgia Engelhard–That Girl Could Climb!

For many years, **Georgia Engelhard** was a regular guest at Chateau Lake Louise. She liked to climb with Swiss guides Ernest Feuz, Rudolf Aemmer, and Christian Haesler. In 1931, she became the second person ever to climb Chancellor Peak (10,761 feet), which she did by way of the southwest arête. In 1932 she and Ernest Feuz traversed the formidable Mt. Bonney (10,194 feet) in the Selkirks, descending via the north face–a most demanding traverse.

In 1933 she traversed Mt. Victoria from the South Peak to the North. This traverse had always been done from the North Peak to the South and then down Abbot Pass back to the Plain of Six Glaciers. This made for a rather long climb and it routinely took from seventeen to twenty-four hours. Georgia wrote of her climb in the 1933 Canadian Alpine Journal.

> *Ernest Feuz, the Swiss guide, and I calculated that the traverse could be made in the reverse direction. It would be a much less arduous undertaking, as a good start could be made from Abbot Pass Hut, enabling the climber to reach the really difficult part of the ridge in fresh condition.*
>
> *We left for Abbot Pass on the afternoon of August 14th, well supplied with extra rope and slings. We reached the hut at about 8 p.m. and after a good supper went promptly to bed. The morning of the 15th was a gorgeous one, cool and clear and wind still. We started up the familiar ridge at 5:30 a.m. The snow was in*

excellent condition, enabling us to reach the main (Centre) peak very comfortably in one hour and fifty-five minutes. Ahead of us stretched the arete, a bristling chain of gendarmes perched on a knife-like ridge, which dropped off on the O'Hara side at an angle of 45 degrees and on the Lake Louise side, about 53 degrees. It was an imposing sight.

In actuality, it was much less formidable than it appeared at first glance. At 7.30 a.m. we started down to the first gap over loose shale and small boulders lying on a steep slope, a pitch that required caution to negotiate. Reaching the first gendarme, we climbed it easily and descended again to the ridge. We climbed up and down practically all of the gendarmes, making only two traverses on the Lake Louise side of the ridge, a procedure that requires care – as the rock was extremely loose and shaly. But on the whole I was agreeably surprised, finding the rock on the gendarmes fairly solid. The ridge itself was less rotten than I had expected, and though it was narrow in places, it never was actually a knife-edge. The hand and footholds were firm and fairly large. We were able to keep up a fairly steady pace and found the going interesting and enjoyable.

After about an hour of continuous steady climbing we reached the pinnacle, and to our astonishment we encountered no difficulty in scaling the southwest face of this gendarme by way of good, if narrow ledges. We stopped for a second breakfast and continued having no difficulty on the remainder of the traverse. The last bit leading to North Peak is very easy. We reached North Peak at 10.30 a.m., exactly three hours from leaving Centre Peak. The day was so fine and the view so magnificent that we stayed on the North Peak till noon, enjoying the sight of old friends such as Sir Donald, Columbia, and Assiniboine. The descent to the Plain of Six teahouse was made in one hour and fifty minutes – the snow being in excellent condition, and permitting several extremely enjoyable glissades on the upper Victoria glacier. The total time climbing from the pass to the Plain of Six Glaciers was six hours and twenty minutes.

Miss Lillian Gest and Christian Haesler repeated the south to north traverse later in the 1933 season. In 1934, Georgia climbed Mt. Quadra (10, 407feet), above the Ten Peaks, with Ernest Feuz, establishing a new route up this glacier-hung peak.

Georgia was an attractive, perky, and intelligent New York socialite. Together with Ernest Feuz, she featured in a Hollywood movie in the late 1930s. It was set on Mt. Victoria and the two climbed the mountain seven times in five days during the filming. . In 1938, she accomplished the first guideless traverse of Mt. Victoria from North to South. Georgia later married **Tony Cromwell,** a climber from Philadelphia. They frequently returned to the Rockies for climbing holidays.

Georgia Engelhard on the summit of Mt. Victoria

Katie Gardiner – An International Climber

Miss Katie Gardiner of England was another attractive young woman from England. A superb climber with amazing stamina, she climbed with Ernest and Walter Feuz in the 1930s. Her love for climbing undoubtedly came from her father, Frederick Gardiner, a famous English mountaineer in his day who climbed in Switzerland, France, and Italy. He frequently took his children on his expeditions. Katie said that she began climbing easier snow peaks in the Alps when she was just ten years of age. She also visited the Rockies and stayed at Chateau Lake Louise with her father on numerous occasions.

In 1931 she completed the first traverse of Mt. Colliers and Popes Peak (above the Plain of Six Glaciers) with **Rudolf Aemmer** and in 1933 she climbed Mt. Storm (10, 372 feet) near Castle Junction. She also climbed Mt. Foster (10,511 feet). With her favourite guides Ernest Feuz and Christian Haesler she and **Lillian Gest** became the first women to climb the formidable Goodsirs – North Tower (11,565 feet) and the South Tower (11,686 feet).

In February of 1933, at the top of the Fox glacier in New Zealand, Katie was trapped for eight days with two guides and a male climber in a crevasse during a violent storm. It was an amazing feat of survival, but undaunted, she returned to the Rockies later that year and with Lillian Gest made the first ascent of Mt. Vaux (10,891 feet). She then went to the Selkirks with Edward Feuz Jr. and traversed Mt. Sir Donald. A few years later, she and Edward Feuz climbed the formidable Mt. Robson.

Katie Gardiner
This gal was an exceptional climber and often climbed with Ernest Feuz when she visited the Rockies.

In December, 1935 Katie returned to New Zealand and was finally able to climb Mt. Tasman. She had tried on five successive seasons to climb the challenging peak but was turned back each time by poor weather. During the 1928–29 climbing season she climbed New Zealand's Mt. Cook (12,349 feet) with guide Vic Williams. A year earlier, a mountain hut was erected on Pudding Rock on the Hooker Icefall approach to Mt. Cook and named the "Gardiner Hut" in her honour. The Hermitage guides Vic Williams and Mick Bowie packed loads of building materials averaging 90 pounds to the site.

Katie Gardiner was the second woman to climb the "king" and the "queen" of the New Zealand's Southern Alps, Mount Cook and Mount Tasman. She retired in Hastings, New Zealand and lived there well into her eighties. She never married and maintained contact with her old climbing friends in both Canada and New Zealand until her death in 1974.

Walter Perren

Walter Perren was the Chief Warden in charge of mountaineering for the National Parks during the 1950s and 60s. Every year at the beginning of the season, the staff at Chateau Lake Louise would assemble in the ballroom and Walter would give a talk on the mountains and the do's and don'ts of hiking and climbing. He had a rather thick, Swiss accent and would always end up his talks with the warning to "Shtay oot of the goolies" (Stay out of the gullies). This was good advice because it's in the gullies that the rock-falls and the snow and ice avalanches usually occur.

Born in Zermatt, Switzerland in 1914, Walter was from a family of famous mountaineering guides in that magical village that is nestled at the foot of the dominating Matterhorn. He climbed this classic peak some one hundred and forty times before coming to Canada.

Walter came to the Rockies in 1950 when he was thirty-six years of age, having already established himself as an excellent, modern guide that used the latest techniques, methods, and equipment. Hired by the CPR at Lake Louise, he lived with the Fuez brothers in the Swiss Chalet beside the Chateau. He soon became popular with both hotel guests and members of the ACC, who eagerly made use of his services. One of his favourite clients was Harry Green and together they made a number of excellent climbs. Walter was the official guide of the ACC summer camp at Lake O'Hara in 1952, the Hooker Icefields camp in 1953, and the Goodsirs camp in 1954.

Harry Green loved to tell the story of he and Walter climbing along the knife-edged ridge of Mt. Victoria. Feeling somewhat nervous at the extreme exposure of the ridge, Harry called out to Walter: "Are you holding me, Walter?" Walter is reported to have replied: "Jump off, Harry, and you'll soon find out!"

Walter joined the National Parks Warden's Service in 1954 and became Chief Warden in charge of mountaineering. Following this, he founded the National Parks Mountain Rescue School and became an instructor for Park Wardens and the RCMP. By this time the older Swiss guides had to retired, and it fell upon Walter to organize and lead rescue parties.

Walter died on December 26th, 1967, and Harry Green, writing about him in the *Canadian Alpine Journal*, stated that: "Walter was always good company. He was gentle, humorous, and kindly and ever ready to cheer the tired or give a quick hand to a clumsy companion, as when he fished me out of the Whirlpool River by one heel." Walter Feuz said that in all of his life, Walter Perren was one of the best men he ever came in contact with. His brothers Ernest and Edward had nothing but praise for him as well.

Only once did I climb with Walter and that was on the southeast ridge of Mt. Whyte above Lake Agnes on the route he pioneered. He was a joy to be with and he taught me a great deal about rock climbing, belaying, and mountaineering in general. Walter introduced modern mountaineering methods and rescue techniques to the Rockies and pioneered the use of helicopters and "long-line" techniques when rescuing stranded or injured climbers. His legacy is well described by Sid Marty in his excellent book, *Switchbacks: True Stories from the Canadian Rockies.*

There was a special quality about Walter Perren that exemplified his life, and that quality is called "integrity." It was easy to see why he was so highly regarded by all who knew him and it was a privilege for me to have shared the trail with him.

Phyllis Munday

Phyllis Munday was without doubt the best woman mountaineer this country has ever produced. She could out-climb most men in her day and she is the only person, male or female, ever to be given honorary memberships in both the American Alpine Club and the Alpine Club of Canada. She was a true pioneer in the days when there were few modern conveniences that made climbing more comfortable. The equipment, tents, clothing and sleeping bags were primitive by today's standard.

Phyllis was a tall, big-boned woman, strong and tough with amazing stamina. Although **Georgia Engelhard** and **Katie Gardiner** were excellent climbers, Ernest Feuz always felt that no one could compete with Phyllis for sheer strength, endurance, and climbing ability on big mountains.

In July of 1924, Phyllis became the first woman to climb Mt. Robson with the famous guide **Conrad Kain**. She described the last few feet of the Mt. Robson climb:

> *"Conrad's on top, thank Heaven!" I thought, for he was gathering in the slack fast. As I stepped up beside him he held my rope and said in a very satisfying tone, "There Lady! You are the first woman on the top of Mount Robson." I said out loud "thank Heaven!" for it was a four-year-old ambition of mine at last achieved. (Canadian Alpine Journal 1924, 72)*

Phyllis and her husband Don made many exceptional climbs in the Rockies and were regulars at the annual ACC summer camps. They were also the first to find and chart the way into Mt. Waddington, the highest peak in British Columbia's Coast Range. Their adventures finding a way through the west coast rain forests to the Franklin, Homathco, and Teedman glaciers and then on to Mt. Waddington required exceptional perseverance, stamina, and ingenuity. The areas the Mundays explored were uncharted and unknown and their encounters with grizzly bears were chilling, as were her stories of building a boat to take their climbing party up the coast from Vancouver to Knight, Toba, and Bute Inlets.

Walter Perren 1914-1967

Walter Perren was one of the finest mountaineers ever to climb in the area. He was born in January 1914 in Zermatt, Switzerland. He first climbed the famous Matterhorn, which dominates that high mountain village, when he was still a teenager. He scaled the mighty peak some 140 times before coming to Canada in 1950. He joined the Warden's Service in 1954 and introduced modern mountaineering and rescue techniques to the Rockies.

H.A.V. "Harry" Green

Phyllis Munday and her husband Don at the Centre Peak of Mt. Victoria.

The Alpine Club Members who successfully climbed Mt. Robson in 1924.
They were all led to the top by Conrad Kain. Don and Phyllis Munday are in
the front row (second and third from the left).

Don's book, *The Unknown Mountain* tells of their adventures in the Coast Range. Mt. Munday, near Mt. Waddington in the Coast Range, was named in their honour.

In her later years Phyllis was a frequent visitor to Lake Louise and Lake O'Hara and on several occasions we chatted as we walked the trail around the lake or hiked up to Lake Agnes. She was a long-time friend of Harry and Fiona Green and lived within a block of them in North Vancouver. While I was at graduate school at the University of British Columbia she would invited me for supper and then we'd talk into the late evening, looking at pictures and slides of her climbs. She also talked about her late husband Don, who was a writer for the *Vancouver Province* newspaper. Often, she'd invite Harry and Fiona Green and we'd have a wonderful time remembering their adventures in the Rockies.

For years Phyllis was the editor of the Alpine Club Journal and when she was not hiking, climbing, and editing, she dedicated her time to the Girl Scouts of Canada—particularly the Vancouver Chapter. As Phyllis grew older and contemplated eternity she wrote the following verse, *I Think What Will Happen To Me*. I discovered it a few years ago and wish that I had written it, for it perfectly conveys my own thoughts and feelings. I knew from the time that I spent with her that we were kindred spirits, with a love for the high mountain peaks, the alpine meadows, and the wilderness. Her expression of her feelings for God's special places cannot help but touch the hearts of all who have found deep joy and delight in nature. They perfectly describe the type of person she was, her faith in God, her uncomplicated, trust and assurance in His goodness, and her love for His creation.

It was a rare privilege for me to have known Phyllis Munday and to have spent so much time with her. She was a remarkable, gentle and unassuming woman. She died in Nanaimo, British Columbia on April 11th, 1990 at ninety-five years of age.

I Think What Will Happen To Me

When my old body is finished and dies, I'm sure my spirit will come to
a place like this: A lovely woodsy trail, a beautiful lake, an alpine meadow,
A ridge and a peak, for all this has been heaven to me while on earth.
They are all God's gift to man.

I will roam, at will, about the alpine meadows, along the happy rippling streams,
the placid ponds and lakes that mirror the grand peaks and passing clouds.
They will catch the early sunrise, with promise of the day, and later the glorious
sunset, the last of the light, then the night sky with bright stars and brilliant moon.

My spirit will wander about in the fields of flowers, revelling in
their unspeakable beauty—it will pause to wonder at a rare treasure on
some secluded spot. My spirit will also be tuned to all bird songs, and
calls of little animals who make their homes in the mountains.

I will ramble high on the ridges where grotesque trees give way to
heather and the highest flowers. Then I will join the fresh breezes, gain strength,

*and rejoice in the rocks and snows of high places. I will travel all over the
glaciers–which I loved so well–and the sparkling snowfields, the deep
crevasses, and shining seracs and the steep snow ridges and rock faces.
And finally, with all the world at my feet, I will sit exulted on the summit, and just
look, and look, and look, and love it, and thank my Maker for the supreme
privilege my old body has enjoyed through the years.*

*My spirit belongs to all of the mountains–for this to me is heaven.
Thank god who has made me like this. How privileged I have been, as Don
(her husband) and Edith (her daughter) shared these joys with me.
If I have been able to pass on, to even one other soul, the great joy and beauty
God gave me in life, then I have been rewarded beyond measure.*

–Phyllis Munday

H. A. V. Harry Green

Harry Green was in his early seventies when I first met him at Lake Louise. He
had been a regular at the Chateau for many years and was an active member of
the Alpine Club of Canada. He'd made some excellent climbs in the Rockies
and returned each year to hike the old familiar trails. Harry was not a large man,
standing just five-foot, four-inches tall. He had a thick Scots accent and always had
a roguish twinkle in his eyes that foretold his fine sense of humour. A well respected
lawyer in Vancouver he possessed a gentle, unassuming disposition. Harry and his
wife Fiona lived in North Vancouver not far from their friend and fellow climber,
Phyllis Munday.

Harry studied law at Edinburgh University and graduated with honours. He
immigrated to Canada in 1912 and worked for the legal department of the CPR
in Winnipeg. After fifty years of service with the railway he retired as the Senior
Legal Advisor to the Western Division of the CPR. He was then retained as Special
Counsel at the CPR's offices in Vancouver. Harry made a genuine contribution
to the City of Winnipeg during his years there and founded the Winnipeg Little
Theatre. He also wrote plays and short stories and published a book of poems. He
received the Canadian Drama Award and was an avid gardener, specializing in
alpine gardens in Winnipeg, and later in North Vancouver.

Harry climbed regularly in the Lake Louise and Lake O'Hara areas and usually
hired Ernest Feuz or Walter Perren as his guide. With them, he climbed Mt. Victoria,
Mt. Hungabee, Mt. Deltaform, Mt. Lefroy, and Cathedral Mountain. He joined the
Alpine Club of Canada in 1948 and became the President of the Club in 1957, a post
he held for seven years.

In 1954, four members of a Mexican climbing team lost their lives in a climbing
accident on Mt. Victoria. Harry and Ernest Feuz organized the rescue operations
with Chateau bellhops **Ray Wehner, Chuck Roland** and **Frank Campbell**. Harry
was part of the rescue team, escorting three survivors down Abbot Pass and back
to the hotel.

Lillian Guest

Lillian was an excellent climber and spent many summers in the Rockies. She climbed with guides Ernest Feuz and Rudolf Aemmer. Lillian once told me that her traverse of Mt. Victoria was her most exciting climb. She also climbed with her friends Georgia Englehard and Katie Gardiner. She and Katie were the first women to climb the Goodsirs with Ernest Feuz and Christian Haesler. She loved Lake O'Hara and wrote a small book about it that is still available at the Whyte Museum in Banff.

Bud Brewster on the great horse "Chief" at Lake Louise
(Photo by Nick Morant)

While at Lake Louise, I spent many hours talking with Harry about the mountains and the climbs he'd done. We would occasionally hike to the Plain of Six Glaciers or to Lake Agnes. I recall he had a fine sense of humour and an endearing way of poking fun at himself. We would have a good laugh as he'd tell of some of the outlandish claims he had to deal with any time a train killed a horse or a cow that wandered on the CPR tracks. No matter how mangy or decrepit the unfortunate beast was, its owner would inevitably claim that it was a proven champion of prime breeding stock, or a racehorse that was a sure-fire contender for the Kentucky Derby.

In his later years Harry and his wife made annual visits to Lake O'Hara where they'd renew old acquaintances and go on hikes with Lillian Guest, Grassi, and Professor Walter Link. When I moved to Vancouver to attend graduate school, I'd frequently visit Harry and Fiona at their home in North Vancouver. Fiona would prepare a roast and Harry would unfailingly serve his favourite single malt Scotch whiskey. After dinner, there was always Drambuie and coffee and then we'd spend a few hours talking and looking at his mountaineering photos.

Harry and Ernest Feuz climbed a direct route up the precipitous face of Mt. Odaray from the Morning Glory Lakes in O'Hara, but he was especially proud of the route he and Walter Perren took up the exposed ridge on Mt. Cathedral in 1951. As one looks out of the window of the Elizabeth Parker Hut in O'Hara, one gets a terrific view of Harry's route up that impressive ridge. Whenever I see it, I always think of Harry – his soft, gentle voice, his dark twinkling eyes, and his unique laugh. Harry died in North Vancouver in 1979 at ninety-one years of age.

Lillian Gest

Lillian Gest was a graduate of Bryn Mawr and Vassar College in New York State and she spent most of her summers in the Rockies, riding and camping. She climbed frequently with the Feuz brothers and with Christian Haesler in the 1930s and 1940s making several first ascents and new routes, including a traverse of Mt. Victoria. Returning to the Chateau for many years long after she was unable to climb, she enjoyed being around the lake and walking along the trails in the area. Whenever I'd come back from a climb, she'd invite me to her room to describe in detail every aspect of my day's adventure. Her eyes would shine and she'd say, "That's just how Ernest, or was it … Christian and I found it when we did it in 1933, or was it in 34? No it was 33, I'm sure!"

Lillian was a long-time friend of **Phyllis Hart** and the Chateau pianist **John Linn**. Whenever she arrived at the Chateau, John made it a special event and would introduce her during his evening concert. Lillian also loved Lake O'Hara and each year she'd spend eight to ten days there, hiking and visiting with old friends who would join her on the trails. She wrote a book called, *A History of Lake O'Hara* in 1961, and in 1986 it was printed for the fourth time. Lillian died on January 5th, 1986.

Marshall Diverty and Bud Brewster

In the 1950s and 1960s, **Mr. and Mrs. Marshall Diverty** were frequent visitors to the Rockies. They'd arrive each year at the Chateau with much fanfare and excitement. Marshall was a huge bear of a man always dressed western-style with cowboy boots, jeans, red shirt, string tie, leather vest and a well-worn Stetson hat. With his wire-rimmed glasses and generous moustache, he resembled Teddy Roosevelt. Also like Roosevelt, he possessed a booming voice, a thunderous laugh, a great sense of humour, and a quick wit. The Divertys, who were in their seventies when I knew them, were always delighted to be back among their old friends who also returned to the Chateau each year. Without fail the Divertys would book a large suite of rooms for two to three weeks and John Linn would always announce their arrival and dedicate at least one number to them during his evening concerts.

Upon their arrival, Marshall's first words were usually, "Where's Bud?" He meant Bud Brewster, the legendary guide, outfitter, horseman, and all round raconteur of the area. Bud kept a herd of about thirty horses at Lake Louise for trail rides from the Chateau, and for taking special guests on private trips into the Pipestone Valley and Skoki.

When the Divertys arrived, a call would be put out for Bud to come over to the Chateau right away as his friend Marshall was there and waiting. Bud would rush over, having had a fresh wash and a shave. His black hair would be slicked back under his battered cowboy hat and he'd always put on a clean shirt for the occasion. Sometimes, but not always, he'd put on a clean pair of jeans.

With much laughter and genuine affection, Bud and Marshall would greet each other with mighty bear hugs. Then Marshall would escort Bud down to the Glacier Lounge for a couple of good stiff drinks before supper to renew their acquaintances. After an hour or so they'd emerge from the lounge – Bud looking a bit the worse for wear, but not so his comrade. Then they'd proceed down the lobby and up the long stairs to the dining room where Marshall had a table reserved for them. Bud would dutifully remove his hat, but he always seemed a bit uncomfortable in the dignified and genteel atmosphere of the formal dining room. He felt more at home, and certainly much more comfortable, on the trail and around a campfire. But Marshall delighted in introducing him to his many friends at nearby tables. With a booming voice he'd announce that Bud was the best rider, guide, and outdoorsman in the Rockies. Bud always blushed at this testimonial and looked a bit shy and embarrassed.

The next morning there'd be no sign of Marshall or Bud. They would be gone at first light, with the horses packed and loaded with gear – headed for some remote valley where the fish were fat and the air was clean. Marshall always packed in a generous supply of his special whiskey for the long nights by the campfire claiming that it warded off the mosquitoes.

Their trip would last for about two weeks, rain or shine. When they returned, the two friends would be weather-beaten and in dire need of a bath. This was delayed however, as they always headed straight to the Glacier Lounge to wash down the trail-dust with a few well-earned glasses of Scotch. There, anyone who'd listen would hear stories about the elk, the grizzlies, the mountain goats, the bighorn sheep, and the monstrous trout the men had encountered. The Glacier Lounge was the place to tell these tales and the men usually found a receptive audience. After awhile, they'd proceed to the dining room, each ordering the biggest steak that chef Ernie Eglie could find.

Marshall's wife never joined them as she had her own table for herself and her travelling companion, Ruth Wooly. She wisely let her husband live his dream each year and seemed to enjoy seeing him in his element with the people he loved more than life itself.

Arnold Brigden

Arnold Brigden, a botanist, and his wife stayed at Chateau Lake Louise during the 1950s and 60s. for two to three weeks each year. Like Marshall Diverty, his first words were usually, "Where's Bud?" A short time later he and Bud would be heading into the high country or some remote valley, where Arnold would collect specimens of alpine plants and flowers. He'd carefully dig them up, plant them in pots, and take them back in special containers to Winnipeg where he'd introduce them to the prairie soil of his alpine garden. It was rumoured to be one of the finest alpine gardens in Canada.

Brigden was a strange and somewhat eccentric-looking man with a salt-and-pepper beard and round, wire-rimmed glasses. He routinely wore a tweed wool cap, a Harris tweed jacket, a wool plaid shirt, thick corduroy trousers and heavy, high-topped hiking boots that laced to just below his knees. The smell of the smoke from the black, twist tobacco in his pipe served to keep away mosquitoes, grizzlies, and cougars. There was a unique softness about this man who spoke with a thick Scot's accent, and it was always a special treat for me to talk to him about his plants, his gardens, and his trail rides with Bud.

An Interesting Ride from Banff

(Parts of this story were told in my book *Lake Louise at its Best*)

While writing this book I discovered some notes I had written in June, 1963, following a chance meeting while hitchhiking. Mrs. Iverson and her mother Mrs. West offered me a ride from Banff to Lake Louise. (Those were the days when a university student could safely hitchhike and actually get a ride.) Here are my original notes.

June 24, 1963

*I rode from Banff to Lake Louise with a **Mrs. Iverson** and her mother **Mrs. West**. Mrs. West was quite deaf, but she was very interesting as she spoke of the history of the Lake Louise area where she had seen many changes take place during her lifetime. Her father ran a lumber camp at the Great Divide in the 1910s, and she and her sister and brother were the first to go to school at Lake Louise. There were eight pupils and the old log schoolhouse was across the tracks from where the Lake Louise station now stands. The school could not be opened unless Mrs. West's three children attended and everyday the engineers on the train would take them to and from school. In the event of poor weather or slides the children would stay with the engineer's wife. Their first teacher was a young woman named Miss Hume.*

*The original name of the village of Lake Louise was "Holt City" where Sam Steele of the NWMP once served. For some unknown reason the name of the little village was changed to "**Laggan,**" but eventually it became known as "Lake Louise" because so many people rode right on through to Field before they realized that they had already passed the point to get off for Lake Louise and the Chateau. At this time the little tramline railroad running from the train station to the Chateau was in operation.*

*Mrs. West also spoke of **Silver City**, a town of almost 2000 people at the base of Castle Mountain near Eisenhower Junction. This was an early mining town, but when little gold was actually found and the railhead pushed on to Golden the town moved overnight to that fair city. The people took all their belongings with them – even the windows and the doors. Mrs. Iverson said that the mounds where the log cabins once stood could still be seen near the Warden's house in a clearing not far from there.*

*I was also told about how **Whiskey Creek** got its name. It seems a gentleman was bootlegging whiskey to anyone in the Banff area who wished to purchase some illegal spirits. This was at the time of the Louis Riel rebellion in the Prairies and there were only two Mounties left stationed at Calgary. The Mounties heard of the goings-on at Banff and on a beautiful afternoon in mid-June two of the finest were dispatched to the little hamlet. They traveled from Calgary to Canmore by steam locomotive and then with all due haste they made for Banff on a hand-car. They were pumped and ready for action when they arrived in Banff at 2 p.m. The bootlegger was tipped off before the constabulary could arrive, however, and managed to sell most of his inventory at "fire-sale" prices to his eager patrons. With moments to go before the raid took place he quickly emptied his last two barrels of booze into the swift running waters of a little creek that from that day forward became known as "Whiskey Creek".*

The bootlegger was arrested and taken to Calgary where he was kept in jail for three or four days. During his time there one of the Mounties asked him what he would do if his cell door was left open one night. To this he replied: "What would you do?" Sure enough, the next night the cell door was left open and the illicit liquor vendor walked out of the jail. He left Calgary with all due haste and soon – much to the delight of his loyal patrons – he resumed his thriving enterprise in the town of Banff. The reason for the cell door being left open was because the Mounties were so busy in Calgary that they didn't have the time to bother with a bootlegger. They had responded to the complaint of bootlegging in the Banff area and had done their duty.

Mrs. West also told of riding the trails from the Great Divide to Banff in the 1910's and 1920's. They had to leave early in the morning (often at 5:30 a.m.) and would arrive in Banff at 7:00 that night.

After the fire destroyed much of the Chateau at Lake Louise in 1924 a new wing was built and the workers lived in tents with their families near the hotel. There were several bears mooching about at the time and one morning a small baby crawled out of the tent. When the mother looked out a huge black bear was between her and her child. The young mother was afraid to scream for fear the bear would grab up her baby and run into the woods with it so she slipped under the back of the tent and ran for her husband. Together they raced to find the Warden but he was off somewhere. They then found a young Mountie who was stationed nearby and together they rushed back to the campsite. The bear was still there when they reached the scene and the Mountie promptly shot it; thus reuniting the mother with her child. Before nightfall however, the Warden, heard of the day's events and arrested the Mountie for shooting a bear in the Park. This bone-headed, bureaucratic move caused a great uproar and the young Mountie was transferred out of the area. Great friction existed between the Mounties and the Warden's Service for many years after that event.

*Mrs. West then talked about the many mountaineering and skiing accidents that had occurred in the area over the years. She told of **Doctor Stone** and his wife from Purdue University, who had been trying to climb Mt. Assiniboine for four years but they had always been turned back by the elements. One fine morning Dr. Stone told some of his companions that he and his wife were planning to climb Mt. Eon and to not worry if he didn't return until late. This time, he said, he planned to make the climb despite the conditions.*

When Dr. Stone and his wife didn't return, search parties were sent out to find them. Two weeks later, a party that was climbing Mt. Assiniboine thought they heard echoes to the yodeling of their Swiss guides—Ernest Feuz and Rudolf Aemmer. Listening more closely the answering calls proved to be from a woman on a ledge on Mt. Eon. They spotted her with their field glasses and guides waved frantically to let the woman know that she had been seen. They then descended Mt. Assiniboine as fast as possible and proceeded across the valley to Mt. Eon. When the guides finally reached a spot near the top of Mt. Eon they found a piton with a rope attached to it that danged over the edge of the cliff. Looking over the edge they then saw Mrs. Stone on small ledge just below them. Quickly, Rudolf Aemmer rappelled down to the ledge where he ministered to Mrs. Stone, tied her to his rope, and helped her to safety as the others pulled her up from above. An improvised stretcher was made and Rudolf, who possessed amazing physical strength, carried Mrs. Stone down to the meadows. In a few hours she was able to tell her story.

Mrs. Stone reported that she and her husband were nearing the top of Mt. Eon when he said that he wanted to make the final ascent alone. He took off the rope and threw her his end. While she was coiling up the rope she heard a great crash from above. She soon reached the spot where she thought her husband had fallen and below her was a ledge. Without hesitation she drove in a piton and rappelled down to the ledge. Unfortunately her rope was too short and she ran through it and dropped to the ledge. Looking around, her husband could not be seen and she realized that she had been mistaken. Now she was stranded on the ledge and her rope was too high for her to reach. For two weeks she survived on that ledge with only a trickle of snow water for nourishment – the rope dangling above her, but tantalizingly, just out of reach. After her story was heard Dr. Stone was found a few days later. Mrs. West reported that he was quite well-preserved in the snow on the other side of Mt. Eon, when he was found by the great Austrian guide, Conrad Kain.

Finally Mrs. West told of the two boys from Banff who were killed in Dennis Pass by an avalanche. It was late February and the boys planned to do a ski-trip from Wapta, up to Lake O'Hara and from there, over Duchesnay Pass and Dennis Pass, to the railroad above Field. The wardens and the guides at Banff and at Lake Louise, tried to persuade them not to attempt such a dangerous trip at that time of the year but the boys were determined and they started out from Wapta with great enthusiasm on a bright, cloudless morning. Sadly they were never seen alive again.

When they didn't return at the expected time search parties were sent out. Most of the able-bodied men in Lake Louise and Field were called upon to join the search party and they followed the boy's tracks up to Lake O'Hara, and then over Duchesnay Pass to the base of Dennis Pass. Here the tracks disappeared – having been obliterated by massive chunks of the snow and ice deposited by the avalanche that had swept the boys away. As the searchers stood at the scene, the guides whistled, and in a few seconds, tons of snow and ice tumbled down into the pass from the cliffs above. The boys were not found until late July the following summer when some climbers spotted the red tip of a wooden Arlberg ski sticking out of the snow at the base of Dennis Pass.

Mrs. West also told me of the tragedies involving the Mexican climbers on Mt. Victoria and the boy scouts on Mt. Temple – stories I'd already heard. It was without a doubt the most interesting ride I'd ever had while traveling from Banff to Lake Louise and I was sorry to see the turn-off for the village come into view. I could have talked to Mrs. West and her daughter for many more hours.

Nick Morant's Grizzly Bear Encounter

Nick Morant was a free-lance photographer living in Banff who often had contracts with the CPR to take publicity photos. Many of his photos were made into postcards and are still sold today. A book has recently been re-released featuring his work called *Nicholas Morant's Canadian Pacific*, by J. F. Gardens. Nick was the only Canadian photographer other than Yousuf Karsh to receive the Order of Canada for his work. His photos of trains are famous throughout the world and some historians consider him to be one of the greatest photographers of the twentieth century. His pictures of Moraine Lake and the Ten Peaks, and Emerald Lake and Mt. Burgess, were once featured on the Canadian ten and twenty dollar bills. Nick always had exciting tales to tell and was routinely treated as a special guest whenever he'd drop in to Chateau Lake Louise for a few days. In July of 1961 he told me the following story as we sat on the porch of the Lake Agnes teahouse, looking out over the broad Bow River Valley and the Pipestone Range.

On September 19th, 1939, Nick and the Swiss guide Christian Haesler took the train from Banff to Wapta Station, just across from Wapta Lake at the top of the big hill running down past the spiral tunnels to the Kicking Horse River and Field. They planned to hike about eight miles along Sherbrooke Creek, then past Sherbrooke Lake to the head of the valley, where they would scout out a good location for the CPR to build a teahouse. It was a beautiful morning—clear, fresh, and sunny, and they were enjoying the crisp fall weather. It was good to be out in the mountains at that time of year and some of the larch trees higher up the slopes had already turned a soft, golden yellow.

Just after they passed Sherbrooke Lake and were heading up the narrow upper valley on the slopes of Mount Ogden, they spied a sow grizzly and her cub. She seemed to pay no attention to them so they continued on. Suddenly, Christian looked back to see the big sow charging them from out of the underbrush. Nick ran left and climbed a tree as fast as he could, and Christian ran to the right and did likewise. The enraged grizzly was at Christian's tree in a flash and as he tried to scramble up beyond her reach, the bear stretched out to almost eight feet tall, opened her mouth, and grabbed Christian's ankle. "The big sow then snatched him out of the tree and began worrying him like a terrier with a rat, as he screamed in pain. I didn't know what to do," he continued with flashing eyes.

"I had to decide whether to go to Chris' rescue then, or wait in the tree until she was finished with him and went away. We didn't have a gun, but I decided that I had to help Chris then. That big bitch was chewing on him pretty good and tossing him around as if he were a rag-doll."

Scrambling down from the tree, Nick grabbed a branch and hit the sow in the back of the head as hard as he could. The next thing he knew the bear was on top of him, biting through his right leg and breaking it. (As if his point needed proving, Nick pulled up his pant leg to show me the ugly scars that still remained some twenty years later.) "She got a hold of my arm and ripped at it, shredding my wool shirt and exposing all the muscles," he continued, as he showed me the scars on his arm."

The bear then went back to maul Chris again, and Nick seized the opportunity to find a place to hide. Too weak to climb a tree, he hid behind one, as he and the grizzly played hide-and-seek. The furious bear was like a cat toying with a wounded mouse or a bird. She ran past Nick and sniffed the air until she picked up the scent of his blood. Then, with a mighty roar, she was on top of him again. He only had one good leg and one good arm, but he somehow managed to kick the big beast in the snout. Enraged, she grabbed his arm and shook him again, tossing his bleeding body onto a pile of rocks.

While the bear was working Nick over, Christian managed to drag himself down the trail to Wapta Lake where he sought help. Meanwhile, Nick lay face down while the snarling bear leapt on his back and shoulders and put her mouth over the back of his head.

"I could smell her horrible breath as I felt her jaws and teeth tighten around my scalp. I thought, 'Here I go,' but then a miracle happened. The sow's cub let out a whimper and the big bitch let go of my head and scrambled over to her young one. Then the two of them started down the trail toward Wapta Lake, following Chris' trail."

"But now this, as miraculous as it was, presented a problem," Nick said, his countenance flushed as if he were once again on that bloody trail. "I knew I couldn't return down the path or I'd run into them again. My only hope was to go the long way, up and over the ridge, and then down to Sherbrooke Lake where I could pick up the trail again."

He was pretty battered up by this time. His right leg didn't work too well and one arm was useless. He couldn't see out of one eye and his scalp and the back of his neck was bleeding badly, but slowly he dragged himself up the long shale slope to the ridge and then across a snow slope to the other side. Below he could see a train chugging up the tracks and he thought he saw a man flyfishing at Sherbrooke Lake. "I could see him as plain as could be. I could see his arm raised to cast a fly. But then I realized that it was just the stump of a tree."

Agonizingly Nick dragged himself over the slide, half-stumbling and falling down the slope to the lake. Then a big, black animal ran out of the undergrowth toward him.

"You know I thought for sure that it was that bear again, but it wasn't," he said. "It was just a Newfoundland dog with a stretcher party behind him. Somehow Christian, although suffering terribly himself, had made it back and had sent help."

They tied Nick to the stretcher, splinted his broken leg and someone gave him a hypodermic needle, which knocked him out. Then he was carried back to Wapta where a train engine with a flatcar was waiting. Once he was on the flat car the engineer had the firemen shovel the coal fast and furious all the way to Banff.

"We just flew through the station at Lake Louise, past Castle Junction, and on to Banff. I was only half-conscious, but I remember the speed we were going as we rumbled down that track. It was pitch dark by then and I still remember how bright the stars were that clear September night and how relieved I felt, just to be alive."

Nick spent many months in the hospital at Banff undergoing a series of operations. After awhile his wounds healed, but the ugly scars remained as evidence of his horrendous encounter with the grizzly. Years later he still had a faint, diagonal, white scar running from the top centre of his forehead, across his left eye, and down his left cheek. He'd been through quite an ordeal all right.

Christian Haesler did not fare as well. He never did recover completely from his horrible mauling and his heroic struggle to get help as he dragged himself battered and bleeding down the trail to Wapta station. He died about a year later having upheld the tradition of the Swiss guides. No Swiss guide in the Canadian Rockies ever lost a client, although it was sure a close call with Nick Morant.

Nick passed away sixty years later in Banff in March of 1999. He was eighty-eight years old. I was privileged to have known him and to have had the pleasure of sharing the trail with him on more than one occasion.

Nick Morant the "Gentleman Photographer of the Rockies" in his studio in Banff in 1988.

Nick Morant's famous picture of Mt. Rundle with a perfect reflection in Vermillion Lake.

Nick Morant's famous picture of a steam engine entering the Spiral Tunnel near Field.

Norm Luxton – A Pillar of Banff

Norm Luxton led a most exciting life. The son of the editor of a prominent Winnipeg newspaper, Luxton had a number of adventures in the newspaper business in Vancouver, British Columbia, before he and a seasoned Danish sailor, Captain F.C. Voss, sailed a thirty-eight-foot, triple-masted, massive dugout cedar canoe from Victoria to Australia. They left Victoria harbour in the Tillikum (the Chinook Indian word for "friend") on May 22nd, 1901 and had numerous adventures as they made their way through the south seas, stopping at forty-two islands along the way. Voss was a tough task master, however, and Luxton only lasted six months with him.

Luxton moved to Banff in 1903 and established the famous *Crag and Canyon* newspaper, which he published and edited until 1951. He also married one of the pretty McDougall girls from Morely in 1904, a first cousin of Minnie Wilson, Tom Wilson's wife. Like Wilson, he was heavily involved in the life of the community. For many years he was a director of Banff Indian Days and the Banff Winter Carnival. He also constructed the Banff Trading Post and Museum of the Plains on the Bow River, and rebuilt the King Edward Hotel after it burned. At it's opening, Norman tossed the key of the front door into the woods; proclaiming that the hotel would never close.

Trusted and admired by the Stoney Indians, he was adopted into their tribe and named "Chief White Shield". The Stoneys said, "White Shield would protect them." When he died in 1962 at the age of eighty-six, his funeral was one of the largest ever seen in Banff attended by scores of townspeople as well as many Stoney Indians in full ceremonial dress.

Norm Luxton riding tall in the saddle at Banff Indian Days

Bruno Engler, 1915–2001

Bruno Engler on The Needles above Lake Agnes

Bruno Engler–A man for the mountains.

Bruno Engler loved life and he, more than most men I have known, lived it to the fullest. I knew Bruno well and climbed with him on numerous occasions when he'd drop by Chateau Lake Louise in the early 1960s. We climbed together on Mt. Lefroy, Mt. Victoria, and Walter Perron's route on Mt. Whyte. Bruno was always fun to be with and he always had exciting, and usually hilarious, stories to tell. He was an outstanding climber, skier and outdoorsman but his true talent was mountain photography. I can almost hear his voice again as I recall his good-natured jesting and his interest in the quality of the light as we sat atop Mt. Lefroy on a cloudless morning in late July of 1960. How he loved the mountains!

Bruno was born in Lugano Switzerland on December 4th, 1915, Bruno trained to become a mountain guide and an outdoor photographer.During the first World War, he commanded a mountain brigade in the Italian Army. When he came to Canada in 1939, he was just twenty-four years of age and quite naturally gravitated to the Banff area, where he became a ski instructor at Sunshine Village. In 1940, he taught a mountain unit of the Canadian Army how to ski and survive in the mountains. In the summers he often worked with the Feuz brothers at Lake Louise as a guide. He guided the likes of Frank Smythe, Georgia Englehard, Katie Gardiner, Pierre Trudeau, Peter Lougheed, and Roland Michener to successful climbs in the Rockies. He was also on the Canadian Mt. Everest Expedition in 1982.

Photography was Bruno's true passion and he was one of the best mountain photographers of his time. In the 1950s he formed a company, Alpine Films, which offered cinematography and mountain safety consulting and guiding services to the giants of the film industry. He was retained on numerous occasions by the National Film Board, Disney Productions, Universal Studios, and Canadian and US television networks.

Bruno himself specialized in black-and-white photography and over the years, amassed a large collection of photos, which included spectacular shots of avalanches and mountain vistas, as well as celebrities such as Paul Newman, Margot Kidder, Jimmy Stewart, and Dustin Hoffman. He pioneered the use of motion pictures and always carried a number of cameras in his large backpack. His favorite place to photograph avalanches was at the Plain of Six Glaciers where he captured many impressive photos of avalanches as they rumbled down the upper slopes of Mt. Victoria, and off the upper slopes of Mt. Lefroy. The first book of his photography, *A Mountain Life*, was edited by R.W. Sandford and published by the Alpine Club of Canada in 1996.

Everyone, who knew Bruno, liked and admired him. I recall Ernest Feuz telling me how much he enjoyed his company. Walter Perron also thought the world of him. He could sure liven up any gathering–whether it was around a campfire, at the pub in Field, or in the lobby of the Chateau.

Bruno was also a dedicated family man. With his first wife of thirty years, Angel, he had ten children. His second wife, Vera Matrasova-Engler, was his constant companion until his death on March 23rd, 2001 at the age eighty-five. In 1999, he started work on a new book that Vera, and his daughter, Susan Engler

Potts, completed after he passed away, *Bruno Engler Photography: Photographs Celebrating over Sixty Years in the Canadian Rockies,* 2002.

Those of us who occasionally roamed the old trails with Bruno were saddened at his passing but his spirit lives on in the mountains that he loved. Those that have passed away must have rejoiced when their old friend finally joined them to wander, climb, and ski those glorious peaks and virgin slopes in the Great Beyond.

Ken Jones

Born in Golden in 1910, Ken was the first certified guide in the Rockies who was born in Canada. He guided in the Selkirks, the Bugaboos and the Rockies. He loved the Skoki area and often worked at Skoki Lodge as a cook and general maintenance man. From 1967 until 1974 he served as the first warden of Assiniboine Provincial Park. He completed degrees in Engineering and Biology by correspondence and maintained an active interest in all matters relating to the mountain environment. He was also an accomplished fly fisherman. Ken passed away at his home in Nanton, Alberta in January, 2004. I always enjoyed the times I spent with Ken in Skoki and at Lake Louise.

Ken Jones – Mountain Man – 1910 – 2004

Hans Gmoser

Born in Braunau Inn Austria in 1932, Hans Gmoser came to Canada in 1951 with his friend and fellow climber Leo Grillmair. Upon arriving the two adventurers first went to Edmonton, and worked in lumber camps until they learned to speak enough English. Hans, who was a trained electrician, some found better work. But steady work in construction was not what they dreamed of as each weekend they headed for the mountains for hiking, climbing and skiing. Fortunately they met an old Swiss mountaineer who trained them as guides and gave them licenses as "official mountaineers."

In 1957 the two friends founded Rocky Mountain Guides Ltd. and began taking clients on climbing trips. They also began to make films of their climbing and skiing adventures and travelled throughout Canada and the United States giving stirring presentations enhanced by their enthusiasm and their thick Austrian accents. They thus became well recognized pioneers in establishing and promoting climbing, skiing, and guiding in the Canadian Rockies.

Hans developed into a gifted and fearless climber in the 1950s he and his colleague Leo Grillmair pioneered several new rock climbing routes on the challenging Yamnuska, just east of Canmore. The Grillmair Chimney, the Calgary Route, and the Diretissimard were all first climbed by this skilled pair of mountaineers.

In 1958 Gmoser was the first Canadian to climb Mt. Alberta and he was a part of the team that may have been the first to climb Alaska's Mount Blackburn. In 1959 Gmoser led successful expedition to Mount Logan (east ridge), and in 1960 he became the first Canadian to climb Brussels Peak In 1963 he led a successful team to Mount McKinley and was the first to climb the formidable Wickersham Wall. In 1964 he climbed Mount Louis via a difficult new route on the treacherous south face.

In the early 1960s Gmoser was also a pioneer in ski mountaineering and led several parties over the ice fields from Jasper to Lake Louise.

In 1965, Gmoser and Grillmair were guiding in the Bugaboo Mountains near Radium, British Columbia when someone suggested that they use a helicopter to ferry people from the base in the valley to the virgin powder snow on the remote peaks. The duo thus became the first in the world to establish a business transporting skiers and hikers to wilderness areas accessible only by helicopter. The first tour in 1965 was comprised of two groups of nine Americans and it was an unqualified success. Soon word spread and it was decided to establish a base in the area. Gmoser then leased an abandoned logging camp near Bugaboo Glacier and used it as his headquarters for three years before eventually acquiring it. The first heli-ski tours cost $260.00 for a weekend. Today the same trip costs $7,500.00, but now one stays in the luxury Bugaboo lodge. Gmoser continued to build his business and named it Canadian Mountain Holidays. As it expanded it required careful ongoing professional management and deep financial pockets so in 1995 Gmoser sold the business to Intrawest, the company that owns and operates Whistler resort near Vancouver.

In 1963 Gmoser was a founding member of the Association of Canadian Mountain Guides (ACMG) and was its first technical chairman. Gmoser was elected an honorary member of The Alpine Club of Canada in 1986 and he was awarded the Order of Canada in 1987, He received the Banff Mountain Film Festival Summit of Excellence award in 1989, and was elected to the Honour Roll of Canadian Skiing in 1989. He was named an honorary member of the International Federation of Mountain Guides Association in 1992, and in 1997 he was elected Honorary President of the ACMG.

Gmoser's clients over the years were among the rich and famous, including the King of Spain, the King and Queen of Norway and, Pierre Elliot Trudeau, who he led up the challenging Bugaboo Spire. Sadly, Hans was killed in a cycling accident while returning to his home at Harvie Heights from a trip to Lake Louise in July, 2006.

In the 1960s and 70s I would meet Hans frequently while climbing. He'd often turn up at Abbot Hut, the Mitchell Hut in the Little Yoho, the Elizabeth Parker Hut in O'Hara, and the W.O. Wheeler Hut at Roger's Pass. At that time, Hans Gmoser and Leo Grillmair were just like other climbers from Banff who were trying to establish themselves. These included, Chic Scott, Tim Auger, Brian Greenwood, Don Vockeroth, and Peter Fuhrman. We'd bump into each other frequently, and Hans would always inquired about Edward and Ernest Feuz as he knew that I knew them as well, and saw them whenever they'd come to Lake Louise. He was always friendly and interested in what I had just climbed, or was planning to climb, and frequently we'd share a Heinekens together as we chatted. I climbed with Hans but once, and that was on Mt. Sir Donald at Roger's Pass.

It was in early September in 1961, and for some reason Hans' clients didn't show up. They left a message at the Summit Gas Station saying that they wouldn't be able to meet as arranged. As I was also waiting for a friend to join me in a few days he asked me if I'd like to climb Sir Donald with him the next day. I was delighted as I knew that Hans was a terrific climber and I looked forward to learning all I could from him.

We left at four in the morning and headed across the nasty moraine and lower glacier and then we scrambled up the messy slabs and scree to the col between Mt. Sir Donald and Terminal Peak. Hans was all business on the mountain and after we roped up he moved quickly and skilfully across the moraine, the glacier and the rock outcroppings. He seemed to never waste any motion as he stepped confidently along at a brisk pace. I was glad that I was in good shape from a summer of climbing, as it would have been difficult to keep up with him otherwise. Once on the ridge, it was a straight forward romp to the summit where we basked in the crisp noon-time sunlight and enjoyed the view and a great lunch of sausage, cheese, buns and apricots. Hans wasn't a gregarious comedian like our friend Bruno Engler, but there was a solid sense of integrity about him.

We wasted no time descending and got back to the Wheeler Hut at five thirty. After a cool beer, that had been cooling all day in the little stream by the hut, Hans hopped into his Volkswagen Van and headed first for Golden, and then for Radium and the Bugaboos. I've always treasured the time I spent with this truly unique personality and I've often thought back on that perfect day that we enjoyed.

Hans Gmoser

Hans Gmoser July 7, 1932 –July 5, 2006
A great mountaineer, skier. photographer, adventurer and visionary. He introduced heli-skiing and heli-hiking to the Canadian Rockies and founded Bugaboo Lodge.

Chapter 8

Two Mountaineering Tragedies

Introduction

Over the years there have been many serious mountaineering accidents in the Rockies and several fatalities. A number have taken place in the Moraine Lake area on some of the Ten Peaks and on Mount Temple, and others have occurred in the Lake Louise area on Mt. Lefroy, Mt. Victoria, and in Abbot Pass. The Tower of Eisenhower at Castle Junction has also claimed its share of climbers, as have several peaks around the Columbia Icefields and in the Selkirks.

Most mountaineering accidents generally result from failing to use basic common sense and accepted mountaineering practices, but some have been the result of freak natural occurrences such as falling rocks, avalanches, storms, whiteouts, and lightning strikes. Several climbers died due to their inexperience or from pushing themselves beyond their capabilities. Some have had limited experience in the outdoors and have been unable to ascertain obvious danger signs and situations. Occasionally, seasoned climbers have suffered from over-confidence and neglected to observe standard safety procedures.

In 1884, the inexperienced **Lou Frissell** from Yale University was badly hurt on the first attempt to climb Mt. Lefroy. It was the first recorded mountaineering accident to take place in the Rockies. In 1892, **Phil Abbot** gained the distinction of being the first mountaineer to be killed while climbing in the Rockies. He took his rope off just below the summit of Mt. Lefroy, and when a large rock pulled loose, he lost his balance and fell to his death. **Charles Thompson** was lucky to escape with his life in 1897 when, unroped,, he fell head first into a crevasse while attempting to climb Mt. Gordon.

Miss Helen Hatch was unroped when she fell to her death on Mt. Avalanche at Rogers Pass in 1907, as was **M. D. Geddes** when he tried to glissade down Mt. Lefroy in 1927. He lost his footing and tumbled to his death as his comrades watched helplessly. Like Abbot, **Dr. Stone** was unroped when he fell to his death from Mt. Eon in 1921. His wife barely survived after spending seven days stranded on a narrow ledge when she rappelled down the cliff-face of the mountain to find her husband and ran out of rope.

Rex Gibson was killed by a falling rock on Mt. Howson near Smithers, B.C. in 1957, and **John Linn,** the pianist at Chateau Lake Louise, was almost killed when he fell into a crevasse on the Lower Victoria Glacier in 1961. (See the full story in my book: *Lake Louise at its Best*). In 1963, **Graham Cooper** was killed at the base of the 3-4 couloir at Moraine Lake, when he was hit in the head by a falling rock shortly after he'd removed his safety helmet.

Over the intervening years there have been several other serious accidents – such is the nature of the sport. On August 29th, 2000 the mountaineering guide **Karl Konrad Nagy** of Canmore was killed instantly when he was hit in the head by a rock as he was testing three aspiring mountaineering guides on Mt. Little, above Moraine Lake. The party was at the base of a rock face near the summit when a large rock was dislodged as one of the climbers scaled the final pitch. The same day that Nagy was killed, **Franz Waibl,** of New Zealand slipped and fell to his death as he descended Mt. Athabaska. Like so many of those who died, he was not roped to his climbing companions.

Shortly after the death of Waibl, **Sylvain Aubin** fell while climbing Mt. Colin near Jasper on September 7th, 2000. He was unroped and when a rock he was using as a handhold pulled loose. He lost his balance and fell to his death. It was reported that the pitch was a relatively easy and he felt that it was not necessary for him to be roped for a belay. In August the following summer, **Diane Volkers** and **Christine Aikens,** two off-duty wardens from Banff, were injured when they slipped on loose rocks near the top of Mt. Lefroy. Fortunately, they were roped together. Miraculously some avalanche debris slowed down their momentum, preventing them from catapulting over a cliff into Abbot Pass. It is not known whether the pair was belaying one another up the dangerous pitch near the summit or whether they were both moving together when one, or both, slipped. Tim Auger, the head of the Mountain Rescue Unit in Banff, told me later that a large rock had let go and pulled both climbers off.

On October 14, 2001, **Gerhard Farmer** sustained severe face, back and leg injuries when he fell some two hundred meters down the glacier on Mt. Aberdeen. Gerhard and his three companions were not roped when he slipped on the icy glacier and could not self-arrest. On December 17th, 2002, two climbers were killed while scaling a frozen waterfall on Cascade Mountain at Banff. **Maxine Arsenault** of Sainte–Foy, Quebec died when, moments after he took off his rope, he slipped and fell twenty meters to the rocks below. Minutes later an avalanche swept down the mountain and killed **Thilo Penzel** of Germany as he and his four colleagues attempted to rappel down to where Arsenault's body lay. A similar accident occurred in the first week of November, 2006 when a pair of climbers were hit by an avalanche while ice climbing near Fortress Lake. One of the climbers survived when he took shelter under an rock outcropping. The other didn't have time to take cover and was buried by heavy wet snow.

In 2004, there were at least three climbing fatalities in the Rockies. One occurred above Bow Lake on Mt. Wilson in late March, when an unexpected avalanche hit an experienced group of mountaineers from Seattle. In mid June, two rather inexperienced lads were killed when hit by an avalanche near the summit of Mt. Deltaform (in the Ten Peaks) as they ascended the Super Coulior route. Climbers should expect sudden avalanches and snow and rock slides in the early part of the season – particularly in June and early July.

On November 7, 2006 a twenty-five-year-old climber died after being buried by an avalanche while ice-climbing with a partner near Fortress Mountain. The accident was the first fatality of the ice-climbing and ski season. The first climber was belaying his partner at the top of a pitch when he saw the avalanche coming.

He yelled out a warning as he took shelter under a large rock. His partner was fully exposed however and he was unable to avoid the tumbling snow and ice.

In general you can expect unstable conditions when temperatures are rising in late October and early November. It is common for the steep slopes to be unstable, with sloughing snow, after a heavy early-season snow storm – especially in east facing alpine bowls with temperatures rising. One must learn to recognize the terrain where avalanches are likely to occur. While both climbers were reported to have a "high level of experience", they seem to have been lacking in "basic mountain savvy" and judgement in the outdoors, and as a consequence, paid a heavy price.

The two mountaineering tragedies that rank as claiming the most lives took place in the mid 1950s in the Lake Louise area. One involved the deaths of three Mexican women and their guide who plunged to their deaths from the icy slopes of Mt. Victoria on July 30th, 1954. The other took place the following year on July 11th, 1955 when seven, poorly-equipped, poorly-prepared, and poorly-led young boys, aged twelve to sixteen years, died on the unforgiving slopes of Mt. Temple. Both tragedies should never have happened. Both were the result of foolhardy actions and could have been avoided with the application of some basic common sense and mountaineering experience. Strangely the stories of these tragedies have never been fully told – although they have been frequently referred to. What follows are the details of both of these accidents as they were told to me by several people who took part in the rescues, and as reported in local newspapers.

Death on Mt. Victoria

The early spring of 1954 had dumped a lot of snow on the Rockies and the peaks around Lake Louise were still heavily laden by mid July. The crevasses and the bergschrund in Abbot Pass were well filled in by the many avalanches that thundered into the pass from the precipitous slopes of Mt. Lefroy and Mt. Victoria. Despite this, few parties had attempted to climb either mountain, as too much unstable snow lay on the standard routes.

Wednesday, July 28th, 1954 was a cloudless day and the temperature was in the eighties (Fahrenheit) at the Lake Louise boathouse. As usual, that afternoon Walter Feuz was on duty on the dock, and the business of renting canoes to the tourists was brisk. Walter's brother Ernest had just returned from taking some clients up The Mitre and was resting on the porch of the Swiss chalet with his climbing boots off, enjoying a hot cup of tea. The big clock on the mantle of the fireplace in the chalet had just struck a quarter to three when a group of seven foreign-looking women climbers and one man appeared from the direction of the parking lot. Ernest watched them stop and ask old Ralph at the Brewster corral for directions. There was a lot of pointing and gesturing toward Mt. Victoria and the snow-covered peaks at the end of Lake Louise. Then Ralph pointed to the Swiss chalet and to Ernest who was still sipping his tea. Seeing Ernest on the porch, Ralph waved at him and pointed once again. With that, the group of seven headed in his direction.

The man and a pretty young woman with raven-black hair led the others toward the steps of the chalet where Ernest sat. They all had heavy packs with mountaineering ropes and crampons attached to them, and each carried a new ice axe. None of the group was more than five-foot six-inches tall, but all were well tanned with dark features and hair. Ernest guessed that they were probably Mexican or South American climbers.

Reaching the steps of the chalet, the woman leading the group asked if he was "Mr. Ernest Feuz." Ernest acknowledged that he was, and then the woman introduced the group as a Mexican women's mountaineering team that had come to Canada to "conquer the peaks." The woman introduced herself as **Ofelia Fernadez,** the leader of the group. She spoke broken English but Ernest could tell that she was well-educated and certainly the person in charge. Ofelia introduced the man, **Eduardo San Vincente** their mountaineering guide. She said that he had climbed Mt. Aconcagua in Argentina, Mt. Chimborazo in Ecuador, Mt. Huascaran in Peru, and Mt. McKinley in Alaska. Eduardo spoke no English but he seemed affable and rather jolly.

Always the hospitable host, Ernest invited them onto the porch and offered them some tea—there was always a large pot on the back of the woodstove in the kitchen and it was always hot.

With the exception of San Vincente, who was forty-three, the members of the group were all in their twenties or early thirties, and all were physically fit. They were also well equipped with modern mountaineering boots, knickers, gaiters, anoraks, and down jackets. Their ropes, carabiners, and crampons were also the best available. Ernest learned that they all belonged to different mountaineering clubs in Mexico and that they had brought their club banners to fly proudly from the peaks that they planned to conquer in the Rockies.

After the tea was served, Ofelia announced that the group wanted to climb Mt. Victoria. She asked Ernest to point out the route for their guide and Ernest described the way to the Plain of Six Glaciers. With a pencil and paper he drew a crude map of Abbot Pass and the route up Mt. Victoria. He stressed that the group should leave Abbot Hut early in the morning in order that their ascent and descent could be made on firm snow. The climbing party should gain the exposed ridge by keeping to the left as they climbed South Peak, and then they should proceed along the ridge to the knife-edged "sickle."

From there Ernest told them to keep to the main ridge over and around the gendarmes to Centre Peak. He repeated the instructions and the details of the climb several times, and Ofelia translated all that he said into Spanish for the benefit of her colleagues. Their guide Eduardo nodded and smiled a lot and indicated that he understood what Ernest was saying. The other women also nodded and smiled frequently to show that they too understood. They were anticipating a great climb.

Ernest suggested that the group leave for the Plain of Six Glaciers as soon as possible and enter Abbot Pass at about seven o'clock that evening. By then the upper glaciers on Mt. Lefroy and Mt. Victoria would be cooling and unlikely to avalanche. He told them to stay in the centre of the pass and to be always on the lookout for avalanches. As they finished their tea, Ernest gave them a few tips about the bergschrund and the crevasses near Abbot Hut. The members of the group then shouldered their packs and each formally shook hands with both Ernest and his brother Walter, who had come over from the boathouse for a cup of tea and to meet the visitors. As they were leaving **H.A.V. (Harry) Green**, a regular guest at the Chateau and the President of the Canadian Alpine Club, arrived to renew old acquaintances with the Feuz brothers.

The heavily-laden Mexican team made good time to the Plain of Six Glaciers arriving at the teahouse at about six fifteen. Here they met **Irene Stanfield** and had another cup of tea and some sandwiches. They soon resumed their trek and proceeded down the trail through the lateral moraine to the lower glacier as Ernest had instructed. At the beginning of the glacier the group roped up on two ropes. Guide Eduardo San Vincente led off with his rope mates and the second rope, led by Ofelia Fernandez, followed smartly behind. Occasionally the party paused to look back at the magnificence of the Chateau and tranquil surface of the jade-green lake as it shimmered in the early evening shadows far below them.

Soon the group passed the flanks of Mt. Lefroy and entered the beginning of the treacherous pass. Here they put on their crampons and followed the tracks of a party that had preceded them two days earlier. They made good time over some minor crevasses and soon came to the bergschrund, which was situated about three-quarters of the way up the pass. There was a good snow bridge over the bergschrund on the left side of the pass that year and the Mexicans had little trouble negotiating it. Keeping up a slow, steady pace, the group seldom stopped to rest on their ascent and soon they could see the hut. At nine-fifteen they mounted the stairs and entered the unlocked door. (In those days all mountain cabins and huts were unlocked).

Getting the woodstove going, the group lit some candles and then put on some hot tea and soup. Out on the porch they could see the twinkling, amber lights of Lake O'Hara Lodge far below them. On the other side, they could look down upon the Plain of Six Glaciers. Above them on their left, were the imposing slopes of Mt. Victoria coated with sparkling bands of ice, snow, and rock. To their right were the equally-menacing snow slopes and rock bands of Mt. Lefroy. After a satisfying bedtime snack Ofelia Fernandez entered the following note in the climber's log that was always kept on the table in the hut.

> *"July 28th, 1954. This is the first feminine expedition organized in the whole world to conquer peaks in other country thousands miles far. Seven women and only one man to help them. [sic]*
>
> *Expedicion Mexicana Femenina. Julio 28–1954*
> *Arrivo-a-esta Refugio—Women–*
> > *Ofelia Fernadez—Jefe (Chief)*
> > *Beatriz Diaz Silva*
> > *Margarita Vivanco*
> > *Carmen Rubio*
> > *Lucia Oscaranza*
> > *Ma Louisa Fabila*
> > *Maria Garcia*

Man—Eduardo San Vincente
        Jefe Tecnico (Technique Chief)
        Conqueror of: "Aconcaqua" Argentina
        "Chimborazo" Ecudar
        "Mt. McKinley" Alaska
        "Huascaran" Peru

Long Live Mexico!"

The only known photograph of the entire group of eight Mexican mountaineers before the tragedy of July 30, 1954. They are (from right to left) Lucia Ocaranza (standing), Margarita Vivanco (foreground), Beatriz Diaz Silva, Maria Garcia, Maria Luisa Fabila, Carmen Rubio, Ofelia Fernandez (leader of the group) and Eduardo San Vincente (guide).

The next morning the group rose at a leisurely hour, having decided to rest that day and climb Mt. Victoria on July 30th. They spent their time taking pictures, getting their equipment in order, napping, and practicing on the snow and ice slopes of Mt. Lefroy within sight of the hut. They planned to take Ernest's advice and get an early start the following morning.

The early morning of July 30th, was clear and cold and the party was ready to leave for their climb at six thirty. **Margarita Vivanco,** thirty-five was not feeling well that morning, so she decided to stay in the cabin to recuperate and prepare a victory dinner for her comrades.

The party divided into two ropes. Guide **Eduardo San Vincente** led the first rope with **Beatriz Diaz Silva, Lucia Oscaranza** and **Ma Louisa Fabila. Ofelia Fernandez** led the second rope with **Maria Garcia** and **Carmen Rubio** as her companions.

The Mexican team on their way up to the Plain of Six Glaciers on July 28th, 1954. They are standing on some avalanche debris along the trail. This picture was in all likelihood taken by their guide Eduardo San Vincente

The previous night had been cold and the snow that morning was rock hard. After negotiating the initial rock bands behind the hut at the base of South Peak they reached the snow. Here they each put on a pair of curious canvass and rubber over-boots over their regular climbing boots. Over these they fastened their crampons.

Moving at a painfully-slow pace the teams followed Ernest's instructions and kept to the left of South Peak as they ascended. They reached the summit of South Peak at approximately nine-thirty and rested for awhile. They enjoyed a remarkable view of Mt. Huber beside them, the Waputik Icefield to the northwest, Mt. Hungabee to the south, and Lake O'Hara below. As the sun began to rise in the deep blue, summer sky, it foretold the promise of a very warm day.

After some picture-taking and a second breakfast the party decided against going to Centre Peak. Rather than returning from South Peak by retracing the route they had taken on the way up, they foolishly decided to descend directly down the face the mountain. It was a rash and risky move – one that Ernest had cautioned them against.

Leaving South Peak at about ten forty-five, they started their descent. They moved cautiously and again, ignoring Ernest's advice, they belayed each other directly down the face of the treacherous mountain in the rapidly-softening snow. Soon they encountered sliding, granular snow over the rock-hard snow and ice beneath. The group now moved at a snail's pace, taking an inordinate amount of time to belay each other down the steepening pitches.

As the snow became softer under the intense sun, it started to "ball-up" in the cleats of their crampons. It was now almost eleven thirty. Walter Feuz, who was monitoring their progress through his binoculars at the Lake Louise boathouse, knew immediately that they were making a fatal mistake. Several bellhops were also taking turns peering at the climbing party through the large brass telescope on the loggia of the hotel. Bellhop **Ray Wehner** and assistant hotel manager **Ray Mackay** were also tracking them through their binoculars and remarked to each other that the group was moving very slowly, and foolishly descending straight down the face of the mountain.

Four members of the Mexican team heading up Abbot Pass on July 28th, 1954. There was a lot of snow in the pass that season. This picture shows the steepness of the pass. The team is about ½ way to the top at this point.

It was quarter to one when Wehner and Mackay rushed ashen-faced from the loggia to the bell-desk, where **Chuck Roland** and **Frank Campbell** were sharing a joke. They breathlessly announced that they had just seen climbers fall from below South Peak, slide down the entire steep slope of the mountain, and then disappear over the precipice into Abbot Pass. The second rope of climbers seemed to be stranded on the snowy face of the peak, about three hundred feet below the summit ridge, and they didn't appear to be moving. What happened next is taken from the personal accounts of **Chuck Roland, Ray Wehner, Frank Campbell,** and **Harry Green.** Chuck graciously allowed me to use the following account for this book.

"Friday, July 30, 1954

> *Shortly after lunch,* **Ray Mackay** *and* **Ray Wehner** *saw a party of seven climbers through the telescope. Soon after, while they were describing the location of the group to* **J. Stephenson** *and the hotel electrician, several of the climbers appeared to slide down the south face of Mt. Victoria. On viewing the scene through the telescope, only three of the party (originally there were seven) remained on the mountain. The time was approximately 12:45 p.m.*

> *Wehner consulted with* **Ernest Feuz,** *who felt that perhaps the party of four had gone in front of the rock bluff, and consequently were not visible.* **Cliff Pethyridge** *(a Brewster mechanic) who had been watching the party closely with his own binoculars stated that four climbers had definitely fallen. Ray Wehner went to the boathouse and there,* **Walter Feuz** *expressed the opinion that there was no doubt about it—the four climbers had fallen.*

> *On hearing the distressing news* **Manager E.C. Fitt** *and* **Mr. Harry A.V. Green** *came down to the boathouse. Manager Fitt immediately formed a rescue squad consisting of Ernest Feuz, Harry Green, Ray Wehner, and two others of Wehner's choosing. He immediately chose Frank Campbell and Charles Roland—both of who were excellent climbers and on duty at the time.*

> *While the rescue party was preparing itself, long shrouds of canvass were cut by the upholsterer to be taken with all due haste to the Plain of Six Glaciers by packhorse. At 2:45 p.m., the rescue party left the boathouse by motor canoe and travelled to the end of the lake. A hurried, but uneventful, hike took them to the Plain of Six Glaciers Teahouse where Irene Stanfield (the manageress) served tea and provided some supplies for the trip to the accident site.*

> *At 4:30 p.m. they left the teahouse and moved on to the end of the trail over the moraine to a spot where they could look directly up Abbot Pass. They stopped and searched the area with binoculars and Ernest saw what looked like two bodies. Someone suggested that the others had fallen into a crevasse. A few probable locations for the bodies were seen and noted and the party, deciding not to wait for the horses and the canvas, started up the pass.*

Ofelia Fernandez – the leader of the Mexican women's team.
This picture was taken near the Abbot Pass Hut the day before the tragedy on July 29, 1954. Mt. Hungabee is in the background to the left.

Arriving at the bodies at approximately 6:00 p.m. the remains of the Mexican climbers were found in a group at one of the spots previously noted from below. All four were together – tangled inextricably in their own rope. Nearly all of their limbs were broken, some in several places. Three had their skulls smashed in as well. It was ascertained that all four were dead and then they moved on quickly for the Abbot Pass hut.

As the rescuers travelled up the pass, they saw the remainder of the party attempting a descent from the ridge on the steep snow slope. They tried to halt them by shouting, and being recognized they felt that they had been successful and that the stranded Mexicans were waiting to be rescued. [They had been petrified

in that spot since just before noon—some six and a half hours.]
As the rescue party climbed, however, they noticed that the party
was still trying to move slowly downward and that their attempts
to prevent this seemed to be to no avail.

At 6:40 p.m. the rescue party reached Abbot Hut and were met at
the door by an unexpected sight. One member of the eight-person
Mexican party had remained. **Margarita Vivanco** *greeted them*
as they arrived. They tried to impart to her the sad news that her
friends had died—but she either did not understand or refused to
believe the awful truth.

Ernest and Harry decided that all of the rescue party need not
continue on up the mountain, and as Chuck Roland was the
freshest of the group, Ernest decided that he should be the one to
go with him. They roped themselves together, gulped down a few
mouthfuls of fruit juice, and left the hut. Those remaining behind
lit the stove, prepared some hot food, and got the cabin warmed
up. Occasionally someone would run outside to check on the
progress of the two rescuers and the condition of the three women
who awaited their rescue. In the cabin Ray Wehner discovered a
plaque inscribed with the national anthem of Mexico. On it, one
of the Mexicans had written the names of the members of their
group and some of the details of their expedition.

After leaving the cabin, Feuz and Roland raced up the southeast
ridge of Mt. Victoria in an effort to reach the survivors before
they too slipped. Climbing quickly over excellent rock and very
firm snow they reached the ridge and proceeded along it until
they were directly above the stranded threesome, who were
roughly two hundred feet below them, and squatting on the steep
snow-slope. [Chuck Roland noted later that: "Ernest usually
goes slow and steady when he's climbing. This time he went fast
and steady. I've never moved so fast on a mountain in my life."
The average time to climb from the hut to the South Peak is about
an hour; Ernest and Chuck did it in thirty-five minutes.]

Tying three climbing ropes together, Ernest carefully belayed
Roland, as he kicked steps down the snow slope and descended
to the three women. At first the frightened women refused to
climb back up to the ridge as instructed—saying that it was too
dangerous. Reaching **Carmelita Rubio***, (the leader of the rope),*
Roland unfastened the end of her climbing rope from her carabiner
and tied it to himself. He then tied her into a position about ten
feet farther along. Belayed from above by Ernest, Roland urged
the women to follow as he retraced his steps up to the ridge. They
displayed signs of great fatigue and nervous exhaustion however
and moved very slowly with great caution.

Six members of the Mexican Women's expedition on the South Peak of Victoria on July 30, 1954. Three fell to their death along with their male guide shortly after this picture was taken. The photo was taken by their guide Eduardo San Vincente.

Mount Victoria showing where the four Mexican climbers fell and their line of fall down the face of the mountain. They fell some 1000 feet and then over the cliff into Abbot Pass

The Mexican survivors at the Plain of Six Glaciers. Left to Right – Maria Garcia, Carmelita Rubio, Ofelia Fernandez (the leader), and Marguerita Vivanco (Photo –The Calgary Herald August 2, 1954)

Ofelia Fernandez the leader of the group.
(Photo –The Calgary Herald August 2, 1954)

The surviving members of the Mexican women's Team at the Plain of Six Glaciers. Following their rescue from the precipitous slopes of Mt. Victoria. The arrow at the top of the pictures shows the spot from which they were rescued and from which their colleagues fell to their death. They are from Left to Right – Maria Garcia, Carmelita Rubio, Ofelia Fernandez (the leader), and Marguerita Vivanco (Photo The Albertan August 2, 1954)

*When they finally reached the ridge, Feuz and Roland removed the Mexican's crampons and their canvas over-boots from over their regular climbing boots. As they did so they related the sad news of their friends' death. Besides **Carmelita Rubio**, the two other survivors were **Maria Garcia** and **Ofelia Fernandez** – the leader of the expedition.*

Re-grouping on one rope they began the descent to the hut with Roland leading and Feuz guiding their descent from above at the upper end of the rope. Leaving the snow, on which the girls were very uncertain, they began their descent on the rocks. At this point the women moved even slower and became more uncertain. Nearly every step on the way had to be carefully pointed out to each of the women.

Abbot Pass and Mt. Victoria

The "X" shows where the climbers slipped and where they came to rest some 3000 feet below in Abbot Pass. (Photo –The Albertan, August 2, 1954)

As they neared the hut, Frank Campbell approached the base of the rocks to meet them and as he watched the rescue party's progress he saw Maria suddenly slip and fall onto Chuck Roland, who at that moment was in a precarious position. Fortunately Roland managed to catch her and maintain his balance. Minutes later they reached the hut with the three survivors. By then it was 9:40 p.m. and almost totally dark.

Hot food and warm blankets awaited the survivors and the men removed the footwear of the traumatized women and rubbed their feet to restore circulation. The women conversed with Margarita but did not inform her of the tragedy. Instead, they told her that the four others had returned to Lake Louise. Privately Maria Garcia revealed the identity of those who had died by pointing to the list prepared by Ray Wehner.

Almost immediately Ernest set about preparing the whole group for the descent down the pass to the teahouse. He led with Margarita and Carmen on one rope and Harry Green, Maria Garcia, and Frank Campbell followed on another. The final rope was made up of Ray Wehner, Ofelia Fernandez, and Chuck Roland. The first and the last parties each carried a small flashlight. Wehner and Roland found the descent quite difficult for with every second or third step Ofelia would slip and fall. The final struggle up the moraine to the path leading to the teahouse was also very difficult. On the descent through the pass, they skirted around the bodies and although the rescuers could see them, none of women were aware of the proximity of the dead.

Reaching the teahouse at 1:00 a.m., Irene Stanfield was awakened and the group was fed. **Jack Caldwell***, a former staff member of the Chateau (1952) was also at the teahouse to greet them. After eating, it was decided that the Mexican women should stay overnight at the Plain of Six Glaciers teahouse because they were too tired to go any further. Harry Green, Ray Wehner and Ernest Feuz returned to the Chateau so that the details could be given to the police. Campbell and Roland were instructed to stay overnight at the teahouse so they could move up to the bodies early the following morning.*

Had the group returning to the Chateau not been so excited by the events of the day and had they not had Ernest for company, the long walk in the inky darkness would have been painful, but it went surprisingly quickly. After talking to anxious members of the staff, searching for food in the kitchen, and taking a short drink to calm themselves postponed their bed time until nearly 4:00 a.m.

Ray Wehner was up shortly after 7:00 a.m. and consulted with the R.C.M.P. while he awaited the arrival of Ernest Feuz and Harry Green. All preparations were made and shortly after 9:00 a.m. they headed back to the Plain of Six Glaciers on horseback. The party included Ernest Feuz, Harry Green, Ray Wehner, **Howard Shrigley***, (the R.C.M.P. constable) and one of the Park wardens. After a short stop at the teahouse they roped up and proceeded up Abbot Pass to where the bodies lay. The wind was strong and they were quite concerned about the frequent falling ice from the Victoria Glacier above them., (Campbell, Green, Roland and Wehner. Unpublished)*

❧

Three of the rescuers
L. to R. Frank Campbell, Charles Roland, Raymond Wehner. All three would become medical doctors. (Photo –The Calgary Herald August 2, 1954)

Swiss guide Ernest Feuz after the rescue.
He was 65 years old at the time. (Photo – The Calgary Herald August 2, 1954)

Meanwhile, Frank Campbell and Chuck Roland stayed the night in one of the cabins at the Plain of Six Glaciers. Here is their account of the part they played retrieving the bodies.

> *We went to bed shortly after 2:00 a.m., but were kept awake by a combination of frequent nearby avalanches and vivid imaginations. Consequently, we had only about two hours sleep when we were awakened by Irene Stanfield at 6:30 a.m.* **Nigel Dun** *of the Calgary Herald and a photographer, had arrived and wanted an interview. We got up, dressed, ate a quick breakfast, and talked to them for a short while. Then, on hearing from Jack Caldwell that a party of five staff had started up the pass, we left immediately in hopes of catching them and turning them back. Hastening to the moraine we picked up four canvasses, added them to our already heavy packs, and started up the pass at 7:45 a.m.*
>
> *At 8:55 we reached the bodies – the other party had too great a start and had pushed on to the hut at this stage. Since we did not want to touch the bodies until we had taken pictures – which we thought might be needed for official records – we moved on up to the large crevasse to wait until the sun had risen higher. After a short wait we returned to the bodies, which we had previously covered with canvas, took our pictures (which did not turn out), and began the grisly task of separating and wrapping the dead.*
>
> *It was necessary to cut the Mexican's rope in numerous places, as it was tangled about their legs in an unbelievably complicated manner. We had previously cut a large shelf with our ice axes just below the bodies. Here we spread the canvasses, one at a time, and began the laborious job of wrapping the bodies and tying them securely for the trip down the pass. (Campbell and Roland – Unpublished)*

In a separate account Chuck Roland described their unsavory task:

> *Both of us (Roland and Campbell) were to enter medical school a few months later and we did not feel prepared for the macabre necessities of that July day. The four climbers were, of course unmoved. One still gazed back up the slope down which they had all tumbled just yesterday. Another gravely contemplated the lower levels of the pass, pale countenance dramatized by an ugly but unbleeding gash down one temple and cheek.*
>
> *Through the morning hours we labored to impress some humanness on the grotesquely bound remains of the climbers. We slashed the rope and tried to separate their bodies. Occasionally*

we dodged small avalanches from the surrounding mountains as the August 1st sun rose and loosened the bind of the snow slopes. As the Mexicans became individuals again, rather than units in a gory quartet, we attempted to cloak each in a canvas shroud. After some struggle with arms and legs frozen stiff, or tight with rigor mortis, we managed to reduce the evidence of the tragedy to four rope-girded canvass masses, seemingly a little smaller than life-size.

About 11:00 a.m. while we were engaged, an avalanche came down from the Victoria Glacier, following the path of the previous day's fall. It forced us to run toward Mount Lefroy as it came right down to where we were working.

Chuck Roland (left) and Ray Wehner just past the end of Lake Louise on the trail to the Plain of Six Glaciers Summer of 1954

*As the hours passed we slid the bodies carefully down the pass and across the glacier. At 1:00 p.m. the rest of the group reached the bodies. The first to arrive was **Raymond Grobet**, who brought a Mexican flag, given to him by the surviving Mexicans, so that he might place it on the bodies and take a picture. He was followed by **Jack Caldwell**, **Ernest Feuz**, **Constable Shrigley**, **Park Warden Ian McKenzie**, and **Ray Wehner**. The group began the descent immediately, with two people bringing down each body – sliding them down the steep slopes of the pass and dragging them across the snow slopes at the bottom.*

Ray Wehner (left) Irene Stanfield, and Chuck Roland
At the Plain of Six Glaciers – Summer of 1954

Chuck Roland (centre) and Frank Campbell (right) with one of the wrapped bodies at the moraine below the Plain of Six Glaciers. They had pulled the body down Abbot Pass to the base of the moraine. (The person to the left is Dave Tilley a CPR constable.)

Pack horses carrying the bodies back from the Plain of Six Glaciers to the Chateau. (Photo –The Calgary Herald August 2, 1954)

Pulling the bodies across the glacier.
Here Jack Caldwell and Ray Wehner haul one of the dead Mexicans, who is wrapped in a heavy canvass shroud, across the snow of Abbot Pass. (Photo –The Calgary Herald August 2, 1954)

*At the base of the moraine we met **Harry Green**, who had brought the stretchers, which had been carried part way the previous day by Jack Caldwell and one other person. At the base of the lateral moraine several others met us including: C.P.R. constables **Ralph Peterson** and **Dave Tilley**, and two newspapermen. The former two were of invaluable help in the backbreaking task of transporting the bodies up the steep, rocky slope of the moraine and along the path to where **Hugh Jennings** waited with the* *horses. This job took two hours. Two of the bodies were carried on stretchers and two were slung on long poles for the journey up the moraine. While Hugh packed the bodies on the horses the rescue party, their responsibility ended, walked down to the teahouse for a cup of tea. From there they returned to the Chateau. The bodies of the Mexican climbers followed on packhorses to the end of the lake, where they were transferred to the warden's truck for removal to Banff. **John Linn** and **Phyllis Hart** went up to the Plain of Six Glaciers early that morning to help take the survivors down to the Chateau." (Campbell, Green, Roland and Wehner Unpublished)*

On Tuesday August 2nd, Ofelia Fernandez told her version of the tragedy to a reporter from the Calgary Herald from her bed at Chateau Lake Louise.

"The seven alpinists were traveling in two groups. The four victims in the lead and three more led by me [Miss Fernandez] coming behind. We had spent about an hour on the south summit and were on our way down. The others were ahead. We were taking every precaution. We knew it was dangerous. We were using ice axes but sometimes we couldn't use them and our crampons were not taking hold because the snow was so loose. I saw position three [the third climber] start to slip and drag the others down. They slid down and then they tangled up together in a ball and rolled down very fast. There was no avalanche. When I saw them fall, I knew it was all over."

Miss Fernandez said that the members of the party recognized the dangers of the route they had taken for the descent, but counted on their experience to surmount the challenge. Stumbling over her words, she recalled the details of what happened after the accident.

"We were shocked. But we are trained when we have an accident to safeguard ourselves as much as possible. We were not panicky. We knew our exact route down. We were going to take the rock route."

This was the route originally recommended by Ernest Feuz, who had advised them earlier to keep clear of the snow slope from which the climbers had fallen. The three women spent nearly seven hours struggling on the slopes after the accident before aid finally reached them. The three survivors said they were sufficiently experienced as mountain climbers to tackle the slope, and were aware of the snow conditions before they started the climb. "It was just an accident," Miss Fernandez cried. "It was just an accident."

In an article on the front page of the August 2nd, 1954 edition of the Calgary Herald, Ernest Feuz was interviewed and gave his version of the tragic events.

Death Lies In Wait On Mt. Victoria

"Victoria can be a dangerous mountain." That's the opinion of Ernest Feuz, 65-year old, Swiss born mountain guide who has climbed the mountain more times than any other man. Feuz has lost count of the exact number of ascents he has made of the 11,365 ft. peak, but he believes the number is about 50. These climbs have been made over the period of 28 years. For 17 years prior to coming to Lake Louise, the diminutive, steel-tough guide climbed in British Columbia's Selkirk range.

Feuz contended the Mexicans should not have used crampons on the soft, rotten snow of the sun-soaked east face. The crampons could not reach the hard snow underneath the slushy upper layer and the climbers therefore were supported only by the unstable surface snow. "If they want to try tricks like that no one can stop them," said the guide. He said they should have used their ice axes to cut steps in the hard snow underneath. Then they would have had firm support for their feet.

The east face of Mount Victoria had been climbed only once before to Feuz's knowledge and that was about 20 years ago. The ascent was made at a point much farther to the right of the route taken by the Mexicans, and two or three unsuccessful attempts were made before the sheer walls were forced. [Val Fynn was the first to climb Mt. Victoria via this direct route]

Feuz said that neither the Mexicans nor any other mountaineer should climb on the east face of Victoria – the route chosen by the ill-fated group.

"That's committing suicide especially in these conditions. The high mountains are in bad shape this year. In all the history we have never had such a hard winter, so much snow, and so late a spring." Apart from the usual ridge route, Victoria has been dangerous to climb so far this season. To his knowledge, the Mexicans' was the first ascent of the south summit that season. None have reached the main peak this year."

"My brother Walter and I warned them to stay to the ridge. If they had kept on the ridge, they would have been alive today." Feuz said.

The guide said that many climbers come to the Swiss for advice on routes and some do not always follow the advice given. Feuz said the guides could only tell climbers what they should do. They could not make them do it.

"Lots of people don't take our advice. Some people think it is an easy mountain, but Victoria can be dangerous."

On Monday August 2nd, Maria Garcia, accompanied by **Bruce Lee,** a Bell Captain at the Chateau, and **John Linn,** the concert pianist, returned to the Abbot Hut to pick up some of the expedition's equipment and personal effects. Some years later, John Linn told me about that trip and how emotional it was for all of them.

On Tuesday, August 3rd, the Mexican government sent a DC-3 aircraft to Calgary to pick up the survivors and the bodies of the deceased. It was decided that an inquest was not warranted. The survivors and the bodies of their ill-fated comrades left Lake Louise station on the train and stayed the night in Calgary. Before leaving the survivors tried to express their gratitude for the way everyone had responded to their plight.

At nine o'clock. on the morning of August 4th, the Mexican DC-3, loaded with the surviving climbers and the bodies of their comrades, taxied down the east-west runway of the Calgary Airport. It took off to the east and gained altitude, then it banked in a slow, 180-degree turn and headed west toward Banff and the Bow River Valley. Flying slowly at about fifteen thousand feet with three quarter flaps engaged, it cruised slowly past Mt. Temple and then it banked slowly to the left and flew directly over the Chateau and Lake Louise. When it was over Abbot Pass and Mt. Victoria, the turbo-prop plane briefly wagged it wings and then made a slow turn to the south, gained more altitude, and finally disappeared from the view of those who stood on the lawn in front of the Chateau.

Harry Green in a later account, written for the Alpine Club Journal analyzed the causes of tragedy:

> *It was a terrible tragedy and all due to ignorance and inexperience. These seven Mexican women and one male Mexican guide were living in tents. They spoke to Walter Feuz, who told them to keep to the ridge. First mistake. They never went up the ridge at all, but out on the dangerous steep snow face. Second mistake is that they had on good climbing boots but over these they had curious-looking canvas and rubber pullovers and then crampons.*

> *Now crampons are good on hard snow and ice but just suicidal on the soft, loose snow they were on. Such snow balls up between the spikes and makes it very easy to slip. One of them slipped and pulled the others down with her. If they had not had on crampons, balled up with snow, they could have easily slid a few feet and stopped as they took about 2 inches in depth of surface snow with them when they started to slip. The under snow was quite firm. I cannot understand why the guide could not stop*

them when the first one slipped. He had only to drive his ice axe in. Having them in such a crazy place, why did he not take care of them? Poor fellow, he is dead and I suppose I should not blame him. Also perhaps he did try to stop them as we found his axe and the point was bent to about 45 degrees. (Alpine Club Journal, 1954)

Chuck Roland came to the same conclusion as he pondered the causes of the accident in an article he wrote for the December 1967 edition of *A Medical Bulletin.*

Mexico has many fine mountains, with exotic names like Ixtachihuatl and Popocatepetl, but these mountains are over 17,000 feet high. The summer sun doesn't have the same effect on their snow, which tends to stay crisp and firm. The Mexican party, climbing in two ropes, had dressed for climbing at higher altitudes than they found in Canada. In particular, they wore crampons, strap-on metal sole frames with sharp spikes so useful to climbers on ice and firm snow. But at lower altitudes, in the hot July sun, the snow was not firm. It became soft, balling up to clog the spikes and impede movement. And the group was not experienced enough to know its danger, or to take precautions to prevent disaster. One climber in the group of four slipped on the steep slope. For some reason the others could not hold the weight, and all tumbled downward, bound fatally together, over fifteen hundred feet of snow slopes and then over craggy rocks to a sheer 2000 foot fall. This occurred not in decent privacy, but before the eyes of scores of on-lookers – telescopes and binoculars had followed the climbers all day. Until the fall, the spectacle had been an exhilarating bonus to jaded tourists. Now horror replaced all other feelings. (Roland, C. A Medical Bulletin, December 1967)

On August 4th the Calgary Herald published an editorial by **Nigel Dunn.** Dunn had rushed to the scene of the tragedy and was on hand to help carry the bodies of the dead climbers from the lower Victoria Glacier to the waiting horses. This article should be read and re-read by park wardens and officials as it captures the essence of the sport of mountaineering.

The Cruel Beauty – by Nigel Dunn

There is perhaps no scene more fascinating that a towering mountain mantled with cold blue ice and dazzling white snow. This is the most simple description which can be given of the Victoria group of mountains at Lake Louise, where four climbers lost their lives last week.

Nature has carved the two major massifs, Victoria itself and Mt. Lefroy, in classic style. The base of both peaks is a desolate and fantastic pile of rubble—the moraine of an ancient glacier now shrunk to relatively insignificant proportions. From the base rise sheer cliffs of more than 1000 feet, jagged and scarred from a relentless bombardment by glacier and avalanche, and the decay of rock developing throughout time.

These multi-coloured walls act as the foundation for the crowning glory of the Victoria group—the hanging glaciers which sweep down from near the summits to the edge of the sheer rock walls. These rivers of ice appear ready at any moment to plunge over the brink of the frightening cliffs, which guard the peaks from the assault of men.

The Victoria group, framed by the heavily timbered slopes of neighbouring and more insignificant mountains, and set off to perfection by the unbelievable colours of Lake Louise, is said to be one of the world's most perfect landscapes. Tourists, admiring this scene from the comfort of the Chateau, see only the beauty. They fail to recognize and appreciate the latent cruelty and the terrible powers of the devastation locked within these mountains. But the tourist alone is not guilty. Many experienced mountaineers lack respect for the peaks of the Canadian Rockies.

Few Alpine accidents happen. Most are caused. More than anything they are caused by a lack of respect by the mountaineer for the monstrous adversary. That is the fundamental cause. A party crosses a slope it should never touch; it fails to take adequate precautions when extreme care is required; it places too much faith in its experience and does not show enough awareness of the unpredictability of unstable snow, rock, and ice.

As in the case of the Mexican mountaineers who died on Mt. Victoria, the warning of a veteran guide, who knew every climbable inch of the mountain and all its changing moods, was ignored. Many people ignore warnings by men who know the mountains and more often than not they run into some difficulty— either death, injury or a few terrifying minutes which could have been avoided.

Should these people be prohibited from entering the mountains without authorized guides? Should authorized guides or wardens be empowered to prohibit a party from climbing on a slope or ridge or glacier, which is in bad condition? I do not think so. Most mountaineers would agree with this.

If the first restriction were imposed on mountaineers, many cautious and skilful climbers might be denied the pleasure of pursuing their sport to ultimate fulfilment. Many amateurs have climbed for years without incident, avoiding obvious risks, adequately protecting themselves on questionable pitches and above all appreciating the risks involved. They have climbed exceptionally difficult peaks without guides.

And why would the second restriction be necessary or desirable? The mountains are public domain and it is right that people should be permitted to go where they will. Furthermore to attempt to enforce such a restriction would be impossible. The National Parks Service now asks that people, who leave the highway for any excursions into more rugged country, report out and report in to either wardens or the RCMP. Few people bother to take advantage of this precaution. It seems to me that this is their own responsibility.

It is true that guides and wardens and even good climbers must risk their own lives to aid those who have ignored good advice and who have thereby found themselves in difficulty. But this is true also of the lifeguard who must rescue a swimmer who swims over his depth or into dangerous waters despite fair warnings. Mountaineers who get into trouble simply have tackled something over their heads.

Ernest Feuz, the veteran Swiss guide at Lake Louise has had to rescue many people from trouble. Often they have been those who he himself warned. He feels that he must warn climbers of potential danger areas, but he cannot stop them from taking their lives into their own careless hands if they wish.

The climber's life is his own. On the mountain he alone is responsible for it. To relieve him completely of that responsibility would be to take the zest out of climbing and the initiative out of climbers. New routes must be tried. It is man's nature to take certain risks whether it is on the highway or on a mountain. Good climbers will find in tragic accidents lessons, which could never be completely learned any other way. They will learn from the deaths of the four Mexicans that mountains can be dangerous; that they must be held in respect; that the risks must be fully appreciated and adequate safeguards against accidents employed.

Cruel though it may appear, mountain climbing accidents serve, if nothing else, to instil in those who follow the trails to the high peaks an appreciation not only of their beauty but of their power.

Mt. Lefroy and the Mitre – far left

Reflections

As I pieced together the details of this tragic accident, I couldn't help but put myself in the boots of the participants. What were the thoughts of the guide, Eduardo San Vincente, as he started out for the climb after talking to Ernest Feuz? As they negotiated their way up Abbot Pass did he have any misgivings, as he mentally assessed the strengths and the weaknesses of each member of the climbing party? They were one of the first parties up the pass that season. Eduardo must have felt elated when the group arrived at the summit of the South Peak of Mt. Victoria. He took a picture of the jubilant young women holding up their flags of Mexico and their mountaineering clubs. It was their first climb in the Rockies.

What possessed Eduardo to permit a descent down the dangerously, steep face of South Peak, when Ernest Feuz had specifically advised them not to do so? Did he not sense the danger, as the snow softened and began to ball-up in the teeth of his crampons? What were his thoughts when Ma Louisa Fabila lost her footing and knocked the feet out from under Beatriz Diaz Silva and Lucia Oscaranza – the two women ahead of her? Could he see the disaster unfolding, as if in slow motion, as he dug in his ice axe and tried to hold the weight of the three women as they gathered momentum?

When the full weight of the three women hit the end of the rope, it bent the pick of Eduardo's ice axe to about forty-five degrees, rendering it useless. What were his thoughts as he was jerked from his feet and fought to find a foot or handhold to stop their deadly slide toward the two thousand foot precipice? What panic filled his heart as he fought vainly to regain his footing and somehow arrest their accelerating fall?

Can't hold on...Axe useless in soft snow...Can't get my feet to hold...Snow balled-up in my crampons...Can't hold them!... Gaining speed...Cliffs approaching....Getting tangled in the rope...Rocks coming fast...Can't hold on now...Tangled in rope...Hitting and bouncing off rocks...Cries of the women...Cliff coming now...Falling!...Women screaming!...Darkness...Sudden excruciating pain...DARKNESS...

What were the thoughts of Ofelia Fernandez and Maria Garcia, and Carmen Rubio, as they watched their comrades slip, yell out an alarm, and then pull each other down the steep, unforgiving slope of snow and ice? What did they think as they helplessly watched their colleagues clawing, grasping, and contorting themselves – trying desperately to hang on to anything that would stop their accelerating slide to death?

What were their thoughts as they watched their friends tangle in the rope and crash headlong into the rock bands at the edge of the precipice and then disappear over the edge – a limp and battered tangle of humanity – not to be heard from, or seen alive again?

The silence must have been deafening as the survivors clung in terror to their ice axes and listened for some sound from their comrades. How their hearts must have been racing as they frantically tried to kick the packed snow from the teeth of their crampons so they could get a firm footing on that wickedly exposed slope of ice and snow. What were their thoughts as they realized that their comrades were surely dead and they were now stranded on the face of South Peak? One false step could mean death for all of them as well. They were undoubtedly petrified with fear and grief over the loss of their friends. It would take superhuman willpower to suppress the horror of the past few seconds, if they were to save themselves. Miraculously they stayed where they were and were seen by those who could rescue them.

What were the thoughts of the rescue party – Chuck Roland, Ray Wehner, Frank Campbell, Harry Green and Ernest Feuz as they rushed from Lake Louise to the Plain of Six Glaciers and then up Abbot Pass to the tangled and broken bodies of the four Mexican climbers near the bergschrund? It was the first time that most of them had encountered a dead and mangled human and now they were looking at four tangled and distorted bodies that hours earlier had been strong, confident, and vital.

What were their thoughts as they pressed on in a desperate attempt to save Ofelia Fernandez, Maria Garcia, and Carmen Rubio who were stranded on steep face of Mt. Victoria? They could see the women holding on about two hundred feet below the summit of South Peak. They yelled loudly in an attempt to instruct the women to stay where they were, and to let them know that help was coming.

What was going through the minds of Ernest Feuz and Chuck Roland as they gulped down some fruit juice and raced up to South Peak to rescue the three stranded women? And what were Chuck Roland's thoughts as Ernest belayed him down the deadly, steep slopes of Mt. Victoria as he kicked and cut deep footholds into the snow and ice on his decent to the three stranded women? How would he get the cold, frightened, and exhausted women back up to the ridge and then to safety?

Could Ernest hold them if one or more of them should slip? Would the women be too cold and traumatized to move safely?

What were the thoughts of Chuck Roland and Frank Campbell the next morning when they went back to untangle the bodies, take pictures for the coroner, and then bind the corpses into canvas sacks? It was a lot to ask of two young university lads in their early twenties—even if they were aspiring medical students. It doubtlessly shaped their conscious and unconscious thoughts for many years.

Finally, what were the thoughts of Ofelia Fernandez, Maria Garcia, and Carmen Rubio as they watched from the cabin windows of the Mexican DC-3 aircraft (carrying the bodies of their comrades) as it flew westward toward Banff, and the Bow River Valley, and then over Chateau Lake Louise, Abbot Pass, and Mt. Victoria? Whatever became of the survivors on their return to Mexico? Did they ever climb again? Did they ever return to Lake Louise? Did they ever seek to avenge the deaths of their comrades by another attempt to climb the mountain that doesn't forgive even the simplest mistake or miscalculation?

Chuck Roland, Ray Wehner and Frank Campbell all went on to become medical doctors practicing in Ontario, Manitoba, and British Columbia respectively. From time to time they return to Lake Louise for reunions and occasionally they hike the old trails again. They don't scale the high, snow-clad peaks anymore, but whenever they look up at those magnificent peaks at the end of Lake Louise, their thoughts surely go back to that tragic day at the end of July, many decades ago, when they rescued three Mexican climbers.

The Rescuers. Ray Whener, Harry Green, Chuck Roland, Frank Campbell, and Ernest Feuz a few days after the rescue.

Tragedy on Mt. Temple: The worst climbing accident ever recorded in the Rockies

Just nineteen days short of the first anniversary of the tragedy on Mt. Victoria, there was an even worse accident on Mount Temple. On Monday, July 11th, 1955 seven young boys from the Wilderness Club of Philadelphia met with death on this the highest mountain in Banff National Park. The group of eleven poorly-prepared, poorly-dressed, poorly-equipped, and poorly-led boys—all from twelve to sixteen years of age—were caught in an avalanche at the nine thousand five hundred foot level of rugged Mt. Temple. When the day was over seven boys were dead from exposure and hypothermia, two were badly injured, and two had miraculously survived and walked down the mountain to get help. It was a day of infamy in the Canadian Rockies that seems to have been all but forgotten, except of course, by the families of the victims.

The tragedy started early in the summer of 1955, when twenty-two boys from some of the most prestigious families of Philadelphia, Pennsylvania, signed up for a summer of high adventure in the Canadian wilderness. The group of adventurers was led by twenty-nine-year old **Oliver Donald Dickerson,** a lecturer in insurance at the University of Pennsylvania, and **William Oeser,** a public school teacher in the Philadelphia area.

The enthusiastic group left Philadelphia on June 22nd, planning to spend some time at Glacier National Park, Banff, Lake Louise, and Jasper. The final adventure was to be a canoe trip in the Fort Francis area of Northern Ontario. They planned to be back home in Philadelphia by August 5th.

The first stop was at Yellowstone National Park, in Wyoming where they limbered up by climbing Swift Current Pass and The Look-Out. Then it was off to Banff, where they planned to do some serious hiking and climbing. The two leaders had never been in the Rockies before, but their experience in the outdoors seemed to be extensive—Dickerson boasted that he had climbed every peak of significance in the eastern United States, and even a peak or two in Colorado. Their leadership skills proved to be sadly wanting however, especially their ability to take charge in an emergency.

The group hiked several trails in the Banff area and stopped by the Warden's office to inquire about the best routes to use when climbing Mt. Rundle and Mt. Temple. Their experience scrambling up Mt. Rundle on July 9th is unrecorded, but on Sunday, July 10th, the boys and their stalwart leaders made camp at a wilderness campground near Moraine Lake.

The next morning dawned clear and bright and after a hearty breakfast, assistant leader Bill Oeser, together with eighteen of the boys, headed up the trail for Larch Valley and the base of Mt. Temple. It was a hot day and the boys enjoyed lunch in the shade of some mountain larch trees that grow beside the little stream that meanders through the pristine, alpine meadows of that high, hanging valley.

After a pleasant afternoon scampering through the meadows and up some of the minor rock buttresses, it was time to return to camp. Eleven of the boys wished to go higher however, and they requested permission to climb part way up Mt. Temple. Their leader, William Oeser, agreed but only on the condition that they would be careful and take their time. Oeser sent the rest of the boys down the trail to Moraine Lake, while he remained in the meadows to take some pictures. It was then approximately two o'clock.

The eleven boys that climbed higher on Mt. Temple were: **Miles Marble**, twelve, twin brothers **Richard** and **James Baylis**, **Luther Seddon**, **Fredrick Ballard**, and **Peter Smith**, aged thirteen, **Jerry Clattenburg**, fourteen, **William Wise** and **Donald Chapman** fifteen; and **William Watts** and **Tony Woodfield**, sixteen.

Tony Woodfield had climbed one or two mountains in the Alps, and so he led the group as they ascended the snow slopes and cliff bands on their way to the distant summit. They were neither dressed nor equipped for such a venture. Some of the boys were wearing only T-shirts, shorts and running shoes. One boy had on a pair of baseball spikes. They carried two thin ropes: one was little more than a clothesline, one-quarter-inch in diameter. The other was not much better – just three-eighths inches in diameter. The combined length of the two ropes was roughly one hundred and fifty feet. Woodfield carried the only ice axe.

When they reached the ten thousand foot level it was approaching four o'clock, and they could hear snow slides and small avalanches around them. Some of the boys kicked rocks down into the snow and started small slides. Woodfield realized that it was too dangerous to continue the ascent, so he called a halt to the climb and instructed the boys to tie on to the rope. The two "end" lads tied on with bowline knots while the others used simple slipknots.

The boys descended slowly, with Tony Woodfield at the end of the rope to serve as the anchorman. They started down amid small snow slides, and then at about the nine thousand five hundred foot level, a larger avalanche hit them.

Woodfield later said that he heard the avalanche coming and yelled to the others to take cover. He dug his ice axe into the slope and hung on. The connecting rope snapped just below him and the other boys were swept down the steep slopes with tons of snow and rock. Unencumbered by the rope, Woodfield managed to fight his way to the top of the sliding snow. Young **Peter Smith**, the second from the front, tried to hang on the rocks with his fingers, but he too was swept down the slope with the others in the full course of the avalanche. At one point, Smith felt the rope tighten around his neck. Miraculously he managed to pull it free and fight his way to the top of the tumbling snow and rock and out of danger.

The boys tumbled about three thousand feet in the avalanche. One of the boys screamed for help and Smith attempted to drag him from the snow, but couldn't. He continued down the mountain as fast as he could to get help. He eventually found Oeser, who was taking pictures of the wild flowers, happily oblivious to the tragedy unfolding above him.

Several accounts tell of what happened next. One version related that rather than attempting to help the boys trapped in the avalanche, Oeser retreated down the trail to Moraine Lake for help. Arriving at Moraine Lake Lodge at about six thirty, he sounded the alarm. Radio phone calls were made to the Warden in the village of Lake Louise and to the Chateau where **Walter Perren** was alerted.

Perrin then contacted **"Beef" Woodworth**, the district warden, stationed at Lake Louise, and then he and **Dr. Sutton**, (the doctor at the Chateau) headed for Moraine Lake at top speed. They arrived at the lodge at about seven fifteen and were joined by Woodworth, and Assistant Warden **Bert Pettiway**. Chief Warden **Herb Ashley** arrived a little later with three or four men from the village. Soon they too were racing up the trail to the avalanche site where the boys lay dead and dying.

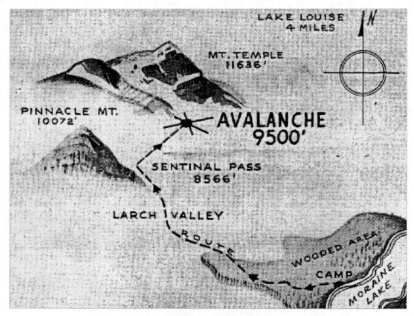

The location of the tragedy on Mount Temple

The site of the avalanche (Photos from Calgary Herald)

Thirteen of the Surviving Boys
Two were in the Banff Hospital at the time. Back Row: L to R) Ted Harris, B. Lambert, Lee Rodgers, C.Vearson, Tony Woodfield, Bert Morton. Middle Row: Oliver Dickerson, Camp counsellor and leader, John Black. Front Row: Perry Anderson, Blair Meglathery, Andy Walsh, Tom Jones, Peter Smith.

Tony Woodfield and Peter Smith (seated in centre). Two of the heroes of the tragedy, tell their friends of the happenings on Mt. Temple. (Photos Calgary Herald)

Chuck Roland and **Ray Wehner**, who had been instrumental in rescuing the Mexican climbing team from Mt. Victoria the previous summer, asked manager **Pat Fitt**, if they could get off work early to assist with the rescue. For some unexplained reason, Fitt refused to let them go. To this day Roland feels that lives could have been saved if they had been allowed to immediately help with the rescue. As it was, they had to wait until their shift was over at eleven o'clock and by then it was too dark and too late. Roland, Wehner, and four other bellboys left for Moraine Lake where they helped carry down the dead and injured boys.

While the rescue efforts were taking shape at Moraine Lake, Tony Woodfield remained on the scene and tried to dig out his friends as best he could. He gave most of his clothes to two of the injured boys to protect them from the near-freezing temperatures. Later, he raced down to Moraine Lake and together with Peter Smith, ordered Oeser back up to the disaster site. The three of them then raced back up the trail to the accident scene to help with the rescue.

One of the boys, **Fred Ballard,** had a six-inch gash in his head. He grew tired of waiting for help to arrive and managed to free himself from the cement-like grip of the avalanche. Alone, he managed to stagger down the mountain, past the Larch Valley meadows and two-and-a-half miles down the trail, where the rescue party met him. He continued on to Moraine Lake Lodge, where he collapsed. The other dead and dying boys were left alone on the mountain until the rescue party arrived on the scene.

It was nine-thirty and almost dark when the first members of the rescue party arrived at the accident scene In all, seven of the boys perished from multiple injuries and exposure—only one of them appeared to have been killed instantly. The rest died from exposure and the trauma of their injuries.

Among the first to arrive on the scene were acting wardens **Jack Schuarte** and **Wes Gilstorf** of the Lake Louise district. Digging as quickly as possible, they managed to free and untangle the dead lads from the grip of the avalanche and the rope that bound them together. Some of the boys lived for some time following the accident, and one died shortly after the rescue party arrived. Doctor Sutton and the Park Wardens who took part in the rescue were convinced that many of the boys were not killed instantly, but died of exposure owing to the light clothing they wore.

Bert Pettiway related that they got one of the boys on a stretcher and while Dr. Sutton went to administer first aid to another boy, the first lad died. He said that the avalanche snow broke off on a steep, open snow-covered slope, which gradually funnelled into a narrow crack leading down hundreds of feet to another open slope. The falling mass of snow stopped just short of the top of the crack. He said that there was water flowing under the snow and that several of the bodies were found in this creek. One of the boys was partially buried by the snow but he had sustained no apparent injuries. Another boy was found, tied by the rope, to two of his companions, buried deeper in the snow. Bert later said that: *"If someone had cut the rope or dug him out, he might have been saved. There didn't appear to be anything wrong with him."* Pettiway also told of finding a small dead figure huddled in the snow, apparently trying to find shelter from the cold wind that swept the ramparts of the mountain. If someone had gone up to help the boys when young Peter Smith told of the accident, perhaps this boy would have been saved.

The rescuers main plan of action was to take care of the injured boys first and do everything possible to get them to safety before moving those who were already dead. Throughout the night they frantically searched with failing flashlights and in the early hours of the morning, the light from the half moon helped illuminate their grizzly task. At six o'clock the next morning, the first group of rescuers came down to Moraine Lake Lodge with the injured boys and five bodies that they had retrieved. Walter Perrin and some other recruits continued to search for the remaining two lads. They were found tied together—buried beneath the spot where another of the dead boys was found. The two remaining bodies were packed out on horses the next morning.

The RCMP in Banff issued a statement.

> Eighteen boys went up the slope Monday morning and got up to the 9,000-foot level. Eleven went up to the 10,000 foot-level and the rest turned back. The going got rough and the boys had seen several small avalanches. They were afraid of further danger, and roped themselves together and started down. They got into a funnel, and were placed diagonally across it when an avalanche started 500 feet above them. It caught 10. The lead man held on with an ice axe and the rope broke. The others were carried 1,800 to 1,900 feet down. One other boy got clear of the rope and rode the crest down. Five were killed and two were found dead later, and two were injured."

The Aftermath

The next day the accusations and counter-accusations flew thick and fast. The party's leader **Oliver Dickerson,** attempted to blame the Park Service—which he said didn't provide him with the information he required before making the excursion. Dickerson had not accompanied the boys on their Mt. Temple adventure, as he had driven down to Lake Louise to buy groceries. Despite claiming to be an experienced outdoorsman, he seemed to have no idea that Mt. Temple was a dangerous environment.

Dickerson claimed that he was not a professional but on the other hand, he was not an amateur. He said that the group had followed a route suggested in the Alpine Club guidebook and that he had consulted maps of the area. He also emphatically asserted that he had left word at the Park Warden's Office in Banff that he and the group intended to climb Mt. Rundle and Mt. Temple. He contended that:

> There were a couple of girls there. They told us a little about Rundle and didn't tell us anything about Mt. Temple. We did climb Rundle, and when we set out later for Moraine Lake, we didn't

bother going back to ask them again about Temple, because they had been so little help the first time. They couldn't even tell us much about Mt. Rundle, right outside their own office.

Dickerson stated that he had returned to Moraine Lake from his shopping excursion, just after one of the injured boys arrived at the camp to tell of the disaster. Once the rangers were summoned, they came quickly. Later, he went up toward Larch Valley. On the way up he met Wes Gistorf, who was carrying one of the injured boys, probably Ricky Ballard. Shortly after this, he met the main search party on its way up to the accident site.

The question that many asked was: What were Dickerson and Oeser doing from four forty-five until about eight forty-five when the boys were dying in the snow from their injuries and hypothermia? Some people felt that if Dickerson and Oeser, together with some of the stronger lads, who were at the Moraine Lake campsite, had rushed up to the accident scene with warm blankets, warm clothing, and hot drinks as soon as Peter Smith had arrived with news of the disaster, they might have saved most of the boys who eventually died from exposure. If they had accompanied Jack Schuarte, Dr. Sutton and Wes Gilstorf when they left for the scene at approximately six thirty, they might have made a difference. As it was, Dickerson did not leave for the accident scene until about eight forty-five. Why did it take these leaders so long to respond to this emergency that threatened the lives of many of their charges?

The morning following the tragedy, the surviving boys were taken to Banff and cared for by Red Cross volunteers in a local church until their parents made arrangements to fly them home. The leaders, Dickerson and Oeser, were both admitted to the Banff hospital – apparently suffering from stress and shock.

On Wednesday, July 13th the Calgary Herald ran a number of stories about the tragedy. It reported:

The one man who could shed some light on the accident refused to talk. He was William H. "Bill" Oeser of Baltimore, a camp counsellor who made the ascent with the boys. Oeser, who was under sedation for most of the day, curtly declined to speak to newspapermen on the subject when he awoke. "When I get married, I'll have my picture in the paper," he said. "But not on a thing like this. And I have nothing to say."

Many people, including **Bruno Engler** offered observations and analysis about the tragedy. Engler offered some sage advice, and remarked that the south face where the slide occurred, is a long shale slope with a drop of about one thousand feet near the bottom. He also noted that the snow conditions on Mt. Temple, and other spots in the Rockies had been exceptionally dangerous that season due to the late spring snowfall. "The snow has been very loose and will slide at the slightest touch." He also observed that it was strange that the party would attempt to climb under such dangerous conditions without first being advised by experts. A veteran guide would certainly have advised against such a trip.

On July 12th **Slocom Chapin,** the vice-president of the American Broadcasting Company (ABC), arrived in Banff to claim the body of his fifteen-year-old son

David. He said he didn't want to see either Oliver Dickerson or William Oeser. The next day the Calgary Herald gave full coverage to the tragedy quoting Dickerson as saying that they had "adequate equipment and that he had instructed the boys in the technique of mountaineering".

In analysing the tragedy *The Herald* commented

> *What is adequate equipment? What are the accepted techniques for a climb of this kind? Veteran mountaineers carry and wear special boots shod with climbing nails, at least 100 feet of nylon or hemp rope specially made for alpine use, for a maximum of four people. They carry crampons (spikes which can be attached to boots for travel on ice) and pitons (spikes to drive into ice to which a rope may be attached).*

> *The experienced mountaineer mostly permits three persons on a rope and never more than four. In addition, he will wear clothes to protect him against exposure should he be stranded on a mountainside. Each climber would have an ice axe.*

> *Here is what the boys had for equipment. Some wore smooth soled scampers on their feet, one had baseball shoes with cleats on them, and others had track shoes with only small spikes on the insole. All had light clothing; only one boy had an ice axe, only one had any pitons, none had any crampons. Moreover, the eleven boys were all attached to the one rope at five-foot intervals. Experienced climbers are roped 30 feet apart. Slipknots on the rope held them together, and when the fall started, the rope tightened about each so that none could escape. Normal practice is to use a bowline, which will not tighten on a person's midriff.*

> *One of the rescue group (Park Warden Bert Pettiway) described the ¼ inch thick manila rope as "unethical as far as mountaineering was concerned." Another mountaineer pointed out that the party would have been better advised to unrope while crossing the snow slope which at this time of year, and at that time of day, might be expected to avalanche.*

Mount Temple and the path of the avalanche that caught up the boys from Philadelphia on July 11, 1955.

Mount Temple and the path of the avalanche that caught up the boys from Philadelphia on July 11, 1955. The black dots indicate where the bodies ended up.

The Inquest

An inquest into the deaths of the seven lads was held in the basement of the Masonic Hall in Banff on July 15th. The first witness was thirteen-year-old **Fred "Ricky" Ballard,** who had just been released from the hospital. He said that before the boys left for their climb about nine o'clock they had had a discussion as to how to use their equipment – led by Mr. Dickerson. Young Ballard reported that seventeen of the boys and Mr. Oeser started out for Larch Valley at the base of Mt. Temple. At one point in the hike, Mr. Oeser stopped to take pictures and some of the boys continued on. William Watts was in charge of the eleven boys who continued climbing up the mountain. As they did so, they could hear avalanches all around them. Eventually, they became concerned about the condition of the snow slope, and so they started down.

The boys decided to rope together as they descended. Tony Woodfield was in front and Watts was behind. Ballard reported that he saw an avalanche on Pinnacle Mountain, and that was the last thing he remembered, before an avalanche struck them. When Ballard regained consciouness he said he was talking to Willy Wise. He couldn't move Wise because as he said: "My legs wouldn't quite work right." He then got cold and walked down the mountain.

Before leaving the stranded boys, Ballard told one of those injured that he was walking down for help – "in case he was still awake." Ballard said that a man [Wes Gilstorf] carried him part way down the mountain. He also told the inquiry that when people at Moraine Lake Lodge were told of their impending climb, they told the boys that they were the first group to attempt to climb Mt. Temple that season.

The second witness was **Peter Smith**. He was second in line, after Billy Watts, as the boys descended. Smith said that he saw the avalanche about thirty feet above him. He held on for a few seconds but then the avalanche took him down with the rest. When the avalanche stopped, he said that he got up but was knocked down again by additional snow. The rope came up around his neck and he slipped it off while falling and crawling over the snow and the rocks. He stated that he heard Willie Wise yelling for help from near a boulder on the avalanche trail. He tried to move him, but found that Willie had a broken hip and a wrist. Ballard said that he put Willie in a comfortable position and told him that he was going for help. He said that he also saw Luther Seden, with a badly broken leg, and one of the Baylis twins. He then ran down the mountain for help. At the lodge, he located the spot of the accident on a map for the rescuers, and then he went back up the mountain with one of the rescue parties.

Smith also reported that each of the bodies had part of the rope around them excepting for himself, as he had managed to get free of it. He said that the boys were roped "for moral support."

Tony Woodfield was the third witness. He told the inquest that he and William Watts had been appointed leaders of the boys that continued to climb further up the mountain. At about ten thousand feet, the highest point climbed, the snow was becoming wet. The boys then held a conference and decided to get off the mountain as quickly and as safely as possible. They roped up and attempted to belay each other down the slope. Except for the two boys at either end of the rope, they used slipknots to attach themselves together.

Woodfield was at the rear of the group with an ice axe when the avalanche struck them. He said that he saw the avalanche and yelled "Avalanche! Head for cover!" He then tried to run to the side and dig in his ice axe. "I held on for a while and then the rope broke. Then I stood up and saw the avalanche stop about fifteen hundred feet below," he said. Later he saw Ricky Ballard, sitting on a rock. Woodfield stated:

> *Ricky Ballard looked all right, but he was apparently in shock. I asked him if he had anything broken and he said no. I gave him my shirt. Then I went down to Willy Wise and he said that he had a broken hip. I took a shirt out of my rucksack and gave it to him.*

He then heard muffled shouts from under the snow above him. He found Watts buried about a foot under the snow and spent almost an hour and a half trying to dig him out with shoes, rocks, and his bare hands. Then some help arrived. At this point he became hysterical and was told to go down to the lodge and get a helicopter and some first aid.

William Oeser, one of the two leaders of the group, told the inquest that he was "not a professional mountaineer and did not like high altitudes." He had gone up to about eight thousand five hundred feet with the boys and, not seeing anything he considered dangerous, allowed them to continue on without him. "I told them that at the first sign of any danger, they were to come down quickly and safely. I told William Watts he would be the leader." Sixteen boys started out on the climb. Five dropped out along the route and rejoined Oeser in Larch Valley where they had left their lunches. Oeser stated:

> *After sitting and talking for a while, I noticed the party was starting down. They were a long way off—just a vertical line in the snow. I saw them come together and stop on a rock, then I noticed them start down again and I noticed something peculiar—something sort of rolling. I thought they were fooling around and when the rolling stopped, I saw people walking around and I wasn't particularly alarmed."*

Oeser related that a few moments after this he thought he heard someone calling for help. He started up the slope towards the spot where he had last seen the boys—still not sure anything was wrong. He then ran into Peter Smith, who had survived the fifteen hundred foot plunge down the avalanche slope, and was coming down to get help. Oeser reported that he and Tommy Jones proceeded as quickly as they could to the foot of the avalanche, where the full magnitude of the disaster struck him. He testified:

I saw four bodies in the snow. Luther Sedon was lying about four feet from the edge of the snow. He had apparently suffered a broken leg and was calling for help. Terry Clattenberg [who was in the hospital during the inquest] was about six feet further on in the snow, in a sitting position. Eight feet further was Richard Baylis. He was unconscious and several feet above and to the left. Townsend Baylis was evidently dead by the colour of his skin and the position of his body."

Oeser testified that he moved Seddon and Richard Baylis to the rocky slope nearby, where they would be in less danger, in case another slide occurred. He then went up the slope to where Tony Woodfield was trying to dig out young Watts, who was buried to his waist. It was bitterly cold by then, and hail and rain began to fall. He felt that it was imperative that he get help, as he could not pull Watts free. Fred Ballard was nearby, bleeding from a gash on his head, but otherwise uninjured. Willy Wise was lying near Ballard with a broken hip. There was no sign of David Chapin and Miles Marble. Woodfield gave most of his own clothing to the injured boys, and then Oeser sent him down with Jones to Moraine Lake Lodge for help. After two hours, when no help arrived, Oeser went down to the lodge, fearing for the injured, who were exposed to the cold rain and sleet. He met the rescue party on its way up, but he was in a state of shock, and was not allowed to go back up to the scene again, although he said he wanted to.

Doctor Pat Costigan, Medical Health Officer for Banff, Yoho, and Glacier Parks, gave his opinion of the tragedy and he didn't mince words in expressing his thoughts on the matter. He was highly critical of the leadership which allowed a large party of pitifully-equipped, inexperienced young boys to roam almost at will in the dangerous high country. "The little T-shirts and socks they were wearing would not even provide sufficient warmth for a short hike across one of the mountain valleys, let alone an attack on Mt. Temple, one of the most formidable mountains in the area. The statement made that the equipment was adequate is absolutely ridiculous. The clothing they were wearing would be more suited for a romp on the beach."

On July 29th, the Crag and Canyon printed the following announcement:

Mt. Temple Becomes Monument to Dead Boy: *The cremated remains of David Chapin, 15 year old Philadelphia Pa. youth, who met his death when caught in an avalanche on Mt. Temple July 11, when climbing with a group of ten other youngsters, were scattered from an airplane over the spot where the tragic incident occurred.*

Thus ended the saga of one of the worst climbing accidents ever to take place in the Rockies

The author on the summit ridge of Mt.Temple

The Elizabeth Parker Hut with Mt. Hungabee on the left and Mt. Biddle on the Left.

Chapter 9

Final Thoughts, Reflections, and Concerns

I've treasured my times in the Rockies – roaming the meadows, sleeping under the stars in the high country, scaling the glacier-hung peaks, fishing the lakes and streams, hiking the trails, and skiing the slopes. I still enjoy hiking and visiting the alpine meadows. Occasionally I tease feisty trout with well-presented dry flies and sleep under the eternal stars – away from the crowded, "designated areas" – with just a sleeping bag and a light tarp or a mountain tent, and listen to the night sounds. But over the past five to ten years, I've become increasingly concerned with subtle, and sometimes not-so-subtle, attempts by Parks Canada to manage, contain, and control tourists, hikers, and climbers who wish to access the backcountry of the national mountain parks.

Aided and abetted by environmental groups, such as the Eastern Slopes Grizzly Bear Project (ESGBP), the Alberta Wilderness Association (AWA), and the Canadian Parks and Wilderness Society (CPWS), Parks Canada has increasingly closed off some of Banff National Park's best and most accessible backcountry in the vicinity of Banff and Lake Louise. Areas such as Larch Valley, Paradise Valley, parts of the Odaray Plateau in O'Hara, the Pipestone Valley, the Boulder Pass/Deception Pass area, and parts of Skoki are routinely closed to hikers. For more details, I suggest reading two recent studies by Dr. Barry Cooper and Sylvia LeRoy, both respected researchers from of the Fraser Institute of Canada. *Off Limits: How Radical Environmentalists are Shutting Down Canada's National Parks* (2000), is available online at: http://oldfraser.lexi.net/publications/pps/45/index.html. and *Science Fact or Science Fiction? The Grizzly Bear Biology behind Parks Canada Management Models* (December 2002) is available at http://fraserinstitute.ca/shared/readmore.asp?sNav=pb&id=457 The Fraser Institute's website is www.fraserinstitute.ca

Science Fact or Science Fiction? released on December 19th, 2002, suggests that the environmentalists that hang about Banff and the biologists within Parks Canada, have a heavily-biased agenda intent on managing, containing, and controlling park visitors and restricting the use of normally accessible backcountry areas that have been enjoyed by hikers, climbers, and adventurers since before Banff National Park was created. This should be a matter of great concern to all who love the mountain trails and the high backcountry meadows – especially for those who are frustrated with ever-increasing bureaucratic rules, regulations, and restrictions designed to contain and control the citizenry. Many in the environmental lobby garner hefty salaries, professorships, and grants at the public's expense and their aim is to close off large sections of the national mountain parks for their own rhetoric filled ambitions. According to Cooper and LeRoy they also have a secondary agenda that involves "rewilding" vast areas of North America. In the language of the conservation biologists the intent is: "to restore diversity, and help wounded lands become self-willed again." Cooper and LeRoy explain:

> *"Rewilding" is to be practically achieved by creating a vast network of "core" wilderness areas, surrounded by wildlife "corridors" stretching across the continent. Proponents of these projects consider them to be the means to implement a "new paradigm" in protected areas of management". A significant implication of the new paradigm is that, where existing property rights, traditional multiple use, and human enjoyment conflict with this aim, they will be subordinated to the overriding ecological purpose of allowing a wounded land to reassert its will."*

The environmentalist's agenda also fosters "mission-focused" research that is spiced with fear-mongering and exaggerated threats of species extinction. It also tends to invent environmental crises that are pure romantic fantasy, and trite terms such as the "Kermode Spirit Bear," the "Great Bear Rainforest," the "Year of the Great Bear," and "Islands of Extinction" that tug at the reader's heartstrings. This hype is enthusiastically embraced by the gullible media who are always eager for a heart-rending story and by Parks Canada bureaucrats, who funnel thousands of dollars into questionable projects and mislead their political bosses into believing that the bear population in Canada is in imminent danger of extinction. Cooper and LeRoy expose this agenda and point out that most provincial counts of the bear population confirm that the opposite is true.

A recent example of how the environmentalist fraternity is never satisfied with the available space for the growing grizzly bear population in Canada was reported in the National Post on March 29th, 2004. It seems that the "principal scientist" studying the grizzly bear population in Nahanni National Park was bemoaning the fact that the 4,765-acre park was not big enough to satisfy the roaming instincts of the many grizzlies residing in the area. The busy researcher, who had occupied himself collecting some 620 different bear hair samples, suggested that these roaming brutes need between 66 and 1380 square miles of home range. To put this into perspective, the maximum area desired would be equivalent to the distance from Toronto to Thunder Bay squared, or from Vancouver to Swift Current squared. The "mad" scientist then ventured the opinion that since some of the bears he'd identified had travelled as far as fifty kilometres outside the park boundary *it was important for the government to expand the park boundary*. He was distressed in the extreme that there were plans to build a road and silver mine near the parks perimeter.

For some time agenda-driven senior bureaucrats in Parks Canada, have attempted to change the purpose and the intent of the *National Parks Act*. They have sought to put a major emphasis on the protection of wildlife in areas where they deem there to be a real or imagined threat to selected species. Relying on the recently proclaimed (June 11th, 2002) *Species at Risk Act* (SARA) – also known as Bill C-5, *"An Act Respecting the Protection of Wildlife Species in Canada* – environmental groups and Parks Canada officials have manufactured the myth that the grizzly bear population in Canada, particularly the cohort in Banff, Yoho, and Kootenay national parks, is either "at risk," "threatened," or "of special concern," or all three. This myth has now become part of the prevailing folk wisdom and provides the rationale for closing off large areas of the national parks and the surrounding lands from what they refer to as "human contamination." Couple this with Parks Canada's lavish funding of mission-focused research projects that have employed questionable computer-modelling techniques to perpetrate the myth that the grizzly bear population is in extreme danger, and the future use and enjoyment of the backcountry in the national mountain parks is in serious jeopardy. This is an issue that should be of considerable concern to all legitimate conservation, outdoors, climbing, and hiking groups across North America.

The National Parks of Canada have been maintained and managed as recreation and tourist destinations for Canadians for almost one hundred and twenty years. The National Parks Act clearly statest: *"national parks of Canada are hereby dedicated to the people of Canada for their benefit, education, and enjoyment."* Cooper and LeRoy suggest that this constitutes a legal invitation for citizens to visit and take their recreation in the national parks, but Parks Canada documents now proclaim that the parks are places for both nature AND people. Cooper warns that this "dual use" policy is now in serious danger of being replaced by a "single use" policy that doesn't include the people.

So long as Canada's national parks are defined as de facto grizzly habitat, and human use is automatically considered to be a disturbance of it, the push to limit human enjoyment of natural areas is bound to increase. "Eventually Canadians will be able to enjoy their wilderness parks, and recreation areas only in some ethereal sense of deriving remote and virtual comfort from the knowledge that they exist. (Cooper and LeRoy)

Fear of lawsuits, real or imagined, as well as a strong environmental lobby, has resulted in a "we know what's best for you" mentality in the management of the national parks. Rather than advising hikers and climbers that a bear, or bears, have been seen in an area and to proceed at one's own risk, the strategy of choice is to close the area completely and invent some tall tale about the area being "traditional bear habitat." From then on, the area is frequently "CLOSED TO THE PUBLIC" and reserved for the bruins – and the environmentalists.

For the past four to five years, Parks Canada officials in Banff and Yoho parks have developed a psychotic paranoia that humans will upset the cohort of grizzly bears they have been encouraging to take up residence in high-use, high-tourist areas of Banff and Yoho Park. As a result, the trails and valleys around Lake Louise, Skoki, Moraine Lake, Larch Valley, and Paradise Valley are regularly closed and intimidating signs, warning of bears in the vicinity, are posted when none have actually been seen for weeks.

My own experience suggests that Parks Canada officials are attempting to establish a grizzly bear population in the Lake Louise area and in doing so they have invented the myth that this area was once traditional grizzly bear habitat. Imposing signs are posted suggesting that the area is alive with ferocious bears ready to leap from behind the nearest tree to maul unsuspecting tourists if they venture too far from the parking lots of the commercial establishments. This scares the wits out of most casual urban visitors, but most locals who know better agree that the campaign is gross over-kill with little to substantiate it.

During the summers of 2003 and 2004, I had to laugh at some intimidating signs posted almost on the front lawn of the Chateau at Lake Louise and at the junction of the trail to Lake Agnes. The signs warned that a GRIZZLY BEAR was in the vicinity – this, in the beginning of August, when these trails were at their peak use and the tourists were so numerous that no self-respecting bear would venture anywhere near the area. In more than forty years of hiking this particular trail as well as others in the area, I have never encountered a grizzly bear. The odd black bear in the early season, yes; but never a grizzly. I've run into the odd grizzly in the backcountry near McArthur Pass, in the Ottertail Valley on the way to the Goodsirs, and near the head of the Yoho Valley past Twin Falls, but never on the trail to the Plain of Six Glaciers or on the way to Lake Agnes in mid summer.

Hiking past the signs and up to Lake Agnes, I continued over The Beehive and then on to the Plain of Six Glaciers. On the way, there was not one sign of a bear of any description – no scent, no scat (droppings) – nothing. The same was true for the return trip via the Plain of Six Glaciers – Lake Louise trail. Despite this, the ominous signs were still in place when I returned. I thought something was fishy and while enjoying a refreshing glass of dark ale in the pub in the lower area of the Chateau, I inquired if anyone had actually seen a bear in recent months. I was told that someone had reported that they had seen a scruffy-looking black bear and her two clubs behind the staff residences in early June, just before the ice had left the lake, but there hadn't been so much as a porcupine seen since then. Someone else reported seeing a marmot on the trail to the Plain of Six Glaciers, just past the end of the lake, but that was all.

The bar-tender suggested that the Parks Canada summer staff loved to strut about, looking officious, and warning people about the dangers of bears, when none had actually been seen in the area for weeks. He then told of a runtish looking grizzly and her cub that had been hanging around the village of Lake Louise and near the campground. Apparently Park officials refused to capture the critters and ship them out of the area. A waiter laughingly reported that Parks Canada was actually trying to encourage grizzly bears, of all animals, to take up residence on the ski slopes of Mt. Whitehorn – not more that a mile from the village. He suggested that the Parks Canada "bear people" were nuts and he resented the fact that several of the trails in the area were being closed for large portions of the summer.

The following morning I planned to hike up above Moraine Lake to Larch Valley. Arriving at about eight o'clock,. we found that the trail near the parking lot was blocked with two crossed poles from which hung a menacing sign saying that the trail was closed because "BEARS" were in the area. I was determined to get up to Larch Valley and asked the boathouse attendant when the last bear had actually been seen. She said she didn't know, but the sign had been up for the past few summers and she thought that one black bear might have been spotted. She also said that it was reported that a grizzly bear was in the upper part of Paradise Valley, but no one she knew had actually seen it. She thought it was probably another of the ones "invented" by Parks Canada staff. She stated that a lot of people were angry that the Paradise Valley trails (to the Giant Steps and to Sentinel Pass) were frequently closed because of a grizzly bear that no one had actually seen. Later on the trail, two young doctors from Calgary, who regularly hike and climb in the area, confirmed this story.

At the beginning of the main trail to Larch Valley was another sign saying something to the effect that bears were in the area and only parties of six or more would be allowed beyond the tree line. Hikers were also warned to stay on the trail and not to doddle. We hiked up the gentle switchbacks of the board trail to the larch meadows and then proceeded to the high meadows on the way to Sentinel Pass. At the crest of the meadows we left the trail and found a pleasant spot to light our small mountain stove, cook some soup, and have an award-winning lunch. Following this, we meandered through the meadows along the stream and eventually back to the main trail. We covered the area pretty well and not once did we see any evidence of bears. Again it appeared that the ominous signs and closures were orchestrated to discourage the use of the area and to contain and intimidate naïve backpackers.

For several years, tenters were banished from the Lake Louise campground because a small sow grizzly and her club were being encouraged to take up residence nearby. Rather than remove the obnoxious and unpredictable critters, as would have been done in the "good old days," they were allowed to rummage and forage about the community and make a nuisance of themselves. When I suggested to a young Parks Canada attendant at the "CLOSED" entrance to the campground, that in the past any bear near the village, particularly a grizzly, would have been rounded up and transported deep into the backcountry for the safety of both the bear and public, she indignantly replied: "This sir is their home and we at Parks Canada are going to keep it that way. The campground is closed to tenters."

It was no use saying anything else. Her superiors had rehearsed her well as to how to handle inquiring campers who might question the closure of the campground they had camped in for many years. I just shook my head and headed for the campground at Protection Mountain. A few days later I got the same response from another Parks Canada attendant at the Information Kiosk in the village. He almost had an apoplectic attack when I told him that I planned to hike into Paradise Valley and sleep under a tarp in the meadows above the Giant Steps. He mumbled something about needing a "back country permit" as I left.

Bears and Humans Don't Mix Well

Sadly for many, the messages emanating from popular TV shows and Disney cartoons are not true. Bears and humans don't mix well—particularly grizzly bears, which are notoriously territorial, unpredictable, aggressive, cunning, dangerously predatory, and downright nasty. This information may come as stunning blow to many of the bear-huggers and environmentalists who hang around Banff, Lake Louise and elsewhere. Thanks to misguided government management practices, most grizzlies and black bears in the area have lost their fear of humans and many have become extremely dangerous and unpredictable. As a consequence the number of predatory attacks by habituated black bears and grizzlies has increased dramatically in recent years. (See *Bear Attacks: The Deadly Truth* and *Bear Attacks II: Myth and Reality* both by *Gary Shelton.*

A tremendous growth industry has developed around "The Kermode Spirit Bear," "The Rainbow Bear," "The Great Spirit Bear," "The Year of the Great Bear," the "Great Rainforest Bear," the "Gummy Bear," and now the "Banff Grizzly Bear." This fact has not gone unnoticed by opportunistic environmentalists and assorted hangers-on in the Banff area and elsewhere. Every time one turns around there's another "Save-the-Bear" group coining trite phases, raising funds, selling buttons, and pontificating about the need for more and more bear habitat. They seem to spring up like mushrooms on a steamy summer night. Sadly, such groups raise thousands of dollars each year and garner significant federal grants and public donations, based on emotional presentations, manufactured myths, and mission-focused research. These groups show little concern for the fact that they frequently distort, or create, data in order to aid their questionable causes.

Parks Canada, always gullible, and ever ready to take on some dim-witted scheme hatched by the environmental lobby, usually takes the bait This was demonstrated in a series of rather hilarious incidents that took place early in the fall of 1999. Cathy Ellis, cub reporter (no pun intended) for the venerable Banff Crag and Canyon newspaper, carefully reported the incredible saga. I have changed a few of the names to protect the innocent – particularly the bears.

Ellis's account provided the heart-wrenching details of how a wiry, middle-aged, female, "bear specialist" from Montana, an equally wiry female researcher from Scandinavia, and assorted "groupies" from Parks Canada, gave chase to a rogue black bear near the village of Lake Louise. Led by a fearless "Wildlife-Human Conflict Specialist" from Parks Canada, the intrepid "B" Team ("B" for bear) and a pack of scruffy, yapping, dogs attempted to roundup the large beast and give him a "scare to remember."

The big bruin had been making a nuisance of itself around the Lake Louise campground and in the village. Fearless Wildlife-Human Conflict Specialist, Cal Modern (not his real name), was quoted as saying that the critter had developed a taste for human food when it found a yummy jar of peanut butter in an "illegal campsite" nearby. After much chasing and hazing, the bear was eventually lured into a mobile barrel trap. The successful team was really pumped at having captured the belligerent brute, and they were determined to give him a scare that his tiny mind would remember for a long, long time. Quickly they hooked the mobile bear-trap to the back of their muscle-bound pickup truck and drove at break-neck speed to the crowded parking lot of the Lake Louise ski hill. Here Ranger Cal and the enthusiastic American bear biologist were just about to release the crazed critter and give him a traumatizing experience, when some quick-witted, and much more level-headed, staff members from the ski hill intervened and shouted:

"Hey! Not so fast! The parking lot's full of people! Someone could get hurt!"

A nasty looking male grizzly.

Don't mess with this critter–he's big, mean, and fast. If you get this close to one try to look "big", talk to him softly but firmly, and slowly back away. As you retreat, get out your "bear spray" and perhaps some bear bangers or a "Cherry Bomb " or two. Stay calm–the bear is probably as surprised as you are and doesn't know what to make of you either. Don't turn your back on the big beast and don't run. If you're charged and there's not a study tree you can climb in a hurry, fall down with your pack still on to protect your back and neck. Clasp your hands around the back of your neck and head and lay still–even if he gives you a good sniff or two and tries to turn you over.

If you have "bear spray" wait until the last second and blast him right in the kisser. It does no good to wildly spray it in the air from twenty feet or so. He has to be close to you so you can give him the full treatment. While he's wiping his stinging eyes, get the hell out of there–fast. If you have a bear banger aim it at him when he's good and close. I prefer a good Roman candle. A few well aimed red, green, and yellow balls from the Roman candle to the bear's face and neck should slow him down quickly. As you leave the area keep a lookout behind you, as grizzlies are notorious for doubling back and tracking a person from behind.

Two friendly black bears

Black bears were once easily chased away with a hefty stick and a few well-aimed rocks but now thanks to goofy government management practices many have become habituated and almost as dangerous as grizzlies. Some have become predatory and are not to be trusted. They are also mean and fast. As with the grizzly if you get close to one try to look "big", talk to him firmly, and slowly back away. He may make a few false charges but stay calm and don't turn your back on it. Don't run but as you retreat and get out your bear spray and bear bangers. If you have to, fall down with your pack still on to protect your back and clasp your hands around the back of your neck and head. Lay still even if he sniffs you and tries to turn you over. If you have bear spray wait until the last second and blast him in the face. If you have a bear banger aim it at him when he's good and close.

As you leave the area keep always keep a lookout behind you as well. If playing dead with a black bear doesn't work, fight back as fiercely as you can with anything you can get your hands on. A good ice axe to the skull should slow it down for a while.

The steadfast resort staff refused to allow the release of the dangerous bruin, and after much yelling and cussing, and a few threatening gestures, the B Team retreated, with the fidgety bear still inside the mobile trap. They were genuinely miffed at the unwanted interference from the lowly ski-hill personnel, and a few hours later returned with renewed determination to give the bear the treatment that he so richly deserved. With fewer people and cars about, the jittery creature was successfully flushed from the barrel trap into the parking lot. It was then chased around for a while with four or five yapping Karelian bear dogs, held firmly on leashes by the resolute American bear biologist and the tenacious Scandinavian researcher. After this cruel and unusual punishment, the B Team shifted into high gear and with unbridled enthusiasm inflicted more "aversion-conditioning" measures upon the bewildered animal. First he was hit about the head, face, and neck with some well-aimed beanbags, fired from a dreaded beanbag launcher. (I'm told that this launcher resembles the equally-dreaded potato gun.) The adrenaline-charged members of the posse also threw several beanbags in the general direction of the stunned bear.

Next, the unfortunate beast received two or three good squirts of bear-spray, right in the kisser and a few other embarrassing parts of its anatomy. Finally, just as the bear was wiping his stinging eyes, Ranger Cal fired a volley of rubber bullets at its tender, round rump. Needless to say, the bear's ears were tightly pinned back against his head as he tore out of the parking lot and into the bushes at break-neck speed. As he disappeared into the undergrowth the American "bear-person" and the Scandinavian researcher were heard to yell some hurtful things at the violated animal, which included: "Get going and never come back!" and "Get the hell out of here you big brute!" This dastardly treatment was all designed to give the bear a horribly, traumatic experience that it would not soon forget. The theory was that if the treatment were sufficiently repugnant, the bear would clear out of the area and never return. If it didn't leave, it was assuredly promised that it would henceforth avoid humans at all costs.

When I was a lad growing up in a quiet southern Ontario village along Lake St. Clair, a large neighbourhood dog of dubious breeding was making a nuisance of himself–killing the odd chicken, getting into garbage cans, and snatching kid's lunches on their way to school. A friend lassoed the mutt and tied a few tin cans to its bushy tail. He then administered a liberal dose of turpentine under the hound's tail and turned it loose. The frisky canine still holds the village speed record for leaving town in a hurry and we never saw it again. I think that the American bear biologist and the Human-Wildlife Conflict specialist may have heard of our cutting-edge techniques to deal with unwanted critters, as they appear to have adopted our methods as a way of giving habituated bears an unforgettable experience.

Later in the fall of 1999, a sow grizzly, affectionately known as "old No. 56," was also making a nuisance of herself around the village of Lake Louise. Crag and Canyon reporter Cathy Ellis also chronicled the details of this adventure and noted that intrepid Ranger Cal and a posse of fleet-footed wardens put in two separate, seven-day efforts to keep the bear away from the village and the nearby campground. They followed her twenty-four hours a day, hazing and spraying her with rubber bullets whenever she ventured near the village or the campground.

Ranger Cal, who if nothing else, is tenacious in his dedication to his duties, was quoted as saying: "We told her the town was not a good place to be." (I guess this bear could understand English.)

The cost of Ranger Cal's round-the-clock, bear-chasing ordeal – in terms of salaries and overtime – was not reported, but the jury is still out as to whether this labour-intensive and costly method of getting rid of overly-friendly bears actually works. Frankly I don't see much chance for its success. The monthly rate for the wiry, American bear biologist and dog handler, plus Ranger Cal's hefty annual salary (not to mention his overtime), plus the cost of the hangers-on from Parks Canada (who also scampered non-stop after the illusive bruin for fourteen days and nights) certainly adds up. I don't know if the gritty Scandinavian researcher was paid – perhaps she simply volunteered her services just to get in on the excitement.

Ironically bear No. 56, the pride and joy of the local bear-hugging fraternity for several years, was killed on the highway near the village of Lake Louise late one night in August of 2001. A speeding transport truck driver, who was seriously behind schedule and rushing through the area, didn't see the scruffy critter when it darted out of the ditch to cross the road in front of his truck. The driver didn't stop to inspect the injured beast or to administer first aid, and I can't say I blame him. It was dark and raining, and the bear might have come to and chewed off his leg – and perhaps a few other things as well. Or one of her shaggy friends might have been lurking in the undergrowth, ready to take revenge. Shortly after this, another sow grizzly was killed by a freight train near the village of Lake Louise. It too had been encouraged to hang around the area rather than being tranquillised and shipped out of town.

Both these deaths were entirely predictable. In both instances the sow grizzlies had cubs with them. I'm told the nimble B Team chased them around for a while, but they eluded capture and disappeared into the woods. Had these bears and their cubs been tranquilized and taken far away into the backcountry to be released, they and their cubs would be alive today. But no! The dopey bear biologists and the gullible Parks Canada officials persisted in their nutty experiment of encouraging grizzly bears to take up residence around the village of Lake Louise.

On June 8, 2004 edition of the Crag and Canyon it was reported that yet another female grizzly had been killed on the highway near Lake Louise. This sow was reported to be eighteen years old and had two cubs with her. Shelley Humpries, a Parks Canada spokesperson stated that she had seen fifteen bears along the highway in the past twenty days. While it is possible that she saw the same bear several times it was reported that since August of 2000, nine grizzly bears, six of them female, had died from "human causes" in Banff National Park.

In a separate article, in the same edition of the Crag and Canyon, it was reported that another grizzly, known to the bear loving fraternity as bear No. 66, was making a nuisance of itself in the Banff area. I submit that it won't be long before this beast is either run down by a truck or a train, or has to be shot for becoming too friendly.

It would seem that crazed wildlife biologists, naive environmentalists, and publicity-hungry bear organizations not only believe their own propaganda which attributes human behaviour patterns, psyches, intelligence, and even feelings to these rather small-brained creatures, but their half-baked schemes are too often warmly embraced by government officials. Parks Canada staff seems to have been sold on the idea that a "scare-to-remember" will overcome the instinct to seek out a free lunch in a garbage barrel, a dump, a picnic cooler, or a camp ground. Somehow, I'm not convinced.

Memo to Bears: Avoid Lake Louise" an article by Randy Boswell appeared in the National Post of May 26th 2004. Boswell reported that a new "landmark" study of bear populations in the Rockies had discovered the obvious – that large numbers of bears are killed on the highway and the railway tracks close to the village of Lake Louise. Some pin-headed professor apparently discovered that the three worst "kill locations" in the Rockies are near the village of Lake Louise, near the town site of Banff, and on a stretch of parkland highway near Red Deer. Apparently 31 of the 297 "human caused grizzly bear mortalities" occurred near the village of Lake Louise and therefore the report insightfully concluded that the big beasts were more likely to die near this village than anywhere else in the central Rockies.

What an amazing finding! I don't know who financed this half-baked effort, or why it took the combined talents of some of the brightest research minds from Parks Canada and the universities of Calgary, and Montana to reach this obvious conclusion, but I would humbly suggest that it was a colossal waste of time, money, and brain-power – although given the conclusions, I'm not too sure about the brain-power. A reasonably astute, sixth-grade student could have arrived at the same conclusions.

If grizzly bears are encouraged to take up residence adjacent to the village of Lake Louise, and along the busy Banff-Jasper corridor, it should come as no surprise to anyone that these critters will become habituated, loose their fear of humans, and be killed in ever increasing numbers by the speeding trucks, cars, and trains that pass through the area. Some will also have to be destroyed for becoming threats to the gentle tourists and residents of the area.

The National Post article also noted that the author the study proffered the ridiculous conclusion that: *"Lake Louise is an indicator, a flagship for what's going on."* The results of this study, together with its astounding findings, were published in the rather obscure journal, *Conservation Biology*. Predictably, the egg-headed professor suggested that his myopic study should: "serve as a wake-up call to federal and provincial officials that the grizzly bear may be facing extinction in Alberta". True to the radical environmentalist's agenda, he concludes with the old scaremonger's threat: "We either have to limit the access to some of the sites or we have to consider that bears might not be there fifty years from now." This guy also naively suggests that "Lake Louise is pristine, a very high-quality area for grizzly bears".

Is this chap the original "nutty professor?" Thousands of tourists, hikers, and climbers visit the area around Banff and Lake Louise each year. It's hardly a wilderness environment where we should encourage bears, of any description, to take up residence and it's certainly not an "indicator" or a "flagship" for what's going on".

It doesn't take a rocket scientist to figure out that bears roaming around Canmore, Banff, Field and Lake Louise will be killed on the highway and the railroad track, and it's no surprise that the recent "landmark" study discovered this obvious fact. Permitting bears to live in high-tourist areas is sheer stupidity for many reasons, not the least of which is the risk to those who visit the area. Notwithstanding the propaganda of the environmental lobby, the only explanation that I can come up with for the sustained and rhetoric-filled attempt to introduce grizzly bears to these high-use, high-tourist areas is that they are not too far from the comforts, the pubs, the cappuccino bars, and the night-life of Banff.

I suggest that once animals, particularly bears, become familiar with the easy pickings of civilization, they will avail themselves of the rich opportunities that it provides and in so doing, make nuisances of themselves, become dangerous, and eventually give someone a good mauling. Bears, cougars, coyotes, and the like, naturally turn to other prey such as small animals, livestock, pets, and sometimes humans, once the easy pick'ns of the campgrounds, the picnic sites, and the town dump are exhausted. Gary Shelton's book, *Bear Attack: The Deadly Truth*, provides ample evidence of this, as does some of Steve Herrero's research. Garbage-eating bears are dangerous bears, as they associate a delectable dinner with humans and lose all fear of them. Once the dumps, their main source of easy food, are closed down, they become downright nasty and too often predatory. Shelton reports that now, some habituated bears, both blacks and grizzlies, have learned to associate gunshots with humans that have just shot a deer, an elk, or a moose. At the sound of gunfire they come running to snatch a free lunch and often give the hunters a mauling for good measure. A few yapping mutts provide little deterrence, as these bears have now lost all fear of humans.

In December of 2002, it was reported that some deep thinker in the higher echelons of Parks Canada had the novel plan of building a high fence around the village of Lake Louise. The object of the plan was to prevent *"deadly grizzly bear encounters and stop the bruins from getting more habituated to people."* This strategy would enable the program of encouraging the establishment of a grizzly-bear population in the area to continue. As might be expected, the suggestion was not greeted with hoarse cries of approval from the residents of Lake Louise. Some suggested that such a fence would turn the pristine village into "Stalag Lake Louise". Others said they didn't want to live and feel like caged monkeys. My fear, however, is that this could result in further restrictions on hikers and climbers who wish to be undisturbed by wardens, naturalists, interpretive guides, and wild-eyed biologists in the backcountry.

The Parks Canada officials, who defended the plan to erect the high fence, suggested that the immediate area is home to one-quarter of the Park's grizzly bear population and therefore it is "critical habitat". This, to my mind, is nonsense, as this area is in no way "critical habitat". If, it is true, then it's time to move the habituated beasts to remote areas of the backcountry in order to prevent more from being killed and to protect the public. There is little evidence that this area was ever traditional bear habitat – except perhaps for the odd bruin passing through on its way to the garbage dump that was once in the bush near Chateau Lake Louise or to the one that was used by the village many years ago. The remote valleys such as the Ice, the Ottertail, the Pipestone, the Red Deer, the Clearwater, and the Panther have traditionally presented good bear habitat and have always supported reasonable bear populations. (Cooper and LeRoy 2000)

Michel Boivin, Parks Canada superintendent of Lake Louise, Yoho, and Kootenay parks, stated that there is a need to build "a wildlife exclusion fence" and to "bubble" the community. He stated: "We're not fencing people in, we're sort of fencing the bears and other animals out."

Many have grave misgivings about this plan, as it fails to take into account the fact that the area around Lake Louise is so popular for sightseeing, backpacking, hiking, and climbing. The introduction and/or the encouragement of a grizzly bear population outside the proposed "bubble-zone" around Lake Louise should therefore be seen as a definite "non-starter". What if people wish to hike and climb outside the fenced area and enjoy the wilderness? Will the entire area be closed off and declared a "Grizzly Bear Zone?" Will a new series of permits and passes, with their accompanying fees, be required to leave the fenced bubble zones of the park? Will there be more red tape, more zealous naturalists, and more officious officials strutting about? Will more areas be closed off completely, season after season, while a few scruffy grizzly bears frolic about?

It is estimated that some 2.8 to 4.0 million people visit Banff National Park annually. This includes tourists that never venture far from their tour buses, the shops of Banff and Lake Louise, or the viewpoints along the way. It also includes those that use the campsites within a mile of the highway and who visit the traditional tourist hot spots such as Takakkaw Falls, Lake Louise, the Lake Louise Gondola Ride, Moraine Lake, Johnson's Canyon, and Banff on their way through. Finally it includes serious hikers, climbers, and mountaineers who venture further into the backcountry – but not usually more than ten miles or so on either side of the highway. This group is a relatively small in number.

The Parks Canada program of encouraging bears, particularly grizzlies, in and around Banff and Lake Louise, and closing large sections of popular wilderness so two or three bears can snuff about undisturbed is flawed in the extreme, as are the efforts of lobbyists that wish to close down the Lake Louise ski area and chair-lift ride during the summer. Not only is this suggestion economically foolish in terms of lost revenue for the area, but the slopes of Mt. Whitehorn are less than a mile from the village of Lake Louise, and not the place to encourage a population of hungry bears. Both Banff and Lake Louise are popular, high-use, high-tourist areas and it is inevitable that when the food supply gets a bit lean on the slopes, the bruins will venture into town and the nearby campgrounds for easier pickings.

Is the Bear Population in Canada at Risk?

The bear population in Alberta and British Columbia, contrary to what hand-wringing bear-huggers and nervous environmentalists would have us believe, is in little danger. Reliable data suggest that the populations of both grizzly and black bears are actually increasing in these provinces. In 1998, Dr. Steven Herrero noted that the British Columbia government estimated a population of some ten to thirteen thousand grizzly bears and one-hundred-and-twenty thousand to one-hundred-and-sixty thousand black bears in that province alone. This exceeds the population of the City of Kamloops – hardly an endangered species.

In *Bear Attacks II–Myth & Reality,* Gary Sheldon wrote that the former provincial New Democratic Party government in British Columbia greatly understated the grizzly bear population in that province, for "environmental and political" reasons. He claims that there are at least sixteen thousand grizzlies in the province and predicts that if the hysterical preservationist ideology in the B.C. Wildlife Branch continues, it will grow to more than twenty thousand in less than twenty years.

Alberta officials report some thirty-six thousand to forty thousand black bears live in their province, along with anywhere from fifteen to twenty-six hundred grizzlies–depending on whose counting. Alaska estimates its grizzly bear population to be a whopping thirty-two thousand. Banff National Park officials estimate that there are somewhere between one-hundred-and-fifty and one-hundred-and-eighty black bears in the park, and from sixty to eighty-five grizzlies–many of them along the Bow River corridor between Banff and Lake Louise.

Given these figures, it must be assumed that the grizzly bear is NOT a threatened species and that the organizations that attempt to the manipulate the data to suggest that it is, have other agendas. For many, manufacturing and perpetuating the myth of imminent disaster for the grizzly bear, and then suggesting that it is representative of the overall state of wildlife in the local wilderness, has brought its rewards. These include generous federal grants and research stipends as well as frequent trips to seminars, round-tables, and symposia where they can tell each other exciting adventure stories about new statistical modeling techniques and cohort survival rates that confound and confuse the public, the civil servants, and themselves.

Cooper and LeRoy conclude in their 2002 study that, contrary to what Parks Canada and the environmental lobby would have us believe, the grizzly-bear population is definitely NOT under pressure in Canada's national mountain parks. They suggest that researchers and environmentalists who raised the "grizzly" alarm, (no pun intended) are engaging in "advocacy science" and are too cozy with Parks Canada. This is not a new or a surprising accusation. Cooper states: *"I would say Parks Canada is complicit in the highly questionable scientific studies that they commission and then act upon."* He suggests that there are some real questions that need to be asked about the research program of the ESGBP, and biologists with Parks Canada–especially since restrictive public policy has resulted from their biased conclusions. The previously-mentioned study that Boswell reported on in the National Post is an excellent example of such research.

In a penetrating analysis of the ESGBP "research," Cooper and LeRoy suggest that the project is long on propaganda and conservationist rhetoric, but short on substantive research methodology that can stand the test of independent, peer review. They also point out that some of the data has been knowingly distorted in an attempt to demonstrate that the grizzly bear population is nearing extinction and/or is under threat if the public is allowed continued access to the backcountry. They also assert that Parks Canada bureaucrats have provided the ESGBP with outrageously large grants from the taxpayer's purse, and then they have used the mission-focused conclusions to formulate restrictive human-use policies in the Parks. In addition, they have attempted to make the case that the area around Lake

Louise is "critical habitat" and this has resulted in the closure of popular hiking trails and backcountry areas.

How to Save the Banff Grizzlies

With the hundreds of thousands, if not millions of tourists, hikers, and climbers visiting the Lake Louise area each summer it is foolishness in the extreme to permit bears of any description to roam about in this high-use, high-tourist area. Knowingly releasing dangerous, habituated bears in the Canmore and Banff areas, or on the slopes of Mt. Whitehorn, less than a mile from the village of Lake Louise and adjacent to the hiking trails to Ptarmigan and Skoki, is an inane move – even if the critters have been given one hell of a scare beforehand. If the cunning beasts act out their revenge by mauling, maiming, or killing an unsuspecting tourist, cyclist, hiker, or, heaven forbid, a wildlife specialist, those involved in releasing them may indeed be criminally and/or civilly liable for their unmitigated stupidity.

Sadly and tragically, this is exactly what happened on June 5th, 2005 when **Isabelle Dube'**, a young mother and outdoors woman from Canmore, just ten minutes drive from Banff, was attacked and killed by a rogue grizzly while she was jogging along a well-used pathway with two friends near the Canmore Silver Tip Golf Resort. On June 7th, the *Crag and Canyon* newspaper reported the incident.

> *Dube' was running with two friends on the trails about a kilometer west of the Silver Tip Golf Resort Sunday afternoon when the trio stumbled on Bear 99, a 198 lb. grizzly that had been removed from the area a week prior but returned Saturday morning (June 4th). As Dube' climbed a tree, her companions ran to the nearby golf course where they contacted Fish and Wildlife officials who [incredibly] were in the area monitoring the bear. The officials arrived on the scene to discover that Dube' has been pulled from the tree and killed. The bear was immediately shot.*

This tragic and needless death should serve as a wake-up call to the over-zealous conservationists, and other bear groupies within Parks Canada who have been encouraging grizzlies to hang around the Banff and Lake Louise. Bear 99 was a well-known trouble-maker. Rather than killing the obnoxious critter a week earlier, wildlife officials released it back into the wilds, not far enough from Canmore. Guess what? The habituated beast returned and killed the young mother as she jogged along a well-used path near the golf course with two friends on a lovely Sunday afternoon. Incredibly wildlife officials were reported to be monitoring the bear at the time! They were obviously asleep at the switch or taking a break somewhere.

In my opinion this mauling should never have happened. I would suggest that and the women's family and loved ones seek legal advice about the possibility of criminal and/or civil redress through the courts. If they did so, perhaps it would put an end to the zany efforts on the part of Parks Canada, researchers, and various other wildlife groups, which encourage unpredictable and dangerous carnivores to take up residence in high-use, high-tourist areas.

It should come as no surprise to anyone who knows anything about animals that these menacing critters easily become habituated, lose their fear of humans, and will eventually attack innocent hikers and joggers who wish to enjoy the outdoors. They will also be killed in ever-increasing numbers by the speeding trucks, cars, and trains that pass through the area. Some will also have to be shot for becoming dangerous nuisances to the gentle residents and tourists who reside in such areas.

A couple of well-fed grizzlies on the prowl

If the real objective is to save grizzly bears, I suggest that the misguided initiative of encouraging them to take up residence in and around the high-use areas of the national parks be abandoned immediately. As many bears as possible should be rounded up, tranquilized, tagged, and transported to remote and safer areas where they can safely feed and cavort. The cost of this strategy would be minuscule in comparison to the cost of fencing "bubble" zones and financing highly-paid wildlife specialists, their hounds, and their questionable "averion-conditioning" schemes.

The downside of this approach is that it may cause some inconvenience to those environmentalists, bear-lovers, and wildlife specialists who like to have an evening cappuccino in the coffee shops of Banff, or a beer in the Cascade Lounge, after a hard day of driving their SUVs between Banff and Lake Louise with their amber lights flashing. They might actually have to hike and/or camp in remote wilderness areas to study the objects of their affection. They might even have to purchase backcountry permits.

If a nuisance bear returns, after being given a one-way ride to a remote wilderness area and becomes a persistent and dangerous problem, it should be shot and stuffed. The mounted bears could then be put near the entrances to the Banff, Lake Louise, and Yoho Visitors' Bureaus, or in front of the village liquor stores where tourists can pose beside them for a memorable photo. Parks Canada could even charge a toonie a pose and make a pot-full of money to fund the OWBTP (the One Way Bear Transportation Program). Several stuffed bears could be placed at these locations—each mounted in a different, menacing pose. This would also give a much-needed shot in the arm to the declining local taxidermy industry.

A fresh snowfall in the larch meadows near the base of Mt. Shaffer in O'Hara

The national mountain parks encompass thousands of acres, and in the remote backcountry there are extensive tracts of excellent habitat for bears to enjoy for a lifetime. There's no need to encourage these large, unpredictable, and increasingly-habituated carnivores, to frolic about near the village of Lake Louise where there is little natural food and where encounters with humans, cars, trucks, and trains are highly probable.

In the meantime, Ms. Dube's loved ones should seek legal advice. I'd love to hear the cross-examination of some of the nutty wildlife officials and "bear specialists" that persist in their misguided belief that bears and humans can amicably co-exist together in the high-use, high tourist mountain parks. I'd also like to hear the interrogation of the Fish and Wildlife personnel who were supposedly monitoring Bear 99's movements. It's a tragedy that never should have happened.

Other Blunders

In addition to the unfortunate program that focuses on encouraging grizzly bears to take up residence in the Banff–Lake Louise corridor, other examples of bizarre Parks Canada programs include the decision a few years ago to kill all the fish in Moraine Lake, including a healthy population of rainbow and cutthroat trout. This action was taken because some obscure bureaucrat somewhere in an Ottawa cubicle, was convinced that Moraine Lake had once been the home of the ignoble Bull Trout. (Related to the Dolly Varden, and a member of the char family, the bull trout, is in my opinion, a greatly inferior breed of fish.) All the feisty cutthroat and rainbow trout in the lake were killed and then the lake was restocked with their sluggish cousin—a fish that seldom rises to a well-presented dry fly and fights like a rubber boot when hooked. Fortunately the cutthroat trout were not totally exterminated for in the summer of 2005 I caught two beautiful, fifteen inch specimens near the end of the lake in less than ten minutes, using one of my specially-tied and highly classified "Moraine Lake Sunrise" flies.

An equally inane decision was the edict to up-root, remove, and eradicate the lovely Icelandic poppies from the grounds around the Chateau at Lake Louise. The management of the Chateau, who were negotiating with Parks Canada with regards to the building of the new convention facility, were was instructed to replace the poppies in most of the flower beds in around the hotel with some rather drab looking native shrubs. The argument supporting this insightful directive was that: "the poppies were not native to the area".

How much are the taxpayers paying the deep-thinking bureaucrats at Parks Canada to come up with their remarkable ideas is not known, but I suggest it's far too much. It's time to return the parks to the people, and in high-use, high-tourist areas, to manage threatening and dangerous wildlife rather than containing the visitors and closing off areas and facilities. Wild carnivores and tourists don't mix well and never will. Trying to pretend they can, and then attempting foolish experimental exercises to test naïve and romantic theories will only lead to dangerous encounters and perhaps the death of unsuspecting tourists or hikers.

It is also time for Parks Canada to stop taking a "we know what's best for you" approach with hikers, campers, and climbers. I suggest that park users be advised that a bear or other dangers may be in an area, and then be allowed to decide whether to camp, hike, or climb at their own risk. Some strategically-posted notices, or warnings, would be sufficient, as most hikers, and even some climbers, can read.

One final point of concern is the manner in which Parks Canada is turning the national parks into cash cows. Each year brings with it a new set of user fees. Vehicle permits (six dollars per person per day or twelve dollars a day for a group of 2–7 persons), camping fees (between thirteen and twenty-five dollars a day per night) and backcountry permits (six dollars per person per night, and a ten dollar $10.00 reservation fee). A seven-day fishing permit is six dollars, and in most instances, you must release the fish. No more fresh trout breakfasts beside an early morning campfire.

While some might feel that these fees are reasonable, I have to question what my excessively high taxes are going for, if every time I turn around, there's another user fee to pay. There should be some things in this country that are free by virtue of being a taxpaying citizen. I would feel a whole lot better about user fees if I knew that the funds raised were being used to improve the parks, the fisheries, the trails, and the shelters, rather than being put into "General Revenue" to be freely spent or diverted, by federal bureaucrats, politicians, and their shadowy friends.

The national and the provincial parks were created for the people to use and enjoy and that should be the focus for the future. The parks and the trails must remain accessible to all, free from all but the most necessary restrictions, rules, regulations, and special fees. The parks and the wilderness are a part of every Canadian's birthright and heritage and they should be available to use and enjoy without being fenced in, managed, and charged at every opportunity.

Finally the national and provincial parks should not be allowed to become the exclusive domain of crazed environmentalists, nutty naturalists, and bear-hugging biologists who have their own agendas, but no higher right to use, enjoy, or study than anyone else. Parks Canada must re-affirm its original purpose and mandate and encourage the use and enjoyment of the backcountry as part of our Canadian heritage. At the same time, ongoing efforts should be continued to ensure the survival of not just the grizzly bear, but also the black bear, the moose, the elk, the coyote, the wolf, the big horn sheep, the Rocky Mountain goat, the mule and the white-tailed deer, the whistling marmot, and the busy pica.

Park Users Must Accept Responsibility for Their Own Stupidity

It's also time for visitors to the National Parks to accept the consequences of their own actions, without always looking for someone else to blame when they get into trouble, or become the victim of their own foolhardiness and lack of judgement. If people wish to venture out into the wilderness, they should be prepared for the fact that things can, and often do, go wrong. They must accept the consequences of their own stupidity and poor decision-making, such as getting wiped out by an avalanche or gored by a frisky elk.

If people are afraid of being mauled by a bear, butted by a sheep, or charged by a marmot, they should stay out of the backcountry. If they're afraid of tipping over in a canoe, they should stay on shore. If they're afraid of bugs and snakes they shouldn't leave home. Finally, if they stub their toe on the trail or get bitten while feeding a ground squirrel, they shouldn't immediately race to the nearest phone to call their favourite litigation lawyer. Thousands more people are killed, maimed, and injured each year on the highways getting to and from the parks than ever get hurt in the backcountry. Parks Canada must abandon its mother-hen mentality about people using the backcountry and deal with its paranoia about people accessing the wilderness for an outbound experience.

Despite my passionate appeal for continued and unencumbered access to the provincial and national parks, I'm pleased to say that the mountains and the high meadows still remain much as Tom Wilson, Jimmy Simpson, Wild Bill Peyto, and Edward Whymper first found them. The wild flowers still bloom in the high meadows, the gentle rain still falls, the sun still shines, and the quality of the air up there is still intoxicating. On clear dark summer nights one can almost reach out and touch the stars and listen to the eternal night sounds of coyotes calling, owls hunting, and avalanches falling from the surrounding peaks. If you listen very carefully, you can almost hear the music of the spheres.

This book has tried to document and recount some of the history and the true tales of the Rockies, much of it told to me many years ago by some of the old-times of the area, and by those that actually lived the legends. I pray that we will always have the freedom to enjoy the mountain trails, the high country, the snow-clad peaks, and the high and windy passes as they did. As Canadians we must always have the opportunity to experience high adventure, mountain challenges, and encounters with nature's elements and the resident wildlife. There may be some accidents, some close calls, and even some deaths from slips, falls, avalanches and/or exposure. Some may also be chased, mauled or killed by unpredictable wildlife, but this is what makes for adventure in the mountains and the backcountry. I trust that new tales and new legends will continue to emerge from the Canadian Rockies and that my grandchildren, and those of others, will have the freedom and the opportunity to enjoy the mountains and the high meadows for many generations to come.

If you have any comments, criticisms, or suggestions, or wish to tell me your stories and/or experiences in the Rockies write or e-mail me at:

Amberlea Press
P.O. Box 1682 Aldergrove, B.C.
V4W 2V1
Tel: 604-859-1432 Cell: 604-626-2517
E-mail: rpatillo@canada.com

Lake Louise and a statue commemorating the Swiss guides

The author and his daughter Kathleen at Lake O'Hara in mid-August. Seven Veils Falls is in the background.

A Glossary of Terms

Arete–a French word often used in mountaineering meaning ridge.

Belay–to bring the rope around some object, usually the climber's body in such a way that should the belayed climber fall, the rope attached to him can be secured to stop the fall. The rope is used to protect another climber from a fall.

Bergschrund–a large crevasse on a glacier where the ice and snow separate from the rock base of the mountain.

Bivouac–a temporary, often unplanned camp made in the course of a climb with only the materials that can be carried in one's rucksack; often on a ledge, but not always.

Buttress–a distinct large bulge of rock against a mountain face, A tower-like projection against the mountain face.

Cairn–a small man-made pile of rocks at the summit of a mountain to marks the first ascent of the mountain or to serve as markers showing the route both up and down the mountain.

Carabiner–an oval or "D" shaped ring with a snap opening that can be clipped on a piton ring or a rope. Usually made of metal alloy or aluminum. Some have screw type locking devices to keep them from opening unexpectedly.

Chimney–a crack in a rock face that is wide enough to allowing one to ascend by wedging your body or arms or legs in it to work your way up by straddling it or other wise. Some chimneys are large enough to wedge your whole body in.

Chockstone–a stone that is firmly wedged in a chimney or crack.

Cirque–a large, concave face usually found high on a mountain near the summit.

Col–the lowest point on a ridge between two mountains. Often referred to as a pass.

Cornice–a build up of snow near the summit or ridge of a mountain caused from the build-up of wind-driven snow and ice crystals on the lee side of a ridge. Over time a cornice may grow to overhang the lee face of the summit. They are extremely dangerous and can collapse and break-off without warning.

Couloir–a wide, natural gully running down a mountain face and down which snow and rock fall. Usually filled with snow, rock scree and or seeping water.

Crampons–a set of sharp spikes that are strapped to the bottom of one's climbing boots. Used on hard snow and ice but never soft snow as it can ball-up causing a nasty fall.

Crevasse–a long, deep and often wide crack running across as glacier. The may be hidden by snow covering them (snow bridges) and they may be fifty to one hundred feet deep or more.

Exposure–a sharp drop over or down which one could easily fall. The degree of exposure is in direct relationship to the distance of the potential fall and one's attitude about it. Walking along a knife-edged ridge with a drop of a thousand feet or so on either side, would be considered to be 'exposed,' by most climbers.

Fixed Ropes–ropes that are permanently attached at the top of a rock face, buttress or chimney to assist one in ascending and descending.

Gendarme–a rock pinnacle on a ridge which requires that one climb up and then down or traverse around in order to proceed along the ridge.

Glissade–sliding down a steep snow slope using just the soles of one's climbing boots and leaning back on the point of one's ice axe for control.

Ice Axe–a mountaineer's axe featuring an adze at one end of the head for trimming up steps cut in the ice and a pick at the other end for digging into the ice and /or snow to cut steps, self arrest or use as a aid in climbing. The shaft varies in length and usually has a spike at the end. They are useful implements and have many uses in addition to mountaineering. i.e. walking stick, emergency can opener, weapon to fend off bears and other critters.

Icefall–where the glacier must flow over steep uneven bedrock, causing the ice to break and crack into big unstable chunks and slabs and to form crevasses.

Primus–the brand name of a small, pack-sized stove that uses white gas as fuel. "Optimus" was another brand name for a similar stove.

Piton–a short, steel blade or chisel-shaped piece of metal with a eye or ring at one end. It is used to hammer into a crack in the rock to provide an anchor for belaying or rappelling. They come in various lengths and thicknesses.

Prussik or Prussic–a knot which permits a rope of smaller diameter to be tied to one of larger diameter. When tension is put on the knot it jams and holds securely. When the tension is released it loosens and can slide up or down the larger rope. Used for prussik stirrups in ascending and descending a rope if jumars (mechanical ascenders) are not available.

Rappel–to descend down a steep cliff of rock face by sliding down a rope in a controlled fashion.

Scree–small pieces of rock and gravel on a mountain slope.

Serac–ice pinnacles and blocks found in an icefall.

Snow Bridge–a bridge of snow covering a crevasse. These can be very unstable and unsafe.

Summit Ridge–the ridge leading to the summit

Talus–larger rocks and slabs usually at the base of a scree slope.

Traverse–to move horizontally from one point to another on a mountain.

Verglas – a thin layer of ice coating the rocks and ledges

Whiteout – a weather condition often found on glaciers or snow slopes, produced by dense cloud, fog or a snowstorm causing the immediate surrounding to appear all white with no apparent horizon, shape or slope. One feels completely enveloped in the "white" fog, snow or mist and quickly loses depth perception and becomes disoriented and confused as to location and direction.

Wrangler – a person who looks after horses, and pack-trains.

Bibliography

Anderson, Ian. *Sitting Bull's Boss* Heritage House, Surrey B.C., V3S 2A7

Cooper, B., Hayes J., LeRoy S. *Science Fact or Science Fiction? The Grizzly Biology behind Parks Canada Management Models,* The Fraser Institute, December 2002

Cooper, B., LeRoy S. *Off Limits: How Radical Environmentalists Are Shutting down Canada's National Parks,* The Fraser Institute, December 2000

Cruise, David & Griffiths Alison, *The Great Adventure – How the Mounties Conquered the West,* Viking Press, Penquin Books, 1996

Denny, Sir Cecil E. *March of the Mounties.* Heritage House, Surrey B.C., 1994

Dodd J. & Helgason G. *The Canadian Rockies Access Guide,* Lone Pine Press, Edmonton, 1987

Dougherty S. *Selected Alpine Climbs in the Canadian Rockies,* Rocky Mountain Books Calgary, 1996

Dowling Phil. *The Mountaineers Famous Climbers in Canada,* Hurtig Publishers 1979

Edwards. Ralph, *The Trail to a Charmed Land,* Herbert R. Larson Publishing Co., Ltd.Victoria, 1950

Fort Macleod Historical Society, *The Story of the Mounted Police,* 1958

Fraser, Esther. *Wheeler,* Summerthought Publications, Banff, 1978

Freeman L. *On the Roof of the Rockies,* Dodd, Mead & Co., New York, 1925

Fergus Fleming *Killing Dragons The Conquest of the Alps,* Atlantic Monthly Press 2000

Fyffe, A. & Peter, I. *The Handbook of Climbing,* Pelham Books- Penguin Group, 1997

Green W.S. *Among the Selkirk Glaciers,* McMillan and Co., New York, 1890

Gest Lillian, *History of Lake O'Hara,* Self Published, Fourth Printed Edition, 1989

Harmon C., *Great Days in the Rockies: The Photographs of Byron Harmon 1907-1934,* Toronto Oxford Press, 1978

Harmon Carole & Robinson B. *Byron Harmon Mountain Photographer,* Altitude Publishing Ltd., Canmore, Alberta, 1996

Hart, E.J. *The Brewster Story – From Pack Train to Tour Bus,* Brewster Transport Company, Ltd., 1981

Hart, E.J. *Diamond Hitch* Summerthought Publications, Banff, 1979

Hart, E.J. *Ain't it Hell – Bill Peyto's Mountain Journal,* Self Published by EJH Literary Enterprises, Banff Canada, 1999

Hart, E.J. *The Place of the Bows* Self Published by EJH Literary Enterprises, Banff Canada, 1995

Hart, E.J. *Jimmy Simpson, Legend of the Rockies* Altitude Press, Canmore, Alberta, 1999

Haydon, A.L. *The Riders of the Plains: A Record of the Royal North-West Mounted Police of Canada, 1873-1910,* Hurtig Books, Edmonton, 1971

J.M. Thorington, editor, *Where the Clouds Can Go,* 1935, Reprinted Boston: Charles T. Branford Co., 1954 by J.M. Thorington

Kallen Urs., *A Climbers Guide to the Yamnuska 2d ed.* Calgary Urd.Kallen, 1977

Kruszyna, R. and Putnam, W.L., *Climbers Guide to the Interior Ranges of British Columbia –South,* Springfield, Mass., The American Alpine Club and the Alpine Club of Canada.

Lunn Arnold, *The Alps,* Henry Holt and Co., July 1914

MacEwan, Grant, *Fifty Mighty Men,* The Western Producer, Saskatoon, Sask., 1958

MacEwan, Grant, *Sitting Bull,* Hertig Publishers, Edmonton, Alberta, 1973

McClung, Nellie L. *Clearing in the West,* Thomas Allen, Toronto, 1935

McWilliams Margaret, *Manitoba Milestones,* J.M. Dent & Sons, Toronto, 1928

Manning Harvey ed., *Mountaineering the Freedom of the Hills,* The Mountaineers, Seattle, 1960

Marty S., *Men for the Mountains,* MacMillan and Stewart, Toronto, 1978

Marty S., *Switchbacks: True Stories from the Canadian Rockies,* MacMillan and Stewart, Toronto, 1999

Morse R., *The Mountains of Canada,* Edmonton, Hurtig Publishers, 1978

Munday, Don, *The Unknown Mountain,* London, Hodder & Stoughton,. 1948 Reprinted, Seattle, The Mountaineers, 1975

Nicol, Eric. Editor, *Dickens of the Mounted*, McClelland & Stewart, Toronto, 1989

Outram Sir James, In the Heart of the Canadian Rockies, Macmillan, 1923

Palmer – *Mountaineering & Exploration in the Selkirks*, Putnam Press, 1914

Parker, Patricia, *The Feather and The Drum, The History of Banff Indian Days, 1889-1978*, Consolidated Communications, 1990

Patillo, R. W., *Lake Louise at its Best*, Trafford Press – 2000

Patterson R.M. *Far Pastures*, Gray Publishing Ltd., Sidney, B.C. 1963

Putnam, W.L. and Boles, G. *Climbers Guide to the Rocky Mountains of Canada-South*, Springfield, Mass. 6th Ed., The American Alpine Club and the Alpine Club of Canada. 1973

Putnam, W.L. Jones,C. and Kruszyna, R., *Climbers Guide to the Rocky Mountains of Canada-North* 6th Ed., Springfield, Mass. The American Alpine Club and the Alpine Club of Canada. 1974

Putnam, W.L., *A Climbers Guide to the Interior Ranges of British Columbia –North*, Springfield Mass., The American Alpine Club and the Alpine Club of Canada. 1975

Putnam, W. and Kauffman L. *The Guiding Spirit*, Footprint Publishing, Revelstoke, B.C. 1986

Thornington, J.M. *A Climber's Guide to The Rocky Mountains of Canada*, Revised Edition The American Alpine Club 1953

Sanford, R.W. *High Ideals – Canadian Pacific's Swiss Guides, 1899-1999* – The Alpine Club of Canada, 1999

Scott, Chic. *Pushing the Limits – The Story of Canadian Mountaineering*, Rocky Mountain Books, 2000.

Sherman Paddy, *Cloud Walkers*. Toronto, MacMillan of Canada, 1965

Shelton J.G., *Bear Attacks,*, Pogany Productions, Hagensburg, B.C., 1998

Shelton J.G., *Bear Encounter Survival Guide Attacks*, Pogany Productions, Hagensburg, B.C. 1994

Smythe F.S., *Climbs in the Canadian Rockies*. New York, Norton and Co. 1951

Steele Sam, B. Forty Years in Canada, Prospero Books, Toronto, 2000

Stewart, Robert. Sam Steele: Lion of the Frontier, Nelson Canada, Toronto 1981

Stutfield Hugh E. M. and Collie J. Norman, *Climbs and Explorations in the Canadian Rockies*, Longmans Green & Co. of London, 1903

Taylor W.C., *The Snows of Yesteryear: J. Norman Collie Mountaineer*, Toronto, Holt, Rinehard and Winston of Canada 1973

Wheeler A.O., *The Selkirk Range of British Columbia (Vol. I)*, Government Printing Bureau, Ottawa, 1905

Wilcox Walter, *The Rockies of Canada*, Putnam, 1909

Journals *The Canadian Alpine Journal* 1907–Present, The Alpine Club of Canada.

Mt. Fay and Mt. Quadra above Moraine Lake

ISBN 1-41205627-6